Weakness of Will in Renaissance
and Reformation Thought

Weakness of Will in Renaissance and Reformation Thought

Risto Saarinen

OXFORD
UNIVERSITY PRESS

OXFORD
UNIVERSITY PRESS

Great Clarendon Street, Oxford OX2 6DP

Oxford University Press is a department of the University of Oxford.
It furthers the University's objective of excellence in research, scholarship,
and education by publishing worldwide in

Oxford New York

Auckland Cape Town Dar es Salaam Hong Kong Karachi
Kuala Lumpur Madrid Melbourne Mexico City Nairobi
New Delhi Shanghai Taipei Toronto

With offices in

Argentina Austria Brazil Chile Czech Republic France Greece
Guatemala Hungary Italy Japan Poland Portugal Singapore
South Korea Switzerland Thailand Turkey Ukraine Vietnam

Oxford is a registered trade mark of Oxford University Press
in the UK and in certain other countries

Published in the United States
by Oxford University Press Inc., New York

© Risto Saarinen 2011

The moral rights of the author have been asserted
Database right Oxford University Press (maker)

First published 2011

British Library Cataloguing in Publication Data

Data available

Library of Congress Cataloging in Publication Data

Data available

Typeset by SPI Publisher Services, Pondicherry, India
Printed in Great Britain
on acid-free paper by
MPG Books Group, Bodmin and King's Lynn

ISBN 978–0–19–960681–8

1 3 5 7 9 10 8 6 4 2

Contents

Acknowledgements

Numerous scholars have generously shared their views and discussed the problems of this book with me. I want to mention especially David Charles, Sabrine Ebbersmeyer, Tobias Hoffmann, Pekka Kärkkäinen, Bonnie Kent, Simo Knuuttila, Jill Kraye, David Lines, Virpi Mäkinen, Jörn Müller, Juha Sihvola, Jack Zupko, and the anonymous referees of the publisher. I am grateful to Roderick McConchie and the editors of Oxford University Press for improving my language and style.

Financial support for this project was provided by the Helsinki Collegium for Advanced Studies and the Academy of Finland, especially through its Centre of Excellence in 'Philosophical Psychology, Morality, and Politics'. The University of Helsinki has always been an inspiring home base for my research activities.

List of Tables

List of Abbreviations

Argyropoulos	Renaissance Latin Translation of EN in Acciaiuoli, *Expositio*
AT	*Oeuvres de Descartes*, ed. C. Adam and P. Tannery
CO	*Ioannis Calvini Opera*, Corpus Reformatorum
CR	Philip Melanchthon, *Opera*, Corpus Reformatorum
CSEL	Corpus Scriptorum Ecclesiasticorum Latinorum
EN	Aristotle, *Nicomachean Ethics*
G	Spinoza, *Opera*, vol. 2, ed. G. Gebhardt
Grosseteste	Medieval Latin Translation of EN in *Aristoteles Latinus*
ICR	John Calvin, *Institutes of the Christian Religion*
Long-Sedley	*The Hellenistic Philosophers*, ed. A. A. Long and D. N. Sedley
LSA	Martin Luther, *Studienausgabe*
MSA	Philip Melanchthon, *Studienausgabe*
PL	Patrologiae Cursus Completus, Series Latina, ed. J.-P. Migne
TC	William Shakespeare, *Troilus and Cressida*
WA	*Martin Luthers Werke*, Weimarer Ausgabe
WABr	*Martin Luthers Werke*, Weimarer Ausgabe, *Briefwechsel*

Introduction

'Weakness of will' is the English equivalent of Aristotle's Greek term *akrasia*, which is extensively discussed in the seventh book of his *Nicomachean Ethics* (EN). A weak-willed or akratic person, the *akratês*, is one who acts against his or her better judgement.[1] Aristotle discusses this phenomenon because, on the one hand, Socrates thought it strange that when an agent has knowledge, something else could master his or her actions. No one acts against what he or she judges best. Given this Socratic position, we cannot act against our better judgement and there is no akrasia. On the other hand, this view contradicts the plain fact that people seem to act akratically fairly often. A philosopher needs to examine whether Socrates is right and, if he is, what seemingly akratic actions are in reality also needs to be explained (EN 1145b22–30).

Weakness of will poses philosophical problems which continue to interest serious thinkers. Since the 1960s especially Aristotle's discussion has prompted a flood of new explanatory attempts. These in part relate to the closer historical understanding of Aristotle's own view, but, and perhaps more importantly, they also address the issue of whether there are truly akratic actions.[2] Recent studies have revealed the amount of reflection devoted to this phenomenon in the history of Western thought.[3] Some earlier studies related sceptically to the relevance of akrasia in the era of Christianity, arguing that the Augustinian concept of will makes akrasia self-evident and that no significant discussion on akrasia took place between Aristotle and contemporary analytical philosophy.[4] A closer look at the sources soon reveals that this is not the case, at least with regard to medieval philosophy and theology.

The medieval period has been particularly productive in the history of the interpretation of akrasia. Once Aristotle's EN had been reintroduced to Western intellectual

---

[1] The present study uses the terms 'akrasia', 'weakness of will', and 'incontinence' as synonyms. The word 'incontinence' derives from the Latin translation of akrasia as *incontinentia*. In the following, akrasia and akrates are written without italics when the phenomenon (and not merely the Greek word) is meant.

[2] A particularly influential turning-point of the contemporary discussion has been the essay by Davidson (1969). For the historical interpretations of akrasia in Plato and Aristotle, see Hardie (1980); Dahl (1984); Charles (1984); Spitzley (1992); Sorabji (2000), 305–15; Grcic (2002); Bobonich and Destrée (2007); and other works mentioned below. Recent comprehensive studies include Mele (1987); Peijnenburg (1996); Stroud and Tappolet (2003); Thero (2006); Stroud (2008).

[3] For historical overviews, see Gosling (1990); Spitzley (1992); Hügli (2004); Bobonich and Destrée (2007); Hoffmann (2008); Müller (2009).

[4] Charlton (1988), reporting other studies.

life in the thirteenth century, it became possible to compare Aristotle's insights with the Augustinian and Christian views of human action. Aristotle prevailed in this comparison to an astonishing extent, but there were also Augustinian and Franciscan critics who did not adopt the Aristotelian view of human action. In addition, new views of action theory emerged in fourteenth-century scholasticism. Although these nominally followed Aristotle and, in some cases, Augustine, they introduced new ways of understanding human action. The discussion of akrasia provided a conceptual laboratory in which new ideas could be tested and their implications spelled out.[5]

The richness of medieval philosophy has been discussed in many specialized studies. The results of this discussion have found their way into the more general historical presentations of akrasia.[6] This interest has not, however, extended to the early modern period. The standard work on philosophical terminology, *Historisches Wörterbuch der Philosophie*, claims, immediately after its elaborate discussion of the medieval period, that 'weakness of will has not been a relevant concept or problem for the philosophy of the modern era. It only begins to be discussed again in the analytic philosophy'.[7] Given that many recent studies deal with akrasia in the writings of Descartes, Spinoza, Locke, Leibniz, and even Kant, this is a suprising statement.[8]

It may, however, contain a grain of truth. In order to find a discussion on 'weakness of will' in these philosophers, the interpreter must define akrasia in broad terms; for instance, as general irrationality in human behaviour. One may doubt whether the non-Aristotelian philosophers of the modern era really are discussing Aristotle's problem. As their conceptual framework appears to be a different one, they may not be discussing akrasia but other problems of irrationality in human action. When Justin Gosling writes that 'between the Middle Ages and the twentieth century... interest in these problems [of akrasia] vanishes',[9] he means that Aristotle's questions no longer appeared as genuine philosophical problems after the decline of medieval Aristotelianism.

My earlier study investigated Augustine's treatment of the so-called 'reluctant actions' (*invitus facere*) in addition to Aristotle's discussion. While that study focused on the medieval commentaries on Aristotle's EN, it also paid attention to the reception history of Augustine's views, claiming that his discussion deals with similar, although not identical, problems of 'weakness of will'. The present study follows the same

---

[5] Saarinen (1994); Hoffmann, Müller, and Perkams (2006) and Müller (2009) offer a comprehensive overview of medieval akrasia. See also 1.3–1.5 below.

[6] Kent (1995); Hügli (2004); Hoffmann, Müller, and Perkams (2006); Müller (2006; 2007; 2009); Hoffmann (2008).

[7] Hügli (2004), 805: 'Für die Philosophie der Neuzeit ist Willensschwäche weder als Begriff noch als Problem von Bedeutung. Zum Diskussionspunkt wird Willensschwäche erst wieder in der Analytischen Philosophie.'

[8] Descartes: Ong-Van-Cung (2003) and McCarthy (2008). Spinoza: Savile (2003) and Koivuniemi (2008). Locke: Vailati (1990) and Glauser (2003). Leibniz: Hintikka (1988); Vailati (1990); Davidson (2005); Roinila (2007). Kant: Hill (2008).

[9] Gosling (1990), 196.

twofold pattern. While the Augustinian discussion needs to be kept distinct from Aristotle's, both discussions are often intertwined in the same sources. My sources do not deal with all the possible problems related to free will and irrationality during the Renaissance and the Reformation. The main criterion of my choice of sources is that they belong to the immediate reception history of Aristotle's and Augustine's treatment of the phenomenon of acting against one's own better judgement.

The present study aims to show that the statement of the *Historisches Wörterbuch* quoted above is wrong, at least as far as the early modern period (*c.* 1350–1630) is concerned. It will be shown that weakness of will was both a relevant concept and a significant problem during this period. In spite of the flood of recent studies on akrasia, this period has remained completely devoid of scholarly attention. Even the extensive and in many respects very useful new volume *Weakness of Will from Plato to the Present* (Hoffmann (2008)) only discusses Dante and Montaigne, two writers whose texts are only distantly related to the interpretation history of akrasia.

The present study makes two distinct but related historical claims. First, the classical problem of weakness of will was the source of lively debates and significant innovations during the Renaissance and the Reformation. These debates and innovations concern both the specific nature of Aristotelian akrasia and the broader discussion on irrationality, desire, and reluctant actions. Second, the study of these debates and innovations sheds light on the general understanding of the human condition during the formative period between medieval times and early modernity. The theological premises of the human condition are visible, moreover, in the Reformation teaching of sin and free will. These doctrines are connected with the philosophical problem of weakness of will in various ways. Furthermore, the philosophical background of the Renaissance and the Reformation is not restricted to Augustinian and Aristotelian features, but Platonism and Stoicism are also reconsidered and re-evaluated. Human weakness, divided will, and the conflict between reason and desire are extensively discussed in Platonic and Neo-Stoic contexts.

In order to make visible the broader significance of our topic for the early modern history of ideas, it is often necessary to treat the theological and philosophical perspectives simultaneously. The authors of our period were for the most part deeply aware of both theological and philosophical traditions. Their understanding of the human condition should not, therefore, be reduced to either philosophy or theology, but the two perspectives need to be combined in our reading of their texts. Although many of the authors of the Reformation period are primarily theologians and many Renaissance authors primarily philosophers, the present study claims that they fundamentally belong to the same tradition of discussing human weakness in its various manifestations.

The present study does not aim at making a sharp distinction between the Renaissance and the different European Reformations. All authors contribute to the ongoing discussion on human weakness; most authors are also connected with the Humanist movement in some way. For the sake of convenience, however, the Renaissance and the Lutheran and Calvinist Reformations are discussed in different chapters. The borderlines between the chapters are flexible: for instance, historically speaking Lefèvre d'Étaples and John Mair (2.4, 2.5) both belong to the Renaissance and the Reformation period, and the section on Luther's Erfurt background (3.1) deals with issues also discussed in the chapter on the Renaissance (2). Some of the Renaissance authors contribute to the Reformation of the Catholic Church and its teaching. Due to many such overlaps, the boundaries between the Renaissance and the Reformations should not be defined in any rigid manner.

The interconnected nature of philosophy and theology has also shaped the selection of source materials. Renaissance and Reformation authors continued to write commentaries on EN VII. *Nicomachean Ethics* remained in the university curriculum at least until the emergence of Cartesianism, and one can therefore easily find long discussions of akrasia in the extant commentaries. Early modern commentaries on EN are an important genre among the sources of the present study.

There are, however, several reasons why commentaries remain a necessary but insufficient part of the whole story. New literary genres, such as textbooks, dictionaries, and monographic treatises emerge in the Renaissance and the Reformation.[10] The relative importance of commentaries is no longer comparable to the medieval period. In addition, many early modern commentaries are humanistic, educational, and philological rather than philosophical in their approach. Although they may explicate text of EN VII at great length, they do not necessarily pose or even recognize its problems in a critical and analytical manner.

Another new factor was introduced by the confessional divide between Catholic and Protestant authors. A fairly extensive theological background is necessary in order to understand the philosophical discussions, since weakness of will is often discussed in theological literature. One important feature of this literature is that both Catholics and Protestants claim that Aristotle and Augustine are on their side. In particular, Augustine's discussion on the phenomenon of acting against one's own will is treated in very different texts, from biblical commentaries on Romans 7 to philosophical treatises intended to heal the divided soul.

It should be added that, even for the medieval period, we now realize that the approach based on the commentaries on Aristotle's EN remains too narrow. The studies that have been published since my *Weakness of the Will in Medieval Thought* (1994) have revealed a great many, highly interesting medieval sources apart from the commentaries.[11]

Given the exponential growth of texts and literary genres in the Renaissance and the Reformation, one needs to be selective with the sources. I have attempted to include the most influential philosophical commentaries on EN, whereas the primarily philological expositions have been left aside. My selection of textbooks and treatises is conditioned by their use of Aristotle and Augustine, but limitations of space also play

---

[10] See Kraye (1988); Lines (2002); Kraye and Saarinen (2005); Saarinen (forthcoming).
[11] See Kent (1995); Hoffmann, Müller, and Perkams (2006); Müller (2007) and (2009).

a role. Authors belonging to certain periods and geographical areas, such as Renaissance Italy from 1350 to 1450 or early sixteenth-century Germany did not produce many innovative commentaries on Aristotle. But these authors, for instance, Petrach or Martin Luther, do interpret Augustine's views on powerless will in a creative and challenging fashion. During Protestant Aristotelianism (1560–1630), the flood of commentaries and textbooks is again massive. Many relevant texts deriving from this period need to be left aside.[12] I have attempted to offer a representative selection.

Most authors of both the Renaissance and the Reformation affirm the Humanist principle *ad fontes*. They are very conscious of the ancient and medieval interpretation traditions, which we need to outline before proceeding to the actual sources. Although Aristotle's discussion remains the standard against which other discussions are measured, it is also essential to sketch the understanding of akrasia in Plato, Stoicism, and Augustine (1.1–1.2). While the precise relationship of these three ancient traditions to Aristotle's discussion can be debated, they all remain important in the course of reception history.

The medieval views are summarized with the help of a threefold classification: the Aristotelian views of Thomas Aquinas and Walter Burley (1.3), the Franciscan voluntarist critique of Walter of Bruges and Henry of Ghent (1.4), and the Augustinian-Aristotelian syntheses undertaken by Albert the Great and John Buridan (1.5). In presenting these three strains of interpretation, special attention is paid to the important new studies which have appeared since the publication of my own study in 1994.

Although the four currents of ancient thought (Plato, Aristotle, Stoicism, and Augustine), and the three classes of medieval interpretation remain ideal types, they are sufficient to capture the sources employed by later Renaissance and Reformation authors. A preliminary typology or 'inventory' of different models of akrasia appears at the end of 1.5. This typology is applied in later chapters to the varying explanations of akrasia during the Renaissance and the Reformation.

Several new studies have argued that the *Quattrocento* was not an innovative period in the history of Aristotelian ethics and that this situation only changed with the publication of the famous *Tres conversiones* of Jacques Lefèvre d'Étaples in 1497.[13] The present study modifies this view, pointing out many different developments during the fifteenth and sixteenth centuries. Francesco Petrarch's innovative treatment of virtues and will in *Secretum* and *De remediis utriusque fortunae* contains noteworthy passages which can be regarded as the beginning of Renaissance discussions on akrasia (2.1).

After Petrarch, we will turn to Donato Acciaiouli as the most influential representative of the reception of Aristotle in Renaissance Italy (2.2). Moving north of the Alps, special attention is then paid to John Versor, Virgilius Wellendorffer, Jacques Lefèvre

---

[12] In particular, philological commentaries and works of Catholic moral theology. See the discussion in the beginning of 2.5 below.

[13] Kraye (1995); Kessler (1999); Lines (2002), 17–18.

d'Étaples, Josse Clichtove, and John Mair (2.3–2.5). The final part of this chapter returns to Italy, dealing with Francesco Piccolomini (2.6).

The third chapter begins with the dawn of the Lutheran Reformation. In order to understand Martin Luther's view of the fundamental incapacity of the human will, it is necessary to begin with some ethical and psychological views of his teachers in Erfurt (3.1). Another important factor was the interpretation of Romans 7 in the Augustinian tradition. In his formative years, Luther expounded this biblical text several times to highlight his own views. For a deeper understanding of subsequent Reformation thought, it is crucial to see whether and in what precise sense Romans 7 relates to akrasia. Given these preliminaries, it is possible to establish Luther's view of weakness of will within its immediate historical context (3.2). The third chapter then proceeds to Philip Melanchthon and Joachim Camerarius, who wrote the first Lutheran commentaries on EN (3.3). The last part of the chapter deals with the Lutheran Aristotelians, Theophilus Golius and Wolfgang Heider (3.4).

John Calvin's *Institutio christianae religionis* contains a thematic discussion on Aristotle's akrasia (4.1). The Calvinist Reformation was often characterized by great academic erudition, which led to conscious renewal in ethics. In addition to Calvin, we analyse the interpretations of akrasia in early Calvinist Ramism (Theodor Zwinger) and Humanism (Hubert van Giffen) (4.2), as well as in Lambert Daneau's programme of 'Christian ethics' (4.3). The systematic textbooks of John Case and Bartholomaeus Keckermann round out the picture of Calvinism (4.4).

The first part of the fifth chapter (5.1) presents an overall summary of our findings, bringing together the materials discussed separately in the three previous chapters. In addition, the fifth chapter briefly discusses the views of some founding fathers of modernity, namely Shakespeare (5.2), Descartes, Spinoza, and Leibniz (5.3). Their understanding of akrasia has to some extent been dealt with in earlier studies, but our discussion situates them within the broader historical discussion on weakness of will.

1

Ancient and Medieval Background

1.1 Plato and Aristotle

Our cursory discussion of ancient philosophy cannot cover the whole variety of interpretations available in contemporary research.[1] We will be content with presenting the basic texts, their well-known problems of interpretation, and the prevailing scholarly views. Our main focus is on those problems that are relevant within the context of the Renaissance and the Reformation.

In *Protagoras* 351–8, Plato describes the view of Socrates, which is later discussed by Aristotle in EN VII. Socrates argues that since agents always choose what they think best, our knowledge cannot be overcome through emotions like pleasure, fear, or anger, although many people commonly say this is the case. When people seemingly act against their knowledge, they in reality do not possess a firm judgement, their judgement following the illusory presentations of the moment. Thus at each moment they in fact do follow their momentary judgement, based on, for instance, the judgement that pleasure is good. Their reason is not overcome by pleasure, but it judges that pleasure should be pursued.

In other words, the person who follows pleasure or fear follows the judgement recommending this course of action. This person remains ignorant of true virtue, but he or she chooses what he momentarily thinks best. Socrates summarizes this view as follows:

No one willingly goes to meet evil or what he thinks to be evil. To make for what one believes to be evil, instead of making for the good, is not, it seems, in human nature, and when faced with the choice of two evils no one will choose the greater when he might choose the less. (358c–d)

In the fourth book of the *Republic*, however, Plato introduces his tripartite division of the soul and compares it with the classes of society. The appetitive and the spirited lower parts of the soul are distinctive of the lower classes and individuals, whereas rationality is distinctive of the ruling class and the philosophers. In this context, Plato allows for a genuine conflict between reason and desires. He seems to admit that many,

---

[1] Bobonich and Destrée (2007), Hoffmann (2008), and Müller (2009) contain new studies and excellent bibliographic information. See also Sorabji (2000), 305–10.

if not most people are governed by their appetite or spiritedness, although their reason keeps warning them. Here Socrates teaches that

> the soul of a man within him has a better part and a worse part, and the expression self-mastery means the control of the worse by the naturally better part . . . But when, because of bad breeding or some association, the better part, which is the smaller, is dominated by the multitude of the worse, I think that our speech censures this as a reproach, and calls the man in this plight unself-controlled and licentious. (431a–b)

Plato's *Republic* thus conveys the classic picture of a struggle between reason and desire. Reason should rule the lower parts and, in a virtuous person, reason in fact rules and prompts good actions. But akrasia remains a genuine possibility in a situation in which the better part stays alive but is mastered by the lower. Thus the *Republic* seems to justify the commonplace view of akrasia which is criticized in *Protagoras*. Although the wise person cannot be akratic, ordinary people often are.

Given these two texts, it is possible to label two different views as 'Platonic'. According to the first view, Plato adopts the Socratic view and denies the possibility of akrasia, even among ordinary people. According to the second view, Platonism holds that (a) the soul is tripartite, (b) that there are, at least in ordinary people, genuine conflicts between reason and desire, and (c) that desire can sometimes overcome the better part of the soul.

There is some evidence that the later books of the *Republic* again revise Plato's view towards the Socratic position. It has been argued that the tripartite division of the soul represents a preliminary stage of psychological analysis and that Plato finally defends the unity of the soul. This unity is forged in the *Republic* V–VII and is based on knowledge and rationality. The picture of true knowledge and love of truth which is achieved in Book VII is similar to that of *Protagoras*.[2] Other scholars maintain, however, that the *Republic* contains two different moral psychologies.[3] Still others consider that the two views can be reconciled through a distinction between first-order and second-order desires (desiring p vs desiring not to desire p); in such a case, the akratic person possesses good judgement only in a second-order sense.[4]

For the purposes of our reception history it is important to note the continuing influence of the two pictures. The 'commonplace' view of the *Republic* IV which allows for the conflicts within the tripartite soul was later employed in order to refute overly intellectualist views, whereas the philosophical view of Socrates became influential as the basis of Aristotle's reflection.

Aristotle begins his discussion by outlining a scale of virtuous and vicious moral states:

> Let us . . . point out that of moral states to be avoided there are three kinds—vice, incontinence, brutishness. The contraries of two of these are evident—one we call excellence, the other

---

[2] Dorter (2008).   [3] Shields (2007), 86.   [4] Bobonich (2007).

continence; to brutishness it would be most fitting to oppose superhuman excellence, something heroic and divine. (EN 1145a15–20)

The commentators of the Renaissance and the Reformation are very interested in these classifications. Although EN VII treats many classifications only in passing, commentators can use Aristotle's brief remarks as a springboard to develop their own views. The basic classification of six moral states presupposes that virtue and vice are the normative standards which are superseded by heroic virtue and brutishness, whereas continence and incontinence represent an underdeveloped stage of virtue or wickedness.[5]

Continence (*enkrateia*) is, therefore, an incomplete virtue, and incontinence (*akrasia*) an incomplete vice. Aristotle also says that the incontinent is half-wicked (EN 1152a18). Later interpreters often understand temperance (cf. EN 1151a18) to be the full virtue to which continence relates as an underdeveloped stage. Accordingly, akrasia is less bad than intemperance. Virtuous and continent people both act well, but the continent person would feel pleasure in acting contrary to reason; he therefore performs a virtuous action with some difficulty. The wicked or intemperate person does not think that he ought to live according to reason, but the akratic person thinks that he should. However, both the intemperate and the akratic person in reality act contrary to reason (EN 1151b–1152a).

In addition to the six moral states, Aristotle mentions some others but leaves their precise role somewhat open. Endurance (*karteria*) and softness (*malakia*) are closely related to continence and akrasia in EN VII, 1. Aristotle concludes that continence is better than endurance. The man of endurance can resist passions but not conquer them, whereas the continent person conquers the passions. The soft person is not defeated by appetites and pains, but he avoids them. Aristotle is critical of softness and seems to consider it a worse state than akrasia (EN 1150a24–b6).

Aristotle distinguishes between variants of softness and akrasia, depending on which intense pleasures and pains cause the deviant action and how. That variant of akrasia which is caused by natural desires, for instance anger and bad temper, is less bad than akrasia caused by the appetite for excess (EN 1149b4–10). Likewise, if a person is defeated by violent pleasures which could conquer most people, he can more easily be forgiven than the man who is defeated by pleasures which most people can resist (EN 1150b6–10). Another category is the so-called precipitate akrasia, in which the person rushes into action without proper deliberation (EN 1150b19–22; 1152a18–19). Later, for instance in Epictetus, this variant of akrasia is discussed as the vice of precipitancy (*propeteia*).[6]

It is common in Aristotelianism to treat the six moral states mentioned in EN 1145a15–20 as the basic matrix. Additional classes, in particular endurance, softness,

---

[5] Bobonich and Destrée (2007) and Hoffmann (2008) contain new studies and good bibliographies on Aristotle's akrasia. Among older works, Charles (1984) remains very valuable.

[6] See Salles (2007), referring to Epictetus, *Discourses* 1, 28, 30; 2, 1, 10; 3, 22, 104; 4, 4, 46; 4, 8, 1; 4, 13, 5.

and the different variants of akrasia, appear to have a contextual character. They are employed in judging the moral quality of particular actions, but their precise meaning depends on the discussion at hand.

Aristotle's philosophical problems do not, however, relate to the issues of classification but to the claim by Socrates that 'there is no such thing as incontinence' (EN 1145b25). According to Aristotle, 'this view contradicts the plain phenomena, and we must inquire about what happens to such a man' (EN 1145b28). The results of this enquiry continue to be debated in today's research, as they were in medieval philosophy. Because of this openness with regard to the possible explanations of weakness of will, the reception history of EN VII remains complex and generates new views of human action. Given that Aristotle classifies akrasia as a basic moral state and discusses its variants and their moral value, it is evident that he does not share the view of Socrates. For Aristotle, akrasia is a common phenomenon in need of closer examination.

At the same time, Aristotle's discussion remains sympathetic to Socrates insofar as the so-called 'clear-eyed akrasia' is concerned. Following many previous studies, I will use the phrase 'clear-eyed akrasia' to depict a case in which the agent with perfect knowledge of the relevant facts and an adequate use of reason acts against his or her better judgement. Aristotle does not allow for this kind of akratic action, setting out to show that the incontinent person ignores something or commits a logical error in his or her akratic action.

Aristotle makes three distinctions with regard to how a person knows the facts relevant to his action. (1) A person may have the knowledge but not exercise it (EN 1146b31–35); (2) a person may know the universal propositions relevant for his action (e.g. dry food is good for you), but ignore some particular proposition (e.g. this food is dry, EN 1147a1–9); (3) some people may even claim to have knowledge but yet do not have it in the proper and effective manner, as is the case with the drunken man who utters the verses of Empedocles (EN 1147a10–23, b12). Common, though not clear-eyed, instances of akrasia can thus take place when the person's knowledge of the good is qualified in one of these three ways.

In addition to these qualifications, Aristotle in this context introduces his famous doctrine of the practical syllogism, a logical framework which explains the emergence of action. Without entering into an extensive discussion of the nature of the practical syllogism, we can briefly describe it as follows: the practical syllogism consists of a major premise which recommends a certain conduct in universal terms (e.g. everything sweet ought to be tasted) and a minor premise which conveys the particular and perceptible circumstances now relevant for the agent (e.g. this is sweet). When the two premises appear together, the soul must in theoretical syllogisms affirm the logical conclusion, but in a practical syllogism it must immediately act (EN 1147a25–30). In other words, the conclusion of the practical syllogism is the action corresponding to the norm or recommendation.

The doctrine of the practical syllogism effectively denies the possibility of clear-eyed akrasia. If the relevant premises are clearly and simultaneously present in the agent's mind, he or she must act according to their outcome; the outcome is in itself the action. Therefore, something must be wrong in the practical syllogism of the akratic person. In this syllogistic context, Aristotle explains the emergence of akrasia as follows:

Since the last proposition (*protasis*) is a belief about a perceptible object and is what determines our action, either a man does not have this when he is in a state of passion or he has it in the sense in which having knowledge is not knowing but merely saying something—as a drunken man may be said to have knowledge of the verses of Empedocles. And because the last term is not universal nor an object of knowledge equally with a universal term, what Socrates was seeking seems to turn out to be correct; for it is not in the presence of what is thought to be proper knowledge that the affection of incontinence arises nor is it that which is dragged about as a result of a state of passion but it is in the presence rather of perceptual knowledge. (EN 1147b9–18)

The precise meaning of this passage has been extensively debated. Aristotle evidently follows a middle way between Socrates and the commonplace view. In Aristotle's view, passion cannot enslave the universal truths which are proper knowledge expressed in the major premise. Passion can, however, influence the perceptual knowledge of the particulars so that something with regard to them remains ignored. Thus the proper action does not emerge, the person acting akratically contrary to the knowledge expressed in the major premise.

What remains debatable in this crucial passage is the actual nature of perceptual knowledge. An obvious and widespread interpretation holds that the details of the minor premise remain to an extent ignored. In my previous study I labelled this interpretation '1a'.[7] A somewhat stronger or more clear-eyed case of akrasia is '1b', an interpretation in which it is claimed that the akratic person can grasp both the universals and the particulars but cannot combine them in a proper syllogistic manner. According to this model, akrasia resembles the logical errors described in *Prior Analytics* (67b5–11).[8] Both of these interpretations take the 'last protasis' to refer to the minor premise.

A third possibility, designated number '2', reads the 'last *protasis*' in EN 1147b9 as pertaining to the propositional conclusion of the syllogism.[9] In terms of this interpretation, it is possible to distinguish between the propositional and the dynamic level of the conclusion and to claim that it is possible to reach the conclusion intellectually and yet act contrary to it. This model is more 'clear-eyed' than 1a and 1b, though not

---

[7] According to Charles (1984), 117, 'most recent commentators' support this view. See also, e.g. Sorabji (2000), 311–12. Bobonich and Destrée (2007) offer new contributions.

[8] For this view, see Hardie (1980), 282–6. See also my discussion in Saarinen (1994), 12–13 and Hintikka (1978).

[9] This, according to Sorabji (2000), 312, is the 'minority interpretation' put forward in Charles (1984) and Dahl (1984); see also Charles (2007).

completely so, since Aristotle in EN 1147b9–18 holds that the last *protasis*, the propositional conclusion, is only grasped by the agent in an imperfect manner.

All three models have found support in modern scholarship; in fact, all three found adherents in medieval philosophy.[10] While 1a and 1b need not assume the existence of propositional conclusion, model 2 has some other benefits with regard to Aristotle's discussion. One of these benefits pertains to Aristotle's notion of choice (*prohairesis*). Since the Aristotelian choice is the state which transforms the results of practical reason into action, it does not choose freely among alternatives but effectively supports the rational judgement. In EN 1152a15–17, Aristotle holds that the akratic person acts voluntarily but is not wicked, since his choice is good. In EN 1111b13–15, Aristotle remarks that the akratic person acts with appetite but not with choice.

Since Aristotle evidently thinks that the akratic person has the good choice, it would be somewhat odd to claim that he ignores the minor premise (1a) or cannot combine the two premises (1b). In these cases, the good choice would not emerge, whereas model 2, in affirming that the akratic reasoning leads to a conclusion and the corresponding good choice, is in keeping with this view of choice. In the model 2, the propositional conclusion and the good choice are formed in the mind of the akratic person, but for some reason they remain imperfect and therefore cannot prevent the emergence of the passionate act contrary to choice. The akratic act is nevertheless voluntary (*hekousion*), since the agent is neither ignorant nor compelled to perform it. It is important to note that the traditional translations of *hekousion* and *prohairesis* do not contain all modern meanings ascribed to 'voluntary' and 'choice'.

We will not discuss further which of the three models should be preferred in the historical understanding of Aristotle's akrasia. All three are Aristotelian in the sense that they deny clear-eyed akrasia but affirm the existence of akrasia as a common moral state. The three models further differ from later non-Aristotelian models in two important respects. First, the models presuppose the overarching importance of the practical syllogism which guides the rational deliberation towards one alternative which is preferred in the final judgement. There should not be lasting internal conflict, the psychology of the mind being harmonious and teleological. Second, there is no 'free will' involved in the sense of later Western philosophy. In these two respects Aristotelianism differs from Stoicism and Augustinianism.

1.2 Stoicism, Paul, and Augustine

Stoicism was an important current in Renaissance and Reformation thought. Most authors want to keep a critical distance from Stoicism, but aspects of Stoic theories of emotions and action are both consciously and unconsciously employed in the discussions on weakness of will. The fragmentary nature of the extant sources makes the

---

[10] For medieval views, see Saarinen (1994) and 1.3–1.5 below.

precise reconstruction of original Stoic positions difficult and hypothetical. The new study by Gourinat reminds us that the words *akrasia* and *akratês* appear only three times in the *Stoicorum veterum fragmenta* and twice in Epictetus. Sorabji holds that Seneca's *impotentia* and *impotens* correspond to Aristotle's Greek terms, but Gourinat doubts this. He is also critical of Zeller's view, according to which Cicero's term *intemperantia* could be a translation of *akrasia*.[11]

There is a much-discussed passage in Chrysippus in which the term *akratês* appears. We will continue the discussion on its interpretation, keeping in mind that Gourinat warns of drawing far-reaching conclusions on the basis of a single occurrence of the word. The passage is particularly relevant for us for two reasons: (1) its description of akrasia resembles Augustine's elaboration of incontinence in *Confessions* 8, and (2) Galen and Chrysippus employ the story of Medea as an illustration of this kind of akrasia. Both *Confessions* 8 and the story of Medea continue to have a formative importance for the understanding of akrasia in the Renaissance and the Reformation.

Galen quotes Chrysippus as follows:

Such states are like those that are out of control (*akrateis*), as if the men had no power over themselves but were carried away, just as those who run hard are carried along and have no control over that sort of movement. But those who move with reason as their guide and steer their course by it, no matter what the nature of the reasoning, have control over, or are not subject to, that kind of movement and its impulses.[12]

A little earlier in the text Galen discusses the story of Medea as portrayed by Euripides and interpreted by Chrysippus. When Medea sets out to kill her children in order to take vengeance on her husband, she says: 'I know what evil I propose to do, but anger rules my deliberations.' For Chrysippus, Medea is a case of akrasia within the unified intellectual soul: she has good judgement, but she nevertheless rationally continues her plan of vengeance. Galen, however, prefers a commonplace Platonist reading which presupposes a threefold division within the soul, holding that Medea's reason was overpowered by the passion of anger.[13]

Recent discussion on the so-called Stoic akrasia has concentrated on the two examples provided by Chrysippus. To understand the cases of Medea and the runner who cannot stop running better, we need a more comprehensive outline of the Stoic theory of action, in which three faculties of the soul contribute to the emergence of action. First, there is impression (*phantasia*) which arises as the result of perception. In

---

[11] Gourinat (2007), 215, 241–4, referring to Zeller (1909), 234 and Sorabji (2000), 54–65. The word *akrasia* appears in the New Testament in Matt. 23:25 (Vulgate: *immunditia*) and 1 Cor. 7:5 (Vulgate: *incontinentia*); the word *akratês* appears in 2 Tim. 3:3. The triad of 2 Tim. 3:3: *akratês, anhêmeros, aphilagathos* (Vulgate: *incontinens, immitis, sine benignitate*) resembles Aristotle's threefold classification of vice. See further Saarinen (2008a), 148–9.

[12] Translation from Gourinat (2007), 241, 244, who also discusses various translation problems. Galen, *Plac. Hipp et Plat*. 4, 4, 24, ed. De Lacy (1978–1984), 256.

[13] Galen, *Plac. Hipp. et Plat*. 4, 2, 27, ed. De Lacy (1978–1984), 244. Euripides, *Medea* 1078–9. See further Gill (1983); Price (1994); Sorabji (2000), 56; Graver (2007), 70–4; Müller (2009), 54–61.

animals, the impression immediately calls forth a second faculty, a desire or impulse (*horme*) to move. In humans, however, reason first passes judgements on various impressions. A third faculty, that of assent (*sunkatathesis*), accompanies the judgement so that the impression is joined with the impulse to move. In humans, assent thus mediates between sensual impressions and impulses to move.[14]

According to Origen's description of Stoicism,

ensouled things are moved by themselves when an impression occurs within them which calls forth an impulse ... A rational animal, however, in addition to its impressionistic nature, has reason which passes judgement on impressions, rejecting some of these and accepting others, in order that the animal may be guided accordingly.[15]

Plutarch reports that the most disputed subject in the Stoic doctrine concerns the view that

without assent there is neither action nor impulsion, and that they are talking nonsense ... who claim that, when an appropriate impression occurs, impulsion ensues at once without people first having yielded or given their assent.[16]

Given this view, 'all impulses are acts of assent'.[17]

This view of assent is a Stoic innovation which has no counterpart in Plato's and Aristotle's theory of action. The classical philosophers understand that rational deliberation results in finding best proper means to reach the one goal. This unified result is expressed in reason's judgement and the corresponding choice (*prohairesis*). The Hellenistic Stoics, however, affirm the possibility of conflicting impressions and conflicting judgements related to them. Although the sage may have learned to eliminate misguided impressions, the ordinary person is surrounded by a variety of different impressions which are not, according to Origen,[18] under our control. Although the Stoic assent is not a faculty of free will but a faculty which coexists with the prevailing judgement, the assent must 'reject some' impressions while 'accepting others', as Origens tells us. In this sense, the plurality of options is expressed more strongly than in classical philosophy. While Socrates and Aristotle believe that rational deliberation finally leads to the judgement related to the one goal, the Stoics locate judgement and assent at the beginning of the road of rationality. Thus the agent needs to operate with an initial plurality of conflicting options.

An important corollary of the Stoic view is that all passions, like anger, fear, and distress, are already judgements assented to and therefore functions of the reasoning

---

[14] Long and Sedley (1987), 321–2. Graver (2007), 67–71 discusses 'the runner who cannot stop running'. Müller (2009), 165–83 deals with Chrysippus's example of Medea. I will not, however, go into their interpretations in detail, but present merely a general outline of Stoicism.

[15] Long-Sedley, 313, quoting Origen, *De principiis* 3, 1, 2–3.

[16] Long-Sedley, 317, quoting Plutarch, *On Stoic self-contradictions* 1057A.

[17] Long-Sedley, 197, quoting *Stobaeus* 2, 88, 2–6.

[18] So Origen, *De principiis* 3, 1, 2–3, as explained in Gosling (1990), 65. Müller (2009), 213–43 studies Origen's concept of akrasia.

faculty. If the impressions lead to impulse only when a rational judgement and assent is given to them, then all passions (desires, impulses, aspects of *hormē*) are by definition judgements. The Stoics want to assert a strong unity of the soul in which all desires express a judgement. Commonplace Platonists like Plutarch and Galen criticize this view as being contrary to our psychological experience which, so they believe, perceives the conflict between reason and the passions. Thus, according to Galen, Chrysippus in his Stoic definitions of passions

completely departs from the doctrine of the ancients, defining distress as 'a fresh opinion that something bad is present' . . . In these definitions he obviously mentions only the rational part of the soul, omitting the appetitive and competitive.[19]

This quote reveals how the commonplace Platonist critique presupposes the threefold division of the soul. By contrast, Chrysippus and his Stoic followers teach that there cannot be any internal conflict between reason and desire, because all impulses emerge as the results of judgement and are thus rational. As the grown-up person is a rational being, all impressions she receives are judgemental. If this person fears, she is not overcome by the desire for fear, but she has judged it fitting to fear. Epictetus says that

it is not things themselves that disturb men, but their judgements about things. For example, death is nothing terrible . . . what is terrible is the judgement that death is terrible. So whenever we are impeded or disturbed or distressed, let us blame no one but ourselves, that is, our own judgements.[20]

Given the Stoic unity of the soul and the judgemental nature of passions it does not seem to make sense to say that somebody acts against her own better judgement or that there is a genuine conflict between reason and passion. All impulses simply represent the rational judgement the person has. According to Plutarch, the Stoics

say that passion is no different from reason, and that there is no dissension and conflict between the two, but a turning of the single reason in both directions, which we do not notice owing to the sharpness and speed of the change . . . For appetite and anger and fear and all such things are corrupt opinions and judgements, which do not arise about just one part of the soul but are the whole commanding-faculty's inclinations, yieldings, assents and impulses, and, quite generally, activities which change rapidly.[21]

Given this analysis of the inner life of the mind, there are no real conflicts but merely sudden changes of opinion. From a commonplace Platonist viewpoint, such a doctrine is contrary to our psychological experience.

Although the Stoic view of judgement and assent differs from Socrates and Aristotle, the Stoics are no less intellectualistic in their theory of action; perhaps they are even more so than the classical philosophers, since they teach that all impulses stem from

---

[19] Long-Sedley, 411–12, quoting Galen, *Plac. Hipp. et Plat.* 4, 2, 1–6.

[20] Long-Sedley, 418, quoting Epictetus, *Manual* 5.

[21] Long-Sedley, 412, quoting Plutarch, *On moral virtue* 446F–447A.

judgement and assent. If this is the whole story, then there is no place for akrasia. If somebody goes wrong, it is due to their poor judgement. There cannot be a case in which the wrong impression is followed while the person assents to the right alternative.

Several scholars have argued, however, that the reality of Stoicism is more complicated, and that the hostile reports that Plutarch, Galen, and others give is a somewhat distorted picture.[22] There are at least two different ways of introducing akrasia into the Stoic discussion. One way proceeds from the so-called *propatheiai*, pre-passions, residual impulses activated immediately by the impressions. In animals and small children the impulses emerge in this manner, without the control of reason's assent. Although rational adults act according to their judgement and assent, they may possess the residual traces of pre-passions. For instance, a trace of natural pre-passion towards some good could be found in a person who acts according to his misguided judgements. In this limited sense there may be some residual 'impulse towards the better' even during the wrong action.[23]

Another theoretical possibility results from the effect of earlier assents which have shaped the person's character and memory to the extent that the person cannot, in spite of new information, avoid acting according to his old habits. The paradigmatic example of such a situation is Medea's line: 'I know what evil I propose to do, but anger rules my deliberations.' Medea knows that murder is wrong and she is conscious of this fact. She has, however, given her assent to the passion of anger for revenge for some time already. In this situation, the reasons for revenge continue to determine her deliberation. The outcome of this long-standing assent is that a later judgement and assent to the sentence 'murder is evil' cannot achieve control over the prevailing assent.

As we saw above, in the crucial passage in which Chrysippus employs the word *akratês*, he compares akratic people to runners who cannot stop running. The runners have first assented to start running, but the subsequent internal effort to stop remains beyond their control.[24] In this sense the Stoic theory would allow for acting against better judgement: an earlier assent which has become a habit continues to rule the deliberation even when the person arrives at a new judgement. In the cases of Medea and the runner who cannot stop running, the Stoic view of conflicting impressions leads, therefore, to a situation which resembles Aristotelian akrasia. In such a situation the reason can grasp the better course of action without accepting it. Moreover, if emotions in the Stoic theory result from mistaken judgements and display a lack of control, then akrasia appears, together with disturbing emotions.

We need not discuss further the respects in which this theoretical possibility for a genuine Stoic account of akrasia is applicable to Hellenistic Stoicism and how much

---

[22] See Gill (1983); Gosling (1990), 48–68; Sorabji (2000), 56–65; Graver (2007). Müller (2009), 155–93 presents an elaborate account of Stoic views of akrasia.

[23] Gosling (1990), 53–5; Knuuttila (2004), 63–8; Graver (2007), 67–9.

[24] Gosling (1990), 59.

support it gets from the available historical sources.[25] Renaissance and Reformation authors sometimes employ the verses of Euripides, but more often they depict Medea's words from Ovid's *Metamorphoses* 7, 20–21: 'I see the better and approve it, but I follow the worse.'

It is also possible to see reason and passion as complementary faculties within a single course of action. Medea's revenge is motivated by her anger, but it also involves careful rational planning. In the context of Stoicism, although anger may loosely be said to overcome reason, the individual cannot perform an action unless he or she has assented to it.[26] Anger does not overcome reason, but concurs with it, since Medea's elaborate revenge is preceded by clever preparation. Later Christian thinkers similarly hold that the wrong desire does not simply 'overcome' a rational person, a sinful act being preceded by a voluntary assent or consent to the persuasion of desire. It is Augustine who strengthens this link between desire and consent in Western thought.

Long before Augustine, however, the apostle Paul in Romans 7 discusses a position which bears some resemblance to Medea's conflict. Paul's discussion has been interpreted in diverse ways in the Christian Church as well as in contemporary exegetical scholarship. The ecclesiastical debates are highly dependent on Augustine's and Luther's reading of Romans 7. We will first present the contemporary view of Paul in biblical scholarship and then turn to the reception of Paul in Augustine's writings.

In Romans 7:15–20 Paul gives his classical account of human powerlessness:

I do not understand my own actions. For I do not do what I want, but I do the very thing I hate. Now if I do what I do not want, I agree that the law is good. But in fact it is no longer I that do it, but sin that dwells within me. For I know that nothing good dwells within me, that is, in my flesh. I can will what is right, but I cannot do it. For I do not do the good I want, but the evil I do not want is what I do. Now if I do what I do not want, it is no longer I that do it, but sin that dwells within me.

One basic problem of this passage is that both before and after it Paul teaches that Christians are liberated from sin. In Romans 6:22 Paul says: 'But now that you have been freed from sin and enslaved to God, the advantage you get is sanctification.' In Romans 8:2 he states: 'For the law of the Spirit of life in Christ Jesus has set you free from the law of sin and of death.' How is this optimistic picture of freedom compatible with the pessimistic view of Romans 7:15–20?

The majority of contemporary biblical scholars explain this discrepancy through postulating a difference of perspectives in Romans 6–8. According to this explanation, Romans 6:22 and 8:2 describe the current, relatively optimistic situation of the Christian writer. The *ego* of Romans 7:15–20, on the other hand, does not refer to

---

[25] For Sorabji (2000), 56, Chrysippus makes 'all emotion involve akrasia', because emotion is nothing else than mistaken judgement and being out of control. For Gourinat (2007), 216, 247, this is exaggerated, but he admits that 'some texts . . . make incontinence, if not the *source* of all passions, then at least the . . . vice *dealing with passions*' (247, emphasis in original).

[26] See Dillon (1997), 213 and Torrance (2007).

Paul's current state, but it is employed as an 'exemplary I' which remains under the law and under sin. The conflict of the 'exemplary I' is, therefore, not experienced at the time of writing this passage. Paul is rather making a retrospective analysis: his new Christian personality now sees clearly the conflict of his former self and describes that past conflict. Moreover, the conflict described in Romans 7:15–20 was never actual and self-conscious: the person under sin did not yet understand his existence in terms of this conflict, and the Christian person now presents this analysis only in retrospect, after he has been freed from sin.[27]

The so-called 'new perspective on Paul', a dominant view in current biblical scholarship, adheres to this explanation, maintaining that the Christian existence is, for Paul, characterized by the freedom from sin. A competing minority position is the so-called 'Lutheran Paul', a view claiming that the situation depicted in Romans 7:15–20 remains permanently relevant for the Christian and has a deeper existential significance.[28] Obviously, this view also needs to explain its compatibility with other and more positive Pauline statements. An additional oddity of the 'Lutheran Paul' is its postulate that the exemplary apostle and saint would have remained permanently weak-willed, continuing to do things he hated. Augustine and Luther already struggled with this problem, as we will see below. Although the 'new perspective' postulates a relatively complex difference of perspectives, the majority of contemporary biblical scholars considers it to be a smaller interpretative problem than the awkward assumption that, for Paul, even exemplary Christians remain permanently weak-willed.

A related but distinct problem of Romans 7:15–20 concerns its historical relationship with Medea's conflict as described by Euripides and Ovid. Many scholars today think that Paul was probably familiar with the general topic of inner conflict as discussed in Hellenistic popular philosophy. They consider it unlikely, however, that Paul in Romans 7:15–20 would directly address Medea's conflict or other similar discussions available, for instance, among his contemporaries Seneca and Epictetus. Paul is rather using a common topic familiar to many of his readers.[29] Scholars also agree that Paul does not aim to make any conscious contribution to the Aristotelian problem of akrasia, but he simply illustrates the existence of humans under the power of sin with the help of the popular topic of inner conflict.[30]

Given this, one can still ask which concept of 'willing' Paul here presupposes. Paul's use of *thelein* does contain some features of intellectual desire, but this verb also expresses a distinct concept which is not reducible to cognitive powers. Paul's conflict

---

[27] Müller (2009), 211–15; Westerholm (2004). These two studies give an overview of exegetical literature. Engberg-Pedersen (2002) and Lichtenberger (2004) are comprehensive new studies on 'I' in Romans 7. My own view is elaborated in Saarinen (2008b).

[28] Westerholm (2004); see also Lichtenberger (2004).

[29] So Theissen (1983), 221 and Müller (2009), 216. Theissen (1983), 213–23, Hommel (1984), and Lichtenberger (2004), 166–76 have collected parallel materials from Hellenistic philosophy. They are discussed in detail by Müller (2009), 216–42.

[30] Müller (2009), 236; Lichtenberger (2004), 143.

between willing and doing is not portrayed as a conflict between reason and desire; this is so, because the concepts of knowledge and emotion are both embedded in the verb *thelein*. Rather, the Pauline conflict is related to the metaphysical duality of the realms of 'spirit' and 'flesh'. As 'flesh', the natural and sinful person cannot will in a manner which leads to right doing.[31] If we follow the 'new perspective', we may conclude that Paul is making a retrospective judgement regarding the powerlessness of all sinful people without the Holy Spirit. Such people 'will' the good and have a certain knowledge of the law, but they cannot follow their good intention in their action.

Paul's concept of 'willing' is not elaborated any closer in Romans 7:15–20. This concept contains knowledge-based and desire-based aspects, but it remains a holistic concept which denotes the fundamental direction of human aspirations without the Holy Spirit. Therefore, Paul's discussion is theological or religious rather than philosophical and it cannot be reduced to any particular philosophical theory of action. The concept of 'willing' in Romans 7:15–20 contains, therefore, elements which can be connected with different theories of action. The *ego* of Romans 7:15–20 has been interpreted in different ways both in the ecclesiastical reception of this passage and in contemporary academic scholarship. Because Romans 7:15–20 leaves room for diverse interpretations, it has fertilized different philosophical and theological theories of human action.

Augustine's writings have a formative influence on medieval philosophy and theology. This influence continues in the Renaissance and the Reformation. Petrarch, for instance, wrote his *Secretum* as a dialogue with Augustine. Martin Luther initiated his career as an Augustinian monk, and both Protestant and Catholic reformers continued to invoke Augustine for their support. The concepts of will and consent are extremely important for Augustine's philosophy of mind, but scholars continue to debate the precise meaning of these concepts.[32]

Augustine has often been regarded as the inventor of the free will (*voluntas libera*) or, more specifically, the free decision of the will (*liberum arbitrium voluntatis*). In my earlier study, I adopted a moderated version of this view, claiming that whereas the Aristotelians understood freedom primarily in terms of freedom from compulsion, Augustine at least sometimes conceptualizes freedom as the 'power of acting or non-acting'. In this kind of freedom, the agent, at least in principle, can choose between two or more alternatives. But Augustine is no voluntarist in the late medieval sense of the term: the will is no separate mental faculty or part of the soul, *voluntas* denoting the human psyche in its role as moral agent.[33]

---

[31] All these aspects are discussed by Müller (2009), 224–42, with reference to contemporary exegetical scholarship.

[32] Recent histories of the concept of the will include Sorabji (2000), 319–40 and Pink and Stone (eds) (2004).

[33] I am for the most part consistent with my portrayal of Augustine's view in Saarinen (1994), 20–43 (here: 23), but the works of Chappell (1995) and Sorabji (2000) have caused some modifications. I also relate Augustine more strongly to the concept of 'Stoic akrasia' than in my earlier work.

It can also be argued that Aristotle and Augustine share many features in action theory, both teaching that voluntary actions are uncompelled, not ignorant, and done in pursuit of perceived attainable goods. While the Greek action theory cannot admit the existence of irrational voluntary actions, however, Augustine approves this possibility, although he cannot explain it. Evil voluntary actions remain inexplicable.[34] Given this, one could also say that Augustine admits the possibility of akratic actions but cannot explain them. Since Augustine did not know EN VII, he does not comment on Aristotle's problems explicitly, but scholars have extensively discussed those features in Augustine's action theory which correspond to akrasia.[35]

My own earlier suggestion in this discussion was that Augustine identifies a specific category of 'reluctant actions' which he often describes by the phrase *invitus facere*, 'to do something unwillingly/reluctantly'. This category is comparable, though not identical, with Aristotle's class of akratic actions. It is employed in Augustine's famous discussion of 'two wills' (*duae voluntates*) and 'incomplete will' (*voluntas non tota/non plena*) in the eighth book of *Confessions*. A person who does something 'unwillingly' (*invito*) in this sense is nevertheless responsible for his actions and cannot be said to have acted under compulsion.[36]

In his autobiographical story of religious conversion, Augustine describes the will's lack of power as follows:

The mind commands the mind to will; it is not something else, yet it does not do it. What is the source of this monstrosity? What purpose does it serve? It commands, I say, that the will-act be performed, and it would not issue the command unless it willed it, yet its command is not carried out.[37]

Augustine explains this inability to act according to one's better judgement by holding that, in fact, two voluntary inclinations exercise an effect within the person's mind, neither of which is the 'complete' will:

But it does not will it completely, and so it does not command it completely. For it commands to the extent that it wills; and what it commands is not done, to the extent that it does not will it, since the will commands that there be a will, not another will, but its very self. So, it does not command with its whole being; therefore, its command is not fulfilled. For, if it were whole, it would not command that it be done; it would already be done. Hence, it is not a monstrosity to will something in part and to oppose it in part; it is rather an illness of the mind, which, though lifted up by truth, is also weighed down heavily by habit; so it does not rise up unimpaired. And, thus, there are two voluntary inclinations (*duae voluntates*), neither one of which is complete, and what is present in one is lacking in the other.[38]

---

[34] Chappell (1995), 198–201, 206–7.

[35] In addition to Chappell (1995), see Rubiglio (2002); Hoffmann, Müller, and Perkams (2006); Müller (2009), 301–66.

[36] Saarinen (1994), 20–30.

[37] *Confessions* 8, 9, 21. This and the following are V. J. Bourke's translations from Augustine, *Confessions* (1966).

[38] *Confessions* 8, 9, 21.

This passage reveals a far-reaching parallel to what we regarded above as the Stoic version of akrasia. A person has had a long-standing assent to a false alternative. This assent has become a habit which continues its influence even when the good judgement concerning the truth emerges. The truth 'lifts up' the mind, but the old habit 'weighs it down', thus preventing the command of the mind being fulfilled. Augustine considers that in such a situation the person has two incomplete wills. In this context, *voluntas* does not mean an effective will, but rather a desire or an impulse to do something. In *Confessions* 8, 10, Augustine describes this inner situation using several allusions to Romans 7, claiming that in some sense this inner division is involuntary, but in another sense the *ego* remains a partial subject of the different impulses concerned.

Yet it must be the case that one of the impulses actually prevails and determines the actual behaviour of the person. Augustine admits this, claiming that when one impulse is chosen, the will becomes one in its operative outlook:

Do not different wills distract the mind when a man is trying to decide what he should choose? Yet they are all good, and are at variance with each other until one is chosen. When this is done the whole united will may go forward on a single track instead of remaining as it was before, divided in many ways.[39]

In the 'akratic' case described here, this means that the will finally sticks to its old habits and cannot choose the truth. The old habits recommend the pleasures under the aspect of goodness, thus distracting the mind from the true good. Although Augustine here maintains that the will is unified in the actual choice, he admits in other contexts that one can act with less than full will.[40]

To understand the reception history of these passages, it is extremely important to follow the story of *Confessions* 8 to its logical conclusion. After this description, Augustine has a vision in which the virtue of Continence appears to him as the spouse of God and as the 'fruitful mother of the children of joys'. Continence advises Augustine not to stand by his own strength but to throw himself on God's mercy, who will heal him so that he can perform the same good actions as the children of joys.[41] This scene is followed by the famous episode under the fig tree where Augustine converts so that 'there was infused in my heart something like the light of full certainty and all the gloom of doubt vanished away'.[42]

Earlier in *Confessions*[43] Augustine had quoted the Vulgate translation of the Wisdom of Solomon 8:21: 'And I knew that I could not otherwise be continent, except God gave it.' After the infusion of certainty, however, Augustine's will was changed so that 'in a single moment' it became free of harmful passions causing the distraction:

---

[39] *Confessions* 8, 10, 24.

[40] *De spiritu et litera* 31, 53 (quoted below). This has been pointed out by Sorabji (2000), 316, as a friendly amendment to Saarinen (1994), 31.

[41] *Confessions* 8, 11, 27. [42] *Confessions* 8, 12, 29. [43] *Confessions* 6, 11, 20.

And this was the result: now I did not will to do what I willed, and began to will to do what thou didst will (*nolle quod volebam et velle quod volebas*). But where was my free decision during all those years and from what deep and secret retreat was it called forth in a single moment (*evocatum est in momento liberum arbitrium meum*).[44]

The conversion of Augustine thus effects a healing which enables him to practise the free decision and, as a result, the virtue of continence.[45] Augustine's use of Romans 13:13–14 in *Confessions* 8, 12, 29 underlines the liberation from harmful desires.

These passages are highly influential for the reception history for linguistic reasons: in medieval commentaries, *akrasia* and *enkrateia* came to be translated into Latin as *incontinentia* and *continentia*; the Latin terms thus had a counterpart in Augustine as well as in the Vulgate. Differences from Aristotle are also apparent: whereas *continentia* for Augustine is a major virtue which is given from above and mainly related to sexuality, Aristotle's *enkrateia* generally pertains to all half-virtuous moral states in which the good choice is followed in spite of the remaining desire to do otherwise. These differences did not, however, hinder the later expositors from establishing links between the two ancient discussions on continence.

It needs to be said in addition that these links are not merely accidental. Augustine's discussion in *Confessions* 8 displays important similarities to what we regarded above as the Stoic account of weakness of will. Augustine is concerned with the problem of controlling the different impulses which have already become a sort of inner 'will'. He further thinks that the actual choice or assent needs to be one; he also recognizes that seeing the better is not necessarily enough, since the long-standing habit weighs more than the new insight. Like Medea and the runner who cannot stop running, the storyteller of *Confessions* 8 cannot proceed to conversion, although he wishes to do so. Although Augustine's solution of this conflict situation is theological, the situation itself reveals a continuity with earlier discussions on weakness of will. The visionary appearance of Lady Continence transforms a classical philosophical problem into a theological one; at the same time, however, the designation of the remedy in terms of continence establishes a continuity from Aristotle to Augustine.

Augustine's discussion of 'two wills' is refined in some other influential writings. In *De spiritu et litera* he holds, for instance, that reluctant actions are in some sense always voluntary and the agent should therefore be held responsible for them:

Yet, on a closer analysis, it appears that even if you do a thing unwillingly (*invitus facere*), you do it by your will (*voluntate facit*) if you do it at all: you are said to do it against your will, that is, unwillingly, because you would prefer to act differently. You are compelled to act because of some evil, which it is your will to avoid or remove; and so you act under compulsion. If your will were strong enough to prefer the suffering of the evil to the doing of the act, you would of course resist the compulsion and refuse the act. Thus if you act, though it may not be with full or

---

[44] *Confessions* 9, 1, 1.
[45] For Augustine's notion of continence, see Schlabach (1999), as well as Augustine's work *De continentia*, dealing primarily with sexual chastity.

free will, it can never be without willing; and since the willing is carried into effect, we cannot say that the actor was powerless.[46]

According to this view, all acts which qualify as human acts are in some sense voluntary, although the latent tendencies to do otherwise characterize the action as reluctant. In a sense, the agent here acts with less than full will. The Augustinian terminology of internal voluntary tendencies and external voluntary acts later developed into even more sophisticated modes of conditional will (If p, then I will that q), hypothetical will (*velleitas*), willing the impossible (*voluntas impossibilis*), and second-order will (I will to will that p). These modes have been discussed in detail in recent studies.[47]

For the purposes of the present study, however, it is necessary to say something more about Augustine's view of consent, including its cognate terms of choice and free decision. Chappell's parallels between Aristotelian and Augustinian theories of action explain why the medieval philosophers could build innovative syntheses of the two. But, as the close reading of *Confessions* 8 indicates, Augustine is finally closer to Stoicism than to Aristotle. This closeness is particularly apparent in his view of desire and consent.

Augustine often claims that the morality of an act is dependent on the consent given to the impression and desire to perform this act.

If consent is given, then a sin is fully committed in the heart, and it is known to God, even though it be not made known to men through the medium of any act.[48]
We do not commit sin in the bad desire, but in our consenting to it.[49]

In this sense both the desires and the external actions are morally indifferent, since the moral quality is attached to the person's intentional consent to act. With some qualifications,[50] this has remained the standard picture of Augustine's moral theory in Catholic theology.

This account of desire and consent is of Stoic origin. The plurality of impressions inevitably leads to a plurality of desires, but we are not fully responsible for these desires before we have given our consent to them. Unlike the full-blooded Stoics in Plutarch's description quoted above, Augustine thinks that desires are no proper judgements but preliminary ones: only the final consent is regarded as the proper judgement of the issue at hand. In this sense, Augustine is close to Origen, who holds that sensual impressions as such are beyond our control, but reason can accept some of them and reject others. One can say, therefore, that Augustine's variant of Stoicism does not approve the unity

---

[46] *De spiritu et litera* 31, 53. J. Burnaby's translation from Augustine, *Spirit* (1955).

[47] Saarinen (1994), 37–86. See also Rubiglio (2002) and Knuuttila (2004), 205–12.

[48] *De sermone Domini in monte* 1, 12, 34. D. J. Havanagh's translation from Augustine, *Commentary* (1951).

[49] *Expositio quarundam propositionum ex Epist. ad Romanos*, PL 35, 2066.

[50] An important qualification concerns the so-called intrinsically evil acts which are wicked irrespectively of the agent's intention. See, e.g., the condemnation of Peter Abelard in Denzinger and Hünermann (1991), 733.

of the soul and the judgemental nature of passions as strictly as is the case in Chrysippus. While the constituents of Augustine's action theory remain those of Stoicism, namely, impression, impulse, and assent, he assumes a fairly clear distinction between impression/impulse/desire on the one hand, and assent/consent/final judgement on the other.[51]

Although this standard view prevails in many works by Augustine, there is some indication that he can also regard desires more strongly as proper judgements possessing moral value. In such a case, the unity of the soul is affirmed more radically and the conscious desires involve some act of consent which can be regarded as sin. This variant of Augustinianism, which is closer to the Stoicism of Chrysippus, becomes particularly apparent in the discussions regarding the sinful desire of concupiscence. This desire exists in people as a punishment for the original sin. Baptism cleanses the moral guilt caused by it, but concupiscence remains even in baptized Christians. When a Christian consents to its suggestions, he again becomes guilty of sin. In itself, however, according to the standard Catholic view, concupiscence is not yet sin but merely weakness. Only when a Christian consents to it, does it become sin.[52]

This clear picture is blurred by the fact that Augustine sometimes calls concupiscence a sin. These sayings gain new importance, as well as relevance for our study, when the Reformation declares that concupiscence is a sin and when the Council of Trent denies that this is the case. Augustine in some cases connects the desire of concupiscence with the judging power of reason. Concupiscence is sin, for instance, when reason learns the command not to covet and this act of learning and recognition evokes the desire. Concupiscence is likewise a sin when it contains a judgement of disobedience and rebellion against the rule of reason.[53] These passages affirm the view of concupiscence as judgement which in itself already involves consent. They break the twofold sequence of desire and consent, and claim in a genuinely Stoic manner that the awareness of some desires already involves proper judgement and assent. For the purposes of the present study, I will schematically distinguish[54] between three phases of Augustine's career, using two criteria: (1) his understanding of Paul's conflict in Romans 7; and (2) whether the concupiscence which remains in the Christian can be called sin.

(i) Young Augustine regards Romans 7 as pertaining to Paul 'under the law', that is, as a worldly person who can distinguish between good and evil. Augustine's *Confessions*

---

[51]   See further Knuuttila (2004), 152–72; Sorabji (2000), 400–17; Colish (1985) II, 142–238.

[52]   For the official promulgation of this view at the Council of Trent (1545–1563), see Walter (2001).

[53]   See Augustinus, *Contra Iulianum opus imperfectum* 3, 210, CSEL 85/1, 503, 11–17; *Contra Iulianum* 5, 43, 8, PL 44, 787: 'concupiscentia . . . peccatum est, quia inest illi inoboedientia contra dominatum mentis'; *De nuptiis et concupiscentia* 1, 23, 25, CSEL 42, 238, 3–13. See the interpretation of these passages in Markschies (2001), 100–4. Walter (2001), 268 even calls this view 'Augustinian' and labels the official Catholic view as 'scholastic'. See also Calvin, *Institutio* 3, 3, 13.

[54]   I am indebted to Timo Nisula for insightful discussions on this matter in Augustine. Schneider and Wenz (2001) offer an overview of the theological reception of these matters. For a short opinio communis, see Burnell (1999). I here revise my earlier view in Saarinen (1994), 26–7.

belongs to this first period. A person under the law remains akratic: he can recognize his faults and wants to improve his conduct, but he cannot accomplish goodness with his own power, because concupiscence effectively leads him to sinful actions. After conversion, however, the new person *sub gratia* can accomplish goodness with divine help. Concupiscence remains in the person, but a Christian need not consent to its temptations. Concupiscence does not pose deep spiritual problems for the Christian existence.

(ii) After 411, however, Augustine considers that Romans 7 does not describe the akratic struggle of a worldly person, but the chapter depicts an enkratic Christian apostle who can resist and conquer concupiscence. The apostle wants to be perfect but, because of the continuing repugnance caused by concupiscence, he remains less than perfect. The speaker of Romans 7 is thus a paradigm of the good Christian, to whom concupiscence is a sparring partner or a domesticated enemy. In this second phase of 'mature Augustine', concupiscence provides continuous opportunities to sin, but cannot compel the person. The enkratic *Paulus Christianus* may complain that he is imperfect and not as free from evil desires as he wants to be, but he can relatively well resist sin.

(iii) During the late debate with Julian of Eclanum, Augustine underlines the sinfulness of remaining concupiscence more strongly than ever. This debate leads him towards a new definition of sin. Especially in his last work, *Contra Iulianum opus imperfectum* (429/430), Augustine sometimes calls concupiscence a sin and teaches that concupiscence can become operative in a compulsory manner.[55] Other late works, in particular *Contra Iulianum* (421/422), already contain remarks pointing to this direction. At the same time, Augustine stresses that Christians do not sin out of necessity, but concupiscence can be resisted with God's help (e.g. *Contra Iulianum* 5, 9). Even the very last writings do not, therefore, change the whole definition of sin, since the peculiar concupiscence which is sin per se remains a special case. But it is nevertheless remarkable that in some cases concupiscence is so strongly present in Christians that it can be called sin.[56]

The identification of these three phases is sufficient for our discussion of reception history. A person who wants to stress the Stoic features of Augustine's view of concupiscence can relate to the late anti-Julian writings and claim that the presence of sinful concupiscence already involves judgement and assent. Protestant Reformers

---

[55] e.g, *Contra Iulianum opus imperfectum* 5, 50 (PL 45, 1485). Müller (2009), 358 argues that the late anti-Julian Augustine moves towards a 'compatibilist' position in which a necessary action can nevertheless be intentional and in that sense free.

[56] Nisula (2010) presents a more detailed account of this topic. Steinmetz (1990), 308 distinguishes between three positions in the reception history of Augustine as follows: Romans 7 (1) as a description of pre-Christian existence; (2) as a description of the imperfectly just believer; (3) as a description of the justified, but imperfectly renewed, believer. Although these two classifications may differ in the closer understanding of renewal, they both aim at making visible the difference between the 'second' and the 'third' position. See also Müller (2009), 355–66 and further 3.2.

(3.2, 4.1) who emphasize the permanent sinfulness of all Christians stress the anti-Julian writings in this manner. Authors like Petrarch (2.1) discuss critically whether the pre-Christian akratic situation of Romans 7 and young Augustine is effectively overcome in religious conversion as *Confessions* claims. The standard Catholic view relies on the mature Augustine, holding that, while all Christians continue to struggle with concupiscence, the presence of this desire is not counted as sin because the person can resist its temptations and remain enkratic.[57] The standard Catholic view thus employs the Stoic notion of consent as the criterion of sin but does not approve the Stoic idea of emotions as judgements assented to.

Monastic and patristic authors employ two different ways of analysing the emotions. Many authors who normally affirm the standard Augustinian view of desire and consent regard the passions as being morally indifferent and beyond human control. Others claim that passions and desires already have moral value and that evil desires can be eradicated, or at least moderated, by ascetic techniques. These authors are fairly close to the Stoic treatment of desire as judgement; they also affirm the unity of mind and the ascetic ideals of life more strongly. Intermediate positions hold that while impressions and impulses are already sinful to an extent, the consent brings the sin to completion. Thus, for instance, Gregory the Great holds that 'the seed of sin is in suggestion, the nourishment of sin in pleasure, and the maturity is in consent'.[58]

We may summarize our discussion on Stoicism and Augustine by introducing three heuristic models of akrasia. The 'strictly Stoic' model holds that emotions are judgements and the soul is one. Within the limits of this model, explanations of akrasia are difficult or even impossible, since all acts take place in accordance with the momentarily prevailing judgement. There is no conflict between different impulses, but only 'a turning of the single reason in both directions, which we do not notice owing to the sharpness and speed of the change', as Plutarch says.[59] The phenomena which look like akrasia need to be understood as actions proceeding from the momentarily prevailing judgement, or sometimes as residual effects of the so-called pre-passions.

A 'moderated Stoic' model holds that some distinction, although no separation, is made between the initial impressions and impulses on the one hand, and the final assent on the other. Although the impulses involve some kind of judgement and assent, later judgements may change the prevailing assent. In such a model, akrasia can be understood as the inability to change the prevailing previous assent by means of new information. The examples of Medea and Augustine's conversion fall under this explanatory model. This model probably even allows for a clear-eyed akrasia in that

---

[57] Steinmetz (1990) has shown that, in addition to this standard view, some Catholics preferred to read Romans 7 as a description of pre-Christian existence. He also points out that, in order to understand the Protestant readings of Romans 7, one needs to distinguish between different ways of conceiving Romans 7 as a description of Christian existence.

[58] Gregory in Bede, *Ecclesiastical History* 1, 27, 9. Knuuttila (2004), 172–95; Saarinen (2007), 271–7.

[59] Long-Sedley, 412, quoting Plutarch, *On moral virtue* 446F–447A (quoted above).

the new insight is fairly clear, but the strength of the old habits continues, as in the case of the runner who cannot stop running.

A third, 'strongly moderated Stoic' or 'commonplace Augustinian' model treats desire and consent as separate faculties. Impressions and impulses/desires may represent preliminary judgements, but they emerge spontaneously and remain beyond our immediate control. One can certainly avoid the emergence of harmful desires indirectly; for instance, by not going to the circus or not smelling the food, but once the objects are perceived, the impulses are not under the will's control. Such desires do not, however, lead to action, since they are only connected with preliminary judgements, like 'this looks good/pleasant'. The decisive judgement and assent is undertaken only afterwards by reason, which freely and voluntarily consents to some impulses and rejects others. The standard Catholic view of consent as the source and criterion of moral quality exemplifies the 'commonplace Augustinian' model. In this model, akratic actions occur as voluntary consent to the wrong alternative.

In the second and third models, the harmful desires appear as pleasant and in that sense good in the preliminary judgement. The akratic person who consents to them does not, therefore, intend evil but is tempted or habituated by the seemingly good pleasure brought about by the desire. Since the commonplace Augustinian model detaches consent from the realm of impressions and impulses, the harmful desire presupposed by this model probably cannot overcome the good consent in the way this occurs in the moderated Stoic model. In order to affirm the possibility of akrasia and to distinguish akratic actions from other vicious conduct, commonplace Augustinianism therefore probably needs to presuppose some error or ignorance during deliberation. Thus 'clear-eyed akrasia' would not be possible.

The 'commonplace Augustinian' model has some affinities with so-called 'commonplace Platonism' (1.1). On closer inspection, however, the models differ considerably. In both, desires are portrayed as relatively autonomous impulses which advocate the akratic action. But while in commonplace Augustinianism rational and free consent is to be held responsible for the actual akratic decision, the commonplace Platonic model portrays the akratic action as irrational behaviour in which desire simply overcomes reason. Commonplace Platonic akrasia thus resembles the behaviour of passionate animals, whereas the commonplace Augustinian thinker holds that even those people who, prompted by their harmful desire, act 'unwillingly' (invitus), nevertheless act by their own will and are responsible for their choices.

1.3 Medieval Aristotelians: Thomas Aquinas and Walter Burley

Robert Grosseteste translated EN in its entirety into Latin in 1246–1247. He added an anonymous Latin commentary on EN VII and some expository notes of his own to his translation, among other texts. Before that, already some details on EN VII were known through the Arabic reception of Aristotle, for instance, the so-called *Summa Alexandrinorum*. Averroes's commentary on EN was translated into Latin in 1240.[60] The first Western commentaries of Albert the Great and Thomas Aquinas were of decisive importance for the philosophical and theological reception of EN VII. We will return to Albert in 1.5 below.

The works of Thomas Aquinas were not only important for the medieval period, but they continued their formative influence through the Renaissance and the Reformation. Thomas's commentary on the EN, *Sententia libri Ethicorum*, follows Aristotle's text closely and expounds it literally, remaining true to the teachings of the philosopher.[61] At times this makes Aquinas's commentary uninteresting, because his own contribution seems to be lacking. This feature has not hindered the enormous popularity of the work. As we shall see, many Renaissance commentaries continue to follow in the footsteps of the *doctor communis*.

According to Thomas's exposition of EN 1147b9–17, the akratic person fails to use the singular proposition of the practical syllogism. Since passion can confuse our senses so that we do not grasp the particular facts properly, akrasia is due to ignorance in the sense of our Aristotelian model 1a. In keeping with this explanation, Thomas holds that the akratic person does not act by choice. On the other hand, Thomas also says that the akratic person has a transitory false evaluation (*aestimatio falsa*) which prompts the akratic action. This indicates that the akratic person in some sense consents to the misguided action.[62]

The theological works of Aquinas, in particular *De malo* and *Summa theologiae*, explain akratic action in a manner which departs more strongly from Aristotle and approaches the Augustinian view of consent to the wrong alternative. In *De malo*, Aquinas maintains that although the akratic person does not sin 'from choice' (*ex electione*), he nevertheless sins 'while choosing' (*eligens*). In *Summa theologiae* he says that the akratês 'chooses to follow' evil passions (*eligit sequi eas*). The moral responsibility and the moral guilt of the akratic person are thus clearly indicated in the theological works.[63]

The basic problem in the reception history of Aquinas's akrasia is, therefore, whether the later Thomists follow the Aristotelian *Sententia* or the more Augustinian theological works and, perhaps more importantly, whether these emphases can be reconciled. In

---

[60] See Saarinen (1994), 87–94. For *Summa Alexandrinorum*, see Fidora (2006).

[61] For Thomas's ethics in general, see Pope (2002). Doig (2001) is a study of *Sententia libri Ethicorum* (= Ethica). Thomas's view of akrasia has been treated in Kent (1989); Saarinen (1994), 118–30; Saarinen (2003); Hoffmann (2006); Bradley (2008) (with an extensive bibliography) and Müller (2009), 512–46.

[62] Thomas, *Ethica*, ed. Leonina, 393, 310–27. For the different expressions of choice, see Saarinen (1994), 118–20. A new and very careful discussion is Bradley (2008), who holds that 'in Aquinas's reading, Aristotle hews closely to the Socratic line and only allows for unknowing or "closed-eyed akrasia"' (p. 97).

[63] *De malo* q3 a12 ad11. *Summa theologiae* II/2 q155 a3. Saarinen (1994), 121–5. Bradley (2008), 98–9 says that 'in his mature works, Aquinas definitely transposes . . . the Aristotelian discussion of akrasia to the plane of will', quoting *De malo* q2 a3 ad 5: 'Principaliter autem est peccatum in voluntate secundum quod malae concupiscentiae consentit.'

my earlier study[64] I argued for a fairly Aristotelian synthesis as follows: in his discussion on akrasia, Thomas presupposes two practical syllogisms, one persuading the agent, the other forbidding. For instance:

Persuading:	*Forbidding:*
Everything sweet is pleasant and pleasure should be pursued	Nothing sweet should be tasted out of season
This is sweet	(At present is out of season)
It follows that:	
This is pursued	

The harmful passion cannot directly obscure the major premises, but it can obscure one of the minor ones, in this case the one in brackets. Given this, the forbidding major loses its dynamic force because it is not found to be relevant in the prevailing circumstances. In such a situation the deliberation is shifted to the persuading syllogism, which is found to be more relevant in this case. This shift does not occur 'from choice' (*non ex electione*), because it is part of the deliberation. Its being wrong or erroneous is due to ignorance in the sense of the Aristotelian model 1a. However, the persuading syllogism which leads to sinful action is followed with choice (*eligens, secundum electionem*). The akratic action thus presupposes ignorance, but this also involves the wrong choice, according to which the harmful action is performed. In this sense the akratic person can be said not to act 'from choice' but nevertheless voluntarily and with choice.

It is therefore theoretically possible to reconcile the Aristotelian view of Thomas's commentary with the more Augustinian view which prevails in his theological works. This 'two-step' model of akrasia is very close to Aristotelian model 1a, because the practical syllogism directs the emergence of human action and because akrasia is explained in terms of ignorance of the minor premise. Thomas's model also involves some Augustinian features of voluntary consent to the wrong alternative, as well as aspects of Augustine's inner struggle between 'two wills' (cf. 2.2 below).

New studies on Aquinas's view of akrasia have refined this 'two-step' model. Denis Bradley argues that Thomas claims in *Sententia libri Ethicorum* that the akratic agent must actively consent to concupiscence before acting from concupiscence.[65] This choice is not, however, 'deliberate' (*ex electione*). In keeping with this idea of consent, the akratic person does not act 'from ignorance' (*propter ignorantiam*), although he acts 'in ignorance' (*ignorans*) of the particular premise. This latter ignorance is a 'vincible ignorance' and, since the akratês does not overcome it, he is in some sense culpable: 'by

---

[64] The following summarizes my earlier account in Saarinen (1994), 125–9. For later scholarly discussion on this, see Pasnau (2002), 241–52; Irwin (2006), 50–8; Hoffmann (2006) and, in particular, the detailed account of Bradley (2008).

[65] Bradley (2008), 98, referring to *Ethica*, ed. Leonina. 315a, 154–63.

volitionally consenting to passion, which consent *follows upon* an erroneous judgement of reason, the incontinent man makes a bad choice . . . The *incontinens* chooses to be in a state of ignorance by freely choosing to follow rather than resist the inordinate inclinations of his sensible appetite'.[66]

Although Aquinas imports an Augustinian view of consent into Aristotle's notion of choice in this way, his view of akrasia remains fairly close to Aristotle's in the sense of our model 1a. Like Aquinas, Aristotle regards the akratic person as culpable, although he can be more easily forgiven than the wicked or intemperate person. Given the dominance of Augustinian theology in medieval Latin Christianity, Aquinas's real contribution consists in his ability to understand Aristotle's akrasia in precise terms and in his adherence to the explanation which regards ignorance of the particular circumstances as the root cause of acting against one's own better judgement.

Aquinas can competently discuss the various Aristotelian subspecies of akrasia (see 1.1) and relate them to different theological topics.[67] Aquinas's theories of perception and practical deliberation can be further refined by concentrating on the so-called 'parts of prudence', among which *eubulia* (EN 1142b32–35) deals with good deliberation and *synesis* (1143a6–15) with a good capacity to judge the particulars perceived. Sense perception is connected with the judgement expressed in the minor premise of the practical syllogism not only in Stoicism but also in the Aristotelian theory.[68]

Most medieval commentaries on EN are Aristotelian in their emphasis that some ignorance must precede akratic actions and that the process of deliberation is presented in terms of a practical syllogism. The commentators normally think that what they present as the Aristotelian view is a philosophically true description of the matters in question. In spite of these similarities, however, their actual expositions of Aristotle's view differ considerably. It seems that individual and innovative views were rewarded in medieval teaching.[69]

Walter Burley's *Expositio super decem libros Ethicorum Aristotelis* is a good example of a commentary which follows Aquinas, but deviates from him in some crucial passages. With regard to akrasia, this strategy is both fascinating and puzzling, and has evoked some scholarly debate.[70] Paraphrasing Aquinas's commentary, Burley first claims that the akratic person is ignorant of particular circumstances in the sense of our model 1a. After the exposition of EN 1147b9–18, however, he adds a note saying that

the proposition with regard to which the akratic person is deceived and of which he is ignorant, is not the minor premise of the practical syllogism, but the conclusion of the practical syllogism. Let us consider for instance the following practical syllogism: nothing sweet ought to be tasted, this is

---

[66] Bradley (2008), 104.
[67] Hoffmann (2006) and Bradley (2008) discuss these in detail.
[68] See Saarinen (2003).
[69] Courtenay (1987), 191.
[70] See Saarinen (1994), 131–46; Wood (1999) and Saarinen (1999) discuss the topic further.

sweet, therefore this should not be tasted. Now, the akratic person is not deceived in regard to the minor premise, since he knows well enough that this is sweet. But he is deceived with regard to the conclusion which he does not actually know because of vehement concupiscence.[71]

This quote offers clear evidence that the so-called Aristotelian model 2 was known in the medieval period. Burley thinks that it is possible to formulate a propositional conclusion and that Aristotle refers to it as the 'last protasis'. Burley also takes very seriously Aristotle's claim that the akratês has a good choice; according to Burley, the incontinent person is prevented from 'executing' this choice.

Burley is further interested in parallels between the practical syllogism and logic in general. Following a suggestion made in Averroes' commentary on EN, he remarks that the akratic person who knows both premises

can be ignorant of the conclusion and be deceived with regard to it. This occurs when he does not actually put the premises together in order to reach the conclusion. But when he does actually put the premises together, aiming at the conclusion, it is not possible to know the premises and ignore the conclusion.[72]

In this connection Burley quotes Aristotle's description of a similar logical error from *Analytica posteriora* (71a21). Averroes and Burley are thus aware of the Aristotelian explanatory model 1b.

Burley does not state unequivocally which solution he himself prefers. According to Rega Wood, Burley explores 'different ways in which to introduce indeterminacy into the intellect'.[73] This conclusion means that Burley is even more intellectualist than Thomas in locating the root cause of akrasia in the failures of our intellectual grasp of the facts. Burley does not stress the role of consent, stating in a truly Aristotelian manner that the akratês has a good choice. For the purpose of our interpretation history, it is important to see that all three Aristotelian explanatory models (1a, 1b, and 2) are present in medieval discussion and that akrasia is often expounded in a truly Aristotelian fashion in the medieval commentaries, without recourse to the Augustinian notions of free will and consent.

1.4 Medieval Voluntarists: Walter of Bruges and Henry of Ghent

Augustine's writings remain fundamental for all medieval Latin philosophers and theologians, but the church father's theory of the will also becomes a point from which two different ways depart. Thomas chooses the Aristotelian way and embeds Augustine's view of consent into the broader framework of the practical syllogism. Taking the other way, many Franciscan theologians highlight the freedom of the will

---

[71] Burley, *Super Ethicorum*, 121 va. Cf. Saarinen (1994), 137–8.

[72] *Super Ethicorum*, 121va. Saarinen (1994), 139.

[73] Wood (1999), 80.

and consider Augustine's views to be in conflict with Aristotle, developing a voluntarism which applies but also extends the framework of Augustine's thought.[74]

The voluntarist approach is less visible in the commentaries on EN. The first Franciscan commentator, Geraldus Odonis, can be regarded as being fairly Aristotelian.[75] John Buridan, who shares many of the new philosophical presuppositions of the voluntarists, nevertheless expounds Aristotle's ethics in a fairly Augustinian and intellectualist fashion (see 1.5). The Franciscans do, however, comment on Aristotle's akrasia in their other writings. These texts reveal the voluntarist stance which sets out to explain incontinent action in terms of wilful neglect rather than ignorance. For many thinkers of this leaning, in particular Walter of Bruges, Henry of Ghent, and Peter Olivi, the mutual relationship between will and intellect is one between king and advisor. Although the ruler needs information and advice, he sovereignly decides what is to be done.[76]

Such a voluntarist image of the mind departs from both Aristotelianism and Stoicism. The free and sovereign will now becomes a reified faculty to which other mental faculties relate as auxiliaries. Reason in particular is regarded as a servant holding the lamp in the darkness so that the master can see, but it is the master, the will, which actually commands the lamp-holder.[77] The will possesses a capacity of self-determination. Although Augustine's view of the 'free decision' (*liberum arbitrium voluntatis*) probably contains the germ of this development, Augustine never reified the faculty of the will in the autonomous manner of the medieval voluntarists.[78]

In his *Quaestiones disputatae*, Walter of Bruges shows that he knows Aristotle's discussion on incontinence well. He is not satisfied with the Aristotelian and Thomist view of ignorance related to akrasia, claiming that the incontinent sinner has a 'sufficient' knowledge of what should be done. If there is some lack of knowledge, it is only because the akratês does not want to have this knowledge and so sins voluntarily.[79] The incontinent act is thus due to voluntary negligence. Walter aims to underline the responsibility and culpability of the akratic person.

At the same time, the will in Walter's view does not will evil as such, always choosing an option which is in some way good. Thus incorrect choices are always willed in some way *sub ratione boni*, under the aspect of goodness. This view means, as

---

[74] See Stadter (1971); Kent (1995); Kobusch (2006).

[75] For Odonis, see Kent (1984) and Saarinen (1994), 146–61.

[76] Kent (1995), 116–29 and Kobusch (2006), 250–3 discuss the 'imperial will' in detail.

[77] Kobusch (2006), 251, quoting Richard of Mediavilla, *In II Sent.* d38 a2 q4, and Henry of Ghent, *Quodlibet* I q14, 90.

[78] Here I side with Chappell (1995) and distinguish myself from Dihle (1982). Sorabji (2000), 319–40 offers a balanced account.

[79] Kobusch (2006), 253, quoting Walter, *Quaestiones disputatae* q4 ad11 p. 45: 'incontinens habet sufficientem scientiam ad judicandum sibi apparens bonum esse malum et esse vitandum; scit enim in universali omnem fornicationem esse malam et vitandam; ex quo concludere posset, si vellet, etiam sibi esse malam et vitandam, et ideo non caret scientia nisi quia vult, propter quod voluntarie peccat.' See also Müller (2009), 559–65.

Bonnie Kent has pointed out,[80] an important departure from Aristotle's ethics in which all alternatives but one are eliminated in the course of deliberation. The view that various alternatives continue to appear *sub ratione boni* is closer to the Stoic and Augustinian theories of action in which the various impressions can evoke different preliminary desires and temptations.

In keeping with this idea, Walter describes the wrong choice as follows:

When the will acts by choosing what is evil or choosing to do nothing or to do what is less good, it wills for the sake of something better, which it itself decides is better at that time, as Adam did—not absolutely, nor having some passion that blinded reason, as the intemperate has, nor even having a passion that would incline appetite to movement and take away judgement in the particular proposition, which happens in the incontinent, as is evident in Book VII of the *Ethics*; but it was decided only by the freedom of the will in commanding reason that it would be better for him to eat from the forbidden fruit tree, against God's command, than to cause his wife's displeasure.[81]

For Walter, the dominance of will over reason is so strong that the free will can shape reason's judgement to make the desired course of action appear better than its alternatives. Their appearance *sub ratione boni* is thus affected by the will's commanding power.

The example of Adam is important, since Adam was considered to have lived in paradise without passions. Thus his acting against better judgement is not due to passion, but is caused by the free will, which in paradise appears to have existed completely detached from desires and impulses. Henry of Ghent also taught that the first man acted directly, without any interference of the passion, against the judgement of right reason.[82] The free will thus enabled a 'clear-eyed akrasia' in the case of Adam. Although fallen humankind cannot exercise free will without the interference of the passions, the faculty of the will is so independent that it cannot be located in the realm of Stoic impulses nor in the animal or rational soul of Aristotelianism. For Walter and Henry, Adam's freedom depicts a sovereignty which exists in addition to the ancient conceptions of freedom. Although Adam's impassionate will can decide in itself which is the better alternative, it must will under the aspect of goodness.

Henry of Ghent presents a thoroughly voluntaristic reading of incontinence in his *Quodlibeta*. Even for a strict voluntarist like Henry akrasia is not a self-evident phenomenon, but a reality which needs to be spelled out carefully in order to refute the Socratic-Aristotelian misunderstandings of the issue.[83] Henry's basic position is that weakness of will is accompanied by some disorder or ignorance in the intellect. This

---

[80] Kent (1995), 174.

[81] Walter, *Quaestiones disputatae* q6 ad14, translation from Kent (1995), 176.

[82] See Kent (1995), 179, quoting Henry, *Quodlibet* V, 128–9.

[83] In addition to Kent (1995) and Kobusch (2006), Henry's view of akrasia has been studied in detail by Müller (2007) and (2009), 569–616.

ignorance is not, however, the cause of akrasia, but vice versa, since the corruption of the will affects the intellect so that it becomes disordered.

For Henry, the incontinent person slides into his or her akratic action gradually. The stages of this slide are fairly Augustinian. First, the person is tempted by pleasure. Second, his or her will consents to the temptation. Third, some forgetting occurs in the reason. Fourth, the will proceeds to the sinful action.[84] The act of consent is free and voluntary in that the akratic person could have prevented it. Even during the third stage, the akratic will could still revise its course, since reason does not exercise any positive causality in the process. Only after the third stage does the so-called *consensus perfectus* determine the course of action. After the third stage, the

sinful action can be said to take place necessarily, since the person has through his consent lost both the use of free decision in the will and the use of right reason in the intellect.[85]

This analysis of akratic action presupposes that the will consents to something which is presented to it under the aspect of goodness (*sub ratione boni*), that is, pleasure. A free will is a rational appetite which does not will wickedly for the sake of wickedness but it can will the seemingly good aspects of the wrong option. Because the process of akrasia is directed by the will and increases gradually, clear-eyed akrasia is possible only in the qualified sense that the free act of the will is not a priori conditioned by ignorance. The consent to the temptation, however, inevitably brings about some ignorance in the intellect. This is voluntary ignorance caused by the will's consent, which occurs a posteriori but immediately and is thus simultaneous with the disorder of the will. The akratic action is thus accompanied by some ignorance and is not clear-eyed.[86]

Henry's view is to some extent conditioned by external reasons. At the University of Paris, a condemnation was pronounced in 1277 which obligated the teachers to defend free will. At the same time, another declaration was approved, namely the so-called *propositio magistralis*, according to which 'there is no evil in the will unless there is error or some lack of knowledge in reason'.[87] Henry shows the sense in which one can affirm this proposition without subscribing to the Aristotelian-Thomist view of ignorance as the cause of evil.

Akrasia thus remained a prominent topic of discussion even in the voluntarist branch of scholasticism. Recent studies ask whether the Socratic intellectualism was 'pushed out of the front door only to be let in at the back'.[88] Although voluntarists like

---

[84] Müller (2007), 10, quoting Henry, *Quodlibet* I, 141–3.

[85] Müller (2007), 11. Henry, *Quodlibet* I, 143: 'Nec est aliquod inconveniens voluntatem sic necessitari in actum peccati, postquam per consensum amisit usum liberi arbitrii in voluntate, sicut rationis rectae in intellectu.'

[86] Kent (1995), 180–1; Müller (2007), 12–15.

[87] For this sentence, attributed to Giles of Rome, see Kent (1995), 79–81, and Müller (2007), 12–15. For the content and reception of the Parisian articles of 1277, see Hissette (1977).

[88] So Kent (1995), 180; cf. Müller (2007), 22.

Walter of Bruges and Henry of Ghent set out to defend free will and moral responsibility, they understand the will as rational appetite which is directed to its objects only when they appear under the aspect of goodness. Although the will is self-determining and can command the intellect, it is also in itself a cognitive and rational faculty and in that sense not fundamentally different from reason. Neither Walter nor Henry teach 'deliberate irrationality', that is, a view which would detach the will from being rational or the most noble part of the soul. Only if free will was separated from cognitive powers could it choose anything that happens to be available, but voluntarists normally do want the will to be the most noble part of the soul, a view which embraces rationality rather than rejects it.

If Aristotle's akrasia exemplifies the mysterious inability of reason to control action, the voluntarist version exemplifies the mysterious corruption of free will after the emergence of misguided consent. For Henry, consent to temptation resembles the act of selling oneself into slavery: once consent is given, free decision and right reason are lost. Voluntarist akrasia is due to a free decision, but this decision cannot be reversed. Consent to temptation brings about a state of ignorance and necessity in which the operative control is lost. Thus the voluntarist account in some ways resembles the intellectualist accounts it sets out to oppose.

In spite of these similarities, the voluntarists proceed on that Augustinian way which emphasizes the will's self-determination and leads away from Aristotelian models. They celebrate free will as the highest faculty of the soul. This view of the will is different from the Aristotelian tradition, since it also develops the Augustinian view of consent in a new direction. Concerning akrasia in particular, the use of Adam's fall as an example is one of the most radical innovations. The role of passions is effectively bracketed by employing Adam as the paradigmatic example and proof of the will's capacity to act against better judgement. In all earlier accounts of akrasia, passions play a major role. We may designate 'Adam's akrasia' as a case in which the person acts against his or her own better judgement so that no passions are involved. Walter and Henry discuss this case in the context of akrasia, but Adam is for them not an example of Aristotle's akrasia but of how a person can go wrong in a clear-eyed manner.

Henry's description of the successive degrees of akrasia imitates the Catholic narrative of the Fall. The Fall is not caused by Adam's ignorance or his passions, but the causality is reversed: Adam's subsequent fallen state is characterized by ignorance and harmful passions which emerge as effects and even punishments of consent to the wrong alternative. Adam could sin freely, but after the Fall he cannot avoid being and remaining a sinner. Adam exemplifies the kind of akrasia in which ignorance and passions belong to the consequences of one's acting against one's better judgement.

1.5 Medieval Syntheses: Albert the Great and John Buridan

Some prominent medieval thinkers in addition to the Aristotelians and the voluntarists attempted to outline a middle way which would integrate the best of the ancient traditions and reconcile them with one another. Albert the Great's commentaries on EN harmonize Aristotle's teachings with the rest of ancient philosophy as well as with Augustinian Christianity.[89] Since the commentaries were written between 1248 and 1267, that is, before the controversies between Thomist intellectualists and Franciscan voluntarists began, Albert's considerations are not inhibited by later doctrinal condemnations. His commentaries had broad influence; among others, Aquinas, Burley, and John Buridan use them extensively.[90] For the purposes of our reception history, the line from Albert to Buridan is instructive, since it establishes a third distinct type of medieval akrasia. We will treat Albert's extensive discussions only insofar as this succession is relevant.

Albert is well aware of Aristotle's intentions and sympathetic to them for the most part. In his first commentary, he claims that the basic explanation of akratic action can be given by maintaining that the incontinent person does not know the minor premise in its full sense. The minor premise is corrupted by passion. Socrates is right in saying that no one violates his own knowledge insofar as the universal knowledge of the major premises is concerned.[91] In this way Albert adheres to model 1a.

In his second commentary, Albert defends the same position in principle. Now, however, he introduces the Stoic-Augustinian concept of acceptance (*acceptio*) more strongly into the context of explaining akrasia. Albert concludes that

in the syllogism of the continent person the last or minor premise and opinion, or the sensual acceptance, is accepted under the affection which qualifies the senses. This minor premise is the ruling principle in our action and work, for all our actions are related to particular concrete situations. As long as the incontinent person suffers the passion of concupiscence, he either does not have this sensual acceptance, or he has it in such way that in such a disposition he cannot truly be said to know rightly what should be done.[92]

On the one hand, this passage indicates the solution that something is wrong with the minor premise (1a). The word 'acceptance', on the other hand, introduces some Stoic-Augustinian features into the syllogistic picture.

---

[89] For Albert's ethics, see in particular Müller (2001). For Albert's akrasia, see Saarinen (1994), 94–118; Tracey (2006); Müller (2006).

[90] Albert, *Ethica* I, *Ethica* II. Saarinen (1994), 94–6. Walsh (1975), 258 documents the use of Albert in Burley and Buridan. They refer to *Ethica* II, whereas Aquinas uses *Ethica* I; see Gauthier (1969) and Müller (2001).

[91] Saarinen (1994), 113–14, quoting *Ethica* I, 532–3.

[92] *Ethica* II, 476; Saarinen (1994), 114.

In this context, Albert claims that 'contrary acceptances' reside in the soul of the continent person who thinks, for instance, that this act is both pleasant and shameful, and therefore inclines towards both committing and avoiding the act in question. Cicero, for instance, uses *acceptio* in the sense of Stoic assent, and it is evident that Albert understands the word to mean a preliminary assent or consent to the action in question. He compares acceptance with an opinion; thus acceptance expresses a judgement which is assented to but which does not yet prompt action. Albert further argues that continent and incontinent actions involve 'not one potency but two', since concupiscence exercises the power towards the pleasant while reason tries to avoid the shameful. The incontinent person has 'contrary acceptances' in his mind.[93] This state of affairs is Aristotelian, but Albert's understanding of it is 'clearly modelled on Augustine's "two wills" which compete with one another'.[94] Augustine's description of inner struggle is thus introduced into the Aristotelian framework. Albert's pupil Thomas Aquinas recognizes some aspects of this struggle; we will return to them in 2.2 below.

Unlike later voluntarists, Albert does not introduce the term 'acceptance' in order to stress the voluntary nature of akratic action. He follows the Aristotelian explanation, insisting that concupiscence obscures right reason and thus enables the execution of akratic action. Akrasia is thus due to ignorance. After the action, concupiscence dissolves and the person can again see clearly and fully what he should have done. Akrasia resembles the state of sleep or drunkenness, during which the person cannot control his or her actions.[95] The Aristotelian model 1a thus prevails.

In both of his commentaries, Albert is interested in the problem of moral certainty. Aristotle's word *akribeia*, 'precision', was translated into Latin as *certitudo*, 'certainty'. Aristotle's remark that we cannot reach the same degree of precision in ethics as in mathematics (EN 1094b2527, 1104a1–6) led Albert to emphasize that we cannot achieve absolute certainty in ethics. In addition, the singular terms of minor premises always report on contingent matters which may be otherwise. Whereas the Aristotelian *scientia* has as its object things which cannot be otherwise (EN 1139b), akratic actions deal with the estimation and acceptance of contingent and uncertain matters. Albert presents these remarks on moral uncertainty in a somewhat unsystematic fashion,[96] but they are of great importance in the ethics of John Buridan.

Buridan's *Quaestiones super decem libros Ethicorum* can be regarded as the richest harvest of medieval Aristotelian ethics. Buridan knows Aquinas, but he mentions

---

[93] *Ethica* II, 474–5; Saarinen (1994), 115–16. As Rist (1969), 140 points out, Cicero uses *acceptio* in the sense of Stoic assent.

[94] So Müller (2006), 1312. He provides extensive information of Albert's relationship to Augustine in Müller (2001); (2006); (2009), 503–11.

[95] *Ethica* II, 476: 'Si autem aliquis quaerat, qualiter in incontinente resolvitur ignorantia quae est ex obnubilatione concupiscentiae, ita quod incontinens rursus fiat sciens et claram habeat acceptionem operabilium. Eadem ratio est quae est de vinolento et dormiente: haec enim passio propriam et separatam ab aliis non habet causam. Hanc autem causam a Physiologis audire oportet, quia ex principiis ethicis non potest determinari.' Cf. Saarinen (1994), 116.

[96] *Ethica* I, 522–3, 530; *Ethica* II, 51–4, 408, 465–7. See Saarinen (1994), 103–12.

Albert more often. Among Franciscan authors, he uses Gerald Odonis in particular. Buridan's discussion on akrasia is an attempt to delineate a middle way between intellectualists and voluntarists. He uses Seneca in particular among the Stoics. Buridan avoids theological issues and does not often quote Augustine, but he pays special attention to his own agreement with the above-mentioned Parisian articles which defend medieval Augustinianism.[97]

Buridan's action theory is a synthesis of Stoic, Augustinian, voluntarist, and Albertian elements. In his view, the self-determination of the will must be affirmed, although it may not be possible to present sufficient rational grounds for the so-called *libertas oppositionis*, the self-regulating capacity of the will, to be determined (everything else being equally disposed) sometimes towards one of the opposites and sometimes to the other.[98] In addition, Buridan affirms the Parisian article which holds that the will can remain in the state of *non velle* in situations in which it is natural for it to be moved.[99] In other words, the will exercises control over the immediate impulses of the animal soul.

In spite of these affirmations, Buridan is not a straightforward voluntarist in the style of Walter of Bruges or Henry of Ghent. He teaches that the will is prepared to action through three stages. The will first receives a judgement of the practical intellect, informing it of various good and bad aspects of the alternatives under consideration. This preliminary judgement does not prompt action but only generates an act of 'complacence' or 'displacence' in the will. It is possible to introduce many different acts of complacence and displacence simultaneously, given that the practical intellect judges that different aspects of the situation at hand appear as under the aspect of goodness or badness (*sub ratione boni/mali*). The cluster of first acts is followed by the second act of the will which is the actual acceptance or refusal (*acceptatio, refutatio*). This act is more specific than Albert's *acceptio*, since the will only accepts one alternative, which is considered to be the best among the candidates introduced by the first act. The second act is in many respects similar to Augustine's consent. But while in the voluntarist tradition the act of consent demonstrates the freedom of the will, Buridan's second act of the will occurs on the basis of accomplished intellectual deliberation. The second act prompts the action if no external hindrance is present. The third act of the will is the action itself (*prosecutio, fuga*).[100]

Buridan's theory applies some Stoic features. It understands that the first act of the will, the desire to do something, occurs in the form of judgement. Although Buridan applies the Aristotelian idea of practical deliberation and syllogistic reasoning, his description of the first acts of the will resembles the Stoic view in which the agent is

---

[97] For Buridan's ethics and action theory, see Krieger (1986); Saarinen (1994), 161–88; Saarinen (2003); Lagerlund (2002); Zupko (2003), 227–70. Pironet (2001) is a valuable electronic edition and commentary. In the following, references are first given to Buridan (1513) and second, in brackets, to Buridan (1637).

[98] Saarinen (1994), 166–7, referring to Buridan, *Quaestiones*, lib III, q1, 36rb, 37rb–va (147–8, 152–3).

[99] *Quaestiones*, 36vb (149). Saarinen (1994), 168. Müller (2009), 692 holds that Buridan takes the topic of *non velle* from Duns Scotus. For Duns Scotus's view of akrasia, see Müller (2009), 636–72.

[100] *Quaestiones*, lib. III q3, 41va–43ra (165–71). Saarinen (1994), 169–70.

confronted with different and contrary impressions and impulses. In order to make a definitive choice between them, an act of assent is needed. This second act is different from the preliminary judgements and preliminary desires, equipping the will with the freedom of not accepting the seemingly good and not refuting the seemingly bad.[101] Buridan is, however, an Aristotelian intellectualist in the sense that he believes in the discerning capacity of practical reasoning between the first and the second acts of the will. His analysis of akrasia shows this in a paradigmatic manner.

The akratic conduct occurs in a situation which is characterized by a 'twofold inclination' (*duplex inclinatio*); that is, a situation in which the person successively inclines towards contrary alternatives. Incontinence is primarily located in the will, because it is the faculty of the soul which can first exercise a choice towards one alternative and then to its contrary.[102] Although the different first acts of the will can exemplify different preliminary judgements, Buridan defends the final unity of judgement and assent. He therefore refutes the view that a person could, strictly speaking, simultaneously have contrary judgements about a particular action. Even in the case of the incontinent person this does not happen, since

the incontinent moves toward contrary positions as follows: when he is not under the influence of passion, his appetite inclines towards avoiding wrong, whereas under the influence of passion it inclines towards pursuing it. But it does not have both inclinations at once. It can also be said that the intellect judges simultaneously that one and the same thing is both pleasant and shameful. Given this, the appetite immediately receives both complacence toward it because of pleasure, and displacence because of shamefulness. In this sense, complacence and displacence are not opposites. But as the intellect cannot judge that this totality must be both followed and avoided simultaneously, so the appetite cannot both accept and refute this totality simultaneously.[103]

Buridan is both Stoic and Aristotelian in his emphasis on the unity of the judgement. Although the first act of the will can generate different and contrary viewpoints which are judgemental since they appear *sub ratione boni/mali*, the complete situation will finally be judged in a unified manner. This is expressed in the second act of the will which prompts action. The second act is not, however, a voluntarist manifestation of freedom, but an intellectualistic affirmation of the best option. Buridan underlines this intellectualist stance in his decisive questions regarding akrasia. In his view, since it is not possible to act against actual, particular, and perfect knowledge, akrasia is accompanied by some ignorance. He further holds that the will necessarily obeys the conclusion of the practical intellect, if this conclusion is argued with full clarity and certainty.[104]

---

[101] *Quaestiones*, 42 va (169): 'est sciendum, quod libertas secundum quam voluntas potest non acceptare, quod sibi presentatum fuerit sub ratione boni, vel non refutare quod sibi presentatum est sub ratione mali, prodest valde nobis in vitae directionem.' See further Saarinen (1994), 171.

[102] *Quaestiones*, lib. VII q3, 141ra–va (576–8). Saarinen (1994), 172–3.

[103] *Quaestiones*, lib. VII q6, 143va (587). Saarinen (1994), 174–5.

[104] See Saarinen (1994), 178–81, discussing *Quaestiones*, lib. VII q7–8.

Given that Buridan also believes in the self-determination of the will and in the *libertas oppositionis*, these are somewhat puzzling conclusions. Buridan evidently thinks that he can combine the requirements of Franciscan voluntarism and Thomist intellectualism. This combination is achieved with the help of two additional postulates: (1) the uncertainty of moral situations, and (2) the ability of the will to withhold the implementation of judgement in uncertain cases. For Buridan, akrasia is a common phenomenon which results from uncertain situations. A person need not implement better judgement, if that judgement remains uncertain and its alternative also appears under the aspect of some goodness.

In discussing akrasia, Buridan undertakes a distinction among four different grades of how the intellect can estimate the truth of its own judgement. (1) The weakest case arises when no reason supports either A or B. (2) Another weak case arises when equal reasons support both A and B. (3) In the third case, there is a stronger reason for A than for B, but some reason nevertheless promotes B. (4) Only when all doubts are removed can the intellect reach a judgement which is neither weak (*debile*) nor faint (*formidinale*). In cases (1)–(3), contrary inclinations and, in turn, akratic actions are possible. In such cases, the will is often advised to use its inherent capacity of *non velle*, of postponing the judgement.[105]

When Buridan investigates the question of whether the will necessarily obeys the conclusion of the practical intellect, he introduces a distinction between uncertain and certain judgements:

If someone judges that something is good for him according to a consistent good reason, so that it appears good according to all good reasons and so that nothing evil follows, then, it seems to me, if this judgement is uncertain (*dubium*), the will nevertheless does not necessarily accept it ... if the judgement in question is totally certain (*certum omnino*), i.e. that the person firmly and sufficiently believes he sees all relevant circumstances and all of the different possibilities, and, after having taken everything into consideration, he firmly believes that the decision in hand will be good for him in any case and by no means bad, then I say that the will necessarily accepts it.[106]

The self-determining capacity of the will thus consists in a far-reaching right of veto: as long as there is some doubt, the will is not required to act. Akratic actions pertain to these cases of uncertainty. Buridan's explanation of akrasia has some affinities with Donald Davidson's view, both maintaining that akratic action pertains to cases in which the intellectual judgement remains conditional or *prima facie*.[107] Only unconditional judgements prompt action necessarily.

Buridan's view applies different elements of the ancient and medieval interpretation history of akrasia. Buridan combines Aristotle's view of inevitable ignorance with the Stoic emphasis on judgement and assent. He takes over the voluntarist idea of the will's

[105] *Quaestiones*, lib. VII q6, 143ra (585). Saarinen (1994), 175–6.
[106] *Quaestiones*, lib. VII q8, 145 rb (594). Saarinen (1994), 181.
[107] See Saarinen (1993).

self-determination, but embeds it in a Thomist framework in which good action is rationally deliberated.[108] Buridan's own contribution can be seen in his consistent distinction between the first and second acts of the will, as well as in his underlining of the weak and uncertain nature of many, if not most, judgements. This contribution reveals some debt to Albert and Augustine, but it is, basically, a recognizable model which can be called a 'Buridanistic' analysis of human action.

In short, the Buridanistic model holds that while different and even contrary alternatives can appear under some aspect of goodness and thus create preliminary acts of complacence or displacence, the final assent of the will is given to one alternative. This alternative, chosen as a result of intellectual deliberation, represents the final judgement. In unclear and uncertain situations, the will can postpone the final judgement, since it need not accept uncertain judgements, but the will is also a rational faculty, not choosing directly against reason. Although clear-eyed akrasia is impossible, akratic actions occur in situations in which the judgement remains uncertain. Some ignorance or at least uncertainty needs to be presupposed in akratic behaviour. Although Buridan teaches the self-determination of the will, he does not appeal to it as the ground of incorrect choices.

We conclude this chapter with Table 1.1 of the models outlined in 1.1–1.5 (see next page). There is considerable overlap among different models, but the three major classes have their distinguishing features. The following chapters will employ this inventory in classifying the different explanations of akrasia. The models will be spelled out in more detail with regard to each author; this inventory only formulates some relevant catchwords.

---

[108] Cf. the insightful discussion of Zupko (2003), 249–51 and my differentiation of prudential deliberation in Saarinen (2003).

Table 1.1 Models of akrasia: a brief inventory

Platonic models. Distinctive feature: reason vs desire (but no syllogism, no assent)
- Socratic-Platonic model: intellectualist action theory, no one goes wrong willingly
- commonplace Platonism: tripartite soul, strong lower part may overcome small higher part, therefore desire sometimes overcomes reason

Aristotelian models. Distinctive feature: the practical syllogism
- 1a: the minor premise is ignored in akrasia
- 1b: when the premises are not properly connected, akrasia can occur
- 2: in akrasia, the propositional conclusion is reached but not followed

Stoic-Augustinian models. Distinctive feature: the concept of assent/consent/free will
- strictly Stoic model: emotions are assented judgements, no real distinction between desire and consent
- moderated Stoic model: emotions are preliminary judgements; later assents play a role
- commonplace Augustinian model: a clear distinction between inevitable desires and free consent; the judgemental nature of desires remains in the background while merit and sin are consequential to the consent
- Buridanism: rational decision-making within the commonplace Augustinian model
- voluntarism: the self-determining will as the supreme ruler; the will represents the most noble part of the soul
- Adam's akrasia: the will chooses freely without interference of emotions; passions and ignorance only emerge afterwards, as the consequence (punishment) of misguided choice
- deliberate irrationality: the will chooses freely; the will does not represent the rational soul or the most noble part of the soul

---

2

The Renaissance

2.1 Petrarch and Augustinian Voluntarism

The reception of Aristotle's ethics in Italy was different from that in France and England. Whereas in Paris lectures on EN are mentioned in 1215, the first teaching appointments in Florence date from 1365 and the statutes mention moral philosophy only in 1387. In Bologna, the earliest records date from 1405 and in Padua from 1465. There is some evidence, however, that Aristotle's ethical works were known by the first decades of the fourteenth century.[1]

On the other hand, moral philosophy was also discussed outside of academic lecture rooms. Francesco Petrarch (1304–1374) writes that he is familiar with Aristotle's ethics. Petrarch is often critical of Aristotle and prefers Cicero and Seneca:

> I have read all of Aristotle's moral books if I am not mistaken. Some of them I have also heard commented on . . . He teaches what virtue is, I do not deny that; but his lesson lacks the words that sting and set afire and urge toward love of virtue and hatred of vice or, at any rate, does not have enough of such power. He who looks for that will find it in our Latin writers, especially in Cicero and Seneca.[2]

Petrarch owned a copy of the *Nicomachean Ethics* and he quotes Aristotle in many of his works, sometimes approvingly. He is better known as a critic of Aristotelianism, however. Petrarch's philosophical sympathies are not with Aristotle, but with a Christianized interpretation of Plato, Cicero, and Seneca. He could not read Aristotle in Greek and was dependent on the medieval translation by Grosseteste.[3]

In addition to his vernacular writings, Petrarch wrote extensive and influential works on moral philosophy in Latin. Petrarch's *Secretum* is a programmatic treatise on the Augustinian issues related to weakness of will. His *De remediis utriusque fortunae* also includes passages dealing with akrasia. Petrarch's eloquence sometimes conceals the fact that his doctrinal positions are actually much closer to the medieval traditions than his classical Latin style. Petrarch considered a religious career seriously and he had

---

[1] Lines (2002), 81–3. The work of Lines offers exhaustive information on the fates of EN in Italy from 1350 to 1650.

[2] Petrarch, *De ignorantia* (*Opere latine* 2, 1106–8); translation from *On His Own Ignorance*, 105–6, quoted in Lines (2002), 213 (Lines omits the word 'moral').

[3] For a detailed account of Petrarch's knowledge of moral traditions, see Trinkaus (1979), 1–26. His critical stance with regard to Aristotelianism is elaborated in detail in *De ignorantia*.

many contacts with the Augustinian eremites in Milan. Scholars have seen in his philosophical works a proximity to the ideas of via *moderna* and to the renaissance of Augustinianism.[4] Petrarch admires Augustine, and his contribution to akrasia is formulated under the preconditions of late medieval Augustinianism.

Although Petrarch is a contemporary of John Buridan and writes at a time when Aristotle's *Ethics* was only beginning to be used in Italian universities, his texts in many ways signal a departure from the scholastic setting. Both *Secretum* and *De remediis* are composed as dialogues which aim to heal the soul.[5] His audience is not the university classroom or academic colleagues, but the literary elite as a whole. Eloquence and practical usefulness are important elements of his argument, whereas technical philosophical terminology is absent. At the same time, however, the differences in style should not obscure the thematic continuation. Petrarch addresses the same problems of human will which had occupied Augustine and medieval scholastics.

At the same time, Petrarch practises philosophical therapy, or philosophy 'as a way of life'. Recent research has emphasized the distinct form of this kind of philosophy which was popular in Hellenistic antiquity.[6] It is evident that Renaissance and Reformation authors revive this philosophical style, suggesting it as an alternative to academic and, in particular, scholastic philosophy. In this spirit, early modern thinkers sometimes argue that philosophy does not primarily seek speculative knowledge but consolation, therapy, improvement of life, virtue, and even eternal bliss.[7]

While it is important to recognize the existence of this mode of argumentation, we will not treat it as a separate branch of philosophy, proceeding from the assumption that the same problems of weakness of will can be treated in different rhetorical genres. It seems evident, however, that religious early modern authors from Petrarch to Luther and Calvin consider Augustine to be the champion of 'philosophy as a way of life' and a worthy counterpoint of Aristotle, who is the embodiment of academic and scholastic philosophy.

The composition of *Secretum* underlines the connections with tradition. The alter ego of Petrarch, Francesco, lies depressed but awake when Lady Truth and Augustine appear to him in a vision. Truth asks Augustine to help her in healing Francesco's melancholy. Augustine agrees, and *Secretum* then reports the therapeutic dialogue between Francesco and Augustine. Petrarch underlines the private nature of this conversation, saying that the volume is not intended for wide circulation.[8] Although it is difficult to say whether Petrarch really meant this, the work, which was composed in 1342–1343 and slightly revised in 1358, did not become public before the author's death.

---

[4] Trinkaus (1979), 52–4.

[5] The English edition of *Secretum* by Carozza and Shey (1989) contains several essays and bibliography. The English edition of *De remediis* by Rawski (*Remedies*) contains extensive bibliographic information and identifies Petrarch's sources in great detail. I give the English quotes from these English editions (page number in brackets). The Latin texts are quoted according to *Prose*, 21–215 (*Secretum*) and *Vita di Francesco Petrarca* (digital edition of *De remediis*, quoted according to book and chapter).

[6] See e.g. Hadot (1995) and (2002); Nussbaum (1994).

[7] For this feature in Petrarch, see, e.g. Vasoli (1988), 62–3; Trinkaus (1979), 22–6.

[8] *Secretum*, 26 (39).

The obvious literary model of the dialogue is Boethius' *Consolation of Philosophy*. Augustine aims to console Francesco and heal his sadness. Another possible model may be the appearance of Lady Continence to Augustine in *Confessions* 8, 11, 27. Continence instructs Augustine how to heal the division of his will; now Augustine teaches this to Francesco. The instruction takes three days: on the first day, Francesco is taught that man can choose to become happy; the second day's dialogue is devoted to liberation from the seven deadly sins; on the third day, Augustine teaches how to release oneself from the chains of love and glory.

Augustine begins his therapy by stating boldly that 'if a man expends every effort to become happy, it is in his power to do so'.[9] Francesco doubts this. Nobody wishes for poverty, grief, disgrace, and disease, and yet it is not in our power to avoid these.[10] Augustine reminds Francesco of the Stoic doctrine that warns of identifying happiness with external circumstances. Francesco agrees, but claims that the problem of unhappiness is a deeper one. People cannot achieve happiness by the effort of their own will, because the will has no such power: 'You are trying to show that no one falls into unhappiness except of his own free will and that no one is unhappy unless he wants to be. It is my sad experience that the opposite is true.'[11] Augustine disagrees, claiming that 'when you said that you were unable to do anything about your situation, what you really meant to say was that you were unwilling to do anything about it'.[12]

Francesco denies this several times, maintaining that he often wanted to do something but remained unable. Augustine relates this complaint to his own struggles before conversion:

it is truer to say that you were unwilling. I am not surprised that you are confused, just as I was when I was contemplating a new way of life... And yet... I stayed the same man until at last a deep meditation brought home to me the full extent of my unhappiness. And so, after I committed my will fully, I was instantly able to act and with amazing and blessed swiftness I was a changed man. I am sure you know all this from reading my *Confessions*.[13]

Francesco realizes that he cannot do what he wants to do and that this situation makes him depressed; Augustine maintains that everyone can do what he or she wants, provided that the will is unified. Next, Augustine sets out to prove that he is right by appealing to reason and conscience. Conscience is the 'infallible judge of thoughts and

---

[9] *Secretum*, 28 (42).

[10] *Secretum*, 32 (44).

[11] *Secretum*, 36 (45–6): 'Hoc igitur unum est, quod me super ambigenda propositionis tue veritate solicitat, qua conaris astruere neminem nisi sponte sua in miseriam corruisse, neminem miserum esse, nisi qui velit; cuius rei contrarium in me tristis experior.'

[12] *Secretum*, 40 (47–8): 'Verba vero, quibus uti te velim, hec sunt: ut ubi "ultra te non posse" dixisti "ultra te nolle" fatearis.'

[13] *Secretum*, 40 (48): 'respondi, imo verius noluisse? Nec tamen admiror te in his nunc ambagibus obvolutum in quibus olim ego ipse iactatus, dum novam vite viam carpere meditarer... Et tamen hec inter idem ille qui fueram mansi, donec alta tandem meditatio omnem miseriam meam ante oculos congessit. Itaque postquam plene volui, ilicet et potui, miraque et felicissima celeritate transformatus sum in alterum Augustinum, cuius historie seriem, ni fallor, ex Confessionibus meis nosti.'

deeds'. If Francesco examined his conscience, he would realize that his wishes remained half-hearted and feeble.[14]

A crucial issue regarding this examination is the meditation on death. Francesco claims that he has meditated on death sufficiently and that his conscience affirms this to be the case. Augustine, however, insists that conscience should be examined more thoroughly.[15] A human being is by definition rational and mortal: but only when he is 'so aware of his mortality that he holds it before his eyes daily', can he have 'true and useful knowledge concerning the definition of man'. Augustine holds that a sufficient meditation of death enables reason to concentrate on the higher being in man.[16]

Francesco's meditation has been hindered by the passions of the body, which confuse him.[17] Through concentrating on death, he can again focus his mind and examine his conscience more profoundly. At the end of the first day, Augustine arrives at a conclusive diagnosis:

It is this plague which has hurt you and will lead you to destruction, unless you do something about it. Overwhelmed by too many impressions made upon it and oppressed by many different worries constantly warring with one another, your weak spirit does not know what care it should attack first, which nurture, which destroy, which drive away . . . The same thing has happened to you as happens to someone who plants too many seeds in one narrow place for them to grow without interfering one another. In your overcrowded mind, nothing useful can take root and bear fruit. You are without a plan and so you are carried this way and that, disorganized and never at full strength. This is the reason that as often as your mind, capable of great things if allowed, comes to meditate on death and other things that might lead it to life and tries with its own keen intelligence to meditate deeply, it does not have the strength and is turned back, driven by a host of various cares. As a result, the beneficial undertaking is weakened by indecision and comes to nothing. And then comes this inner discord, about which we have said much, and that torment of a mind which is angry at itself.[18]

This passage contains Petrarch's most elaborate and analytical account of weakness of will, in which the introspective account of Augustine is spelled out more fully than in *Confessions* 8. The root cause of akrasia is seen in the plurality of 'impressions'

[14] *Secretum*, 44 (50): 'Ut certius credas conscientiam ipse tuam consule. Illa optima virtutis interpres, illa infallibilis et verax est operum cogitationumque pensatrix. Illa tibi dicet nunquam te ad salutem qua decuit aspirasse, sed tepidius remissiusque quam periculorum tantorum consideratio requirebat.'

[15] *Secretum*, 48 (52).

[16] *Secretum*, 52–4 (54–5).

[17] *Secretum*, 64 (60).

[18] *Secretum*, 66–8 (61–2): 'Hec tibi pestis nocuit; hec te, nisi provideas perditum ire festinat. Siquidem fantasmatibus suis obrutus, multisque et variis ac secum sine pace pugnantibus curis animus fragilis oppressus, cui primum occurrat, quam nutriat, quam perimat, quam repellat . . . idem tibi contingit, ut in animo nimis occupato nil utile radices agat, nichilque fructiferum coalescat; tuque inops consilii modo huc modo illuc mira fluctuatione volvaris, nusquam integer, nusquam totus. Hinc est ut quotiens ad hanc cogitationem mortis aliasque, per quas iri possit ad vitam, generosus, si sinatur, animus accessit, inque altum naturali descendit acumine, stare ibi non valens, turba curarum variarum pellente, resiliat. Ex quo fit ut tam salutare propositum nimia mobilitate fatiscat, oriturque illa intestina discordia de qua multa iam diximus, illaque anime sibi irascentis anxietas.'

(*fantasmas*) which disturbs and weakens the mind. This plurality inhibits effective deliberation which could lead to unified action. Weakness of will is not primarily due to ignorance but rather to an overload of conflicting impressions. Stoic and Augustinian motives (cf. 1.2) are employed to create a picture of indecision. The inner discord which causes Francesco's depression and frustration is a consequence of the overcrowded mind.

This diagnosis is also intended to explain the origin of the harmful desires in Francesco. The inner discord and weakness of will generates anxiety and self-hatred (*sibi irascendi anxietas*), which in turn lead to sadness. This bears some resemblance to Sorabji's reading of Chrysippus (1.2), in which akrasia is related to the emergence of harmful desires. Such desires are, by definition, mistaken judgements, and their eradication requires a new cognitive stance. Augustine sets out to heal Francesco by means of cognitive therapy.

The church father believes that the new cognitive insight can be reached through meditation on death. Like his historical model (*Confessions* 6, 11, 20), Petrarch's Augustine believes that the strong will is finally a gift of God, alluding to the Wisdom of Solomon (8:21): 'A man cannot be continent, unless God gave it.'[19] Discussions on the second day deal with the eradication and moderation of the passions which accompany the impressions and lead to the seven deadly sins. Among these, lust is particularly related to the notion of continence.

For Petrarch's Augustine, a significant feature of lust is that it can prevent knowledge. Referring to Plato, Augustine teaches that 'nothing prevents one from knowing the divine so much as one's carnal appetites and inflamed desires'. 'Familiarity with Venus takes away the ability to see divine things', Augustine further claims.[20] It is unclear how well Petrarch knew Plato; this view resembles the so-called commonplace Platonism (cf. 1.1). Augustine's discussion tries to increase Francesco's awareness and clarity of mind. Although Francesco is overloaded with impressions, not ignorant, his mind is confused and he needs to examine his conscience in order to be liberated from the passions. In that limited sense his weakness of will is due to non-awareness created by various harmful passions.

Augustine returns to the mutual relationship between lust, confusion, and weakness of will on the third day. Francesco has meanwhile admitted that Augustine is right in making him aware of the various disturbances of his mind, but Augustine has kept the most difficult therapy to the third day. Now he argues that Francesco is bound by two chains which finally prevent him from focusing his will:

Augustine: You see very clearly the chains that hold you, but you are blind to the fact that they are chains. What blindness! You delight in the very chains that drag you to your death, and what is saddest of all, you glory in them.

---

[19] *Secretum*, 100 (82).
[20] *Secretum*, 102–4 (83–4).

Francesco: What are the chains you are talking about?
Augustine: Love and glory. [21]

The third day is devoted to the eradication of these two emotions. Francesco is advised to abandon his fame and glory as poet. But even more crucial for his happiness is the renunciation of his love for the woman he has loved since his youth. Francesco is horrified by this proposal and sets out to show that love and glory are his 'fairest ideals' and represent 'the clearest faculties' of his soul.[22] Augustine is, however, persistent in his claims. When Francesco claims that his love for the woman ignited his love of God, Augustine declares that, on the contrary, 'she has distracted your mind from the love of heavenly things'.[23]

To convince Francesco, Augustine asks him to review his youth and tell the church father when and why he went wrong. Francesco responds as follows:

When travelling the right road I had with temperance and modesty reached the fork in the road and was ordered to take the right turn, I turned to the left, whether out of carelessness or perversity I do not know. What I had often read as a boy was of no help [he quotes the *Aeneid* 6, 540–543, describing the crossing between Elysium and Tartarus]. Although I had read this before, I did not understand the passage before my experience. From then on, I was lost on this twisting and dusty pathway and often turning back in tears, I could not find the way to the right; because once I had left it, then, yes it was then that the confusion in my life began.[24]

This description of akratic choice reveals some important features of Petrach's account. It is less important whether the akratic choice occurs out of ignorance or wickedness, but full understanding only takes place afterwards, when it is too late to reverse the course of things. Here as well, the state of confusion is not the cause of akrasia, but a consequence of it.

Augustine then asks Francesco to compare the date of turning left to the date of meeting the woman, and to his own astonishment Francesco notes that the dates coincide.[25] Augustine further increases his attack on Francesco, urging him to abandon his love; otherwise he could not get rid of the harmful desires. Cognitive arguments, introduced with the imperative: consider (*cogita*), are an important instrument of this therapy. Francesco should consider the nobility of the soul, the shortness of life, the harmful effects of shame and wasted time. All these should lead him away from his love.[26]

The treatment of glory proceeds in a somewhat different, although not less difficult fashion: Francesco should 'cultivate virtue and ignore glory'. Glory can follow him, but only when he does not seek it. Instead, Francesco should count all these things as secondary, take control of himself and begin to meditate on death.[27]

The end of *Secretum* is puzzling. Francesco thanks Augustine and promises: 'I shall be as true to myself as I can, collect the scattered fragments of my soul, and diligently aim

---

[21] *Secretum*, 132 (102).   [22] *Secretum*, 132 (102).
[23] *Secretum*, 146 (110).   [24] *Secretum*, 150–2 (111–12).   [25] *Secretum*, 152 (112).
[26] See, e.g., the series of arguments in *Secretum*, 184–8 (129–31).   [27] *Secretum*, 206–8 (140–1).

at self-possession.'[28] After saying this, however, he adds that many important matters await his attention and that he must hasten to these tasks. He can only return to Augustine's considerations once they are finished. He adds:

I am not ignorant, as you were just saying, that it would be a much safer course to tend to the care of my soul and set myself straight on the road to salvation, avoiding the byways. But I cannot restrain my desire for study.[29]

To this Augustine resignedly remarks: 'We are slipping back into an old argument. You are labelling the will as lacking in power (*voluntatem impotentiam vocas*). Well, let it pass, since it cannot be otherwise.' Francesco bids farewell to Augustine saying: 'May God lead me safe and whole from so many winding ways. And as I follow His voice, may I raise no cloud of dust before my eyes.'[30] Thus Petrarch's alter ego remains in a state of ambivalence. While he returns to his old habits, he is grateful to Augustine for showing him the causes of his unhappiness and he hopes to have become more clear-eyed than before. At a theoretical level, Francesco has learned how it is possible to obtain a unified will which can effectively bring about happiness.

At the practical level, however, Francesco thinks that the price of this therapy is too high. Even Augustine admits in his final riposte that 'it cannot be otherwise': people continue to complain that their will lacks power. Augustine's conversion story is thus not repeated in *Secretum*; on the contrary, Francesco remains in his state of divided and overcrowded mind. The vision of the overcrowded mind bears some resemblance to Buridan's analysis of the akratic situation in that both Petrarch and Buridan presuppose a plurality of conflicting impressions or first acts of the will. Petrarch, however, describes this situation in more dramatic terms, the plurality of impressions paralyzing the mind and preventing the formation of resolute judgements.

When this paralysis and depressing discord is healed, Petrarch advocates a voluntarist stance with regard to human actions: when people focus their minds and exercise a truthful introspection, they can see that the will does not fundamentally lack the power to do good. At the same time Petrarch trusts that, when the intellect is educated and healed, it will see and approve this underlying capacity of the will. In fact, Francesco is healed in this sense, since he is no longer ignorant, but realizes that his conduct reflects the preferences of his will, not its powerlessness. At the beginning of *Secretum*, Francesco complains that he acts against his better judgement; in the end he sees that this complaint was based on an illusion. The intellectualist descriptions of akrasia thus appear to be illusory and false, since in reality Francesco follows his own preferences.

---

[28] *Secretum*, 214 (144): 'Adero michi ipse quantum potero, et sparsa anime fragmenta recolligam, moraborque mecum sedulo. Sane nunc, dum loquimur, multa me magnaque, quamvis adhuc mortalia, negotia expectant.'

[29] *Secretum*, 214 (144): 'non ignarus, ut paulo ante dicebas, multo michi futurum esse securius studium hoc unum sectari et, deviis pretermissis, rectum callem salutis apprehendere. Sed desiderium frenare non valeo.'

[30] *Secretum*, 214 (144).

When the narrative of *Secretum* is stripped of its dramatic elements and rhetorical points, Petrach's position is surprisingly close to that of Henry of Ghent.[31] Both stress the capacity and responsibility of free will; both investigate the claims of ignorance and disorder in detail but consider them of only secondary importance. Petrarch's description of the fundamental akratic choice bears a resemblance to Henry's view of gradual consent.[32] The person freely chooses the wrong option. This choice is not caused by ignorance and disorder, but brings about disorder and ignorance in will and intellect as its immediate consequence, so that the akratic person cannot reverse the course of his life and remains on the wrong road. He may turn back, but remains confused, not finding the right road again. In this sense, Petrarch adheres to the voluntarist picture of Henry of Ghent. Free will remains the cause and master of all things, but ignorance and disorder, consequences, and even punishments of the original wrong choice, appear to be the primary problems of the incontinent person. They can be remedied in cognitive therapy so that the person can see his voluntarist nature in a truthful light.

Following this lead, the ending of *Secretum* can be regarded as a small footnote and caveat to the voluntaristic picture. Does Francesco simply choose to study, or is he also serious in saying that he 'cannot restrain' his desire (*desiderium frenare non valeo*)? In the latter case, the will has a limit: not all desires can be eradicated, some of them remaining necessarily. Such a picture of remaining assented desire resembles that variant of Augustinianism which holds that some concupiscence continues to be counted as sin, since it involves a judgement and assent (cf. 1.2). Even an enlightened person cannot be without this sinful desire, since some assented concupiscence inevitably remains. There is no return to the original state of Adam. If the last words of the *Secretum* are interpreted in this manner, they do not witness a free humanistic choice, but exemplify a more radical version of sinful concupiscence, which Francesco finally returns to Augustine. When Francesco finally rejects the optimistic Augustine of *Confessions,* he in a way approves the pessimistic anti-Pelagian Augustine who was more inclined to think that some desires cannot be restrained (1.2). This caveat sets a limit to voluntary self-realization without calling the voluntaristic picture into question.

Petrarch's voluntaristic view of free will and akrasia is supported in his other major work in moral philosophy, *De remediis utriusque fortunae.* This work in a peculiar way resembles Peter Abelard's *Sic et non* and later scholastic quaestions, but the resemblance sometimes approaches parody. Each 'question' is a brief dialogue between a problematic emotion and reason. In the first book, reason for the most part moderates the emotion of joy, whereas in the second book reason often consoles and encourages sorrow. Sometimes the emotions of hope and fear are moderated in a similar manner. The questions frequently appear as pairs, so that for instance in Book 1 Ch. 67 reason moderates the joy caused by a fertile wife, whereas in Book II Ch. 22 the sorrow of

---

[31] See Müller (2007) and 1.4 above. Trinkaus (1979), 53–6 compares Petrarch and *via moderna*. Courcelle (1989) emphasizes Petrarch's connections with the Augustinian eremites in Milan.

[32] *Secretum,* 150–2 (111–12). Cf. 1.4 above.

having a barren wife is consoled. Reason aims at finding a balance between the emotions of joy, hope, sorrow, and fear.[33]

Petrarch's method marks a conscious departure from scholasticism. Whereas scholastic questions are formulated in a universal and impersonal manner, the joys and sorrows of De remediis concern individual people and their accidental matters, given or taken away by fortune. The same reason can provide different advice, depending on the emotional state of the dialogue partner. The basic idea is nevertheless that emotions are for the most part harmful and reason steers the course of life so that emotional upheavals can be avoided. Reason is employed as a therapeutic instrument which can offer remedies for both prosperity and adversity, not relativized.

Book II, chapter 104, 'Lack of Virtue', is a dialogue between Sorrow and Reason which is similar to the dialogue between Francesco and Augustine in Secretum. Sorrow complains of the lack of virtue. Reason points out that this lack is not due to fortune or nature, but to one's own voluntary decision, since each person can direct and exercise his own will as he sees fit. 'Nobody suffers a lack of virtue unless he wills it so.'[34]

Sorrow now presents the argument from akrasia: 'What if I want to have virtue but cannot attain it?' This argument is, however, based on self-deception. People 'think they want what they do not want', but in reality they desire something other than the good.[35] The problem is not weakness of will, but the wrong turn of the will. After this reply, Sorrow reformulates the issue: 'I know I want to do good the right way, but I just do not seem to be able to do it.' But Reason is not convinced: 'If this is so, then your willing is just not good enough. One must desire to do it—not moderately so, but with great vehemence! You, however, desire most fervently what is harmful, and only in a lukewarm fashion what is good.'[36] Again, the problem lies in the fundamentally wrong choice by the will.

In spite of this criticism, Reason is optimistic. A person can pursue virtue if he really wants to, but the will needs to be uniform and steadfast:

If you really want to be good, do not procrastinate; begin right now. If the smallest of things cannot be had without effort, what do you expect of virtue, not as a pastime and relaxation from the business of living, but as the only straight way to happiness? Make time for virtue and pursue it with the greatest of effort and the whole strength of your mind.[37]

---

[33] Rawski's introduction in Remedies 1, xxii–xxiii describes the argument of the book. His extensive commentaries (Remedies, vols 2 and 4) analyse the background of the work in detail.

[34] De remediis Book 2, Ch. 104 (Remedies 3, 251–2): 'D. At virtutis inops sum. R. Verum damnum iustus dolor, nisi quod alie omnes inopie naturales, aut fortuite, aut violente esse possunt, hec una proculdubio voluntaria est . . . hec una autem in voluntate consistit, quam pro arbitrio sibi quisque moderatur atque efficit . . . Atque ita virtutis inopiam non patitur, nisi qui vult.'

[35] De remediis 2, 104 (3, 252).

[36] De remediis 2, 104 (3, 252): 'D. Scio me velle, nec posse ideo bonum fieri. R. Ut sit ita, velle non sufficit: desiderio opus est, eoque non modico, sed vehementi. Vos autem mala vestra ferventissime cupitis, bona vultis tepidissime.'

[37] De remediis 2, 104 (3, 252).

Such effort also demands the 'heavenly wisdom, which is the best healer and counselor'. Petrarch again quotes the Wisdom of Solomon 8:21: 'No one can be continent except God gave it.' Sorrow remarks that 'no matter how much I desire to be good, I am not'. But Reason considers this not to be true: 'How much you desire to be good the facts will tell.'[38]

This dialogue repeats the position of *Secretum* in a nutshell: the will can always proceed to virtue if the person really tries. If a person claims that he wills the good but is not able to pursue it, he deceives himself and others: either he wills something in reality, or has not realized that he in fact can do what he wants. Petrarch's stance is again voluntaristic: perverted will, not ignorance, is the ultimate source of wrong actions. Ignorance may accompany wrong choices, but it is not their ultimate cause. In addition, ignorance can be healed so that the foundational role of the will becomes evident. Akratic actions are thus ultimately instances of that Augustinian inner discord in which the weightier part of the will prevails. The Augustinian discord is interpreted in the light of Franciscan voluntarism: if the akratic person is healed and educated, he can see how the will is basically responsible for his actions.

Many other passages in *De remediis* complement this voluntaristic picture. For Petrarch's Reason, to obtain 'righteousness, moderation, thrift, honesty, godliness, mercy and charity' only requires 'a willing mind' (*opus est . . . sola animi voluntate*).[39] Lethargy of mind is the result of imperfect will (*voluntas imperfecta*). Lethargy can be healed when the will begins to desire what is good so that the will changes to ardor and drive (*ardor, impetus*).[40] The reverse situation is that of power. When Joy claims that 'I can do whatever I want', Reason warns of wanting to do evil. It also adds that 'genuine and lasting power is based on virtue'. All external power is subject to the change of fortune.[41]

In sum, the will can bring about goodness and virtue, but this needs to be distinguished from external power which is dependent on circumstances. It is important for Petrarch's moral philosophy to see the foundational power of human will. Philosophical dialogue aims at lifting the veil of ignorance so that people can see the true power of the will. In addition to this cognitive therapy, Petrarch also proposes a therapy of harmful desires in which reason can moderate joy, sorrow, hope, and fear and thus bring about sound judgement. In *Secretum*, however, the limits of this therapy also become evident: Francesco achieves a clear cognitive stance, but he cannot restrain his desire for study.

Francesco's reluctance has been interpreted by some scholars as the turning point between the Middle Ages and the Renaissance since, when he affirms these desires, he turns away from the Augustinian ideals of spiritual life.[42] It is, however, also possible and perhaps more plausible to interpret this feature in terms of medieval voluntarism.

---

[38] *De remediis* 2, 104 (3, 252–3). Wisdom 8:21 is also quoted in Book 2, Ch. 23 (*De remediis* 3, 73).

[39] *De remediis* 2, 81 (3, 184).

[40] *De remediis* 2, 109 (3, 260).

[41] *De remediis* 1, 91 (1, 243–4).

[42] See Carozza (1989) and Trinkaus (1979), especially 83–5.

A sinful person cannot simply return to the previous event of wrong choice, since concupiscence and other inevitable passions now surround his voluntary life. As Henry of Ghent points out (cf. 1.4), some corruption of will and intellect necessarily remains in the person who feels the passions. There is no return to the dispassionate choice Adam had. Although Augustine urges Francesco to leave all harmful desires behind so as to completely heal the will, the participants in the dialogue must finally admit that some desires cannot be eradicated. Intellect can be enlightened so that it sees the primacy of the will, but the realm of desires, impulses, and will nevertheless remains disordered. Thus the picture of Francesco, who cannot restrain his desire for study, is not merely an embodiment of Renaissance man, but a more pessimistic picture of Augustinian voluntarism.[43]

Petrarch does not relate his discussion to EN VII explicitly; his conscious focus remains on the Augustinian problem of weakness as explained in *Confessions* 8. Petrarch alludes to EN in *De remediis* fairly often.[44] He mentions the word *incontinentia* twice. Once Reason says that green places incite the mind of pleasure-lovers to incontinence and lust.[45] Reason also warns that some odours provoke carnal passion and lead to incontinence. Reason mentions 'the books on ethics' in a passage which resembles Aristotle's discussion on tasting the sweets in EN VII:

Some odors provoke gluttony, others carnal passion. Appetite for these leads straight to incontinence. Other odors are desired for their own sake . . . like the scents of women's creams and of delicacies . . . The same is true of those pleasures which appeal to the eyes and ears. If you have ever studied the books of ethics you know this.[46]

Basically, Petrarch shares the Augustinian sense of *incontinentia* as sexual lust and misbehaviour. Given his good knowledge of Aristotle as well as Aquinas[47] and the detailed treatment of *impotentia voluntatis* in *Secretum*, it is reasonable to assume that he was also familiar with the Aristotelian problem of akrasia. It is also evident that he does not approve of the Aristotelian explanations which postulate some forgetting or ignorance as the cause of akrasia. For Petrarch, everything stands and falls with the nature of the will. Ignorance may be a side-effect and consequence of the will's disorder, but it does not provide the true explanation of akrasia.

Another recurring theme which distinguishes Petrarch from Aristotle and connects him with Stoic and Augustinian thought is that of conscience. In *Secretum*, conscience appears as an infallible judge of thoughts and deeds.[48] In *De remediis*, a clear conscience is the

---

[43] See 1.2, in particular the discussion concerning the Augustine of *Contra Iulianum* who regards concupiscence as sin. This feature also links Petrarch with the Reformers (3.2, 4.1), as Trinkaus (1979), 52–4 has argued.

[44] See the quotes in *Remedies* 5, 416–17.

[45] *De remediis* 1, 58 (1, 174).

[46] *De remediis*, 1, 22 (1, 65). In Book 1, Ch. 21 (*Remedies* 1, 64) Petrarch elaborates extensively with Aristotle's description of sleep in EN I.

[47] See the quotes in *Remedies* 5, 535–6.

[48] *Secretum*, 44 (50) (cf. above).

greatest enjoyment.[49] The testimony of conscience is the glory of the human being.[50] In his sorrows, the individual should take comfort of his good conscience.[51] True virtue is sufficiently rewarded by good conscience.[52] For Petrarch, conscience provides immediate access to a person's inner life. No practical syllogism in the Aristotelian sense needs to be assumed, since conscience can judge thoughts and deeds immediately. The fact of conscience provides a person with a deep awareness of his or her own moral state, because of which it is possible to see the inner power of the human will.

The strong doctrine of conscience thus rules out those intellectualist accounts of akrasia which are based on transitory forgetting or ignorance. Petrarch's notion of conscience is predominantly epistemic and not operative, in that conscience gives testimony but it does not direct practical deliberation. It is will as such which guides human actions; the role of conscience resembles the task of the lamp-holder in voluntarist theories (cf. 1.4). This is an important role which enables the individual to judge his situation truthfully; for instance, that one is a sinner or that one is not as powerless as one claims to be. But it is not an operative task of achieving virtue and living in accordance with it. This task is reserved to the will.

2.2 Donato Acciaiuoli's Modified Thomism

During the fifteenth century, interest in Aristotle's ethics increased rapidly in Italy. The most important achievements of this new interest were two new translations of EN produced in Florence. Leonardo Bruni's translation, written in elegant and rhetorically persuasive Latin, dates from 1416–1417.[53] The translation of John Argyropoulos, begun around 1457 and completed in 1478, is based on his profound knowledge of Greek. Many later commentaries, in particular Donato Acciaiuoli and Jacques Lefèvre d'Étaples, expand on Argyropoulos's translation. The three well-known Latin translations, Grosseteste, Bruni, and Argyropoulos, were all printed in the so-called *Tres conversiones*, a widely circulated volume of moral philosophy to which we will return in 2.4. The translation by Argyropoulos continued to be printed in the seventeenth and even the eighteenth century.[54]

In fifteenth-century Italy, the new interest in classical ethics also meant an improved knowledge of Greek and an increasingly classical Latin style. Philosophically, however, the new commentaries often followed the medieval models, in particular Thomas Aquinas. Authors who pleaded for a radical break with the Aristotelian tradition, such as Lorenzo Valla, did not write commentaries on EN. David Lines, who has surveyed the fifteenth-century reception of EN in Italy, notes Niccolo Tignosi's (1402–1474)

---

[49] *De remediis* 1, 101 (1, 273–4)

[50] *De remediis* 1, 11 (1, 31), quoting 2 Cor. 1:12.

[51] *De remediis* 2, 25 (3, 75–8).

[52] *De remediis* 2, 28 (3, 83).

[53] On Bruni and his translation of EN, see Copenhaver and Schmitt (2002), 76–84.

[54] Lines (2002), 50–1.

unprinted commentary, which uses Bruni's translation and borrows material from many medieval traditions, reconciling their differences. Tignosi applies rhetorical techniques to his exposition and pursues the ideal of clarity.[55]

The influential commentary by Donato Acciaiuoli (1429–1478), *Expositio super libros Ethicorum*, displays many similarities to Tignosi's work. This commentary, based on Argyropoulos's translation, was composed between 1457 and 1478. It was first printed in Florence in 1478 and received twenty-one more printings up to the end of the sixteenth century.[56] Acciaiuoli often follows Aquinas; Lines even remarks that this 'commentary seems to have been written with Thomas's *Sententia* constantly to hand'.[57] He also uses Albert the Great and Walter Burley.[58] Acciaiuoli's Latin is more eloquent than that of scholastic authors, but it nevertheless remains closer to medieval expositions than to Petrarch's classical style.

Referring to EN 1145b8–20, Acciaiuoli lists six widely held doctrines or opinions (*probabilia*) that are critically discussed when continence and incontinence, as well as endurance and softness, are being treated:

(1) Continence and endurance are praiseworthy, whereas incontinence and softness are blameworthy.

(2) A continent person is synonymous with the constant person who obeys reason, whereas an incontinent person is synonymous with the inconstant person who does not obey reason.

(3) The incontinent person does wrong knowingly because of passion, whereas the continent person does not go wrong.

(4) Some people identify continence with temperance and constancy, whereas others make a distinction between these notions.

(5) Some people hold that prudent agents cannot be incontinent, whereas others think that this can be the case.

(6) Incontinent agents can be incontinent with regard to passion (concupiscence), anger, honour, and greed.[59]

---

[55] Lines (2002), 192–217.

[56] Lines (2002), 489.

[57] Lines (2005), 19.

[58] Bianchi (1990), 43–51.

[59] Acciaiuoli, *Expositio*, 325: 'primo quod continentia et constantia videntur esse laudabilia et studiosa cum sequantur rationem; incontinentia econtra et mollitudo esse improba quaedam et vituperanda... Secunda fuit opinio eorum qui putant quod idem est continens et constans, et persistens in ratione, et incontinens et rationem egrediens. Et haec opinio non videtur vera ut apparebit... Tertia fuit opinio eorum qui dicebant quod incontinens est is qui sciens improba agit ob cupiditatem, continens vero contrario modo, ut patet... Quarta fuit opinio, quod continentia, constantia et temperantia essent idem, quanquam eorum nonnulli dicerent haec non esse omnino idem, quidam vero penitus idem, interdum etiam asserunt. Quinta fuit opinio de prudentia et incontinentia, quia aliqui putabant prudentem non posse incontinentem esse, quidam vero econtra fieri posse censebant, ut prudentes et habiles incontinentes essent... Sexta fuit quod continentia non solum sit circa voluptates, sed etiam circa iram, honorem, et lucrum.'

Aristotle discusses the doubts concerning these six opinions in EN 1145b21–1146b7. In his exposition of this passage, Acciaiuoli notes how the doubts are removed. The third opinion is examined first (EN 1145b21–1146a4). The basic doubt is the classical problem of akrasia: 'In what way can the person whose reason is not corrupted act against his reason?'[60] Then follows the treatment of fifth, fourth, second, first, and sixth opinions,[61] the list of six opinions and the sequence of doubts concerning them being taken from Aquinas's *Sententia*.[62] Acciaiuoli adapts the discussion of Aquinas to the new translation of Argyropoulos, but the philosophical content is to a great extent taken from Thomas. At the same time, however, Acciaiuoli extends the discussion of Aquinas. It is evident that he aims for clarity, but it is more difficult to judge how he defends positions which are not found in Aquinas.

A good example is the passage in which Aristotle says that the view of Socrates contradicts the plain phenomena and that the incontinent person evidently does not intend to do wrong before he gets into a state of passion (EN 1145b27–31). This belongs to the treatment of the third opinion, where Aquinas paraphrases Aristotle.[63] Acciaiuoli extends the final consideration of Aristotle and Aquinas, who simply say that the incontinent person was already aware of the wrongness of the action, as follows:

For before the emergence of passion he knows, and then during the passion he seems to be ignorant . . . and he resembles the drunken person who knows but does not act according to his knowledge. But he acts like children who recite songs which they do not understand, so that they cause disgrace which they hardly recognize. A third time is when, having done the wrong, the person returns to awareness and knows. And below the Philosopher approves to an extent the doctrine of Socrates which he has above refuted.[64]

The example of children reciting obscene songs relates to EN 1147a21–23; Aquinas interprets these lines as referring to children who put words together without understanding them.[65] Acciaiuoli gives examples and connects the discussions with one another.

This extension hardly contains anything original or philosophically innovative. Acciaiuoli clarifies Aristotle's discussion and creates a bridge to EN 1147a21–23 as

---

[60] *Expositio*, 326: 'Quomodo hoc fieri possit ut habeat rationem incorruptam, agat tamen contra rationem?' Cf. Aquinas, *Ethica*, 384, 32–385, 35: 'Quomodo aliquis qui habet rectam existimationem est incontinens operando contraria.' Argyropoulos, EN 1145b21–22: 'Dubitaverit autem quispiam, qui fit ut recte quispiam existimans agat incontinenter.'

[61] *Expositio*, 326–9.

[62] *Expositio*, 325; Aquinas, *Ethica*, 382, 195–234. Thomas does not yet give explicit numbering, but on l. 232 he says that there are six *probabilia*. *Expositio*, 326–9; *Ethica*, 384–7. The numbering occurs in Walter Burley (1521), *Super Ethicorum*, 117ra–rb.

[63] *Ethica*, 385, 53–63.

[64] *Expositio*, 327: 'Nam antequam fit in perturbatione, est sciens, et postea quando est in perturbatione videtur quasi ignorans . . . et est similis ebrio qui habet scientiam, et non agit secundum illam scientiam, sed agit quasi sint pueri, qui dicunt carmina quae non intelligunt, et sic illi proferunt labiis esse turpe quod tunc vix mente cognoscunt. Tertium tempus est quando peracta re turpi rursus redit ad scientiam et cognoscit. Et inferius acceptabit Philosophus aliqua ex parte sententiam Socratis, quam supra visus est refellere omnino.'

[65] *Ethica*, 392, 206–14.

well as to EN 1147b12, in which the example of the drunken man is given. He also informs the reader that although Aristotle refutes the view of Socrates, the subsequent discussion brings him again closer to the Socratic view. Acciaiuoli in fact says in many places that Aristotle mediates between Socrates and the 'plain phenomena'.[66] The merits of such discussions largely consist in making the exposition of Thomas Aquinas available to a larger Renaissance public in a lucid and didactic fashion.

In spite of this heavy dependence on Aquinas, there is one innovative feature in Acciaiuoli's commentary which deserves attention. The medieval expositors are very restrictive in their use of examples, very often only using the examples given in the text which is being exposed. Acciaiuoli introduces some new examples and illustrations of akrasia. The technique of using *exempla* is a common rhetorical device in Renaissance literature, and Acciaiuoli is following the practice of his times.[67] Akrasia is, however, a topic which is very sensitive to examples and illustrations: the understanding of the details of human action is dependent on the phenomena to which it is compared.

The above-mentioned list of six topics continues to be discussed after the preliminary explication of doubts concerning them. Throughout the present chapter, our discussion focuses on what Acciaiuoli calls the 'third common opinion' and the 'first doubt' with regard to it. According to Aquinas and Acciaiuoli,[68] Aristotle elaborates this topic in more detail in EN 1146b8–1147b18. This theme, 'whether the akratic person acts akratically knowingly',[69] is the classical problem of akrasia, which is of major importance in all commentaries. The other five topics are often, although not always, discussed in the commentaries. Our study pays attention to them occasionally, but the limitations of space do not allow treating all six in full detail.

The 'big difficulty' concerns the issue of 'whether the incontinent person acts knowingly or not knowingly, and if knowingly, in what way'.[70] Acciaiuoli follows the basic solution of Aristotle, and Aquinas in particular. There are three distinctions with regard to knowing something. First, one can know something actually or habitually. Acciaiuoli here employs Thomas's example of the geometrian and introduces the example of a guitar player. When the geometrian and the guitar player are asleep, they possess their knowledge in a habitual but not in an actual sense. The akratic person may also possess knowledge in this habitual sense since he considers something as good but does not put this knowledge into actual use. It is not possible for the incontinent person to have both habitual and actual knowledge.[71]

---

[66] See, e.g., *Expositio*, 333, 338.

[67] See Lines (2002), 7.

[68] Cf. Aquinas, *Ethica*, 390, 34–8; Acciaiuoli, *Expositio*, 331.

[69] Acciaiuoli here (*Expositio*, 331) has the formulation: 'solvere intendit primam dubitationem... utrum incontinens agat sciens incontinenter.'

[70] *Expositio*, 331: 'considerandum esse utrum sciens vel non sciens incontinens agat, et si sciens, quonam pacto, haec enim est magna difficultas.'

[71] *Expositio*, 333.

Acciaiuoli also extends Thomas's discussion through another illustration, namely, the scholastic distinction between the first and the second act. This illustration is taken from Walter Burley's commentary. The first act equips a person with a potency and a habit of acting, whereas the second act is the actual performance. In the case of akrasia, the incontinent person possesses the first act or potency but he fails to activate this knowledge in his behaviour. It only becomes actual afterwards. Thus the akratic person is guilty of having not properly attended (*non respicit*) to his habitual knowledge.[72] Acciaiuoli further claims that Aristotle wants to show a middle way between Socrates and the common opinion: according to Aristotle, the akratic person to an extent knows and to an extent remains ignorant.[73] As these observations are not developed further, they serve the purpose of pedagogical clarity rather than philosophical sophistication.

Aristotle's second distinction is that between the universal and particular proposition of the practical syllogism. It is possible to know the universal and ignore the particular so that the corresponding action does not follow. In outlining this possibility, Acciaiuoli again follows Aquinas, but adds his own examples. Interestingly, the syllogistic examples now deal with theoretical knowledge, for instance: 'every magnet attracts iron, this is a magnet', 'all rhubarb cures cholera', 'the angles of every triangle equal 180 degrees'. These examples do not appear in Aristotle, Aquinas, or Burley; Acciaiuoli attempts to show that the failure of the akratês is comparable to other logical errors. For instance, a person may know that rhubarb cures cholera while not knowing that this particular plant is rhubarb.[74]

Aristotle's third distinction between having knowledge and using it pertains to cases in which a state of passion or perturbation prevents the use of knowledge. With regard to this discussion, Acciaiuoli again follows Aquinas, mentioning the boys who recite obscene songs without understanding them.[75]

Given that Acciaiuoli follows Aquinas so closely, one does not expect innovations in EN 1147a24–b18, the crucial passage in which the cause of akrasia is explained. But now Acciaiuoli suddenly deviates from Aquinas, stating that the practical syllogism consists of opinions in the following manner in his exposition of EN 1147a24–28:

It is the case that one of them is a universal opinion, the other a singular opinion, pertaining to the singular actions to be taken, which concern the senses. These two opinions result in *a single opinion and a single sentence* which the Philosopher understands to be *the conclusion, not the minor proposition*, as some expositors claim.[76]

---

[72] *Expositio*, 333, cf. especially: 'culpa sua est quod non respicit eam cum agit, sed post habet et dimittit ut praesentem sequatur voluptatem.' Burley, *Super Ethicorum*, 120rb.

[73] *Expositio*, 333: 'Nam antea vidimus quod nonnulli priscorum dicebant incontinentem scientem esse. Socrates vero dicebat fieri non posse, ut sciens sit incontinens. Philosophus vero medium tenens, partim scientem, partim non scientem esse voluit, afferendo distinctionem de modo sciendi.'

[74] *Expositio*, 333–4.

[75] *Expositio*, 334–5.

[76] *Expositio*, 335: 'Nam sit hoc modo quod quaedam est opinio universalis, quaedam singularis, quae est circa res agendas singulares, quarum est sensus. Ex iis duabus opinionibus fit quandoque *una opinio, et una*

Aquinas as well as the translation of Argyropoulos state here (EN 1147a27) that 'a single reason' (*una ratio*) follows from these two opinions. Why does Acciaiuoli underline that this is an 'opinion' and a 'sentence' which expresses the conclusion of the practical syllogism? And who are the expositors against whom he argues?

An obvious medieval parallel to this statement is Walter Burley's exposition of EN 1147a24–b18. After following Aquinas's exposition throughout this passage, Burley adds a note claiming that the proposition with regard to which the akratês is deceived is not the minor premise but the conclusion of the practical syllogism.[77]

Aquinas reads the passage so that the opinion concerning the singulars (EN 1147a25–26) is identical with the 'last proposition and opinion about perceptibles' mentioned in EN 1147b9–10. This opinion is the minor premise of the practical syllogism, which remains ignored to an extent in the akratic action (model 1a in 1.1 and 1.3). For Acciaiuoli there is a third 'opinion' involved in addition to the major and minor premise, namely, the end result or conclusion of the practical syllogism. This conclusion is not only an opinion but also concrete execution of the corresponding action:

When a universal and a particular opinion are put forward, they generate a *third opinion* which is the *conclusion and execution of it* as follows: everything sweet is to be tasted; this is sweet; and immediately comes the execution and pursuing of this which is the active conclusion.[78]

In the statement quoted above, Acciaiuoli deviates from Aquinas and follows the suggestion made by Walter Burley, but he also deviates from him, because Burley explicitly denies that the executive act is identical with the conclusion.[79] Burley wants to make a consistent distinction between the propositional conclusion and the dynamic process of action, claiming that the conclusion of the practical syllogism is a *sententia* which is followed by choice and action.[80] Acciaiuoli, however, sets out to show that the conclusion of the practical syllogism has a dual nature as *both* an opinion *and* an executive act.

Acciaiuoli's many comparisons between theoretical and practical syllogisms serve the purpose of showing how the conclusion emerges from the premises as a 'third' opinion. In this context, he discusses the syllogism 'Every animal is substance; Socrates is animal; ergo Socrates is substance', stating that when the two premises are given, the mind

---

sententia, quam intelligit Philosophus esse *conclusionem, et non minorem propositionem*, sicut aliqui dicunt expositores.' (Italics added.)

[77] Burley, *Super Ethicorum*, 121va. See Saarinen (1994), 137–40 and (1999); Wood (1999).

[78] *Expositio*, 335: 'ubi ponitur universalis opinio et particularis, ex quibus fit una *tertia*, id est *conclusio et executio* ipsa hoc modo: omne dulce est gustandum, hoc est dulce, et statim sit executio et prosecutio illius quae est conclusio active.' (Italics added.)

[79] Burley, *Super Ethicorum*, 121 ra: 'ita in practicis et factivis ex opinione universali in actu et opinione singulari in actu necessario sequitur opus, non sicut conclusio ex premissis, sed tamen sequitur sicut posterius sequitur ad prius.'

[80] Burley, *Super Ethicorum*, 51 ra: 'Electio est quasi conclusio que sequitur ad sententiam factam de operabili que proprie est conclusio sillogismi practici.' For the interpretation of this idea, see Gomes (1973), 330–40 and Saarinen (1999), 67–9. Acciaiuoli does not follow Burley at this point in EN III. 3.

necessarily assents (*necessario assentitur mens*) to the conclusion.[81] This example is employed by Burley but not by Aquinas. Burley does not use the Stoic verb *assentire*, merely saying that the conclusion of the theoretical syllogism 'necessarily follows' from the premises just as the action 'necessarily follows' from the premises of the practical syllogism.[82] For Acciaiuoli, even the conclusion of the theoretical syllogism displays a kind of dual nature, being not merely a conclusion which logically follows, but an *assented* conclusion.

At the same time, it is instructive to keep in mind Acciaiuoli's above-mentioned examples of logical errors: one can fail in the evaluation of singulars (e.g. 'this is rhubarb') so that the conclusion does not emerge. Burley compares akratic reasoning to other syllogistic errors.[83] These commentators are similar in their tendency to make syllogistic comparisons. Acciaiuoli has taken some of these comparisons from Burley, but he has added some Stoic or Augustinian ingredients to his own understanding of them.

Acciaiuoli underlines Aristotle's doctrine that the agent who reaches the conclusion must immediately act (EN 1147a28). While the mind in theoretical matters assents to the conclusion, it is the peculiar nature of the practical syllogism that it prompts action. 'In theoretical matters it is enough to know the conclusion, but in practical matters the conclusion is not only drawn but also acted upon, because its execution takes place immediately after deliberation.'[84] The conclusion of the practical syllogism is thus both an opinion and an executive act.

To understand Acciaiuoli's argument properly, it is important to see the dual nature of the conclusion of the practical syllogism. If the conclusion was only the action, then all propositional opinions regarding particulars would take the role of minor pre-mises—and this Acciaiuoli denies. If, on the other hand, the conclusion was merely propositional, then the effective cause of akrasia would be detached from the Aristote-lian model of the practical syllogism. Acciaiuoli avoids both of these alternatives, affirming a position in which

in the consideration and deliberation [of an action], a conclusion follows from the universal and the singular. [The akratic person] deserts this conclusion not only in the realm of thinking, as happens in theoretical inference. But he also deserts it in the actual execution of the passionate act which overcomes reason.[85]

---

[81] *Expositio*, 335.

[82] Burley, *Super Ethicorum*, 121 ra.

[83] Cf. Saarinen (1994), 139–44. Bianchi (1990), 43–51 discusses Acciaiuoli's use of medieval commenta-tors. Gomes (1973), 512–14 points out that Burley denies the real distinction between speculative and practical intellect in a Scotistic manner and restores the function of the speculative intellect in ethical theory. It may therefore be the case that both Burley and Acciaiuoli affirm the unity of intellect more strongly than Aquinas. See Saarinen (1999), 61.

[84] *Expositio*, 335: 'Nam in speculativis satis est nosse conclusionem, sed in in activis non tantum est conclusio quae infertur, sed etiam quae agitur, cum statim post discursionem illam fiat executio.'

[85] *Expositio*, 336: 'Verum discursionis et ratiocinationis eius ex universali et singulari sequitur conclusio, quae non desinit in cognitione tantum, ut in speculativis: sed in opere et executione rei secundum appetitum, a quo ratio superatur.'

In Acciaiuoli's view, the practical syllogism produces conclusive opinions immediately when major and minor premises are connected. In such a model, it cannot simply be said that akrasia is due to an imperfect grasp of the minor premise. Because both the propositional and the dynamic aspect of the conclusion emerge when proper deliberation occurs, the agent reaches the conclusion to the same extent as he grasps the minor premise.[86] Given this, the akratic person also reaches the conclusion (cf. our 'model 2' in 1.1), in addition to the minor premise. The conclusion is to an extent reached and abandoned in the akratic action.

In spite of this deviation from both Aquinas and Burley, the syllogistic analysis of the akratic situation can be presented in a fairly Thomist fashion. Like Aquinas, Acciaiuoli considers that the incontinent person accepts two conflicting universal propositions, both of which can match with the singular facts. The akratês focuses on the wrong universal and subsumes the particular facts under it so that the akratic action emerges. The right universal premise is not forgotten, but the akratês does not attend (*non respicit*) the relevant particulars with regard to this universal.[87] Acciaiuoli states that the two syllogisms struggle with one another in the mind so that passion overcomes reason.[88]

The picture of struggle (*pugna*) indicates that the elements of the correct syllogism are not merely ignored but continue to exercise some influence. Aquinas teaches that concupiscence causes some repugnancy (*repugnantia*) which, through the inadequate consideration of particulars, obscures right reason.[89] Acciaiuoli's notion of struggle has a slightly more Platonic feel. He says in this context, perhaps following Albert the Great, that the akratic person continues to have some knowledge of the right, but this knowledge is not proper *scientia*, but a more inchoate *cognitio quadam*.[90] In the akratic struggle, this cognition of the right continues to exercise influence. Such a conflict resembles our 'commonplace Platonic' models of inner strife (1.1).

Compared to the innovative features in EN 1147a24–b3, Acciaiuoli's exposition of EN 1147b9–18 does not offer much that is new. Following the translation by

---

[86] See the previous footnotes and *Expositio*, 335: 'Primo enim habemus aliquam cognitionem sub qua ponimus aliquam particulam, et postea infertur conclusio ex illis, id est operatio et executio, si non prohibetur.'

[87] *Expositio*, 336: 'Incontinens vero cum habeat et percipiat illas duas universales propositiones, quod nullum dulce est gustandum, et quod omne dulce affert voluptatem; exemplo cum advenit hoc dulce cupiditate urgente, quae est contraria negativae propositioni, quia illa vetat gustare, cupiditas suadet, incontinens ponit singularem illam sub affirmativa, et concludit affirmative, operando ut potiendo illo dulci. Et oblitus pene dum est in illa perturbatione primae propositionis bonae negativae vetantis eum gustare, cuius scientiam habet in habitu, sed in operando eam non respicit, quare dicitur quod aliquo modo sciens, aliquo modo non sciens operatur.'

[88] *Expositio*, 336: 'Et notandum quod fit pugna inter ista, quia scientia et cognitio illa universalis coniuncta cum ratione adversatur opinioni particulari non de se, sed opinioni coniunctae cupiditati, et fit pugna, et in ipso incontinente superatur ratio.'

[89] Thomas, *Ethica*, 392, 247–50; 393, 285, 298.

[90] *Expositio*, 336: 'Et cum dicimus incontinentem habere scientiam in habitu eo pacto et non actu, non sumimus scientiam proprie dictam, sed largo modo pro cognitione quadam, quam ille habet universalis illius propositionis et huiusmodi.' On Albert's notion of *cognitio*, cf. Saarinen (1994), 106–8.

Argyropoulos, he says several times that the last proposition is 'an opinion concerning perceivable things' and that this opinion is 'the master of actions to be taken'. The akratic person possesses this opinion imperfectly, since perturbations confuse his mind.[91] The universal proposition remains inactive in the akratic person, who loses full grasp of the particular facts in the state of passion.[92]

In sum, Acciaiuoli deviates from Aquinas in his elaboration of the nature of the syllogistic conclusion. Acciaiuoli presents his own innovative remarks proceeding from EN 1147a24–28. He leans on Walter Burley's commentary, but his view finally also deviates from Burley. Acciaiuoli's original contribution does not concern the exegesis of any individual passage, but can be summarized as three closely related but distinct claims:

(1) The conclusion of the practical syllogism is both an opinion and an executive act.

(2) The akratic person reaches this conclusion in some imperfect way and deserts it.

(3) The perception of singular facts under some universal premise evokes both the minor premise and the corresponding conclusion, so that opinions concerning particular facts are the 'masters of our actions'.

Given (3), it is not crucial for Acciaiuoli to discuss whether the akratic person ignores something in the minor premise or the conclusion. Since the opinions concerning particulars are decisive for our actions, the akratês ignores something both in the minor premise and the conclusion. This result, however, is not a recourse to the Thomist model 1a, since Acciaiuoli pays a great deal of attention to the emergence of the 'third opinion', that is, the syllogistic conclusion. He is closer to Walter Burley's model 2, according to which the akratic person is deceived with regard to the conclusion of the practical syllogism.

Finally, Acciaiuoli approaches Burley's model with some Stoic elements. He thinks that our perception of particulars involves a judgement-like opinion which incites an impulse to act. In the syllogistic reasoning, this means that, because the minor premise and the conclusion go together, both need to be neglected or abandoned in order that the wrong syllogism can become operative. When Acciaiuoli links the sensual perception (minor premise) with the impulse to act (conclusion) in this way, he approaches the Stoic action theory in which the impression cannot be detached from the impulse (1.2).

Acciaiuoli's view of akrasia thus contains no less than three layers: first, he attempts to present a Renaissance version of Aquinas's *Sententia libri Ethicorum*. Second, he modifies Aquinas with some features taken from Burley's commentary. Third, he

---

[91]   *Expositio*, 337–8.

[92]   *Expositio*, 337: 'duas diximus incontinentem habere propositiones, universalem et singularem et haec ultima est rei sensibilis opinatio, quae dicitur domina rerum agendarum, quia actio est rerum singularium. Nam si afferatur sola universalis, nunquam fiet actio: incontinens igitur, cum agit adveniente cupiditate, habet quidem sopitam illam universalem, singularem vero quae est domina rerum agendarum aut non habet, quia non utitur ea, aut si habet non animadvertit secundum eam, nec percipit se habere.'

develops both towards a view in which the perception of singulars implies assented opinion and operative impulse, thus bringing Stoic-Augustinian ingredients to the Aristotelian syllogistic action theory.

2.3 French and German Thomism: John Versor and Virgilius Wellendorffer

If Acciaiuoli's work was the most widely read Italian commentary of the *Quattrocento*, the *Quaestiones super libros ethicorum Aristotelis* of John Versor (died 1485) had a comparable importance in France and Germany.[93] Versor taught at the university of Paris. Since his commentaries were often printed later in Cologne, Versor's thinking exercised a long-term influence from France to Germany and even Denmark.[94] Versor was a Dominican and usually considered to have been a Thomist, but it has also been argued that he became an independent authority who mediated between the followers of Albert the Great and Thomas Aquinas.[95] Versor's ethical writings have not been extensively studied. Gauthier raises some doubts with regard to the authenticity of Books VII–X of the commentary on EN, but they appear in all printed editions and were certainly read by later generations as Versor's teaching.[96]

Versor's *Quaestiones* follow the medieval pattern of presenting extensive questions on the material of EN. The questions are sometimes accompanied by a brief introduction, titled *sciendum*, 'it should be known that'. Thomas Aquinas did not expound EN using questions. Albert the Great, Walter Burley, and Donato Acciaiuoli likewise prefer a continuous exposition of the text, although their commentaries sometimes approach the format of questions. In some sense, Versor's *Quaestiones* and John Buridan's *Quaestiones super decem libros Ethicorum* remain the two most popular and widespread commentaries on EN which consistently and systematically treat akrasia through questions.[97]

In the opening question of the whole commentary, 'whether there can be a practical science regarding human conduct or moral virtues which is distinct from other sciences', Versor discusses the differences between Thomas Aquinas and Albert the Great. According to Thomas, moral philosophy treats teleological human action. For Albert, moral science deals with the goodness of the individual. Versor mediates between these positions. For Albert, the goodness of the human being consists in

---

[93] We will use the 1494 Cologne edition, as reprinted (1967). The first printed edition is Cologne 1491. On Versor's life and career, see Gauthier (1970), 140–1; for his commentaries, see Lohr (1971), 290.

[94] Ebbesen (2003) reports that Versor was still influential in Copenhagen in the seventeenth century.

[95] Rutten (2005). Rutten does not deal with ethics.

[96] Gauthier (1970), 141.

[97] Gauthier (1970), 120–40, presents an overview of commentaries on EN from Albert to Versor; cf. also Saarinen (1994); Lines (2002); Hoffmann, Müller, and Perkams (2006). I assume that unprinted commentaries, e.g. those of Albert of Saxony and Henry of Friemar, were not influential; Gerald Odonis does not present questions on akrasia.

active and contemplative happiness. Versor remarks that the first book of EN discusses active happiness, whereas the tenth book discusses contemplative happiness. There is no real difference between Albert and Thomas, because Thomas focuses on the goodness of the individual in active life, while Albert extends his discussion from the active life towards the contemplative. For Versor, ethics is a science which covers 'human actions or the good of the human being' (operationes hominis seu bonum hominis).[98]

Is this reconciliatory tone apparent in all parts of Versor's commentary? Although Albert and Thomas share many philosophical convictions, their writings on akrasia differ, as we noted in 1.3 and 1.5. While Thomas consistently explains akrasia within the Aristotelian model of the practical syllogism, Albert employs notions from the Stoic and Augustinian traditions, often interpreting the akratic situation in terms of conflict and acceptance.

The treatment of continence and incontinence occupies no less than fourteen questions (Book VII, q3–16), some of which are fairly sophisticated. Versor repeats the six common opinions (probabilia) and six open questions (dubitationes) mentioned by Thomas Aquinas.[99] He also pays attention to the difference between the Augustinian and Aristotelian sense of incontinence:

Second, it should be known that the term 'continence' can be understood in two different ways. Some people call 'continent' a person who abstains from all sexual pleasures... Others say that continence means resisting all vicious concupiscence which is active in the person. In this book, the philosopher understands continence in this manner. A person who has this habit remains reasonable, fights the concupiscence and acts contrary to it.[100]

This distinction is a medieval commonplace which can be found in Albert the Great and John Buridan.[101] In Versor's exposition, the distinction is embedded in question 3 of Book VII, 'whether continence is a virtue'. For Versor, Aristotelian continence is not a perfect virtue, but it 'has something of virtue and lacks something of virtue'.[102]

As in the case of Acciaiouli, we will concentrate on the classical problem of akrasia; namely, whether one can act against one's own better judgement. Versor formulates this issue as his question 4: 'Whether somebody can act incontinently against his own knowledge, maintaining the right reason.'[103] Arguments against this view proceed

---

[98] Versor, Quaestiones, 1rb.

[99] Quaestiones, 57ra–rb; 58vb. Cf. Thomas, Ethica, 382, 195–234 and 2.2 above.

[100] Quaestiones, 57rb: 'Sciendum secundo quod hoc nomen continentia accipitur dupliciter a diversis. Nam quidam continentiam appellant per quam aliquis ab omni delectatione venerea abstinet... Alii vero dicunt continentiam esse propter quam aliquis resistit concupiscentiis pravis que in eo vehementes existunt. Et sic capit philosophus continentiam in hoc libro, ut videlicet est habitus quo habens ipsum se tenet cum ratione et pugnat contra concupiscentias operando contra eas.'

[101] Albert, De bono, 130–5; De natura boni, 32–3; Buridan, Quaestiones, 141vb–142ra (580–1). Cf. Saarinen (1994), 95, 172.

[102] Quaestiones, 57rb: 'habet aliquid de virtute et deficit in aliquo a virtute'.

[103] Quaestiones, 58vb: 'Utrum aliquis possit operari incontinenter contra suam scientiam, ratione in eo recta permanente.'

from the Socratic position that the lower parts of the soul cannot overcome the higher part. Aristotle, however, wants to affirm this view.[104]

Before coming to his conclusions, Versor states some preliminaries (*preambula*) which concern practical knowledge. Like many others, he compares theoretical and practical syllogism, maintaining that the minor premise concerns particular facts and the conclusion is the action. Given this, the question can be understood in three different ways. First, whether one can act against the universal premise. Second, whether one can act against habitual but not actual knowledge. Third, whether one can act against the actual and habitual knowledge which is 'bound', as in the case of a drunken person. These three ways correspond to Aristotle's discussion in EN 1146b30–1147a23.

The first conclusion of Versor is similar to Aquinas's and Buridan's:

When the person has permanent and clear right reason which actually pertains to both major and minor premise, it is not possible to act incontinently. But when the permanent right reason actually pertains to the major premise, it is possible to act incontinently.[105]

The proof of the first claim shows that Versor considers the conclusion of the practical syllogism to be the action:

The first is true because otherwise the incontinent person would act in contrary ways. For the major and the minor in a practical syllogism yield an action as conclusion. If the minor is put under the major the conclusion is immediately known ... An example of a practical syllogism which works in this manner is this: no adultery should be done; some adultery is pleasant; therefore, not every pleasure should be pursued.[106]

Versor's point is clear: when the major and the minor of the right reason are sufficiently known, they can effectively prevent the emergence of incontinent actions. But if the minor is not actually known, it is possible to act akratically.

The second conclusion makes the point that it is possible to act akratically when the knowledge of particulars is 'bound' or 'not actually considered'.[107] Thus the outcome of the question is affirmative:

reason is not completely extinguished in the incontinent person. Although he has the true knowledge in the universal—for instance, if he possesses this universal proposition of the reason: nothing sweet is to be tasted, and concupiscence also says: everything sweet is pleasant—the appetitive passion then captures the judgement of the reason regarding the minor premise and

---

[104] *Quaestiones*, 58vb.

[105] *Quaestiones*, 59ra: 'Recta ratione permanente et integra quo ad maiorem et minorem secundum actum non potest quis incontinenter agere, sed ratione recta permanente secundum actum quo ad maiorem tamen potest quis incontinenter operari.'

[106] *Quaestiones*, 59ra: 'Prima pars patet, quia sic contraria operaretur. Maior enim et minor in syllogismo practico conclusionem habent in opere. Si igitur minor debite sumatur sub maiori necessaria conclusio cognoscitur ... Exemplum de syllogismi practici qui potest sic dari: nulla fornicatio est facienda, sed aliqua fornicatio est delectabilis, ergo non omne delectabile est faciendum.'

[107] *Quaestiones*, 59ra.

subsumes it under the universal provided by the appetite, not under the universal of the reason, and so the incontinent action emerges.[108]

This solution is identical with the view of Thomas Aquinas. Although Thomas's terminology to an extent varies between *Sententia libri Ethicorum* and the theological writings, he nevertheless consistently holds that the incontinent person first moves from the consideration of the proper syllogism to the consideration of pleasure, and, second, he constructs a false syllogism which leads to incontinent action.[109] Versor adheres to this explanation which corresponds to our model 1a.

This discussion does not take a clear stance with regard to the personal responsibility of the incontinent person. But Versor adds a *dubium* to the question which makes this an issue: 'Is it possible to prevent one's own actual consideration in a habitual manner?'[110] Versor affirms this possibility, teaching that it can occur in different ways. First, the person may not want (*non velit*) to consider the case. This occurs when desire inclines the person in another direction, so that passion drags the will with it. Second, the passions may cause bodily changes as is the case with drunk and mad people.[111]

In keeping with these two ways, the sensitive appetite can extinguish the judgement of reason in the state of passion. First, the appetite, insofar as it is natural, need not obey reason, but desires the objects in its own way. This is the case, for instance, with the so-called 'first movements', for which the person is not morally responsible. The appetite obeys reason only insofar as it belongs to the rational soul. When passion is vehement, the will of the incontinent does not want to listen to reason, but turns away from it and consents to passion. Second, the sensual impressions can become modified in incontinent people just as happens with drunken people.[112]

Versor in this way ascribes personal responsibility to the akratic person, who willingly follows passion and consents to its temptations. This voluntary aspect becomes apparent in the first counter-argument to the question, which is that one cannot act against knowledge because the sensitive appetite cannot overcome reason. Versor responds to this by stating that the will of the incontinent person can follow the sensitive appetite

---

[108] *Quaestiones*, 59ra–rb: 'in incontinente non totaliter extinguitur ratio. Quamvis scilicet in universali habeat scientiam veram, ut puta si ex parte rationis hec propositio universalis: nullum dulce est gustandum, et ultra concupiscentia dicat: omne dulce est delectabile, tunc passio appetitus absorbet iudicium rationis quo ad minorem, et subsumit sub universali appetitus et non sub universali rationis, et sic sequitur operatio incontinentis.'

[109] Saarinen (1994), 126–8.

[110] *Quaestiones*, 59rb: 'Utrum possit impedire actualem considerationem eiusdem secundum habitum?'

[111] *Quaestiones*, 59rb.

[112] *Quaestiones*, 59rb: 'Similiter multis modis contingit quod appetitus sensitivus passionatus extinguit iudicium rationis. Uno modo quando appetitus vehementer fertur in suum appetibile tanquam in finem. Unde appetitus inquantum corruptibilis est, naturalis est, et sic non est obediens rationi. Sed inquantum ab anima est, obedit rationi, igitur primi motus non sunt criminosi. Allicitur igitur voluntas appetitu sensitivo tanquam vehementer moto ex pulsu rationis, et sic ei consentit et avertit se a iudicio rationis, nec vult audire rationem. Secundo modo contingit hoc ex parte fantasie quemadmodum enim organum sensitivum ebrii impeditur per motus fumorum. Sic in incontinente impeditur per motum passionum.'

because the wrong syllogistic reasoning, based on false estimation of the particulars, enables the will to do this.[113]

Versor does not intend to be a voluntarist in the sense of Henry of Ghent (1.4). He grants the possibility that some akrasia is due to bodily changes and may occur almost involuntarily. And when he concedes that the consent of the will contributes to the emergence of akrasia, he nevertheless underlines the natural causes of vehement passions. This emphasis may be related to Albert the Great, who employs the picture of conflict between cognitive faculty and sensuality which causes an inner struggle. Albert's use of the notion of acceptance (acceptio) in this context resembles the Augustinian doctrine of consent.[114] Perhaps Versor, through introducing the voluntary consent and the struggle with the natural causes of passions in this dubium, extends the Thomist discussion of akrasia in the Albertian direction. But these additional features are also found in Aquinas and may be interpreted as a typically Thomist reconciliation between Aristotle and Augustine.[115]

One problem with regard to which the voluntary nature of akrasia is particularly relevant is question 16 of Book VII, 'whether the incontinent person can be prudent'. Some preliminaries to this issue are already set out in question 12, in which Versor explains how the intemperate person is worse than the incontinent. Like Aquinas, Versor considers that the intemperate person acts 'with choice' (cum electione) and 'from choice' (ex electione), whereas the akratic person acts 'contrary to choice' (praeter electionem).[116]

The intemperate person is worse than the akratic, because his choice is vicious and he enjoys his sins without repenting, whereas passion draws the akratês to akrasia. Versor points out, however, that sinful actions are done voluntarily. Both the akratês and the intemperate person sin voluntarily, but the intemperate person sins more gravely, since his will is not only inclined to sin because of transitory temptation, but because it is habitually inclined towards misguided goals.[117]

Although the akratic person does not act from choice, his will is inclined to sin because of passion.[118] Because of the voluntary nature of the akratic action, incontinence is not merely ignorance but also a character trait in need of cure:

---

[113] Quaestiones, 58vb, 59rb.

[114] Müller (2006), 1312. Albert, Ethica II, 474–6. Cf. 1.5 above.

[115] Aristotle says in EN 1152a15–17 that the akrates acts voluntarily and contrary to his own good choice; Grosseteste's translation: 'Et volens quidem. Secundum modum enim quendam sciens et quod facit et cuius gracia. Malus autem non. Eleccio enim epieikes.' (Aristoteles Latinus 26, 3, 290). This passage gives the commentarors the possibility to hold that the akrates sins willingly. In Thomas, the voluntary aspect of akrasia is more emphasized in his theological works than in Ethica; cf. 1.3 above and Bradley (2008).

[116] Quaestiones, 65vb–66ra.

[117] Quaestiones, 65vb.

[118] Quaestiones, 65vb: 'In incontinente voluntas inclinatur ad peccandum ex aliquo passione.'

For the healing of the incontinent person knowledge is not sufficient. An external medicine is needed, namely admonition and correction which help the person to begin to resist the concupiscence.[119]

These remarks show that Versor is not simply content with Aristotle's solutions, also introducing the Augustinian concepts of will and concupiscence into his discussion. The remarks on the will, not being found in Aquinas, may relate to Albert's commentary. Albert describes the effects of concupiscence in akratic people extensively using medical vocabulary. He also points out that the akratic person can be persuaded to follow virtue more easily, since his conscience is not habitually vicious.[120] The Augustinian remarks on the will and concupiscence presented here are, however, so general that they can also be understood as basically Thomist modifications of the Aristotelian view that the akratic person does not choose to act against reason.

In question 16, Versor sets out to show why the akratic person cannot be called prudent. Interestingly, the counter-arguments now combine intellectualist stances with Augustinian views. The first counter-argument claims that the akratic person is prudent because he has right reason. The second proceeds from Augustine's favourite biblical verse, the Wisdom of Solomon 8:21, which claims that nobody can be continent without divine help (cf. 1.2, 2.1). Because people cannot be blamed for actions which they cannot avoid by themselves, the akratic person is not vicious and can thus be prudent. The third counter-argument holds that all sin consists in reason's judgement. Because this judgement is overcome by other powers, the akratic person is not guilty of sin and can thus be good and prudent.

Versor teaches that the akratic person cannot be prudent, since prudence guides our good actions and is connected with them. Since the akratês acts wrongly, he cannot be prudent, but the akratic person resembles the prudent person in that both have right reason. But they differ 'in respect of their choice', as Aristotle says (EN 1152b13–14). The prudent person follows the choice, whereas the akratic person does not follow it, but the akratês nevertheless sins willingly because he in some way knows the universal good. His choice is good, but this means that it is good when he is not in the state of passion. When passion comes, the good choice is corrupted. The incontinent person is half-wicked, not entirely wicked.[121] This explanation is taken from Aquinas almost verbatim.[122]

The response to the first counter-argument is obvious: the akratic person knows the right reason in an insufficient manner. To the second and third counter-argument Versor responds as follows:

---

[119] *Quaestiones*, 66rb: 'ad sanationem incontinentis non sufficit sola cognitio, sed adhibetur exterius remedium ammonitionis et correctionis, ex quibus aliquis incipit concupiscentiae resistere.' The so-called fraternal correction referred to here is an old Christian practice based on Matt. 18:15.

[120] Albert, *Ethica* II, 485–7, 492–3.

[121] *Quaestiones*, 68vb.

[122] *Ethica*, 421.

To the second it is said that human being cannot avoid evil and pursue the good without divine help. But the fact that human being needs divine help in order to be continent does not rule out incontinence being sin. For as it is said in the third book of Ethics: what we can do with friends we in some sense can do by ourselves. To the third it is said that the judgement of reason is overcome in the incontinent person. The deed does not, however, proceed from such a necessity as would remove its sinfulness, but proceeds from a certain negligence of inconstant people who aim at resisting passions with the judgement of reason.[123]

While Versor in his actual conclusions follows Aristotle and Thomas Aquinas, the context of the question allows more scope for the Augustinian themes of responsibility and sin. In both q12 and q16, Versor points out that the akratic person can be held morally responsible for his sinful action. Although the akratic action is not chosen, it displays negligence and lack of virtuous character. While Versor in this manner introduces Augustinian elements into his commentary which are not found in Thomas's *Sententia libri Ethicorum*, his exposition remains true to Aquinas. While Versor does not interpret the Augustinian ideas of will and concupiscence in a voluntarist manner, his position resembles Thomas's views in *Summa theologiae* and *De malo*.[124]

Perhaps this strategy is also intended to integrate some features of Albert the Great's ethical theory into the Thomist framework. As these features remain generally Augustinian, one can also say that Versor simply means to show the compatibility of Thomas's ethics with the standard theological views of human will, sin, and concupiscence. Versor's commentary does not develop positions which could be labelled Albertian or the author's own innovation. His *Quaestiones* is a systematic exposition of and apology for the conventional Thomist interpretation of Aristotle's ethics.

Versor's syllogistic explanation of akrasia follows Thomas's model 1a. The Augustinian elements introduced in the context of this explanation do not change Aquinas's model, merely showing the compatibility of some basically Augustinian theological notions with this model. Like Acciaiuoli, Versor 'upgrades' Thomas's ethics to meet the needs of the Renaissance. While Acciaiuoli sometimes significantly departs from Aquinas, however, Versor's contribution is limited to a systematic presentation of the Thomist thinking regarding akrasia.

The extensive commentary of Virgilius Wellendorffer (1460–1534), *Moralogium ex Aristotelis ethicorum libris*, printed in Leipzig in 1509, employs Aquinas above all, as well as Walter Burley and Donato Acciaiuoli to defend an intellectualist account of human action. Aquinas is frequently referred to either by name or as *doctor sanctus*, and the

---

[123] *Quaestiones*, 69ra: 'Ad secundam dicitur quod homo potest vitare et facere bonum, non tamen sine divino auxilio, sed per hoc quod homo indiget divino auxilio ut sit continens, non excluditur quin incontinentia sit peccatum. Quia sicut dictum est in tercio huius, que per amicos possumus aliqualiter per nos possumus. Ad terciam dicitur quod in incontinente vincitur iudicium rationis. Non quidem ex necessitate quod aufert rationem peccati, sed ex negligentia quadam homines non firmi intendentis ad resistendum passioni per iudicium rationis.' The quote is from EN 1112b27; Thomas uses this quote in *Summa theologiae* II/1 q5 a5 ad 1.

[124] For this, cf. 1.3 and Saarinen (1994), 121–5; Bradley (2008).

marginal notes of the Leipzig 1509 edition often cite passages from Thomas's *Summa theologiae*.[125] Wellendorffer's commentary did not share the popularity of John Versor's work, but it nevertheless witnesses the relevance of Thomas's views in Germany on the eve of the Reformation. This voluminous textbook has not interested modern scholarship.[126]

Wellendorffer expounds EN by presenting a great number of 'conclusions' which are discussed with reference to both Aristotle and his commentators. Sometimes these are complemented by 'arguments' which investigate possible counter-examples and detailed questions. In the exposition of the seventh book of the EN, Wellendorffer mentions several commentators by name: Eustratius, Averroes, Robert Grosseteste, Albert the Great, Walter Burley, Jacques Lefèvre d'Étaples and Donato Acciaiuoli, Heinrich of Friemar, and John Buridan.[127] He also mentions Seneca and Cicero fairly often, remarking that they employ the concept of *continentia* in a non-Aristotelian manner, referring to chastity or to a contempt for desires.[128]

Although Wellendorffer's commentary reflects the erudition of its author, the frequent name-dropping does not imply any thorough discussion of the various positions. Wellendorffer presupposes a harmony or at least complementarity between various commentators. He does not play them off against one another, all bearing witness to the correct understanding. In spite of this approach, Wellendorffer has his own preferences, as will be shown below.

The third chapter of EN VII is devoted to the traditional problem of akratic knowledge. In his expositions of EN VII, 2 Wellendorffer remarks in a Thomist manner that one needs to consider three different times with regard to which this problem is discussed. Before and after the perturbation, the akratic person knows clearly, but during it some ignorance occurs in the akratic mind. In this second phase, the akratic mind resembles the state of drunkenness or children singing songs which they do not understand.[129] In the margin, Donato Acciaiuoli is given as the

---

[125] Wellendorffer wants to show his agreement with this work. Although his discussion often also matches with Thomas's *Sententia libri Ethicorum*, this work is interpreted, as is shown below, in the light of Walter Burley and Donato Acciaiuoli.

[126] On Wellendorffer, see Collijn (1934); Lohr (1982), 229; Moss (2003), 135–41.

[127] At least the following quotes appear in the passages on akrasia: Eustratius (*Moralogium*, 104va, 106r, 108rb–va, 112va, 113ra), Averroes/Commentator (110va), Grosseteste (105vb,108ra) Albert (106v), Burley (105rb, 107ra, 111va, 112ra, va, 113rb, 115ra), Lefèvre d'Étaples (105rb, 111va, 112ra, va), Donato Acciaiuoli (105rb–va, 106r, 107ra, 111va, 112ra), Heinrich of Friemar (112va, 115rb), Buridan (112vb, 115va–vb). Thomas's ethics is thus received through Burley and Acciaiuoli; Versor is not mentioned in these passages.

[128] *Moralogium*, 107ra.

[129] *Moralogium*, 105rb–va: 'Tria sunt tempora consideranda. Primum est quando incontinens non est in perturbatione, et tunc est sciens. Secundum tempus est quando actu est in perturbatione constitutus, et tunc videtur quasi ignorans et est similis ebrio qui scientiam habet et non agit secundum eam actu. Sed agit instar puerorum dicentium carmina que non intelligunt et sic illi proferunt labiis esse turpe, quod tunc vix mente cognoscunt. Tertium tempus est, quando re ipsa per acta et commissa peccaminosa et turpi redit ad scientiam et cognoscat que facta sunt.' Cf. Acciaiuoli, *Expositio*, 327.

source of this consideration. A little later, Wellendorffer again quotes Acciaiuoli: the akratic person to some extent (*partim*) knows and to some extent remains ignorant.[130]

Wellendorffer's conclusion 312 states his basic position with regard to akratic knowledge: 'The incontinent person is said to know and to be ignorant in a variety of ways. The philosopher shows this in the text in three ways.'[131] The three ways pertain to Aristotle's distinctions in EN VII, 3 between having and using knowledge, actual and habitual knowledge, and universal and particular knowledge. Like many other advocates of the Aristotelian-Thomist model 1a of akrasia, Wellendorffer claims that it is not possible to act against actual knowledge of particular facts, since some perturbation in this knowledge must occur in order that akratic actions can take place.[132]

Wellendorffer then compares the theoretical and practical syllogism. The practical syllogism of the akratic person resembles the errors of the theoretical syllogism as follows:

The practical syllogism is finally ordered towards drawing a conclusion regarding what we should do. Thus we argue in the universal mode: every evil is to be avoided. Fornication is evil. Thus fornication is to be avoided. Or: every good is to be practised. Praying and fasting is good. Thus they should be followed and practised at all times. For in the syllogism of the temperate person who is not affected by the concupiscence fighting against reason, what is concluded is necessarily chosen and done. But this is not the case in the practical syllogism of the incontinent and the intemperate person: in them concupiscence fights against reason and prevents the execution of the good.[133]

This syllogistic analysis evokes the issue of the nature of the conclusion. In the seventh book, Wellendorffer often quotes Burley and Acciaiuoli who, as we saw in 1.3 and 2.2, both tend to distinguish between the propositional conclusion and the actual execution of the act. In the passage quoted above, Wellendorffer claims that the execution of the proper act is impeded in the case of akrasia. He further distinguishes between conclusion, choice, and execution.

Given this, Wellendorffer's syllogistic account not merely follows Aquinas, but leans towards model 2, as defended by Burley and Acciaiuoli. According to this model, the akratês reaches the good propositional conclusion of the practical syllogism at least to some extent, but fails to put it into practice. Wellendorffer continues to explain his

---

[130] *Moralogium*, 106r: 'quia incontinens partim est sciens et partim nesciens'. Cf. *Expositio*, 333.

[131] *Moralogium*, 106r: 'Incontinens dicitur sciens et nesciens multipliciter. Quemadmodum philosophus in textu ostendit tripliciter.'

[132] *Moralogium*, 106r: 'contra scientiam in particulari et in actu non potest quis agere. Unde ebrii propter ebrietatem, et incontinentes propter incontinentiam ita perturbantur quod non considerant quod agant atque dicant.'

[133] *Moralogium*, 106v: 'Syllogismus practicus est qui ordinatur finaliter ad concludendum conclusionem operabilem a nobis sic arguendo in universali: Omne malum est vitandum. Fornicari est malum. Igitur fornicari est vitandum. Vel omne bonum est faciendum. Ieiunare orare est bonum. Igitur quodlibet horum est prosequendum atque faciendum. Nam in syllogismo temperati qui non habet concupiscentiam rationi repugnantem, tunc conclusum necessario eligitur et operatur. Secus tamen est in syllogismo practico incontinentis et intemperanti, ubi concupiscentia rationi repugnat et prohibet boni exequutionem.'

conclusion 312 by referring to different authorities. He first quotes Thomas's view that
the judgement of the intellect is often impeded by the powers of the sense organs.[134]

Wellendorffer then extensively discusses the position of Albert the Great, according
to which the akratic person has two different syllogisms and four premises in his or her
mind. On the one hand, Wellendorffer grants that since the akratês does not apply the
minor premise properly under the major (*minorem indebite applicat*), there is something
wrong in the minor premise (our model 1a). On the other hand, Wellendorffer also
holds that the akratic mind reaches the propositional conclusion, or, actually, two
contrary conclusions:

Under these two syllogistic forms two different conclusions emerge, one concluding that
fornication is to be avoided insofar as it is a disordered vice, the other holding that it is to be
followed insofar as it is pleasant. These two conclusions are apprehended simultaneously and they
express contrary simultaneous judgements concerning the same issue.[135]

Wellendorffer quotes Albert the Great, who considers that the incontinent person
performs two contrary and simultaneous acceptances so that his appetitive powers have
contrary inclinations simultaneously.[136] As we noted in 1.5, this feature of Albert's
discussion combines Aristotle's syllogistic analysis with Augustine's discussion of 'two
wills'. The theme of contrary and simultaneous appetitive powers is later discussed by
Luther and his Erfurt teachers (see 3.1, 3.2). The theme of two wills is thus not only
passed from Augustine and Petrarch to Luther, but also exercises an influence within
scholastic Aristotelianism.

In Wellendorffer's exposition, this theme serves primarily as an illustration of his
view of the practical syllogism. Wellendorffer is clearly sympathetic to the view of
Burley and Acciaiuoli according to which the propositional aspect of the conclusion
can be detached from its actual execution. Since the akratic person grasps both the
minor premise and the propositional conclusion of the practical syllogism in a somewhat defective manner, he is to an extent ignorant, but he also knows about his
situation. It is noteworthy that Wellendorffer does not quote those passages in Aquinas
which clearly favour the Aristotelian-Thomist model 1a, but he does quote a fairly
irrelevant passage from *Summa theologiae* I q84, which is then connected with the view
that the akratic mind reaches the propositional conclusion.

In this manner, the Thomist analysis (model 1a) is complemented by Walter Burley's
analysis (model 2), which emphasizes the parallelism between the theoretical and
practical syllogisms. This position is very close to the commentary by Acciaiuoli, but

---

[134] *Moralogium*, 106v. Thomas, *Summa theologiae* I q84 a8.

[135] *Moralogium*, 106v: 'Et sub istis duabus [syllogismos] diversimode fit subsumptio atque conclusio, quia
concludit quod fornicatio inquantum est inordinata est vitanda, sed quantum delectabilis prosequenda. Nam
ille conclusiones sunt simul apprehense et contraria iudicia de eiusdem sunt simul.'

[136] *Moralogium*, 106v: 'Et ideo Albertus dicit quod incontinens ambas conclusiones sui syllogismi simul
accipit quia causantur ex motu rationis concupiscentiam refrenantis, et ex motu appetitus in contrarium
inclinantis.' Cf. Albert, *Ethica* II, 474–5; Saarinen (1994), 115–16; Müller (2006), 1312.

differs significantly from the views of John Versor. It is noteworthy that Wellendorffer, in spite of his extensive use of other commentators, does not pay any attention to Versor's commentary in the discussion on akrasia.

Although Wellendorffer's view of the practical syllogism also deviates from Thomas's *Sententia libri Ethicorum*, he declares his allegiance to *Summa theologiae* in many ways. After the quotes from Albert's commentary, conclusion 312 continues with a reference to *Summa theologiae* II/2 q156 a1, in which Thomas teaches that incontinence primarily pertains to the soul and secondarily to the body. In keeping with this teaching, Wellendorffer explains that akrasia is primarily due to negligence and lack of caution, vices that relate to the soul. Although the intellect of the akratic person works properly, the will 'does not permit' him to apply knowledge to the particular facts properly. The will is captured and driven by the vehement concupiscence in this process; thus it may happen that the intellect deviates from its proper judgement.[137]

This explanation matches well with the overall message of conclusion 312 that the intellect reaches a conclusion or some kind of judgement but, because of the influence of the bad will and concupiscence, particular facts are not properly attended to and so the conclusion does not stand firmly. Although Wellendorffer uses Thomas's terminology, his position does not merely follow the angelic doctor. Thomas does ascribe akrasia to negligence and he does say that the mental powers of intellect and will are the primary causes of akrasia. Thomas's discussion does not, however, presuppose any internal conflict between intellect and will: both are equally driven by passion. Whereas Thomas states that 'the will is prevented by the passion' (*voluntas impellitur a passione*),[138] Wellendorffer holds that the will does not permit the intellect to work properly. Thus Wellendorffer in fact reads the conflict of simultaneous contrary acceptances into Thomas's text. He does not do this, however, for voluntaristic reasons, but rather in order to safeguard his intellectualist view, which holds that the akratic intellect can reach the proper conclusion to an extent.

Conclusion 312 is followed by an *argumentum* in which the Socratic opinion that nobody acts contrary to his or her knowledge is highlighted from the perspective reached in the stated conclusion. Wellendorffer first advances the common Aristotelian-Thomist argument that the akratic person knows the universals which express proper knowledge but remains ignorant with regard to particular facts. He then gives two original examples which illuminate his position.[139]

---

[137] *Moralogium*, 107ra: 'Incontinentia enim pertinet a corpus occasionaliter sed ad animam per se, quia non resistit passionibus. Vincitur enim a passionibus incontinens non simpliciter tangentibus, sed vehementer impellentibus, et ita propter incautam resistentiam et ex negligentia. Nam voluntas tracta atque allecta a concupiscentia non permittit intellectus applicare cognitionem quam habet in universali ad singularia, quia habet habitum ligatum in singularibus practicum, ut dictum fuit. Et ita egredit a proprio iudicio.'

[138] See Thomas, *Summa theologiae* II/2, q156 a1, ad1, and ad3.

[139] *Moralogium*, 107rb. He says here that the first example appears in 'commentatores' but does not give any names.

The first example concerns a seaman:

A good and skillful seaman knows in universal terms that all danger is to be avoided, and he actually considers that he wants to avoid danger. He also knows in particular terms that in this current or part of the sea there is danger, because seafarers report the dangers of the sea. He also knows how to travel safely, but because he does not actually know that he is in the place of danger while he is there, nothing prevents him from getting into danger because some particulars have not been considered.[140]

The first sentence of this example tells us that the seaman knows both the universal premise and, to an extent, the conclusion regarding his own actions. The next points go through various particular facts relevant for the minor premise, finding that something remains unconsidered. This inconsideration makes it possible to act 'akratically'.

The example fits well into Wellendorffer's intellectualist account, since it shows how a proper, though imperfect, judgement concerning one's own action can be achieved, although some ignorance of the particulars remains. At the same time, we may wonder whether the first example really depicts akrasia or merely an error. But Wellendorffer's point is to show how a good conclusion regarding action can be reached while some ignorance of the particulars remain. Given the results of conclusion 312, one should probably complement the example by saying that the 'akratic' seaman has two syllogisms in his mind, one attending to the dangers, the other recommending a safe passage. While the conclusions of both syllogisms are to an extent apprehended, the akratic action is due to the primacy of the wrong syllogism.

The other example is again taken from *Summa theologiae*. According to this far-fetched example, the leaders of the Jews knew that Christ was the Messiah, but because of their envy and hatred they were blinded so that they did not apply this knowledge to their own actions.[141] Given that Wellendorffer employs this example as an illustration of akrasia, it again shows that akratic people know the moral situation at hand intellectually, but can nevertheless be so blinded that they act otherwise. The two examples given in the *argumentum* can thus be understood as ways of examining model 2 of akrasia, in which the akratic person arrives at a partial good judgement while he or she also commits some kind of logical error. Wellendorffer's eclectic use of Aquinas does not actually make his action theory Thomist, rather approaching Acciaiuoli and Walter Burley.

As Wellendorffer is no voluntarist, his discussion on choice in EN VII, 8 does not reveal any features which would emphasize consent or the conscious decision to do evil. On the contrary, he states in Aristotelian terms that the akratic person differs from

---

[140] *Moralogium*, 107rb: 'Bonus et artificiosus nauta scit in universali omne periculum esse fugiendum, et actu considerat velle fugere periculum. Etiam in particulari scit in tali fluminis sive maris loco esse periculum, quia qui navigant mare enarrant pericula eius. Scit etiam in mari tutum iter, sed cum non considerat se actu esse in illo passu periculi, cum tamen ibi fuerit, nihil prohibet ipsum periclitari propter inconsiderationem particularis.'

[141] *Moralogium*, 107rb: 'Sic Iudei maiores, scribe, principes atque pharisei (non crucifixores) Christum verum messiam fuisse secundum habitum scripturarum bene cognoverunt. Sed invidia, odium et malicia excecavit illos, ut scripturas prophetarum non actu adverterent.' Thomas, *Summa theologiae* III q47 a5.

the intemperate with regard to choice: while the intemperate remains firm in the chosen vice, the akratês repents. Incontinence is a partial vice and the akratic person is half-wicked.[142] The incontinent has a good choice; he or she is overcome by passion without choice (*ineligibiliter vincitur a passione*).[143]

Wellendorffer's conclusion 341 insists that no incontinent person acts deliberately (*ex consilio eligenter*) contrary to the judgement of right reason.[144] Referring to John Buridan, Wellendorffer holds that while the precipitate akratês does not consider the relevant facts properly, the weak akratês does possess some kind of right consideration of the pertinent facts. However, this is not perfect deliberation and does not prompt the corresponding action.[145] Conclusion 341 clearly leans towards the view that the weak akratês is fairly well informed of the situation and is led to the akratic action without exercising his or her own choice.

Although Wellendorffer's discussion of choice is not very elaborate, we may again conclude that his position remains closer to Burley than to Aquinas. Burley teaches consistently that akratic actions take place 'without' choice, but Aquinas seems, at least in his theological works, to ascribe some role to consent or choice in all blameworthy actions.[146] When Wellendorffer holds that no incontinent person acts *eligenter* contrary to right reason, he is therefore stretching his intellectualism beyond the view of Aquinas. His view differs in this respect from John Versor and approaches the views of Acciaiuoli and Burley.

2.4 Humanism and Platonism: Jacques Lefèvre d'Étaples and Josse Clichtove

The so-called *Tres conversiones* by Jacques Lefèvre d'Étaples (1460–1536) has often been regarded as the first 'predominantly humanist exposition of the Ethics' to have been printed.[147] This huge work, first printed in Paris in 1497 and reprinted there at least eighteen times before 1553,[148] became extremely influential in continental Europe. The first part of the work contains the translation by Argyropoulos and the commentary by Lefèvre. We will first focus our attention on this commentary.

Tres conversiones also contains the translations of EN by Leonardo Bruni and Robert Grosseteste, as well as some shorter texts on moral philosophy, among which

---

[142] *Moralogium*, 112rb–vb, 115vb.

[143] *Moralogium*, 115rb; 114rb.

[144] *Moralogium*, 115rb: 'Nullus incontinens ex consilio eligenter agit contra iudicium recte rationis incontinenter.'

[145] *Moralogium*, 115va: 'Et si debilis [incontinens] consiliatur, tamen non immanet consilio, quare non operatur ex consilio . . . Hic incontinens secundum Buridanum prevolans fit sine deliberatione ex vehementi passione. Sed incontinens debilis fit cum aliquali ratiocinatione, sed non perfecta.' On Buridan, see 1.5 and Saarinen (1994), 161–87.

[146] See 1.3 and Saarinen (1994), 144–5; Saarinen (1999); Kent (1995), 156–74; Wood (1999).

[147] So Lines (2002), 17–18, referring to Kraye (1995), 104 and Kessler (1999).

[148] Lines (2002), 488.

Lefèvre's own brief introduction is interesting for the understanding of akrasia.[149] After 1505, this introduction was often printed separately, together with the commentary by Josse Clichthove (1472–1543). Clichtove expands Lefèvre's discussion on akrasia in important ways. We will return to this text, *Artificialis introductio in X libros Ethicorum, elucidata commentariis Clichtovaei*, in the second part of this chapter.[150]

Lefèvre was a leading French humanist and theologian, who influenced both the Catholic and the emerging Protestant learning in many ways. He edited classical philosophical and theological texts, seeking to establish better access to the original sources. His translation of the New Testament was criticized by the Sorbonne, but he could continue his humanist career under the protection of Francis I. *Tres conversiones* demonstrates Lefèvre's encyclopedic humanistic activity: the scholars could now compare the three different Latin translations with one another and, using Lefèvre's running commentary and brief introduction, obtain a systematic view of Aristotle's discussion.

Lefèvre begins his discussion in the scholastic manner, introducing the six probable opinions and six doubts concerning akrasia. The first doubt is again 'whether one can act incontinently while having knowledge and right estimation'.[151] Lefèvre's expositions remain short. Although problems related to the first doubt occupy his main interest in discussing akrasia, the length of his deliberations does not concur with Acciaiuoli or Versor. The exposition of EN VII, 3 (EN 1146b8–1147b18) contains less than two pages. Lefèvre first offers some brief notes explaining Aristotle's terminology. He does use new examples; for instance, he illustrates Aristotle's remark that universal knowledge can be had in two ways (EN 1147a4–5) by saying that it is one thing to know that an average of two amounts is the mid-point between them and another thing to know that 24 is the midpoint between 22 and 26.[152]

One interesting note concerns the difference between what is false and what is absurd. Lefèvre remarks that the ancient authors do not declare akrasia to be impossible:

---

[149]   The 1497 edition contains, according to Lohr (1976), 730: '1. *Opus de moribus ad Nicomachum*, Joanne Argyropylo Byzantio traductore, adiecto familiari Jacobi Stapulensis commentario, 2. *Magna moralia*, Georgio Valla Placentino interprete, 3. Leonardi Aretini, *Dialogus de moribus*, 4. Jacobi Stapulensis *Introductio moralis in Ethicen Aristotelis*, 5. *Ethica ad Nicomachum*, interprete Leonardo Aretino, 6. *Ethica ad Nicomachum*, antiqua traductio.' In addition to these, the 1497 edition contains registers and (pp. 331–2) Baptista Mantuano's poem on virtues. I have consulted the editions of 1497 and 1505, neither of which has page numbers. I give the chapter numbers and the digital page numbers available of the 1497 edition at http://www.hab.de

[150]   I use the Paris 1514 edition. Lefèvre's text in this edition is identical with page 347 of the 1497 edition of *Tres conversiones*. Clichtove's other moral work, *Dogma moralium philosophorum*, Strasbourg 1512, does not discuss akrasia. It presents some basic notions as they appear in Cicero and Seneca.

[151]   Lefèvre, *In Ethicam* VII, Ch. 2, p.138: 'An contingit scientem recteque existimantem incontinenter agere.'

[152]   *In Eth.* VII, 3 in the 1505 edition. Missing from the 1497 edition.

the authors do not want to avoid only what is false but also what seems absurd. It seems absurd that somebody knows in a universal and particular manner and nevertheless acts against this knowledge and judgement, although he could do this from his absolute freedom.[153]

Given this, a voluntarist stance would be theoretically possible, but the Socratic-Aristotelian position is more reasonable.

Lefèvre presents three conclusions with regard to EN VII, 3. The first is that incontinence pertains to the same passions as continence and intemperance. The person is said to be akratic with regard to these passions. The second conclusion is that one is similarly akratic with regard to true opinions as to knowledge. Lefèvre also presents his syllogistic account of akrasia in the context of this second conclusion. Although he explains the text in an intellectualist manner, he also grants the voluntarist possibility as a theoretical though highly improbable option. For instance, he concludes that while there is nothing absurd or odd (nihil incommodi absurdique) in ignoring the universal premise, it would be 'exceptional' (mirabile) if someone acted akratically while applying the universal premise correctly to the particular facts.[154] Clear-eyed akrasia could thus theoretically occur, but it would be highly exceptional.

In other respects Lefèvre's syllogistic explanation is close to the intellectualism of Aquinas and Burley. His comparison between theoretical and practical syllogism comes very close to saying that one can reach a propositional conclusion which is first known (cognita quod conclusum est) and then acted upon.[155] In that sense, he is close to Burley, but he does not reflect on this matter more closely, and his description of the right and wrong practical syllogisms which compete in the akratic mind is very close to Aquinas. The harmful desire, cupiditas, causes the state of confusion in which the right major premise is not applied to the relevant facts, the particular facts being evaluated from the viewpoint of pursuing pleasure.[156] The third conclusion is that Socrates is basically right. The last proposition or opinatio rei concerns singulars and also directs our actions. The akratic person either does not have it or possesses it in an ineffective manner, but proper knowledge pertains to the universals, and this knowledge is not affected by the perturbations which only affect

---

[153] In Eth. VII, 3, 140: 'Non modo vitant autores dicere que falsa sunt; sed et ea que videntur absurda. Ut absurdum videtur quod quis sciat universale et particulare, et nihilominus agat contra huiusmodi scientiam atque iudicium, quamvis ex eius libertate absolute possit.'

[154] In Eth. VII, 3, 140–1.

[155] In Eth. VII, 3, 141: 'Opinionum enim alia universalium est et alia singularium, quibus iam ipse presidet sensus. Et cum in contemplativis ex universali et singulari una ratiocinatio fit, ut anima id quod conclusum fuerit dicat acceptetque necesse est, ita in agendis ex universali et singulari ratiocinatione cognita quod conclusum est, ut agat ipse, si potest et non prohibeatur, oportet.'

[156] In Eth. VII, 3, 141: 'Cum ergo una erit universalis opinio agere vetans, ut que dicit, nullum dulce gustare oportere, et altera dicit, omne dulce dulce delectabile esse, et insuper hoc esse dulce, secundum ultimam fiet operatio, atque huius dulcis prosecutio. Et illa forte est que a cupiditate nascitur. Et prima idem dulce non gustare atque fugere dictabat, sed cupiditas vincit. Movere enim partes vel singulas potest. Quo fit ut quodam modo a ratiocinatione ac opinione incontinenter agant, ut ea quam suscitat cupiditas.'

the particular facts related to perception. In this sense, Socrates is right that knowledge cannot be overcome by passions.[157]

This end result resembles the intellectualism of Albert, Aquinas, and Versor. Lefèvre in fact stresses the correctness of the Socratic position even more strongly than his predecessors. The strong presence of syllogistic comparisons connects him with Burley and Acciaiuoli. Lefèvre does not clearly say whether the 'last proposition' refers to the minor premise or to the propositional conclusion. His expression *opinatio rei* comes from Argyropoulos (EN 1147b9–10), but Lefèvre's use of it makes it sound like a judgement or a cognitive outcome of the issue. This impression is strengthened by his long discussion of the second conclusion, which relates opinion and knowledge. At the same time, Lefèvre's discussion remains too brief to allow for far-reaching conclusions. Since he does not intend scholastic sophistication, simply a general evaluation of the matter, he can mention the voluntarist possibility of absolute freedom while stressing that the Socratic position is very reasonable.

Lefèvre's intellectualist stance is also apparent in his discussion of akrasia and choice. In his exposition of EN 1152a8–35, he concludes that the akratic person cannot be prudent. Even the akratic person who claims to know better speaks like a drunkard. At the same time, he acts voluntarily, knowing in some way the motives of his akratic action. The akratic person is half-wicked because he possesses the good choice but cannot persist in it.[158] These conclusions are similar to Aquinas and Versor, simply elucidating Aristotle's text without anything original.

Lefèvre's other ethical treatise, *Artificialis introductio*, classifies the central concepts of Aristotelian ethics. The class of *continentia* consists of twenty-one elementary questions, each formulated and responded to in a single sentence. Because the set of questions primarily defines the notions of continence and incontinence, no argument occurs. Aristotle's basic question, that is, whether the akratic person goes wrong knowingly, is significantly missing. The most relevant question is 18: 'Whether the akratic person acts proceeding from the deliberation of right reason.' The answer is very short: 'No one who is guided by the deliberation of the right reason acts wrongly.' To question 16, 'whether the akratic person is wicked without qualification', Lefèvre replies that 'the person whose choice is good is not wicked without qualifications'.[159]

Lefèvre's introduction only offers a didactic memorandum of the basic concepts and cannot therefore shed more light on his view of akrasia. Important to the reception history is that this text was often printed together with the more elaborate commentary by

---

[157] *In Eth.* VII, 3, 141: 'Quodammodo recte evenit quod Socrates investigabat, ut presente scientia non fiat incontinens. Nam cum recte rationis ultima propositio ac opinatio rei sit singularis atque eadem actionum domina, aut hanc incontinens in perturbatione non habet, aut sic eam habet ut ligata compeditaque sit . . . et quia etiam in agendis ultimus terminus ultimaque propositio non est universalis neque ad scientiam eque et universalis pertinere videtur. Evenit igitur quodam modo recte quod Socrates investigabat. Nam ea scientia (que proprie scientia est) presente non fit perturbatio, neque ob perturbationem distrahitur, sed singularis sensitivaque quedam.'

[158] *In Eth.* VII, 10, 151.

[159] Lefèvre, *Introductio*, 36v (p. 347 in the 1497 edition).

Lefèvre's pupil Josse Clichtove. While Lefèvre's entry on *continentia* occupies less than a page in the 1514 edition, Clichtove's exposition takes three-and-a-half-pages, with a significantly smaller typeface. Clichtove goes through all twenty-one questions. Before doing so, he discusses Aristotle's terminology in an original manner, inventing new examples and strategies of interpretation. We remarked above that scholars generally regard Lefèvre's influential volumes as a humanist turning point in the history of ethics. In the case of akrasia, the new features which continue to permeate later commentaries are not found in Lefèvre's own text but in the innovative commentary of his pupil Clichtove.

Clichtove introduces two powerful illustrations of the akratic situation. The first illustration personifies reason and appetite. The sensitive appetite can behave like a wild animal and draw people into all kinds of irrational actions, but when it is 'domesticated by reason', it relates to reason as a master relates to a slave, obeying the master's will. This is the natural state of the appetite. But if the will is overcome by the appetite, then the slave drags the master about (cf. EN 1145b25).[160] The appetite which obeys reason can also be compared to a good son who obeys his father, while the disobedient appetite resembles the rebellious son who disagrees with his father. Reason relates to appetite like a master and teacher relates to his pupil: it is necessary to educate the pupil, because otherwise he would oppose reason.[161]

Continence is for Clichtove a state which is characterized by an intense internal struggle between reason and passion, and in which reason succeeds in gaining the upper hand over the passions without extinguishing them. Continence is not a real virtue, but a 'road towards virtue' (*via ad virtutem*).[162] Although this characterization resembles Aristotelian views, it can also be said that the strong personification of appetite brings Clichtove's discussion close to the view which we called 'commonplace Platonism' in 1.1. On this view, the appetitive powers represent a fairly autonomous entity which needs to be educated by reason and which has the tendency to rebel against higher mental powers.

This tendency also permeates Clichtove's definition of incontinence:

The incontinent person is one who, instead of choosing rightly, follows the abundance of the soul's passions and perturbations related to the pleasures of taste and touch. As when there is a severe struggle between the irrational appetite directed towards wickedness and the reason which resists and warns, a person who neglects reason so that his desires lead him to the acts recommended by the sensitive appetite is called incontinent.[163]

---

[160] Clichtove, *Introductio*, 36v: 'cum vero domitus fuerit [appetitus] per rationem, similis est mansuete fereque suo paret domitori, seque manu prestat tractabilem quocunque volet homo, parata se ferre. Est propter ea ratio ut dominus, appetitus autem sensitivus ut servus. Est enim appetitus sua parte natura ipsi rationi subiectus. Et cum voluntatem que ad dominam dum data est superat, tunc tanquam servus dominum trahit captivum.'

[161] *Introductio*, 36v.

[162] *Introductio*, 36v.

[163] *Introductio*, 36v–37r: '[incontinens] est qui ob passiones perturbationesque animi et non ob electionem voluptatum gustus et tactus sequitur abundantias. Ut cum gravis est pugna inter appetitum irrationalem ad turpia trahentem et rationem obluctantem atque reclamantem, et quis ratione neglecta victus cupiditatibus suis pertrahitur ad ea que suadet appetitus sensitivus, is est incontinens.'

While Lefèvre's exposition remains intellectualistic, stressing the role of the practical syllogism and ignorance in explaining akrasia, Clichtove's emphasis on the quasi-autonomous nature of the appetitive powers gives the discussion a new direction. He does not characterize akrasia in terms of syllogistic deliberation, but the akratic situation is that of an *agon*, an ongoing, vehement struggle (*pugna*) between reason and appetitive powers. In this sense, the commonplace Platonism of *Republic* IV and Galen (1.1–1.2) is reintroduced into the Aristotelian discussion. As Clichtove's description of this struggle does not employ the ideas of consent or free will, his view is closer to commonplace Platonism than Augustinian and voluntarist views.

The second illustration used by Clichtove is Medea as depicted in Ovid's *Metamorphoses* 7, through whom Clichtove exemplifies the third and most standard subclass of akratic people, the 'weak' ones (*debiles, infirmi*):

Weak and powerless people are those incontinents whose previous deliberation does not persist during the perturbation and who are overcome by it. They resemble those who first actively resist the enemies but surrender when they run out of power. Such is Medea in Ovid: she first reflects whether she should, after deserting her father and birthright, follow the foreign stranger Jason whose vehement love has captivated her. But finally she surrenders to the perturbation of love and is overcome by appetite. In her deliberation one can distinguish between reason and appetite as follows: Reason: 'Come, thrust from your maiden breast these flames that you feel, if you can, unhappy girl. Ah, if I could, I should be more myself.' Passion: 'But some strange power holds me down against my will. Desire persuades me one way, reason another. I see the better and approve it, but I follow the worse.'[164]

Clichtove quotes Ovid extensively here (*Metam.* 7, 17–38), transforming Medea's inner monologue into a dialogue between reason and passion.

It is *Metamorphoses* 7, 21: 'I see the better and approve it, but I follow the worse' in particular which the later sixteenth-century interpreters of akrasia will continue to explicate. This verse seems to reveal a non-Aristotelian 'clear-eyed akrasia' which Clichtove here interprets in a commonplace Platonist manner: the human soul is characterized by a continuing and self-conscious struggle between reason and passion.

We saw in 1.2 that Euripides's version of Medea serves as an example of the Stoic discussion on akrasia. In that case, Medea's 'I know what evil I propose to do, but anger rules my deliberations' (Euripides, *Medea* 1078–79) pertains to her decision to kill her children. The two situations of Medea are similar in the sense that both can be

---

[164] *Introductio*, 37r: 'Debiles autem et infirmi sunt incontinentes qui deliberatione prehabita ob perturbationem non persistunt tandem victi. Et assimilantur eis qui in principio quidem hosti acriter resistunt, cui tandem defectis viribus succumbunt. Qualis fingitur Medea apud Ovidium primo consultans an deserto patre et solo natali Jasonem exterum et alienigenam, cuius vehementi amore capta fuit, sequi deberet. Sed tandem amoris perturbatione victa succubuit appetitui. Alternantque vices in sua consultationes nunc ratio, nunc appetitus sensitivus, hoc modo: Ra. Excute virgineo conceptas pectores flammas, /Si potest, infelix, si possem sanior essem. /Ap. Sed trahit invitam nova vis, aliudque cupido /Mens aliud suadet. Video meliora, proboque, /Deteriora sequor.'

interpreted in a commonplace Platonist fashion, that is, as a struggle between reason and passion. They can also both be interpreted in a 'quasi-Stoic' fashion, that is, as Medea's inability to control her passion in spite of her reaching the judgement concerning the better alternative. But it is more difficult to combine the example of Medea with the intellectualist, that is, Socratic and Aristotelian, accounts of akrasia.

There is also a notable difference between the two examples. Euripides' verse exemplies anger, whereas Ovid refers to the passion of love. Given that Aristotle treats akrasia predominantly with regard to pleasures and only secondarily with regard to anger, Ovid's example fits better into the Aristotelian framework.

Clichtove sets out to expound Lefèvre's elementary questions and answers using his own Platonic framework. He explains the traditional view that the 'weak' incontinent people are better than the 'precipitate' ones by referring again to Medea's conflict:

Precipitate people are overcome due to a lack of consideration . . . but the weak and powerless deliberate to an extent. Ovid says of Medea: '. . . loved at sight with a consuming flame. Although she struggled to suppress her desire, she was unable to restrain herself; she fought against it in vain'.[165]

This picture of Medea is consistently accompanied by the idea that the akratic person acts out of passion instead of reason. Clichtove states that while intemperate people act from choice, akratic people act 'from passion' (ex passione).[166]

The Stoic and Augustinian views presuppose that akratic actions nevertheless proceed from consent, whereas the intellectualist tradition postulates some kind of ignorance. In contrast to both of these traditions, the commonplace Platonist view considers reason and passion to be the two driving forces which struggle with one another until one prevails. Adhering to this view, Clichtove defines continence and incontinence as passions. Continence is for him a passion which helps reason to overcome harmful urge towards pleasure.[167] Temperance is a habitus but continence is a passion.[168] In this sense, continence is not a virtue but a 'road towards it', as we saw above.

When Clichtove explains the relationship between intemperance and incontinence, the nature of akrasia as passion becomes clearer:

First, the intemperate person follows the desires of taste and touch habitually and with choice. The incontinent person does not follow them in this manner, but he only acts with the affections and passions of the soul. Second, because the intemperate has a corrupted rational appetite and reason. The incontinent does not have these faults, but his appetite is corrupted. At the same time he has a sound deliberation and right judgement, judging that what he does should not be done.

---

[165] Introductio, 37r (cf. Ovid, Metam. 7, 9–11.).

[166] Introductio, 37r '[Questio 4: circa que] . . . temperantia et intemperantia circa eas versantur ex electione, continentia vero et incontinentia ex passione.'

[167] Introductio, 37r '[Questio 1: quid? Continentia] est passio qua qui rationi parens vehementes gustus et tactus delectationes ad turpia trahentes superat.'

[168] Introductio, 37v, response to q9.

But because the perturbation overcomes him he does not follow this judgement and does not act according to the right reason.[169]

Whereas the Aristotelian and Augustinian traditions consider that some higher and 'voluntary' power must direct akratic actions, Clichtove takes only two powers, reason and passion, into account, claiming that the akratic action is due to passion which simply overcomes reason. The akratic person is characterized by the corruption of the sensitive appetite in that while reason and will remain intact, the corruption of lower appetite already makes the akratês vulnerable to passions.

Intemperance can also be distinguished from akrasia with regard to repentance. The akratic person repents, whereas the intemperate person does not. But if the akratês continues to act akratically, his passion may become a habit so that he becomes intemperate.[170] Thus repeated incontinence leads to intemperance. Given this straight-forward dynamic of two competing powers, Clichtove does not need Aristotle's syllogistic analysis of wrongdoing. Outside of passion, the akratic person chooses well but, when passion moves the mind, the good choice is impeded and perverted.[171] While in the Aristotelian framework, passion can only indirectly overcome the good choice by means of ignorance and shift of attention, Clichtove teaches that passion can move the mind without presupposition of ignorance.

Because of this commonplace Platonism, Clichtove can affirm a clear-eyed akrasia:

The incontinent person acts wrongly, thus he does not act according to the deliberation of right reason. Although he deliberates now and then, he does not follow the right deliberation. He rather acts contrarily to the dictate of right reason.[172]

This basic picture of akrasia is valid with regard to the passion of concupiscence. With regard to anger, the situation is somewhat different, since anger presupposes a reason to be angry.[173] This qualification shows, however, that Clichtove's position with regard to the 'standard' akrasia occasioned by pleasure is a considered and consistent view.

In his discussions of standard akrasia, Clichtove does not appeal to ignorance or to incomplete deliberation. Because continence and incontinence are passions of the soul,

---

[169] *Introductio*, 37v: '[Decima. Quo differt incontinens ab intemperato. Responsio.] Primo. Nam intemperans voluptates gustus et tactus per habitum et electionem sequitur. Incontinens vero non, sed solum per affectionem et passionem animi. Secundo. Quia intemperatus appetitum rationalem habet corruptum rationemque depravatam. Incontinens autem non, dum habet appetitum corruptum, immo et sanum habet consilium et rectum iudicium quo iudicat ea non esse facienda que facit. Verum perturbatione victus non sequitur huiusmodi iudicium neque recte rationi conformiter operatur.'

[170] *Introductio*, 37v, q10, third point.

[171] *Introductio*, 38r, q16: 'incontinentis autem electio bona est precipue cum extra perturbationem fuerit. Nam tunc eligit ea que bona sunt et honesta. Ubi vero animus passione commovetur, huiusmodi electio ex vehementia affectionis impeditur et pervertitur.'

[172] *Introductio*, 38r, q18: 'Incontinens autem turpe operatur, igitur incontinens non agit consilio recte rationis. Quamvis enim interdum consultet, tamen non sequitur consilium rectum, immo contrarium eius quod recta ratio dictat, facit.'

[173] *Introductio*, 38r, q13: 'incontinentia tactus non sequitur rationem, sed ex impetu concupiscientie precipitat ad turpia. Incontinentia vero ire rationem sequitur.'

their seat is the sensitive appetite. While a continent person can resist the passions, the occurrence of akrasia witnesses the corruption of the sensitive appetite. At the same time, the akratic person may possess an uncorrupted reason, will, and good choice. The commonplace Platonic approach allows the possibility that a vehement passion can directly overcome reason. In order to become enkratic, this person therefore needs to improve his passions.

Although akrasia in this manner proceeds without the cooperation or even permission of higher intellectual powers, the akratês is morally responsible for the state of his passions. Clichtove discusses the 'healing' of various incontinent manners at some length. He also teaches that akrasia is always blameworthy, because there remains the possibility of overcoming the passions. The akratic person fails to accomplish this in his struggle.[174]

Clichtove's position thus deviates from that of his teacher Lefèvre, as well as from the tradition of medieval commentaries. These either follow Aristotelian intellectualism or develop the Augustinian view of consent towards voluntarism. Clichtove argues that akrasia is due to the straightforward conflict between reason and passion in which passion gains the upper hand. He does not need the presupposition of ignorance or the Augustinian view of consent to explain this phenomenon. He can affirm a variant of clear-eyed akrasia which is not due to free will but to the relative autonomy of the appetitive powers.

The example of Medea as well as the introductory picture of master and slave illustrate Clichtove's position impressively. Passions need to be domesticated in order to achieve a virtuous life. Without this process of domestication, passions can act like rebellious slaves who overcome their master. No intellectual or volitional failure on the master's side need be assumed. And yet the akratic person is not innocent, and can be blamed because he has not cultivated his passions properly. This view of Clichtove's is new with regard to the medieval tradition, but it basically represents the commonplace Platonism of *Republic* IV as well as of Galen.

2.5 John Mair's Refined Buridanism

Although the fifteenth century brought about the full blooming of the Renaissance, the phenomenon of 'Renaissance philosophy' continued until 1600 or even 1650.[175] The middle and northern parts of Europe were so heavily affected by the different religious Reformations that the time after 1515 in those countries deserves to be called the Reformation period. With regard to our study, the year 1515 is significant because Martin Luther then began his *Lecture on Romans*, a theological exposition which decisively shaped the later Reformation understanding of human will and its weakness (see 3.2).

---

[174] *Introductio*, 38r, q19–20.
[175] For the issues of periodization, see Kraye (1988); Lines (2002); Copenhaver and Schmitt (2002).

The indirect impacts of the Reformation changed the conditions of intellectual life even in countries and universities which were not directly affected by the confessional controversies. New printing houses and universities produced an enormous quantity of books. New literary genres, such as textbooks and systematic treatises, replaced or at least complemented the traditional commentaries. New theological and confessional issues, for instance with regard to the freedom of the will, were reflected in philosophical literature from various new perspectives.

Ethics itself was no longer a merely philosophical subject, becoming increasingly integrated into theological teaching. Protestant authors wrote textbooks on 'Christian ethics' and Catholic theologians developed the new discipline of 'moral theology'. The practice of writing philosophical commentaries on Aristotle's EN continued. Towards the end of the sixteenth century the new genre of philological commentaries emerged.[176] The development of philological commentaries remains beyond the scope of our study.[177]

Because of these multifaceted simultaneous developments, we will discuss the sixteenth century in three thematically distinct but chronologically overlapping chapters. The present chapter continues the treatment of the Renaissance. Chapter 3 deals with the Lutheran Reformation and Chapter 4 with the Calvinist Reformation. Although we will discuss the most influential and most representative texts on akrasia in each of these movements, our choice of materials remains selective.[178] With regard to the sixteenth-century Catholic Renaissance, we will restrict our discussion to two influential authors, John Mair and Francesco Piccolomini.

John Mair (1467–1550) was an influential Scottish philosopher, theologian, and humanist who commuted several times between Scotland, England, and Paris. His extensive *Commentary on Nicomachean Ethics*, printed in Paris in 1530, remained his last major publication after an extensive teaching career at the University of Paris. Mair influenced many later Reformers, for instance, John Knox, but remained Roman Catholic himself.[179] His commentary on EN contains a passage in which John Wyclif and Martin Luther serve as examples of how one can remain stubbornly in error.[180] It

---

[176] For these developments, see Lines (2005); Saarinen (2006); Saarinen (forthcoming).

[177] Among these, Denys Lambin's *In libros De moribus ad Nicomachum annotationes*, Venice (1558), and, in particular, Pier Vettori's *Commentarii in X libros Aristotelis De moribus ad Nicomachum*, Florence (1584) deserve to be mentioned. On the non-philosophical nature of Vettori's commentary, see Lines (2002), 238–46.

[178] Some prominent commentaries do not include EN VII, for instance, Petrus Tartaretus, *Expositio in sex priores Aristotelis libros Moralium*, Paris 1496 and Petrus Vermigli, *In I–III libros Ethicorum commentarius*, Zürich 1563. But many other commentaries, listed in Lohr (1975–1982), dealing with akrasia simply remain to be discussed by later scholarship.

[179] See Broadie (1987) and (1990). For the disputed issue of Mair's relationship to Calvin, see Ganoczy (1966) and 4.1 below. The Latin title is *Ethica Aristotelis Peripateticorum principis, Cum Ioannes Maioris Theologi Parisiensi Commentariis*, Paris (1530). It is noteworthy that Mair here uses the title 'theologian'.

[180] *In Ethicam*, 108r: 'de malo in peius descendit, ut Vuicleff superiore seculo nostre Britannie propudium, et nunc Martinus Luther Germanie dedecus, qui cum cuculla omnem probitatem cum suis affectis exuit. Tales inanes glorie famelici, demonstrationes non sudiunt, sed rimas sinistras elabendi invenire satagunt, ut delira dogmata protegere videantur.'

can be assumed that the commentary is not positively influenced by the emerging Reformation.

The translation of Argyropoulos is printed with Mair's commentary. The text is expounded with the help of clarifying paraphrases and explanations. Critical questions (*dubium, obiectio*) occur regularly and are often treated at length. Sometimes, for instance, in the crucial passages on akrasia in EN VII, 3, several *dubia* and counter-arguments are presented successively so that their treatment resembles a scholastic question. Other commentators are not mentioned by name, but Mair employs biblical examples as well as Augustine and the Parisian articles of 1277. Although Mair follows the scholastic paths in many ways, his commentary is an original work.

In his comments on EN VII, 2, Mair first lists the traditional six opinions and six open questions regarding akrasia (cf. 2.2). The order of these six points differs somewhat from Acciaiuoli and Versor, but Mair basically follows the list which appeared in Thomas Aquinas's *Sententia libri Ethicorum* and was followed by later commentators. Mair focuses on the third opinion, which holds that the akratic person goes wrong knowingly because of perturbation.[181] Mair carefully explains the teaching of Socrates according to which nobody goes wrong knowingly because nothing can be stronger than knowledge. On the other hand, since we recognize something is wrong but do it nevertheless, we should investigate whether some ignorance occurs during the action and what kind of ignorance it might be.[182] Mair further lists the three traditional temporal moments and argues that the incontinent person knows rightly before and after his action. During the passion, however, akratic people behave like children who recite songs which they do not understand.[183]

Although the comments on EN VII, 2 are for the most part traditional, remaining a preliminary introduction of the opinions and problems concerning akrasia, Mair does make some original remarks. In three different passages of EN VII, 2, he discusses the role of conscience in akratic behaviour. Although these comments have no obvious counterpart in the tradition, they resemble to some extent the remarks of Albert the Great (1.5) and Petrarch (2.1).[184] Mair first points out that it is one thing to have scruples and another thing to act contrary to conscience. The fact that a person cannot choose against harmful passions does not liberate him from the guilt resulting from acting against conscience. Although Aristotle says that akrasia is no real vice and continence no real virtue, he also says that akrasia is morally wrong.[185] In his second

---

[181] *In Ethicam*, 107v: 'Et a tertia opinione ceteris difficillima exorditur. Quaerens primo an fieri queat ut quispiam recte existimans incontinenter agat. Dicebat enim tertia opinio, incontinens enim improba sciens ob perturbationem ac cupiditatem agit.'

[182] *In Ethicam*, 107v.

[183] *In Ethicam*, 107v.

[184] For Albert's *agere contra conscientiam*, see Müller (2006).

[185] *In Ethicam*, 107v: 'Hinc est aliud agere contra scrupulos conscientiae, et aliud contra conscientiam. Si contra vehementes cupiditates et impulsus non persistat, at pravitati non est danda venia nec alii cuiqumque vituperabilium. Insultas, Philosophus dixit continentiam non esse virtutem nec incontinentiam vitium, nunc [EN VII, 2] vero incontinentiam pravitatem dicit esse.'

remark, Mair teaches that the incontinent person has a conscience which keeps warning him or her, whereas the intemperate person has a misguided judgement.[186] The third remark relates to Neoptolemus (EN 1146a19–21), whose conscience told him not to lie.[187]

Since the three remarks pertain to the common opinions concerning akrasia, they should not be taken too seriously. It is nevertheless significant that Mair sees conscience—a concept which does not appear in Aristotle's text—so strongly at work in the akratic awareness of wrongdoing. The wording of the three remarks implies that some awareness continues even at the moment of wrongdoing. Since the akratic person deliberately neglects the voice of conscience, Mair turns away from explaining akrasia merely in terms of temporary ignorance. The akratic person acts against his conscience and is thus both morally guilty of wrongdoing and capable of formulating the correct judgement.

Mair's exposition of EN VII, 3 is devoted to the Socratic problem of acting against knowledge. The first half is a careful exposition of Aristotle's teaching. Mair evidently employs earlier commentators: although he does not mention anybody by name, his examples derive from well-known sources. He sorts out the three different ways of knowing something. First, although a person habitually knows that all mules are sterile, he may actually think that a fat mule which he sees is pregnant.[188]

The second difference between knowing the universal and the singular premise is illustrated by Acciaiuoli's example of knowing that rhubarb cures cholera while not knowing that this particular plant is rhubarb.[189] The third difference of having and using knowledge pertains to the cases of drunkenness and emotional perturbations.[190] The akratic person may know the universal moral truths and even declare that he is fully aware of the case, but his utterances then resemble the words of actors and poets who do not really mean what they are saying.[191]

As for so many earlier commentators, Aristotle's solution of incontinent behaviour is for Mair in the closer analysis of the practical syllogism. Mair's approach to this issue proceeds from the observation that there are simultaneous 'different' (*diverse*) propositions regarding the matter in hand. These propositions may seem contrary, but closer inspection shows that they are not really 'contrary' to one another, since one

---

[186] *In Ethicam*, 108r: '[incontinens] ipse percipiat se perperam agere, at tamen illud exequitur, aliter agit quam ratio ipsi ostendit. Habet conscientiam remurmurantem, quid igitur opus extrinseco monitore habet, intemperans habet iam iudicium corruptum.' For the comparison between akrasia and intemperance, see *In Ethicam* VII, 8 and 10, discussed below.

[187] *In Ethicam*, 108r: 'Neoptolemus...persuasione Ulyssis mentiebatur reluctante conscientia atque mordente.'

[188] *In Ethicam*, 109r. John Buridan, *Quaestiones* VII q7, 143vb (587), connects this example with akrasia.

[189] *In Ethicam*, 109r. Acciaiuoli, *Expositio*, 334 (2.2).

[190] *In Ethicam*, 109v.

[191] *In Ethicam*, 109v: 'Quare existimandum est quod ut histriones ac ludii poemata in scenicis ludis recitant, haud secus incontinentes sententias proferunt... Quando incontinens est in opere incontinentiae, si interrogatur, forte recte responderet, sed hoc est a casu. Est enim prorsus distractus et ignarus eorum quae ore exprimit. Ac puero et ludioni ludo scenico ludenti confertur.'

proposition can be apprehended at the same time as the other is assented to.[192] At this point, Mair refers to Aristotle's propositions 'nothing sweet is to be tasted' and 'everything sweet is pleasant'. As Aristotle says, these propositions are only 'incidentally'contrary when the appetite draws the person towards tasting sweet things.[193]

John Mair refines this claim in the second half of his exposition of EN VII, 3, but he first completes the exposition of Aristotle's teaching. He concedes that the akratic person is in some sense ignorant during the perturbation, but when the perturbation evaporates, he regains the full and clear use of his knowledge. Knowledge in the proper sense is not, however, lost, because this knowledge pertains to the universals and the akratês only loses his right estimation of the particular facts.[194] Because of this, Socrates does not speak foolishly, since only the perception of the singular facts is dragged about by passion, not proper knowledge.[195]

This explanation of akrasia follows an intellectualist path, ascribing incontinent conduct to the ignorance of particular facts and considering that the akratic person can nevertheless retain the right estimation of universal moral truths. Immediately after giving this Aristotelian explanation, Mair nevertheless asks how this view relates to the freedom of the will. He gives a blunt answer which seems to go against the aforesaid intellectualism:

It may be asked whether somebody can assent perfectly and actually to the major and the minor premise of the practical syllogism and then act contrary to the concluding judgement with his free will. The answer is affirmative. There is the common magisterial teaching that some sin is from weakness, as when someone acts wrongly being overcome by perturbation; other sins emerge from ignorance; and a third group when somebody acts wrongly from industriousness, from choice and knowingly.[196]

The 'magisterial teaching' refers to Thomas Aquinas's *Summa theologiae*, II/1 q78 a1. Mair also gives biblical references in which somebody is reported to go wrong knowingly and willingly. Reason further proves the same; for instance, when many people commit sins with the intention of repenting later. Some passages in Augustine witness to sinning knowingly and willingly for Mair. And when Aristotle in EN III, 5

---

[192] *In Ethicam*, 109v: 'Nunc [EN 1147a25] philosophus accedit ad solutionem...de eadem re diverse propositiones esse possunt, quae a non considerantibus contrarie putantur, nullo tamen modo sunt contrarie. Nec ignoro quod apprehensio unius contrariorum stat cum assensu alterius.'

[193] *In Ethicam*, 109v. EN 1147b2, Mair here uses the phrase *per accidens* from the translation of Argyropoulos.

[194] *In Ethicam*, 110r.

[195] *In Ethicam*, 110r: 'Evenit igitur quodammodo non inepte quem Socrates percontabatur. Universalis est firma atque perseverans, qua praesente non est perturbatio. Neque ob passionem scientia distrahitur, sed singularis et sensitiva quaedam.'

[196] *In Ethicam*, 110r: 'Dubitatur an aliquis potest assentiri maiori atque minori perfecte et actu in agibilibus, et contravenire iudicio conclusionis per libertatem voluntatis. Affirmative respondetur. Pertrita enim est distinctio illa magistralis: aliquod est peccatum ex infirmitate, quando quispiam perturbatione victus perperam agit. Aliquod ex ignoratione emergit, et tertium quando quispiam ex industria, electione et scienter male agit.'

says that we are masters of our actions from the beginning to the end, he actually means this continuous consciousness. Mair finally mentions that some Parisian articles of 1277 point out that sins proceed from free will.[197]

Mair's strategy of collecting both intellectualist and voluntarist evidence is reminiscent of another Parisian commentator on EN, John Buridan (1.5). Buridan likewise underlines the importance of the Parisian articles and their alleged voluntarism while arguing that the akratic reasoning proceeds in an Aristotelian manner. There is also a strategic similarity between Mair and Buridan: Mair first portrays the Aristotelian view and then asks critically how it relates to the Christian view of the freedom of the will. Buridan first adheres to Aristotelian intellectualism but finally holds that, because of faith and moral responsibility, the freedom of the will must be believed in. This twofold strategy is then applied to Buridan's extensive discussion on the Parisian articles, Aristotle's theory of action, and akrasia.[198]

Like Buridan, Mair wants to defend the final compatibility of Aristotelian action theory with free will. He begins his discussion by offering three 'solutions'. The first and second concern the will's own activity in its relationship to the intellect:

First, I answer that the will prompts action if it is not prevented. But it can be prevented by the effective opposition of the will. Second, the Philosopher thinks that when reason is used, perturbation can blind it unless forcefully resisted. The perturbation can lead a person like roped cattle so that action follows. The powerless person does not then obey the power of the intellect and its judgement but acts from evil will.[199]

The first point resembles the view of the Parisian articles and Buridan which ascribe to the will a right of veto, the possibility of remaining in the state of *non velle*.[200] The second point interprets Aristotle in a somewhat 'commonplace Platonist' manner (cf. 1.1), claiming that the conflict between reason and desire features prominently in action theory and that desire can sometimes overcome reason. We already saw in the

---

[197] *In Ethicam*, 110r: 'A stipulatur deiloquus Lucas 12. capite sui evangelii scribens: Servus qui cogovit voluntatem domini sui et non facit, plagis vapulabit multis. Et Iacobus cap. 4 scribit: Scienti bonum facere et non facienti peccatum est illi. Ratione idem patet: Multi enim peccat cum propositio poenitendi de hoc quod agunt. Huius sententiae est August. super illud passum: Forte vivos deglutissent nos, Ubi ait vivi absorbentur qui sciunt malum esse et consentiunt [Augustine, *Enarr. in Ps.* 123, 5]. Idem super illud: fiat mensa eorum coram ipsis in laqueum, quod est scientes vitio consentire. Ecce noverunt muscipulam et imittunt pedem. [*Enarr. in Ps.* 68, 7]. Et Aristoteles quinto capite tertii ethicorum ait: Actuum enim a principio usque ad finem domini sumus, habituum vero principii. Ad hoc sunt articuli aliquot Parisienses bene stringentes.'

[198] See Buridan, *Quaestiones*, Book III q1–5 and Book VII. Saarinen (1994), 166–83.

[199] *In Ethicam*, 110r: 'Nunc autem superest autoritatem (gratia cuius in hanc dubitationem incidimus) evacuare. Plurifariam respondeo, tum primo quod voluntas operatur si non impediatur. Impeditur autem per efficax reluctamen voluntatis. 2. intelligit philosophus stante rationis usu, perturbatio homini rationem nisi viriliter renitatur adimit, ita quod pecuino more in capistro abducitur, et sic sequitur operatio, quia homo ignavia succumbit non vi intellectus aut eius iudicii sed ex voluntatis malitia.'

[200] See Saarinen (1994), 168. One Parisian article, see Lerner and Mahdi (1989), 350 holds that it is erroneous in philosophy to claim 'that it is impossible for the will not to will (*non velle*) when it is in the disposition in which it is natural for it to be moved and when that which by nature moves remains so disposed.'

cases of Acciaiuoli (2.2) and Clichtove (2.4) that this kind of conflict or struggle *(pugna)* was increasingly associated with akrasia during the Renaissance.

The third solution compares akrasia with the so-called mixed actions which are discussed in EN III, 1 (EN 1110a8–11):

Third, Aristotle speaks of the major premise of the practical syllogism as something to which the will adheres; for instance when I want to save my life in a seastorm and judge that the only means of achieving this is to throw my things or goods overboard; then this volition of throwing goods overboard is naturally followed. This is applied to Aristotle's example as follows: pleasure offers a reason concerning the end, and this end is desired as such. With regard to actions, the end is a moving principle so that when somebody effectively wills pleasure with this woman and considers that this is the only means of achieving pleasure, he necessarily proceeds to this means.[201]

Although Buridan also speaks of akrasia as involving a mixed will,[202] this comparison is original in its claim that Aristotle's discussion of the mixed actions in EN III, 1 resembles akrasia, although the person in the storm does not ignore or forget anything.

Mair considers that all three solutions are compatible with the Parisian articles and the will's freedom.[203] While he has shown that the will prompts that action which has been deliberated and commanded by the intellect, he has also pointed out that the will plays some autonomous role in the process of such deliberation.

Now, given that right reason is blinded and the deliberation proceeds with the wrong syllogism, which recommends pleasure, the third solution holds that the goal of pleasure and the means leading to it are followed if no external hindrance is present. Yet it is also the case that the will has freely chosen its adherence to the wrong major premise; this elicited act pertaining to the end of pleasure is then followed by the 'natural' emergence of the external action (in contrast to free will) by means of the practical syllogism. Mair also remarks that this description of akrasia presupposes that the imperative of misleading major premise and conclusion *(est gustandum)* is not understood as a statement of moral worth but as a kind of effective indicative; that is, as a rule which prompts action.[204]

---

[201] *In Ethicam*, 110r: '3. sic Aristoteles loquitur de maiore ut est practica, cui voluntas consonat. Ut si in periculo maris volo servare vitam, et iudico hoc medium solum mihi relictum, eiicere meas arcas aut merces in mare, naturaliter volitio extrudendi communicatur. Et applica id ad Aristotelicum exemplum sic, delectatio habet rationem finis et per se appetibilis a tali, in agibilibus finis est principium, ita quod cum efficaciter vult delectationem cum hac muliere, et censet hoc medium solum relictum, de necessitate in illud medium fertur.'

[202] Buridan, *Quaestiones*, 143va (587). Saarinen (1994), 175.

[203] *In Ethicam*, 110r: 'Ex nulla harum trium solutionum sequitur aliqua diaphania cum articulis Parisiensibus aut libertate voluntatis.'

[204] *In Ethicam*, 110r: 'Secunda via loquitur de ratione adempta. Prima et secunda ratione facta, omne dulce est gustandum, hoc est dulce, proinde hoc est gustandum, capiendo gustandum ut tantum valet quantum gustabitur et non dignum gustari. Modo volens efficaciter aliquem finem, sciens hoc esse medium ad illum finem, de necessitate operatur si non praepediatur. Tametsi voluntas suum actum elicitum libere eliceat, illa volitio naturaliter actum exteriorem obice secluso producit; et volitio finis cum notitia medii ad illud finem, medium ponit, si obex non ponatur.'

Although this logically precise formulation of akratic action should be regarded as Mair's original contribution, the inner dynamic of this solution is fairly close to the model advanced in Thomas Aquinas's theological works. In Thomas's 'two-step' model of akrasia, the slide or shift from the right reason to the wrong syllogism occurs without conscious choice (first step). However, when the akratic person then follows pleasure, he or she adheres to the wrong major premise and to the goal of pleasure with choice (*eligens*, second step; cf. 1.3). When Mair claims that the akratic will adheres to (*consonat*) and freely chooses (*libere elicit*) the wrong major premise and the goal expressed by it, he is basically making the same claim as Aquinas with regard to the so-called 'second step'.

In spite of this affinity with Aquinas, Mair's style and strategy is finally closer to Buridan's explanation of akrasia. Mair and Buridan underline the voluntaristic nature of the Parisian articles and seek opportunities to show their compatibility with Aristo-telian action theory. Although Thomas also defends free will and the consent theory of morality, especially in his theological works, Buridan and Mair are closer to voluntar-ism than Aquinas.

After offering these solutions, Mair discusses four counter-arguments or questions. The first deals with the possibility of having simultaneous contrary judgements, a theme which already played a role in Albert and later in Buridan and Wellendorffer (1.5, 2.3). Unlike Albert, Mair denies any real contrariety, claiming that the right and the wrong major syllogism are just 'different judgements' (*diversa iudicia*) which are by no means contrary to one another.[205]

This claim is fairly close to Aristotle's syllogistic discussion in EN 1147a28–b3. Mair draws the further conclusion that the following two propositions are compossible: 'Nothing shameful is to be followed' and 'Something shameful is to be followed'. The second proposition does not then express a moral judgement but again expresses an effective indicative, that is, a statement which prompts action.[206] With regard to the history of akrasia, this semantic duality of the expression *est faciendum* needs to be identified as Mair's own innovation, which allows him to preserve the action-prompt-ing stringency of Aristotle's practical syllogism while also claiming that the two major premises available in the akratic mind do not involve contrary judgements.

We have seen that for both Albert the Great and Wellendorffer the akratic phenomenon does involve 'contrary acceptances' or 'contrary judgements'. For Bur-idan, the presence of akrasia implies a 'twofold inclination' of the mind. To avoid

---

[205] *In Ethicam*, 110r: 'In proposito nostro de eadem re diversa iudicia nullo modo contraria ad contrarium scopum tendentia insudant. Mulier est speciosa, hoc pacto allectiva ad sui copulam. Ratio ex contrario syllogisat: nullum inhonestum est patrandum, coire cum hac est inhonestum, itaque non est patrandum. Ecce discursum secundum rationem. Ex altera parte: omnis speciosa foemina est cognoscenda, hec est huiusmodi, igitur. Nulla est contrarietas inter has maiores. De singularibus propositionibus non est questio, illae enim nec inter se nec cum aliis pugnant.'

[206] *In Ethicam*, 110r: 'Iterum dico quod hae duae se mutuo compatiuntur: nullum inhonestum est faciendum, aliquod inhonestum est faciendum, capiendo faciendum in negativa pro illo quod est factu dignum, et in affirmativa pro illo quod fiet.'

simultaneous contrary judgements, Aquinas prefers to underline the temporary ignorance of one of the two incompossible alternatives. Mair offers a new solution: the
major premise of that syllogism which becomes operative in the akratic mind does not
grasp the phrase 'is to be followed' as a moral judgement but as a performative or
effective indicative. Thus *non est faciendum* (as moral judgement) and *est faciendum* (as
effective indicative) are compossible.

The second and third questions deal with the inner dialogue that takes place in the
akratic mind.[207] Mair replies that the voice of conscience causes dissent within the
akratic soul. This can be compared to the situation of the greedy merchant who needs
to throw goods overboard in a storm at sea. The arguments of conscience point
towards honesty while the passion prompts the soul in the other direction so that the
intellect also invents sophistical reasons in favour of pleasure. This inner conflict is not,
however, an elaborate discourse but either a quick judgement or an apprehension
leading towards pleasure.[208]

Mair's references to the mixed actions (the merchant in the storm) as illustration of
akrasia highlight an essential and original feature of his interpretation of EN VII: the
akratic mind need not, strictly speaking, ignore anything, as the various reasons are not
logically contrary to one another but remain compossible. Logically speaking, there
may be clear-eyed akrasia in which the person follows the effective indicative (*pro illo
quod fiet*) while knowing in his or her conscience that such actions are not worthy (*non
est factu dignum*). In a similar, although not in all respects identical manner, the merchant
in the storm neither ignores anything nor has contrary judgements. He willingly
follows the alternative which he chooses; in doing so, he employs a syllogistic structure
but is also aware of other options.

It should be remembered that Mair is defending 'clear-eyed akrasia' throughout the
second half of his exposition of EN VII, 3; that is, the thesis that because of free will one
can know the right major and minor premise perfectly and nevertheless act contrary to
their conclusion. The introduction of 'mixed actions' as a parallel case to akrasia serves
the purpose of showing how clear-eyed akrasia can occur. Likewise, the introduction
of the dual sense of the phrase *est faciendum* shows that the agent can keep the right
major and minor premise in mind while acting akratically. Because of this overall
purpose, some discrepancy between the first and the second half of the exposition of
EN VII, 3 finally remains. The first half discusses Aristotle's teaching in which some
ignorance is presupposed. The second half shows that one can embrace Aristotelian

---

[207] *In Ethicam*, 110r: 'Secundo, quomodo fuit hic discursus. Tertio, an opus est hoc longo discursu,
incontinenti ut habeat duas maiores cum duabus aliis propositionibus.'

[208] *In Ethicam*, 110r–v: 'In ipso incontinente si remorsus consciencie insurgat etsi doctus extiterit est civile
dissidium, sicut in avaro mercatore . . . Ita est in ipso incontinente, signanter non deiecto animo, honestum
provocat eum ne in foedum ruat, et deum irritet, et famam denigret, passio stimulans facit intellectum
invenire sophismata pro illius inclinatione. Interdum non est iste discursus mente sed iudicium sine discursu,
vel simplex apprehensio, ita quod appetitus sensitivus ad delectabile inclinatus maiorem et conclusionem
supplet, quicunque sit syllogismus ad partem inficiatoriam.'

ideas, such as the practical syllogism, and yet claim that clear-eyed akrasia is possible. In showing this, Mair employs Aquinas and Buridan, but he actually goes beyond both in his non-Aristotelian claim that clear-eyed akrasia is possible.

The fourth and final question is whether concupiscence can move the human potencies to action. Mair's answer is affirmative: when concupiscence is judged 'under the aspect of goodness' (sub ratione boni), it moves the will towards action, given that the mind is perturbed and regards something as good which is otherwise regarded as bad.[209] To prove this, Mair gives quotes from the Bible and Aristotle. He also teaches that the will as an intellectual appetite tends to descend to the level of the sensitive appetite if reason does not inform it otherwise. The desires of the sensitive appetite may further obscure the reason and thus affect the will indirectly.[210] All these points are basically corollaries of the above-mentioned second solution, showing that Mair in his peculiar way continues the notion of commonplace Platonist conflict between reason and passion.

The last sub-theme of the fourth question is how this influence of concupiscence relates to the Aristotelian doctrine that the higher potency moves the lower one. Mair replies that the will moves the sensitive appetite like a politician or a ruler moves his subjects: they cooperate under the leadership of the higher power but cannot be forced. Paul's example in Romans 7 shows that the will cannot be effective without the cooperation of the lower powers. On the other hand, the will can autonomously refuse its cooperation with the lower powers and so prevent the sinful actions.[211] This possibility of non consentire is basically the phenomenon which is described in the first solution above.

John Mair's discussion on akrasia in his exposition of EN VII, 3 is particularly rich and innovative. He combines various medieval and Renaissance traditions in an original but nevertheless highly consistent manner. He is also able to offer new insights into the difficult problems of intellectualism and voluntarism, as well as the logical and semantic analysis of the practical syllogism. He is thus philosophically more innovative than the earlier Renaissance commentators discussed in 2.2–2.4.

At the same time, Mair belongs to the era of scholasticism rather than to the humanist movement. Although his Latin is considerably richer than that of the medievals, his argumentative style and method are reminiscent of Thomas Aquinas

---

[209] In Ethicam, 110v: 'Ad quartum an concupiscentia hominem ad inique agendum moveat. Respondetur affirmative, apprehensum sub ratione boni voluntatem movet ad persequendum, quando quispiam perturbatur censet nonnihil esse bonum quod alioqui malum censeret.'

[210] In Ethicam, 110v.

[211] In Ethicam, 110v: 'Insultas, voluntas appetitum sensitivum movet primo ethicorum, modo movens non movetur ab eo quod movet, ut sit motio reciproca octavo physicorum. Respondetur quod voluntas appetitum sensitivum motu politico et non despotico movet. Non enim principatur illi more heri in servum, sed more principis in subditum, cui plerumque recalcitrat nisi homo obsistat, etiam in viris heroicis teste deiloquuo Paulo ad Rom. septimo. Non enim quod volo bonum hoc ago, sed quod odi malum illud facio. Non enim potest voluntas agere quin appetitus sensitivus insurgat, sed potest illi non consentire, et facere ne ullum sit peccatum.'

and, in particular, John Buridan. Unlike Acciaiuoli, Mair does not merely propose upgrading the scholastic positions using more elegant language and better translation, but primarily intends to deepen the philosophical issues. Unlike Clichtove, Mair is not interested in inventing new examples and defending clear-eyed akrasia with the help of commonplace Platonism. Although Mair highlights the conflict between reason and desire in somewhat Platonic terms, his intellectual focus remains on the syllogistic explanation of the theoretical possibility of clear-eyed akrasia. Because of all these features, Mair's discussion is both highly traditional and highly original. In terms of our classification in 1.5, Mair belongs to both Buridanism and voluntarism; his model could be called 'logically refined Buridanism'.

Mair's later chapters on akrasia also offer philosophically interesting and original material. We can only highlight a couple of exemplary texts. In his discussion on akrasia and good choice in EN VII, 8 and 10, Mair basically follows the Aristotelian view that the akratês has a good choice and that he therefore does not sin 'from choice' (*ex electione*). Because the intemperate person sins from choice and does not repent, his human condition is worse than that of the akratic person.[212]

In this connection, Mair evokes the issue of whether continent actions could nevertheless be more meritorious than temperate actions. Because continent people need to struggle with harmful desires, they need more effort to do good; thus their personal merit might be greater than that of temperate people who can easily do good. Mair considers that merit and culpability need to be seen in relationship to the particular issue, since it may be that some continent actions are more meritorious than some temperate actions.[213]

In keeping with this idea, Mair also teaches that the akratic person's sin may be more grave than that of the intemperate. The general condition of the intemperate person is in many respects worse than that of the incontinent, and Aristotle's classification should be understood from that point of view. The akratic person nevertheless sins more gravely,[214] because the akratic person knows the good and thus sins against conscience, whereas the intemperate does not violate his conscience in the same way.[215]

Although this non-Aristotelian conclusion may seem surprising, it is in keeping with the decisions undertaken in the exposition of EN VII, 2–3. Since Mair has pleaded for

---

[212] *In Ethicam*, 115v; 117v.

[213] *In Ethicam*, 116r.

[214] *In Ethicam*, 116r: 'Dico etiam incontinentem plus peccare circa eandem materiam quam intemperatum, attamen est in deteriori casu cum difficulter sit emendabilis, et sic est peior incontinenti. Adde quod saepius in demeritorum cumulo ob defectum poenitudinis illaqueatus, et sic est incontinenti deterior. Ex hic Aristotelem intelligere potes. Licet intemperatus ex sua culpa conscientiam violavit, cuius conscientia primo erat semilacera, postea prorsus conculcata, et sic ex sua culpa agendorum ignorantiam contraxit, et per consequens non est excusandus. Nihilo tamen minus incontinens crebriter gravius quam intemperatus peccat, etiam ante poenitentiam, quia omnia illa solum finite aggravant peccatum intemperati.'

[215] *In Ethicam*, 116r: 'Unus actus incontinentis vel actus eius communiter contingentes sunt deteriores quam actus similes intemperati. Monstro id, incontinens contra suam conscientiam peccat, non autem intemperatus. Servus autem sciens voluntatem domini sui, et non faciens eam, plagis vapulabit multis, Lucae 12.'

clear-eyed akrasia, ignorance is no longer an alleviating circumstance. We saw that Mair had already highlighted the role of conscience in his exposition of EN VII, 2. Now he draws the conclusion that the akratic person acts against his conscience, whereas it is the intemperate who remains in some sense ignorant of the relevant moral truths. It is also remarkable that Mair distinguishes between better and worse human conditions on the one hand, and the quantity of merit and culpability on the other. This non-Aristotelian distinction allows him to hold that an agent with a better general condition may nevertheless be more culpable than some other agents whose general condition remains worse. In some sense, Mair thus replaces Aristotelian virtue ethics with another scale of merit and culpability.

Another original topic is evoked in the context of EN VII, 10, in which Mair asks whether somebody can be continent without the gift of God.[216] The formulation relates to the Wisdom of Solomon 8:21, a biblical text which was relevant for Augustine's *Confessions* (1.2) and was later occasionally quoted in the context of akrasia. Since in scholasticism ethics was taught in the philosophical faculty, a theological issue such as this is not normally discussed as a distinct topic. Mair explicitly says that he now will proceed from philosophy to theology. He quotes several passages from the Bible and Augustine to show that this kind of special help (*auxilium dei speciale*) is needed for continence.[217]

The objections to this view ask whether the requirement of divine help means that no human action can take place autonomously. This seems not to be the case; for instance, Socrates can abstain from fornication without special divine help. Mair replies that God gives this help to everyone in principle; in addition, human activity is needed to produce good works. He also holds, in keeping with the general idea of the freedom of *non velle* discussed above, that no special divine help is needed for acts of abstaining from some evil. If the person could not refrain from acting, he would not be free (*libertate potest non agere, alioqui non sit liber*). Mair adds, however, that the church fathers can also speak of divine aid of this kind.[218]

These exemplary texts testify to Mair's ability to formulate new and original views as well as his aim of integrating philosophical and theological issues. Although Mair in many ways remains on scholastic grounds, the innovative features of his exposition actually depart from medieval Aristotelianism. Such features include (1) a postulate of dual meaning in the imperative verb of the practical syllogism; (2) an understanding of Aristotle's 'mixed actions' as a parallel to akrasia; (3) arguing for the possibility of clear-eyed akrasia with the help of (1) and (2); (4) systematic integration of the notions of free will and conscience into the discussion on akrasia; and (5) an understanding of merit and culpability as relatively independent from Aristotelian virtue and vice.

---

[216] *In Ethicam*, 118r: 'An quis potest esse continens sine munere dei, hoc est speciali dei ope.'

[217] *In Ethicam*, 118r. For the notion of *auxilium speciale* in late medieval theology, see Burger (1981).

[218] *In Ethicam*, 118r–v.

These points allow Mair to argue that human action takes place within the structure of the practical syllogism while it also proceeds from free will. The akratic person acts against his own conscience and is therefore gravely culpable. At the same time, the akratic action is not merely the fruit of irrationality or a despotic will, also proceeding under the aspect of goodness and within the Aristotelian framework of the practical syllogism. Because Mair originally combines strongly intellectualistic and strongly voluntaristic features, his view of akrasia is not easy to classify in terms of our heuristic models. His model is in many respects close to Buridan, but while Buridan holds that the free will must be believed without philosophical proofs, Mair presents new arguments which show the compatibility of free will and Aristotelian action theory. His view of akrasia can therefore be labelled 'logically refined Buridanism'.

2.6 Francesco Piccolomini's Harmonization of Different Traditions

The *Universa philosophia de moribus* by Francesco Piccolomini (1523–1607) enjoyed great popularity during the last decades of the Renaissance. The work appeared first in Venice in 1583 and was then slightly revised in the second edition in Venice 1594. This edition was reprinted in Frankfurt in 1595, 1601, 1611, and 1627 as well as in Geneva in 1596.[219] As the publication of several editions in Frankfurt shows, the work was widely read and commented on in Protestant universities. Recent studies have underlined the theoretical and systematic significance of Piccolomini's work for the history of ethics.[220]

De moribus is not a commentary on EN but a systematic textbook of ethics. Its immediate historical context belongs to a controversy between Jacobo Zabarella and Piccolomini regarding the correct pedagogical method in teaching ethics. Piccolomini adheres to a somewhat non-Aristotelian 'analytical' method in which the teacher begins with lower and more immediate topics and proceeds to the higher goals and the final nature of things only towards the end of his presentation.[221] Because of this procedure, the work is divided into ten 'steps' (*gradus*): the first step deals with the perturbations of the soul, the fourth step with the virtues, and the ninth step with the highest good.[222] The discussion on continence and incontinence takes place at the third step, entitled 'On half-virtues and powers leading to virtue' (*De semivirtute et viis ad virtutem*).

---

[219] Lines (2002), 511. I use the Frankfurt 1595 edition.

[220] Schmitt (1983b); Kraye (1995); Lines (2002), 254–5. Lines (2002), 254–88 informs of the historical context and basic content of Piccolomini's work.

[221] On this method and controversy with Zabarella, see Lines (2002), 254–65.

[222] On all ten steps and their mutual relation, see Lines (2002), 264–5. The steps are different from the five 'loves' discussed in Ficino's *De amore* 6, 8 (Ficino, *Commentary*, 118–20), but both exemplify a certain Platonic elevation of virtue.

Throughout his work, Piccolomini is concerned with the relationship between Plato and Aristotle. He often points out the differences between the two philosophers but also attempts to reconcile their teachings. He does not claim to have achieved a perfect reconciliation but does highlight their distinct emphases and their positive value.[223] Piccolomini is mostly critical with regard to Stoicism.[224] He employs a great variety of classical, patristic, medieval, and Renaissance sources, underlining the positive significance of Christianity, that is, Counter-Reformation Catholicism, for ethics.[225] But, as the popularity of his book among the Protestants shows, this feature does not obscure his philosophical discussion, which is dominated by the attempt to mediate between Plato and Aristotle.

The discussion on akrasia takes place in chapters 13–21 of the third step. While this discussion is focused on the classical problem of acting against better judgement, the focus is broadened from the text of EN to include not only Plato but the general problem of sinning knowingly and voluntarily as well. The chapter headings are as follows:

Ch.13: On endurance and continence, whether they exist.

Ch.14: What are continence and endurance?

Ch.15: Whether one sins knowingly.

Ch.16: Whether one can err with regard to moral knowledge.

Ch.17: Whether man becomes evil and sins voluntarily, Plato's opinion.

Ch.18: Whether man becomes evil voluntarily, Aristotle's opinion.

Ch.19: The refutation of arguments presented in favour of the Platonists.

Ch.20: Whether Aristotle can be reconciled with Plato.

Ch.21: Who sins more, one who goes wrong voluntarily or one who goes wrong reluctantly?[226]

Although the Aristotelian problem of akrasia is discussed primarily and explicitly in chapter 16, the chapters form a systematic unity. Chapters 13 and 14 give a basic definition of concepts. The problem of sinning knowingly and voluntarily is then systematically treated in chapters 15–21. Piccolomini also keeps in mind the Aristotelian concepts of endurance and softness. Instead of the usual Latin term *constantia*, he

---

[223] Lines (2002), 281–4 discusses these features in detail.

[224] Lines (2002), 266.

[225] For Piccolomini's sources, see Lines (2002), 266–85.

[226] *De moribus*, 252–68: '13 De tolerantia et continentia, an sint.

14 Quid sit continentia, et tolerantia.

15 An sciens peccat.

16 An sciens in attinentibus ad mores errare possit.

17 An homo sponte fiat malus, sponteque peccet, opinio Platonis.

18 An homo sponte fiat malus, opinio Aristotelis.

19 Diluuntur rationes pro parte Academicorum formata.

20 An Aristoteles cum Platone conciliari possit.

21 Qui peccet magis, num qui sponte, vel qui invitus aberrat.'

translates endurance as *tolerantia*, probably because the term constancy expresses a higher virtue. While akrasia and continence deal with passions related to pleasure, softness and endurance are concerned with resisting the passion of anger. Continence and endurance thus relate to obedience in the inner life of the soul.[227] Piccolomini can say that whereas continence relates to 'internal enemies', endurance is concerned with the 'external' ones, meaning that the objects of anger are found in the external world.[228] We will focus our analysis on continence and incontinence.[229]

According to Aristotle, Socrates denies the existence of continence when he is said to claim that there is no such thing as incontinence (EN 1145b25). The same doctrine is expressed in Plato's *Protagoras*: in this dialogue Socrates teaches that nobody is evil voluntarily and that no one can sin knowingly. All sin is due to ignorance. Reason and knowledge direct action so that everyone aims at achieving some good.[230] Therefore, all who choose between the greater and the lesser good, choose the greater good. As a result, the Socratic and Platonic view denies incontinence, because the akratic person 'sees the better and approves it, but follows the worse', as Ovid says of Medea.[231] And if there is no akrasia, neither is there any continence, because the same reasoning pertains to both: seemingly akratic actions can be reduced to intemperance, whereas seemingly continent behaviour is indistinguishable from temperance.[232]

It is important to see that Piccolomini does not refer here to the so-called 'commonplace Platonism' which would admit a real conflict between reason and desire, following instead the strictly Socratic-Platonic logic of *Protagoras* (cf. 1.1). He underlines this by saying that reason is the leading power of the soul and that the appetitive part does not desire anything else than that which has been judged to be good. Such knowledge cannot be obscured by the adverse powers which do not represent knowledge. If desire prevails, it is only a weak opinion, not knowledge that has been overcome.[233]

---

[227] *De moribus*, 252; EN 1145a35–b20.

[228] *De moribus*, 254.

[229] The theme of endurance only plays some role in chapter 14. Although Piccolomini says in the beginning of chapter 15 that the issues at stake pertain to continence and endurance similarly, his later discussion focuses on to the problems of akrasia and voluntary wrongdoing.

[230] *De moribus*, 252: 'inquit Aristoteles in septimo moralium Nicomachiorum, capite secundo. Socrates, perinde quasi nulla sit continentia... Haec legere unusquisque potest apud Platonem in Protagora: in eo enim dialogo Socrates cum Protagora disputans nititur ostendere, neminem sponte esse malum, scientem non posse peccare, sed omnes, qui peccant, per inscientiam delinquere. Vis autem rationis eius in eo est posita: quia omne agens agit in gratiam boni.'

[231] *De moribus*, 252–3: 'omnis electio est ipsius boni, minus bonum relatum ad maius obtinet locum mali, quare a nullo minus bonum eligitur, dum iudicat id esse minus bonum. Ex quo infertur non dari incontinentiam, nam incontinens ille dicitur, qui videt meliora, eaque probat, tamen deteriora sequitur.'

[232] *De moribus*, 253: 'Si autem non datur incontinentia, apparet neque continentiam dari posse, quia oppositorum eadem est ratio. Sed ut incontinentia ad intemperantiam redigitur, ita continentia a temperantia non distinguetur.'

[233] *De moribus*, 253: 'scientia est habitus firmus et constans, est dux humanarum actionum, proterea dum ea viget, et per adversam inscitiam non obumbratur, necesse est ut ducat. Appetitus autem nil aliud appetit, nisi id quod iudicio approbatur, nec alio tendit, quam quo a scientia et cognitione ducitur... si nonnunquam videmur aliquid approbare, et aliud sequi, id evenit, quoniam ea non est scientia, sed opinio, quae ab opposita potentiore vincitur.'

Aristotle, on the other hand, affirms the existence of incontinence, arguing contrary to the Platonic view. Aristotle holds that our experience teaches that there are incontinent and soft actions. In moral matters, experience is to be regarded as a particularly strong argument (*ratio efficacissima*).[234] We know from experience that an akratic person who is asked whether he acts rightly answers that he deserts the better alternative and follows the worse. Such a person does not assert that the desire is to be preferred; he only considers that he is weak or impotent and cannot resist passions.[235] In this manner, 'the common consent of humankind discloses this truth: all people affirm that there are those who "see the better and approve it, but follow the worse"'.[236]

The truth of Medea's statement is apparent in the behaviour of wrongdoers. Although their passions lead them to akratic deeds, they warn their friends and relatives not to do the same.[237] When people follow their passion contrary to reason, they are ashamed. In such a case, we perceive the inner struggle and the internal reproach saying, for instance: 'Why am I doing this insane thing?' In this way, the inner compunction of the akratic person prevents his or her full enjoyment of the desire. Such experiences prove the existence of akrasia abundantly.[238]

Because Piccolomini intends lively and many-sided description rather than conceptual precision, this portrayal of akrasia raises some questions. The akratic behaviour described here seems to go beyond Aristotle in claiming that there is clear-eyed akrasia in which the person is led by the passions contrary to the continuous warnings of reason. Medea's words depict a clear-eyed akrasia which is not, as we have seen in the case of Clichtove (2.4), an Aristotelian way of describing weakness of will. Piccolomini's claim that the akratic person does not assert that the passion is good, simply assenting his or her powerlessness, likewise runs contrary to the Aristotelian scholasticism in which the alternative effectively willed must appear 'under the aspect of goodness'. A declaration of powerlessness resembles the 'commonplace Platonist' (1.1, 2.4) struggle between reason and desire. Piccolomini thus connects Aristotle's affirmation of akrasia with 'commonplace Platonism'.

---

[234] *De moribus*, 253.

[235] *De moribus*, 253: 'Experimur enim, quod vir incontinens, dum labitur in voluptates, et vir mollis, qui non tolerat dolores, interrogati an recte agant, ipsimet fatentur se vitium sequi, se deserere id quod melius, non autem asserunt se voluptatem pluris existimare. Solum aiunt se impotentes esse, et non posse vehementibus perturbationibus obsistere, et unusquisque insemetipso id ipsum experitur.'

[236] *De moribus*, 253: 'communis hominum consensio hanc veritatem patefacit, omnes enim uno ore affirmant inveniri eos, qui vident meliora, probantque, deteriora sequuntur.' For the sentence of Medea (Ovid, *Metam.* 7, 20–1), see 1.2 and 2.4.

[237] *De moribus*, 253: 'Insuper illimet, qui perturbatione ducti scelus patrant, frequenter filios et amicos rogant, ac deprecantur, ne idipsum agant, et nedum deprecantur, verum etiam imperant illis, quibus imperare valent.'

[238] *De moribus*, 254: 'Dum derelicta virtute per rationem approbata, voluptatem sequimur, verecundamur; ac insuper internam percipimus pugnam, internam reprehensionem, internumque rationis sermonem dicentis: Quo tedis miser, quo infamis progrederis? Cur tam perdite ruis? Cur ita insanis? Quae interna compunctio non permittit, ut toto animo voluptate fruamur. Haec adeo manifeste nobis vim incontinentiae patefaciunt.'

At this point (Ch. 13) Piccolomini is only interested in showing that there is something which can be called akrasia. The next chapter (Ch. 14) defines akrasia in more detail. Piccolomini first distinguishes continence from temperance in a traditional manner: a temperate person does not need to struggle with her passions; her virtuous life is without struggle (*sine pugna*). The continent person continues to struggle with bad desires, her life being characterized by this struggle (*cum pugna*). Piccolomini asks the same question as John Mair (2.5): if the continent person needs to struggle, does she then display a greater virtue than the temperate person? Piccolomini does not, however, introduce the concept of personal merit in this context. He answers the question with reference to the objective order of goodness in which temperance represents a true virtue, whereas continence remains a half-virtue.[239]

Piccolomini describes the Aristotelian distinction between weak and precipitate akrasia; he also considers that a person can be soft (*inconstans*) in these two ways. He defines continence as 'a virtuous affection which follows right reason so that a person can abstain from the remaining passions of lust'.[240] A continent person is 'like a soldier who constantly fights with a powerful enemy'.[241] The vision of struggle (*pugna*) brings Piccolomini's own view again close to the model of 'commonplace Platonism'.

At the beginning of chapter 15, Piccolomini introduces his two major questions to be asked in this context: first, whether one can sin knowingly, and second, whether one becomes good or wicked willingly or reluctantly.[242] The first problem is discussed in chapters 15–16 and the second in chapters 17–21. As can be seen from the chapter headings and later formulations, Piccolomini varies his formulations of the problems. Basically, the first question is Aristotle's problem in EN VII; the second investigates Plato's claim in *Protagoras* that no one does wrong voluntarily and Aristotle's discussion of it in EN III, 5. As there is considerable overlap between the two questions in chapters 17–21, one could also say that the first question represents a narrower special case, whereas the second investigates the general problems of voluntary action.

With regard to the first question, Piccolomini introduces the tripartite division of knowledge into theoretical, practical (moral), and productive. Piccolomini shows that one can consciously act contrary to one's own knowledge in the realms of theoretical and productive knowledge. A physician who uses medical knowledge to kill somebody is an example of the latter kind; the phenomenon of telling lies is often an example of the former. Thus there is hardly any controversy with regard to these two modes of knowledge; however, the first problem evokes many difficulties with regard to moral knowledge.[243]

---

[239] *De moribus*, 254–5.

[240] *De moribus*, 255: 'Continentia...est enim affectio proba sequens rationem rectam, qua homo se abstinet a voluptatibus repugnante cupiditate.'

[241] *De moribus*, 255: 'Continens se habet ut miles, qui constanter cum hoste forti pugnat.'

[242] *De moribus*, 256: 'Ut exacte pateant pertinentia ad continentiam et tolerantiam, duo magni ponderis, accurataque consideratione digna explicare tenemur. Primum est, an sciens peccare valeat; alterum vero, an homo sponte vel invitus bonus vel malus fiat.'

[243] *De moribus*, 256–7.

Chapter 16 is devoted to these difficulties. Piccolomini first repeats Plato's view that knowledge cannot be overcome by lower powers and one can thus err only because of ignorance. In addition, Piccolomini says that Aristotle seems to contradict himself (*a seipso dissentire videtur*). On the one hand, Aristotle shares the view that nothing is stronger than knowledge and holds that desire must be intellectually judged to be good in order to be followed. On the other hand, Aristotle's discussion on akrasia seems to say that 'the incontinent sees the better but follows the worse'.[244]

To resolve this alleged discrepancy, Piccolomini makes three traditional distinctions in chapter 16. The first and third distinctions are taken from EN VII, 3: one can know something either actually or habitually, and one can know something either in universal or in singular terms. The second distinction is made between exact and perfect knowledge on the one hand, and uncertain opinion on the other. The distinction between knowledge and opinion is made by both Plato and Aristotle (EN VII, 2). With the help of these distinctions, Piccolomini draws two conclusions or 'assertions'. First, one can go wrong in moral matters when something is known habitually but this knowledge is not actually used.[245]

The second assertion is also traditional:

A person can err when he knows something in a confused and unclear manner, or when he knows the common terms but not the singulars, or when he knows something under the cloud of strong perturbation, not knowing precisely. Plato in *Protagoras* calls such seduction under perturbation great ineptness. This shows that Aristotle neither dissents from himself nor from Plato.[246]

At the end of chapter 16, Piccolomini repeats twice that the akratic person knows his error habitually but not actually.[247] Thus his discussion of Aristotle's akrasia in chapter 16 follows the traditional lines of medieval intellectualism. What is original is the comparison with Plato and the attempt at reconciliation between the two philosophers. Because of this reconciliation, Aristotle is read in chapter 16 in a fairly intellectualist manner.

It is nevertheless strange that Piccolomini first appeals several times to Medea's case as a proper illustration of Aristotle's akrasia and then claims that the incontinent person cannot know the relevant facts in a clear and distinct manner. Piccolomini's answer to his first question is therefore not altogether consistent, at least compared to many careful scholastic commentators. Piccolomini does not intend any scholastic sophistication of the issue. Medea and Aristotle both witness the existence of akrasia, which is basically proved by our everyday experience of situations characterized by an inner struggle

---

[244] *De moribus*, 257–8. This is already the third time (cf. above) that Piccolomini alludes to Ovid's Medea as a proof-text of Aristotelian akrasia.

[245] *De moribus*, 258–9.

[246] *De moribus*, 259: 'homo sciens confuse, non distincte, sciens communem, non singularem enuntiationem, sciens sub nube vehementis alicuius perturbationis, non autem conspicue, errare potest. Hanc a perturbatione seductionem Plato in Protagora summam nuncupavit inscitiam. Ex his constat, Aristotelem secum non pugnare, nec a Platone dissentire.'

[247] *De moribus*, 259.

between reason and desire. Piccolomini teaches that in this struggle we (i) claim like Medea that we know the better but follow the worse; but we also (ii) ignore something, as Aristotle claims. Piccolomini is not worried about the tensions between (i) and (ii).

Piccolomini's own interest is, however, predominantly focused on the second question, which he considers to be a much more difficult one.[248] Although the second question is also connected with the traditional problems of akrasia, its immediate Aristotelian context is EN III, 5, in which Aristotle refutes the Platonic view that 'no one is voluntarily wicked' (EN 1113b15–17).[249] Piccolomini here employs the conceptual pair *sua sponte–invitus* which is taken from the Latin translation of EN III, 5 by Argyropoulos, but also reflects the Augustinian use of language (1.2). Piccolomini's second question therefore also returns to the Augustinian issues of voluntary behaviour discussed, for instance, in Petrarch's *Secretum* (2.1).

Piccolomini first lays out the Platonic doctrine in chapter 17. He employs several dialogues of Plato, including *Protagoras, Gorgias,* and *Laws,* to show that Plato considers that all men aim at the apparent good. He also refers to Aristotle's mention of this Platonic doctrine in EN III, 5 (1114 b1).[250] In chapter 18, Piccolomini sets Aristotle's opinions against this view. As Aristotle says, it is false to claim that 'no one is voluntarily wicked' (*sponte improbus nemo*, EN 1113b5). People are naturally masters of their actions, and this principle also pertains to their wrong or wicked actions. In Piccolomini's view, Aristotle defends free decision (*liberum arbitrium*) when he argues in EN III, 5 that it is within our power to do wrong and not do wrong.[251]

In chapter 19, Piccolomini explains why Aristotle is closer to the truth than Plato on this issue. Although one can say that some goodness moves the reason towards action, there are different kinds of goodness:

'Good' is of three kinds: honest, useful, or pleasant. Although the true good is only that which is honest, the human being often freely and voluntarily (neglecting honesty) follows that which is useful or pleasant. He is then not ignorant that this makes him wicked. Let it be added that when committing some crime the human being does not want to be guilty nor wishes to be wicked, but he wants the useful or the pleasant. This thought is reflected in Plato.[252]

---

[248] *De moribus,* 259: 'Altera dubitatio . . . quae proculdubio obscurior est, et maioris momenti, de qua summopere dissentire videntur Plato et Aristoteles.'

[249] Argyropoulos: 'Dicere enim sua sponte neminem pravum . . . sponte autem nostra pravitas'; Grosseteste: 'Dicere autem quod nullus volens malus . . . malicia autem, voluntarium.' Piccolomini refers to Aristotle recognizably but freely; cf. Lines (2002), 279–81.

[250] *De moribus,* 259–61. On page 261 Piccolomini quotes freely EN 1114a32–b8.

[251] *De moribus,* 261–2. Cf. in particular the following (p. 261): 'Ostensiones potiores Aristotelis hae sunt. Prima ducitur ex definitione nostri liberi arbitrii, ac ita formatur. Id dicitur positum in nostra facultate, quod et agere et non agere valemus, et cuius oppositum in nostra facultate est positum' [it follows a broader allusion to EN 1113b 6–14].

[252] *De moribus,* 262: 'Bonum triplex est, honestum, utile, delectabile. Et quamvis re vera bonum id solum sit, quod est honestum, homo tamen frequenter, libere et sponte (neglecto honesto) sequitur utile, vel delectabile, non ignorans se ob id reddi improbum. Addebatur, quod homo in patrando scelere non vult, nec optat improbitatem, sed utile, vel delectabile; reflectitur haec ratio in Platonem.'

Piccolomini further points out that although some ignorance is involved in many sins, people are often responsible for their own ignorance, as is the case with drunkenness (EN 1113b31) or self-inflicted illnesses (EN 1114a16). Aristotle is thus right in holding that many wicked acts are voluntary.[253] If reason considers something to be good or bad, the will cannot simply will contrary to such reason. In that sense we are not doing evil contrary to knowledge. On the other hand, these considerations are within our power and we often cause ourselves to regard something as good which is in fact evil. Thus people are often said to make themselves blind.[254]

In this manner, Piccolomini can rely on Aristotle and refute Plato's view. At the same time, he again wants to embrace both intellectualism and a sort of voluntarism: like Plato, Aristotle proceeds from the axiom that the will is directed to the good. Piccolomini further allows voluntary ignorance as well as a differentiation among kinds of goodness from among which the wrong kind of goodness can be voluntarily chosen. But given this, Piccolomini is not simply mediating between Plato and Aristotle, but also reconciling Aristotle's teaching with the more voluntarist view of sin which is intentionally, though not fully, irrationally consented to. Aristotle thus becomes a defender of Augustinian 'free decision', as Piccolomini says explicitly in chapter 18.

In chapter 20, Piccolomini first points out that one should not reconcile Plato's teachings with Aristotle in all respects. While Aristotle defends our ordinary use of language, Plato often uses metaphors and presses the meaning of concepts. Keeping this difference in mind, both Plato and Aristotle apparently defend a view that people wish to act rationally in the sense that they intend some good.[255] While Plato and Plotinus focus on the conduct of the pure mind, Aristotle pays attention to the factual human condition, in which human actions are not pure but 'mixed' (*mixtae*). In mixed actions, appetitive perception and reason struggle (*pugnant*) with one another.[256]

Aristotle is thus again made a representative of 'commonplace Platonism', while Plato exemplifies the state of the person without perturbations. Platonism and Aristotelianism agree on the natural orientation towards goodness; they only differ over the particular context of the human agent. The apostle Paul in Romans 7, for instance, consents to the law which is spiritual. In doing so, he exemplifies the fundamental striving towards goodness, although he still remains in the struggle with sin.[257]

In Piccolomini's view, Plato takes into account the 'seeds of our future life', whereas Aristotle speaks in the 'common and popular' manner. When theologians assert that

---

[253] *De moribus*, 262–3.

[254] *De moribus*, 264: 'si concedimus iudicium visionemque boni et mali natura nobis competere, nec esse in nostra facultate, et ob id non sponte nostraque voluntate reddi pravos, pari ratione nec sponte, nec nostra voluntate erimus probi. Par enim est ratio utriusque, ut conspicuum est. Per instantiam vero diluitur: quia falsum est id iudicium et visionem aliqua ratione in nostra facultate non esse positam. Nos enim ob nostrum vitae genus, obque improbas assuetudines, frequenter sumus causae, ut ea, quae mala sunt, videantur nobis bona. Ac ita frequenter homines semetipsos dicuntur reddere caecos.'

[255] *De moribus*, 264–5.

[256] *De moribus*, 265.

[257] *De moribus*, 265–6.

people will to do evil without qualification, they also follow this popular way of speaking, bearing in mind that the doctrine that 'no one is evil voluntarily' can easily be misused by criminal minds. At the same time, deeply Christian authors like the apostle Paul and Dionysios Areiopagita can affirm the idea that the fundamental goal of human striving is goodness.[258] The last chapter (21) briefly explains the Aristotelian view (EN 1140b23–24) that in moral matters it is worse to go wrong willingly than unwillingly.[259]

Piccolomini's discussion of his 'second question' (Chs 17–21) strengthens the impression we have already formed with regard to his preceding discussion of akrasia (Chs 15–16). Although Piccolomini formally prefers Aristotle's views, he wants to reconcile them with Platonic doctrine as well as with the voluntarist views of Christian theology. In this reconciliation process, Aristotle emerges as a sort of 'commonplace Platonist' who teaches that the human condition is characterized by our continuing struggle between reason and the sensual perturbations. In this struggle reason can be overcome so that people follow their passions and thus sin voluntarily. Reason is, however, only indirectly overcome, since the passion must appear under the aspect of some goodness and the knowledge of the true good should be obscured to some extent.

Because of this wide-reaching attempt to reconcile all different traditions, Piccolomini's view of akrasia is not very coherent. His discussion lacks scholastic precision, seeking to overcome the differences by adhering to a sort of middle position between the various views. It may be, however, that the success of Piccolomini's textbook lies in this strategy of *via media*. The straightforward portrayal of Aristotle's akrasia as a conflict between reason and passion in which the akratic person sins voluntarily but not altogether irrationally may appeal to readers who prefer to have a harmonious doctrine rather than the problem-orientated approach of scholastic philosophy. Piccolomini's textbook has been called a 'systematization' of ethics.[260] With regard to akrasia, however, the end result rather deserves to be called a harmonization of diverse traditions.

My discussion of 'Renaissance philosophy' has included eight authors: Francesco Petrarch, Donato Acciaiuoli, John Versor, Virgilius Wellendorffer, Jacques Lefèvre d'Étaples, Josse Clichtove, John Mair, and Francesco Piccolomini. We have seen how medieval traditions have been continued and transformed: Petrarch, Mair, and Piccolomini elaborate on Augustinian and late medieval voluntarism, while Acciaiuoli and Wellendorffer relate themselves to Walter Burley's intellectualism. Most of these authors see themselves in some doctrinal continuity with Thomas Aquinas, but Versor may be the only strictly Thomist thinker of this group.

The Platonism of Clichtove and Piccolomini can be regarded as a non-medieval feature, but it also exemplifies a return to the ancient sources. At the same time, most

---

[258] *De moribus*, 267.
[259] *De moribus*, 267–8.
[260] Schmitt (1983a), 128; Lines (2002), 265.

are in some way innovative in their explanation of akrasia: some medieval views are refined, others abandoned, and new Augustinian-Stoic features become associated with Aristotelianism. As our discussion of the Renaissance overlaps temporally with the Lutheran (Ch. 3) and Calvinist Reformation (Ch. 4), I will present an overall discussion of the findings in 5.1.

3

The Lutheran Reformation

3.1 The Erfurt Background: Usingen and his Colleagues

In Martin Luther's debate with Erasmus of Rotterdam around 1524–1525, the free-dom of choice became one of the great discussion topics of the Reformation.[1] This debate was preceded by Luther's criticism of scholastic theology, which in his view affirms the capacity of the human being to produce good works too strongly. In the following we will look at these debates from the perspective of weakness of will. This perspective can shed some light on Luther's early debates with scholastic theology in particular. At the same time, it needs to be stated that the Aristotelian problem of akrasia is not a major issue in Luther's theology, only becoming a significant theme after Philip Melanchthon and John Calvin. Our limited perspective cannot resolve the complex theological issues which Luther debated with Erasmus, but it can illustrate the particular ways in which the young Luther adhered to Augustinian views.

Luther knew Aristotle's philosophy well. He began his academic career by lecturing on Aristotle's ethics in Wittenberg in 1508–1509. These lectures have not survived, but we know that the young Luther knew Aristotle well.[2] His teachers at the university of Erfurt, Bartholomaeus Arnoldi de Usingen (1465–1532) and Jodocus Trutfetter (1460–1519), were established experts in the *via moderna* style of Aristotelianism.[3] Their understanding of Aristotle became Luther's target of criticism. To understand Luther properly, it is first necessary to outline this view of his real and imagined opponents.

Young Martin Luther was a devoted member of the Augustinian eremites and possessed a thorough knowledge of Augustine's writings. Luther had already worked through many early writings of the church father during 1509–1510, including the *Confessions*. He was by then familiar with *De civitate Dei* and *De doctrina christiana* as well. From a letter dated October 1516 we know that Luther was already enthusiastic about the late anti-Pelagian writings of Augustine. This Augustine became for him the real and authentic church father. At the same time, this clear evidence does not rule out the possibility that Luther read Augustine before 1509, nor that he was familiar with the

---

[1] New historical studies of these debates are Wengert (1998) and Kolb (2005).

[2] Dieter (2001). See also Zumkeller (1984), 492–502 and Bayer (2003). The standard biography is Brecht (1993–1999).

[3] On Usingen and Trutfetter, see Lalla (2003); Kärkkäinen (2005); Pilvousek (2007).

anti-Pelagian Augustine before 1516. Indeed, scholars generally assume that this is the case.[4]

Augustine became for Luther and later Reformers, in particular John Calvin, the philosophical and theological point of departure from which a proper view of human action could be developed. If we are to speak of 'weakness of will' in Luther, we therefore need to focus on the Augustinian variants of this theme. As in the case of Petrarch (2.1), our discussion will consider the reception history of *Confessions* 8. In the case of Luther and Calvin, however, we also need to understand the differences between *Confessions* and the bishop of Hippo's late anti-Pelagian writings. Luther and Calvin read Augustine's theory of the will in the light of these writings.

An example which highlights this state of affairs is the understanding of the Apostle Paul's discussion in Romans 7. In this biblical passage, the Apostle claims that he does not do what he wants but the very thing he hates (Romans 7:15). Such comments offer the Reformers a platform to discuss the insufficiency of will in human action. As we noted in 1.2, Augustine changes his interpretation of this passage. Luther and Calvin are very conscious of this shift in Augustine's view and interpret it in a particular manner. It is the anti-Pelagian Augustine who can provide the true answers regarding human weakness and strength.

Before proceeding to the Reformation, we discuss briefly the understanding of Aristotle and Augustine in Luther's immediate surroundings, that is, at the University of Erfurt and the monastery of Augustinian eremites. Simplifying complex matters to an extent, it can be said that the academic discussion on human action in Erfurt offers a portrayal of Luther's enemy, who is combatted with the help of Augustinian views, which for Luther represent the truth regarding the human condition. Given the enormous number of studies on Luther's background and the dawn of the Reformation, our decision to portray Aristotelianism in Erfurt by referring to the philosophical psychology of Bartholomaeus Arnoldi de Usingen (1464–1532) and his colleagues remains illustrative rather than comprehensive.[5] One advantage of this approach is, however, that Usingen explicitly mentions akrasia and embeds it in the late medieval Augustinian and Aristotelian theories of action.

In his *Parvulus philosophie naturalis* (1499), Usingen sets out the freedom of the will as follows:

[the will] has two kinds of acts. Of the first kind are the acts of complacence and displacence with regard to which the will is not free. These acts are formed with natural necessity so that when a pleasant object is presented to the will, it wills, nills, and chooses it with the act of complacence. Similarly, when a painful, ugly, or loathsome object is presented to the will, it chooses the act of displacence. In these acts the will does not act sinfully because it is not free with regard to them. According to both moral philosophy and the Catholic way of speaking, the sinful act proceeds

---

[4] Luther, WABr 1, 17–24; Zumkeller (1984), 485–92; Wriedt (2007); Hamm (2007).

[5] For comprehensive overviews, see Oberman (1989); Zumkeller (1984); Dieter (2001); Bultmann, Leppin, and Lindner (2007).

from free decision insofar as the agent can consider other alternatives. And according to Augustine, sin is thus free; and if it does not occur freely, it cannot be sin.[6]

Usingen here follows action theory as it is formulated in Buridan's commentary on EN.[7] As we noted in 1.5, Buridan represents the 'commonplace Augustinian' understanding of the interplay between desire and consent; that is, a view in which the impressions evoke desires which are not consented judgements. They remain inevitable passions which do not necessarily lead to action and for which a human person cannot be held responsible. For Usingen, this is the correct Augustinian and even Catholic interpretation of the will.

Concerning the second act of the will, Usingen again follows Buridan:

Of the second kind are those acts of the will which follow from the first ones. These are of two kinds, namely contrary and contradictory. The acts of willing and nilling, accepting and refuting are contrary acts. In these acts, the will is not free towards both of them with regard to the same object, as it cannot both will and nill, or both accept and refute. For the will cannot nill or refute an object which is recognized to be good. Nor can it accept or will a bad object: the will does not accept or will anything except under the aspect of goodness, because goodness or apparent goodness is the object of volition and acceptance. Nor can the will refute something unless it appears to be bad.

But the will is free towards one of them, as it can will and accept the object which appears to be good. For it can also refrain from accepting it, suspending its own act. And with regard to bad objects, the will is free to nill and to refute in the same manner, as the philosophers commonly teach. These are contradictory: will, not to will; refute, not to refute; accept, not to accept. With regard to these alternatives, the will is free concerning its relevant object. With regard to a recognized goodness the will is thus free to will or to refrain from willing. For it can suspend its own act to investigate the goodness of the case at hand more closely or to exercise its own freedom.[8]

---

[6] Usingen, *Parvulus*, 63v: 'Habet autem duplices actus. Primi sunt complacentia et displicentia, in quibus voluntas non est libera, sed per modum naturalis necessitatis format tales, ut presentato voluntati obiecto delectabili cognito tali velit, nolit, elicit actum complacentie. Similiter presentato tristi et difformi ac despecto elicit displicentiam. Quare in illis actibus non peccat, cum non sit libera in eis, sed actus peccaminosus sive moraliter, sive catholice loquendo procedit a libero arbitrio inquantum tali, ut habet videri alibi. Et secundum Augustinum peccatum adeo liberum est, quod, si non libere fieret, peccatum non esset.' I use 'nill' to translate the active 'nolle' and 'not to will' to translate the passive 'non velle'.

[7] See Saarinen (1994), 161–87, and 1.5 above.

[8] Usingen, *Parvulus* 63v: 'Secundi sunt, qui sequuntur primos, et tales sunt duplices, scilicet contrarii et contradictorii. Contrarii sunt ut velle, nolle; acceptare, refurare. Et in illis ambobus voluntas non est libera circa idem obiectum, cum non possit idem velle et nolle, acceptare et refutare. Non enim potest bonum cognitum tale nolle vel refutare. Nec malum, ut sic acceptare et velle, quia nihil acceptat et vult, nisi sub ratione boni, quia bonum vel apparens tale est obiectum volitionis et acceptationis. Et nihil refutat, nisi appareat malum. Sed est libera in altero, tamen ut circa apparens bonum in velle et acceptare. Posset enim non acceptare, sed suspendere actum suum. Et circa apparens malum libera est in nolle et refutare simili modo, secundum quod communiter loquuntur philosophi. Sed contradictorii sunt: velle, non velle; refutare, non refutare; acceptare, non acceptare. Et in illis actibus ambobus est libera circa obiectum proportionatum, ut circa bonum cognitum tale est libera in velle et non velle, quia potest suspendere actum suum propter melius deliberare et inquirere de bonitate, vel propter experiri suam libertatem.'

This analysis of freedom occurs in the third book of Buridan's commentary; it is applied to akrasia in the seventh book of this work. The Parisian articles of 1277 already grant the will the freedom of *non velle*.[9] Usingen's teaching basically concerns Augustine's view of consent as it is interpreted in the tradition of the 'commonplace Augustinian' theory of will (see 1.2, 1.5). The person may experience contrary desires simultaneously, but he cannot consent to both of them at the same time. The freedom of consenting to one alternative basically means either willing it or lacking this will. In addition, the consent needs a reason, a feature which is given in the scholastic requirement of an object appearing 'under the aspect of goodness' (*sub ratione boni).*[10] The inevitable first acts of the will can produce such reasons; the freedom of the will in its second act pertains to the acceptance or non-acceptance of these reasons. The free will can thus choose from among contradictory alternatives, but it cannot effectively will two contrary alternatives simultaneously.

It is highly significant that Usingen presents this analysis as a Catholic and Augustinian doctrine. His colleague in Erfurt, Jodocus Trutfetter, describes the same theory in his *Summa in totam physicen* in a somewhat more restrained manner. He concedes that this is a common opinion, but adds that William Ockham and Gabriel Biel understand the will differently. Trutfetter reports that it is commonly taught that the will is free with regard to contradictory alternatives, although it cannot will and nill simultaneously. He qualifies Usingen's view slightly by saying that the will cannot will against the 'total judgement' of the intellect, but it can will against a 'partial judgement'. He gives the example of adultery as a case in which something is both willed because of pleasure and nilled because of shamefulness.[11]

We cannot enter into the complexities of this discussion in detail. For the purposes of our study, it is essential to see the prominence of Buridan's analysis in Erfurt and its straightforward use by Usingen. In his *Compendium naturalis philosophie* (1507), Usingen

---

[9]   On Buridan and this Parisian article, see Saarinen (1994), 168–82, and Dieter (2001), 225–8. As Dieter points out here, Luther's criticism of this view is in fact an unintentional criticism of the anti-Aristotelian stance of the Parisian articles.

[10]   For this feature, see 1.4; Kent (1995), 174–81; Müller (2007), 12–15.

[11]   Trutfetter, *Summa in totam physicen*, fol. Gg 2v-3r (Quid obiectum voluntatis): 'Licet frequentior et communior sit opinio, quod obiectum voluntatis sit bonum verum vel apparens, sic quod voluntas non possit velle illud, in quo nulla apparet intellectui ratio bonitatis, et ita suo modo nec nolle illud, in quo nulla apparet ratio malitie vel fugabilitatis. Licet possit actum suum suspendere non volendo aut non nolendo, ut prius fiat inquisitio, si apparenti bonitati sit annexa malitia aliqui, vel malitie bonitas. Quia id, quod aliquod apparet malum, potest velle et ita nolle, quod aliquod apparet bonum (Verbi gratia: adulterium potest velle ratione delectationis et nolle ipsum ratione inhonestatis.) Atque hinc voluntas nihil possit velle aut nolle contra totale iuditium intellectus, licet bene partiale. Nec velle malum sub ratione mali, nec nolle bonum sub ratione boni, licet id, quod prima facie apparet bonum, possit non velle, nec secundo id quod prima facie apparet malum non nolle, aut illud, in quo simul apparent rationes boni et mali, velle et nolle. Secundum quod etiam communiter dicitur, voluntatem esse liberam in actibus contradictoriis (quales sunt velle: non velle, nolle: non nolle), sed non contrariis (ut puta his: velle: nolle, acceptare: refutare). Tamen Guilhelmus q. 13 lib 3. (et post eum Gabriel dist. 43 lib. 2 eiusdem memit) probabiliter tenet et probare contendit quod obiectum voluntatis non sit bonum sed ens in genere.' For the Buridanian terminology in this passage, see Saarinen (1994), 166–72.

again outlines Buridan's theory, teaching that the concupiscence-related part of the sensitive appetite strives towards that good which is pleasant. The will belongs to the intellect; in its first act, the will wills that which appears to be pleasant or nills that which appears to be painful. These acts are not free and cannot be called sin.[12] In its second act the will is free to choose that which is judged to be under the aspect of goodness or refrain from choosing it, but it cannot simultaneously will and nill the same object.[13]

Usingen also calls the will a 'blind potency' (potentia ceca). The will does not evaluate its object autonomously, but is dependent on the appetitive desires evoked through the senses as well as on their judgement by reason. For Buridan as for Usingen, the first act of the will is accompanied by a preliminary judgement,[14] but it is only the second act of the will which corresponds to the Augustinian notion of consent. The first act is morally irrelevant and occurs without the controlling powers of the will and intellect. The end result of this action theory is a model in which the initial desires remain inevitable and morally irrelevant, whereas free will pertains to the second act of acceptance or refusal.

In his Exercitium de anima (1507), Usingen applies this view to akrasia. He asks whether contrary appetitive powers can be active in the same part of the soul, responding that this is not the case. The phenomenon of incontinence seems, however, to prove the activity of contrary powers. Because of this objection, Usingen admits the activity of contrary powers in different parts of the soul but not in the same faculty. In the case of akrasia, one power is active in the sensitive appetite, another in the intellect. As these powers pertain to two different faculties, they are not contrary to one another in the proper sense.[15]

Usingen clarifies the issue further by investigating the argument that the sensitive appetite cannot conflict with the intellectual appetite because both are the same thing, namely one soul, and one thing cannot be contrary to itself. Furthermore, the judgement of the intellect and the judgement of the senses (iuditium sensus), as well as the corresponding appetitive powers, cannot be contrary because the sensual part of the virtuous person obeys reason.[16]

---

[12] Usingen, Compendium naturalis philosophie, fol. Miiii r.

[13] Usingen, Compendium, Miiii v.

[14] Usingen, Compendium, Miiii r. For Buridan, see Saarinen (1994), 169–70.

[15] Usingen, Exercitium, P4r-v 'Utrum in eodem animali appetitus sit contrarius appetitivi ... Respondetur ad questionem: in eodem animali secundum eandem potentiam appetitus con contrariatur appetitui sed bene secundum diversas ... Arguitur ... motus incontinentium sunt ad contraria septimo ethicorum, ergo in eodem appetitus contrariantur. . . . Ad secundum dicitur secundum quosdam illos motus non esse contrarios proprie loquendo quia unus est sensitivus et alter intellectivus.' The last remark of the question 'referendam esse ad idem tempus' (Q1r) underlines the simultaneity of the contrary powers.

[16] Usingen, Exercitium, Qr1: 'Arguitur appetitus sensitivus non contrariatur intellectivo in homine, ergo. Antecedens probatur quia sunt una res scilicet anima. Sed idem non contrariatur sibi ipsi. Item iuditium sensus et intellectus non contrariatur, ergo nec appetitus iuditia illa presupponentes. Antecedens probatur quia in homine virtuoso sensus obedit rationi.'

Usingen responds that the sensitive appetite is not contrary to the intellectual appetite according to its substance, but according to the judgement and the action concerned. This mode of being contrary occurs in the case of continence and incontinence. Whereas in the case of virtuous and bestially vicious people no repugnancy (*repugnantia*) can be observed,[17] continent and incontinent people display a twofold movement as follows:

Some people are continent. They act well but with some pain and resistance because their sensual part is not completely subject to reason. But reason nevertheless overcomes and conquers the sensual part. In these people the sensitive appetite is contrary to the intellectual appetite. Some people are incontinent. They act badly with some pain and resistance because their reason is not completely extinguished and subjected to the sensual part. But when passions emerge in the sensitive appetite, the sensual part overcomes reason. When passions and titillations are not active the incontinent person judges that adultery is to be avoided. But when the passions emerge, the sexual lust makes the person to rush into bed like an ox attacking its victim. These people have contrary appetitive powers.[18]

In this characterization of akrasia, Usingen is in many ways close to John Buridan's q3 and q6 of the seventh book of the *Quaestiones*. For Buridan, akratic and enkratic behaviour occur in situations with a double inclination (*duplex inclinatio*) and involve both the sensitive appetite and the will, which is the intellectual appetite.[19] Usingen's whole discussion on the contrary powers presupposes the Buridanian analysis of the first and second acts of the will.

In spite of his obvious proximity to Buridan, Usingen's analysis contains some aspects which differ slightly from Buridan's views. Buridan says explicitly that he does not regard the double inclination as consisting of a conflict between the sensitive appetite and the will, ingredients of both appetitive powers being found on both sides of the conflict.[20] Because Buridan teaches that the mind must finally reach one conclusive judgement in a situation of double inclination, he further responds negatively to the question of 'whether one can possess simultaneously contrary judgements about a particular action'.[21] Although Usingen likewise teaches that two contrary appetitive powers cannot be active in the same faculty of the soul, he grants the

---

[17] Usingen, *Exercitium*, Qr1. The term *repugnantia* appears here twice in the phrase 'contrarietatem et repugnantiam'. For the occurrence of *pugna, repugnantia* in the Renaissance, see 2.2 and 2.4, and in Luther, see 3.2.

[18] Usingen, *Exercitium*, Q1r: 'Continentes, qui operantur bona, sed cum luctu et renitentia propterea quod sensualitas non est omnino rationi subiecta. Vincit tamen ratio sensum atque debellat et in illis appetitus sensitivus contrariatur intellectivo. Incontinentes, qui operantur mala cum luctu et resistentia propterea quod ratio non est omnino suppressa atque sensualitati subiecta. Vincit tamen sensualitas rationem in surgentibus passionibus in appetitu sensitivo. Iudicat enim incontinens non esse fornicandum, dum non pulsatur passione at titillatione et pruritus passione insurgente tradit arma duciturque fune veneris ad clinopalim, sicut thaurus imolandus ad victimam, et in illis etiam est contrarietas appetituum.'

[19] Saarinen (1994), 173–5 and 1.5 above.

[20] Saarinen (1994), 173, referring to Buridan, *Quaestiones*, 142rb (581).

[21] Buridan, *Quaestiones* VII q6, 142va (583). Saarinen (1994), 174.

existence of simultaneous contrary judgements in different powers or faculties. The unity of the human mind does not seem to worry Usingen as much as it worries Buridan.

This difference may be small, as both Buridan and Usingen hold that one of the two tendencies created by these judgements must remain latent. Usingen, however, interprets the Buridanian framework in a more 'commonplace Platonist' manner; that is, he allows a coexistence of reason and passion in which the lower potency can directly overcome the higher. The discussion quoted above employs neither the notion of consent nor explains akrasia in terms of ignorance. It simply depicts akrasia as a conflict situation between reason and passion, in which passion gains the upper hand.

In addition to Buridan, Usingen here follows the *Exercitium librorum de anima* (1482) by Johannes de Lutrea (died 1479). Lutrea asks the question whether the appetite can be contrary to an appetitive power.[22] He aims to show that the will and the sensitive appetite may be contrary to one another in the so-called intermediate class of people (*homines medii*). While the sensitive appetite of virtuous people follows reason and the extremely vicious people are guided by the sensitive appetite without reason, the intermediate class of human beings is characterized by the contrariety of sensitive and rational appetite.[23]

Like Usingen, Lutrea teaches that both continent and incontinent people are characterized by the contrariety of sensitive and rational appetite. The continent people do good with some resistance. Akratic people display some use of reason, but their sensual passions nevertheless overcome their reason.[24] Usingen follows this response almost verbatim. In addition to Lutrea's teaching, Usingen teaches the impossibility of contrary appetitive powers in the same faculty in a Buridanian manner. In referring to the intermediate class of continent and incontinent individuals, Lutrea wants to affirm the simultaneous activity of contrary powers.

Lutrea's discussion contains a noteworthy passage in which he divides the class of vicious people into two parts. Whereas the extremely vicious person does not use reason at all, the less blameworthy displays a contrariety of reason and sensitive appetite. In the mind of such people, the sensitive appetite 'does not wait for the judgement of reason but becomes itself the judgement of reason'. As a result of this, the emerging judgement is related to perception and to the sensitive appetite. This judgement

---

[22] Lutrea, *Exercitium*, 70v: 'Utrum appetitus sit contrarius appetitivi.'

[23] Lutrea, *Exercitium*, 71r: 'non semper contrariantur appetitus sensitivus et intellectivus quia in hominibus virtuosis non contrariantur.... Item in hominibus pessimis appetitus sensivitus et intellectivus non contrariantur quia ratio non dominatur sed est omnino depressa. Sic ergo solum in hominibus mediis appetitus sensitivus est contrarius intellectivo.'

[24] Lutrea, *Exercitium*, 71r–v: 'Quidam sunt continentes et sunt illi, qui operantur bona cum luctu et resistentia. Quia in illis hominibus sensualitas non est omnino depressa, nec etiam appetitus sensitivus est omnino subiectus rationi, nihilo minus tamen habet dominium et vincit iudicium sensus. Et in illis appetitus sensitivus est contrarius appetitui intellectivo. Quidam sunt incontinentes et sunt, qui operantur mala cum luctu et resistentia. In illis etiam appetitus sensitivus et intellectivus contrariantur, quia in illis ratio non est simpliciter depressa, nihilominus sensualitas vincit rationem, et ibi etiam appetitus est contrarius appetitui.'

prevails, remaining contrary to the judgement of reason. The sensitive appetite can thus become connected to the higher powers which control the action, so that the sensitive and rational powers are contrary to one another 'in action'.[25] Like Buridan and Usingen, Lutrea here explicitly talks of the judgement (*iudicium*) which is related to the sensitive appetite. Passion does not merely mean an inordinate desire, but involves a judgement.

Usingen does not quote this passage. Lutrea's longer discussion, however, clarifies Usingen's brief statement that the 'bestially vicious' people represent a particular class. More importantly, Lutrea's passage clarifies Usingen's teaching that the contrariety at stake here pertains to judgements and action rather than to any different substance inherent in the appetitive powers. Lutrea's class of less blameworthy people in fact depicts the incontinent agents who are better than the fully vicious people whose reason is completely extinguished. In the less blameworthy, or 'intermediate' class of vice, the sensitive appetite offers its own judgement and replaces the rational judgement. The sensitive appetite uses this procedure to direct the higher powers of the soul and change the course of action. At the same time, the judgement of reason is not completely extinguished but remains latent, causing the state of contrary appetitive powers with regard to the judgement and the corresponding action. The struggle thus continues and the mind is not really unified.

This analysis of akrasia is not completely different from the intellectualist accounts which we have encountered in the Thomistic tradition. In Thomas's view, the right syllogism is also replaced by the wrong syllogism, allowing the argument from pleasure to become operative. In the case of Acciaiuoli (2.2), we noted that he takes over Thomas's notion of *repugnantia*, interpreting it as a struggle (*pugna*) between the opinions of reason and passion.

While the Thomist analysis explains this phenomenon as temporary forgetting or ignorance, Lutrea's and Usingen's analyses are more straightforward. The Erfurt textbooks do not mention ignorance, nor do they employ syllogistic analysis, simply stating that the sensitive appetite can replace the correct judgement with its own judgement. This straightforward explanation of akrasia not only deviates from the intellectualist account of Thomas, Acciaiuoli, and Versor, but also simplifies the account given by Buridan. Neither Thomas nor Buridan would allow a contrariety in which the sensitive power simply pushes its own judgement into the controlling seat of action. At least some transitory forgetting or lack of consideration needs to precede this intervention. In their emphasis on the relative autonomy of the sensitive appetite,

---

[25] Lutrea, *Exercitium*, 71r: 'Sed in hominibus viciosi et in malis ibi appetitus sensitivus contrariatur appetitui intellectivo quia appetitus sensitivus non expectat iudicium rationis sed pervenit iudicium rationis. Quia ibi sequitur iudicium appetitus sensitivus quid est contarium iudicio intellectus et rationis. Sic appetitus sensitivus est contrarius appetitui intellectivo in actibus suis. Recte sicut potentia sensitiva et intellectiva contrariantur in actibus suis.'

Lutrea and Usingen approach the psychology of William Ockham, which presupposes a real distinction between the sensory and the intellectual form of the soul.[26]

In their account of akrasia, Usingen and Lutrea nevertheless primarily employ Buridan's theory of action, in which a plurality of different first acts of complacence and displacence emerge in the agent's mind. Like Buridan, they insist that the agent needs to accept one course of action and that, in uncertain situations, later reconsideration may reactivate the latent reasons to do otherwise. Thus akratic and enkratic actions are characterized by a twofold tendency towards contrary options.

Usingen and Lutrea differ from Buridan in their simplified account of this situation. Buridan favours an Aristotelian rational decision-making theory regarding the deliberation that proceeds from the initial desire to the final and informed consent which unifies the mind in its conclusive judgement. Usingen and Lutrea, however, teach that the situation of inner struggle with its contrary judgements is in itself sufficient to create akratic actions. Given that the desire appears 'under the aspect of goodness' (*sub ratione boni*), this judgement relating to the sensitive appetite can overcome the judgement of reason. Because of the lasting conflict between reason and passion, Usingen's psychology does not achieve the same kind of final unity as it has in Buridan's theory, rather reflecting an Ockhamist real distinction between the sensory and the intellecual form of the soul.

As Usingen and Lutrea do not stress the notion of consent but focus on the struggle between reason and sensitive appetite, their analysis of akrasia to some extent resembles the commonplace Platonism of Josse Clichtove. It may be safer, however, to interpret their view of akrasia in the light of Usingen's broader action theory. As we have seen, Usingen considers (i) that Buridan's analysis of the first and second acts of the will corresponds to Augustine's view of desire and consent; and that (ii) this synthesis is held to be the Catholic way of speaking of merit and sin. This late medieval framework of 'commonplace Augustinianism' receives (iii) some new colour from those Renaissance discussions (Acciaiuoli, Clichtove) which emphasize the ongoing struggle, the *agon*, between reason and passion. Features (i), (ii), and (iii) continue to be relevant to discussing Luther's criticism of the Aristotelian theory of action.

In order to round out the picture of Luther's teachers, it is necessary to discuss briefly the understanding of Augustine in Erfurt. The criticism of Aristotle had deep roots in the theology of this order. Adolar Zumkeller, in particular, has argued that the criticism of Aristotle available in the works of Simon Fidati de Cascia (died 1348) and Hugolin of Orvieto (died 1373) plays a significant role in Luther's understanding of Aristotle and Augustine.[27] The problem of this thesis is that it remains hypothetical, as the mere observation of interesting parallels cannot prove the assumed influence. But the theology of Augustinian eremites connects Luther in some way with Petrarch, another early critic of Aristotle. Petrarch had close contact with the Augustinian eremites of

---

[26] For Ockham's view of sensory and intellectual soul, see Adams (1987), 654–69 and Hirvonen (2004).

[27] Zumkeller (1984); Wriedt (2007) surveys this discussion.

Milan. Charles Trinkaus observes several 'sweeping comparisons' between the Augustinianisms of Petrarch and Luther,[28] but they remain too vague to be discussed further in our study.

To obtain a less uncertain picture of the roots of Luther's Augustinianism, it is instructive to look at the theological work of Johann Staupitz (1468–1524). Luther certainly knew the theological position of his immediate mentor at the monastery of Erfurt. In his work on the theology of Staupitz, Adolar Zumkeller summarizes his main findings by mentioning four points on which Luther's mentor shows a distinct profile with regard to his contemporaries:

1. Staupitz focuses so strongly on the work of the Holy Spirit that the gift of created grace remains in the background.
2. He ascribes the merits of the good works of the Christian to God in a fairly monergistic manner. Human cooperation is not denied, but it remains insignificant.
3. Staupitz emphasizes the sinfulness of human beings. Even Christians always remain sinners.
4. Because of sin all human works remain imperfect and are tainted with sin.[29]

Since all four points have been regarded as important traits of Luther's theology,[30] this list is interesting and exemplifies the reception of the late anti-Pelagian Augustine (see 1.2). Zumkeller nevertheless concludes that Staupitz remains a true Catholic. He states that the four points only describe tendencies which do not question Staupitz's adherence to the standard Catholic understanding of Augustine.[31] We will briefly look at some texts in which Staupitz deals with the passions, the will, and action in the light of this statement.

In his Tübingen sermons, preached around 1497, Staupitz often discusses the interplay between passions and sin. He teaches that since passions do not yet prompt action, the passions of the sensitive appetite are not sinful as such, only becoming actual sin when consent is given to them.[32] At the same time, passions are not morally neutral, often being considered to be harmful. The passion of concupiscence is a natural vice (vitium naturae) which continues to struggle (pugnat) against grace in baptized Christians. Although sin strictly speaking only results from consent, concupiscence belongs to the 'law of sin' (lex peccati, Romans 7:23) which makes the body sinful (corpus peccati).[33]

Given this continuing influence of concupiscence, a Christian should not say that he has no sin (cf. 1 John 1:8). Such a claim would in itself be a sign of false pride and therefore self-contradictory.[34] While a good Catholic should therefore say that he does not consent to sin, he cannot claim to be without sin. The human person is subject to

---

[28] Trinkaus (1979), 29–30, 53–4, 60–1. Courcelle (1989), 217.
[29] Zumkeller (1994), 230.
[30] Regarding 3. and 4., see Schneider and Wenz (2001). For 1. and 2., see Pesch and Peters (1981).
[31] Zumkeller (1994), 230.
[32] Staupitz, Sermo 31, 50–65.
[33] Staupitz, Sermo 32, 245–63; Zumkeller (1994), 37–8.
[34] Staupitz, Sermo 26, 113–15; Zumkeller (1994), 45.

all kinds of passions through his life; Paul even says that it is problematic to live without passions (*sine affectione*, 2 Tim. 3:3). A life without passions is only possible when there is no more sin.[35] Staupitz comes close to saying that Christians remain sinful because of the continuing struggle with concupiscence, but he does not really cross the line because he also chooses to remain within the boundaries of Augustine's consent theory of merit and sin.

At times, Staupitz can state in a fairly voluntarist manner that the will is the ruling principle of the soul (*domina in regno animae*), and that free will distinguishes humans from animals, who move according to natural appetite or desire. This statement is not, however, a consistent anthropological doctrine, but rather a way of speaking related to his exhortation that Christians should turn away from animal desires and live according to their good will.[36] In his Latin writings, Staupitz neither quotes *Confessions* 8 nor employs Augustine's discussion of the 'two wills' or 'incomplete will'. On the contrary, he emphasizes the unity of the will.[37] Staupitz grants that human will and action remain uncertain compared to God's firm intentions,[38] but he does not offer any refined analysis of uncertainty or inner conflict. Although he adopts the Augustinian way of speaking of the Christian striving for perfection as struggle against concupiscence, he does not develop a theory of contrary appetitive powers. He rather defends the unity of the mind in its act of consent.

This brief look at Staupitz's view of the passions, the will, and action confirms Zumkeller's statement. Although Luther's mentor emphasizes the continuing rule of passions and the sinful nature of all humanity, he nevertheless adheres to a fairly 'commonplace Augustinian' theory of action which clearly distinguishes between desire and consent and ascribes sin and merit to the consent. As Staupitz is not interested in the conceptual refinement of action theory, the four points mentioned above remain disparate tendencies which do not constitute a new theoretical viewpoint. With regard to these four points, Staupitz may be fairly close to Luther, but his view of human action nevertheless follows the standard Augustinian framework of many medieval theologians. Given this, it is better to interpret Luther's new view of will and action as a reaction to the philosophical schools of Erfurt than as a continuation of the Augustinianism available in his own order.

3.2 Martin Luther: No Akrasia

With the exception of one remark on Medea's akrasia, to which we will return at the end of this chapter, Martin Luther (1483–1546) never treats the Aristotelian problem of incontinence directly. His indirect contribution to the topic of our study is, however,

---

[35] Staupitz, *Sermo* 33, 122–35.
[36] Staupitz, *Sermo* 25, 50–65; Zumkeller (1994), 132–3.
[37] Staupitz, *De predestinatione* XVIII, 153, 3.
[38] Staupitz, *De predestinatione* XXII, 231.

remarkable in at least two respects. First, later Protestant commentators on EN pay attention to the theological achievements of the Reformation, presupposing the theological framework construed by Luther tacitly and sometimes explicitly. Second, Luther discusses the Augustinian side of our problem extensively. His view of human will follows the teachings of the bishop of Hippo, whom Luther studied extensively at the monastery of Augustinian eremites in Erfurt. It is above all the anti-Pelagian church father who becomes his definitive authority, but Luther also employs terminology available in *Confessions*.

Luther very rarely uses the term *incontinentia*. When he does, its meaning is determined by the Pauline usage in 1 Cor. 7:5, as well as by Augustine's understanding of *continentia* as sexual abstinence. The most important occurrences of this term are found in *Against Latomus* (1521), to which we will return below.

The Augustinian situation of a baptized Christian who continues to battle concupiscence is, however, very familiar to the German reformer. In his early comments on Peter Lombard's *Sentences* (1508–09), Luther concludes that

the intermediate, that is, Christian life is a middle from which a person can incline in both directions. It is difficult but not impossible to incline towards good; it is easy to incline towards evil, but the Christian life does not mean an inevitable servitude to evil. Non-Christians cannot incline towards good but remain in servitude to evil. Christians cannot proceed towards good easily while the blessed people [i.e. those in the heavenly afterlife] can; it is not impossible for the Christians to do good, whereas the condemned people cannot do good.[39]

This early description resembles Johannes de Lutrea's characterization (3.1) of the 'intermediate' human beings who are neither truly virtuous nor bestially vicious. Young Luther regards good Christians as able to become enkratic in this life.

Luther's *Lecture on Romans* (1515–16) reveals a similarity with the problems discussed by his Erfurt teachers:

In the light of these points it is obvious that the idea of the metaphysical theologians is silly and ridiculous, when they argue whether contrary appetites can exist in the same subject, and when they invent the fiction that the spirit, namely, our reason, is something all by itself and absolute and in its own kind and integral and perfectly whole, and similarly that our sensuality, or our flesh, on the contrary likewise constitutes a complete and absolute whole. Because of these stupid fantasies they are driven to forget that the flesh is itself an infirmity or a wound of the whole man who by grace is beginning to be healed in both mind and spirit. For who imagines that in a sick man there are these two opposing entities?[40]

---

[39] WA 9, 71, 1–20: 'Sed vita media i. e. Christiana quasi medio etiam modo se habet ad utrunque flexilis, difficilis ad bonum, sed non impossibilis sicut illa, et facilis ad malum, sed non necessaria servitute sicut illa. Nec est tam facilis ad bonum sicut beati nec tamen impossibilis ad bonum sicut miseri.'

[40] WA 56, 351, 23–352, 8. My English translations for the most part follow *Luther's Works, American Edition*. For the interpretation of this passage, see also Dieter (2001), 130–1. One aspect of Luther's criticism is directed against the Ockhamist tradition of assuming a real distinction within the one soul; see Hirvonen (2004). For Luther, the dichotomy between the spirit and the flesh is possible because the spirit comes from outside.

Luther here criticizes a dualistic anthropology which allows two contrary powers to be simultaneously operative within the same subject. While the metaphysical theologians consider reason and sensitive appetite to be two autonomous powers within the human mind, Luther wants to affirm the unity of the individual. Given that we have observed an increase of dualism in the work of Clichtove (2.4) and Usingen (3.1), this affirmation is understandable.

Luther's exposition of Romans 7:7–15 is of primary importance for his treatment of all phenomena relating to the power of the human will.[41] We shall therefore first outline the basic argumentative framework of this passage and then concentrate on some particular phrases and examples. Throughout the passage it is necessary to keep three complementary points in mind: first, Luther is not a philosopher but a theologian interpreting the Bible. Second, in spite of this basic interest, his points remain consistent and relevant for the action theory in the Augustinian tradition. Third, although Luther focuses on the 'spiritual' individuals, his discussion pertains to all who want to do good. In this sense he believes in the universal validity of his claims.

For Luther, the speaker of Romans 7:7–15 is the Christian Apostle in his spiritual struggle. The passage does not give a retrospective account of Paul's carnal past. Luther is familiar with *Retractationes* 1, 23, a passage in which Augustine mentions his own change of mind on this issue.[42] When Luther gives his arguments in favour of this position, he often quotes Augustine's *Contra Iulianum*, maintaining that the mature church father not only speaks of a Christian struggle but teaches that the remaining harmful desires are already in themselves sinful.[43] For Luther, the very fact that Paul acknowledges his own imperfection in Romans 7 proves that the speaker must be a spiritual person. While a carnal person would boast of his spirituality, a truly spiritual person remains humble and aware of his imperfection.[44]

Luther can defend his reading of *Paulus christianus* with the help of this argumentative figure, which bears a resemblance to Johannes de Lutrea's distinction between really vicious people and the less blameworthy *homines medii*. Both Lutrea and Luther hold that the worst class of people display a unified mind, whereas the less blameworthy are aware of an inner tension. While the vicious person commits sin with conscious choice and unified will,[45] the spiritual person remains in the state of struggle.

Given that the inner tension is evidence of a better spiritual state than the consciously evil will, it would be misleading to read Romans 7 as a report of the actual sins committed by the speaker:

We must not think that the Apostle wants to be understood as saying that he does evil which he hates, and does not do the good which he wants to do, in a moral or metaphysical sense, as if he did nothing good but only evil; for in common parlance this might seem to be the meaning of his words. But he is trying to say [Rom 7:15–16] that he does not do the good as often and as much

---

[41] WA 56, 339, 5–354, 26.   [42] WA 56, 339, 8–15. Cf. 1.2.   [43] WA 56, 340, 25–347, 14.
[44] WA 56, 340, 24–5.   [45] WA 56, 341, 14; 343, 5–7.

and with as much ease as he would like. For he wants to act in a completely pure, free, and joyful manner, without being troubled by his rebellious flesh, and this he cannot accomplish.[46]

When Luther's opponents read Romans 7 as a report of Paul's pre-Christian existence, they do not understand the sinful nature of the remaining concupiscence properly. It is entirely possible that a spiritual person can continue to speak of sinful desires which remain in his struggle:

Our theologians...have come to believe that sin is abolished in baptism or repentance and consider as absurd the statement of the Apostle 'but the sin which dwells within me'. [Rom 7:17] Thus it was this word which gave them the greatest offense, so that they plunged into this false and injurious opinion that the Apostle was not speaking in his own person but in the person of carnal man, for they chatter the nonsense that the Apostle had absolutely no sin, despite his many clear assertions to the contrary.[47]

For Luther, the speaker of Romans 7 is a Christian person who is distinguished from both truly perfect individuals who are completely pure, and carnal people who would not acknowledge the struggle between spirit and flesh. Paul and other exemplary Christians are *homines medii*; they participate in the *vita media* which can incline towards either direction. Because Romans 7 is an introspection of such spiritual people, it is not a description of sinful deeds. This exegetical and theological view has implications for the understanding of human action.

Before turning to these implications, we need to see why and in what sense Luther is against the idea of contrary appetitive powers. Although Luther affirms the theological view that the flesh is against the spirit, he does not want to reify these two realities as autonomous faculties within the individual. In the statement quoted above he considers the flesh to be the 'wound of the whole man' (*vulnus totius hominis*). The wrong opinion is that the two contrary faculties are two things (*duas res*), but the truth is that a person in the process of healing consists of one body (*idem corpus*). Such a person, or a house under construction, are one thing (*eadem res*). A process approaching completion may have an incomplete and a complete stage, but the two stages are no separate or contrary things.[48]

In sum, Luther sees the good Christians in *vita media* as agents who are neither perfect nor completely malicious. At the same time, their intermediate state is not the result of two different powers or faculties, since they are in a process of learning or healing. Luther's own discussion is not without inner tension, since he wants to affirm the unity of the mind while also underlining the residual power of sin. The strong view of sin contains some dualistic tendencies: because sin is not seated in an autonomous human faculty, it resembles an impersonal power, like illness or other external force attacking the human mind.

---

[46] WA 56, 341, 27–33. Luther's reading of Romans 7 is fairly close to Augustine's exposition in his *De nuptiis et concupiscentia*, 1.
[47] WA 56, 349, 24–30.   [48] WA 56, 352, 1–20.

Given this overall picture, we can have a closer look at human action. Paul's exemplary actions lack perfection and remain contaminated by flesh. Luther gives the following example to clarify his point:

It is as with a man who proposes to be chaste; he would wish not to be attacked by temptations and to possess his chastity with complete ease. But his flesh does not allow him, for with its drives and inclinations it makes chastity a very heavy burden, and it arouses unclean desires, even though his spirit is unwilling.[49]

The example resembles the conduct of continent people in the Aristotelian tradition. The flesh acts like the sensitive appetite, causing repugnancy.

Another illustration is the distinction *facere–perficere* employed by Augustine in *Contra Iulianum* (3, 26, 62). An exemplary person like Paul can 'do' the good but not 'accomplish' the good. To 'accomplish' means to fulfil what one wishes or desires. Accomplishing good means the perfect purity of virtue, whereas accomplishing evil means a clear consent to evil. Doing good means trying and willing to act well. Doing evil (Rom 7:19) does not necessarily mean consenting to evil, but it can refer to those blameworthy deeds to which the flesh and concupiscence sometimes draw spiritual people without their consent.[50] An exemplary person can thus will the good and do the good, but not accomplish it. He also sometimes does evil, although he does not will it. Thus he does not 'accomplish' evil, for such action would require consent to evil. It is easy to accomplish evil, while doing good is difficult.[51]

A third illustration depicts the spiritual person who sins without consent. It is not this person himself who does it, but sin within him. This person does not do the good which he wants to do (Rom 7:19–20).[52] Such a person is

like a horseman: When his horses do not trot the way he wants them to, it is he himself and yet not he himself who makes the horse run in such and such a way. For the horse is not without him and he is not without the horse.[53]

So, even a spiritual person can act wrongly. He resists evil and does not consent to it, but the flesh draws him against his good will. In such a case it is both true to say that he acts and that he does not act.[54]

A fourth illustration is that of a boxer between two contrary laws (Rom. 7:23). The pugilist is 'serving the one law . . . standing up to the other law which attacks him and is not serving it, rather that he is serving against it'.[55] A fifth illustration depicts a wound in the flesh. Flesh and spirit are not two faculties, but one thing, as the wound and flesh are one. Flesh is the infirmity or wound of the spirit.[56] All these illustrations ascribe the true subjectivity to the spirit, while the flesh is an imperfection or parasitic reality. With this argumentative strategy Luther wants to strengthen his point that the 'spiritual man'

---

[49] WA 56, 341, 33–342, 3.   [50] WA 56, 342, 6–29; 353, 11–354, 13.   [51] WA 56, 342, 25–8.
[52] WA 56, 342, 30–343, 2.   [53] WA 56, 343, 3–5.   [54] WA 56, 343, 1–2.
[55] WA 56, 346, 10–15.   [56] WA 56, 350, 22–351, 2.

should be regarded as the subject of Romans 7 and that the struggle between spirit and flesh does not constitute a dualistic anthropology.

Although Luther's terminology as well as his intentions remain theological, one can draw fairly clear conclusions with regard to his Augustinian theory of action. For Luther, there are basically two kinds of human action. All those in which the mind consents to evil are sinful and carnal deeds. The other category consists of those actions in which the Christian does not consent to evil. They exemplify the conduct of the spiritual person, resembling the Aristotelian category of continent or enkratic actions. These acts are characterized by a twofold inclination. Since the flesh always causes some repugnancy, nobody in *vita media* can 'accomplish' good; that is, bring about perfect and pure virtue. Luther however denies that the twofold inclination implies a dualistic mind.

There is, in addition, an interesting subgroup within the actions of the spiritual person. Sometimes the flesh forces even the spiritual person to act wrongly. The person does not consent to this act; thus he does evil without 'accomplishing' it. In Aristotelian terms, such actions would be compulsory rather than akratic. Luther's examples of this subgroup include the unskilled horseman and a temporary setback in a healing process. Such actions or events do not qualify as akratic; they are due to compulsion.

This theory of action does not leave any room for a distinct category of akrasia. All voluntary sins stem from consent, which in turn reflects the dynamic unity of mind and flesh in the 'carnal' person.[57] With regard to voluntary sins, Luther's view of action is fairly close to Henry of Ghent and other voluntarists (1.4). There is no mitigating circumstance of weakness observable in voluntary sins: they all proceed from one will. Contrary to this, the spiritual actions of the individual reflect the situation of double inclination. Such actions are either continent actions or involuntary sins which occur without consent. Involuntary sins are compelled, rather than akratic. The category of incontinent action is thus effectively denied.

While Luther employs the Augustinian vocabulary of divided will, he embeds it in a specific framework which is not available as such in *Confessions*, but rather in Augustine's late anti-Pelagian writings. In the medieval tradition, the 'conditional', 'mixed', and 'partial' volitions of weak-willed persons are normally considered to be an alleviating circumstance.[58] Luther, however, employs this phraseology to show that even the spiritual person remains sinful in his enkratic actions. Although Romans 7 offers a prime example of this, Luther employs the vocabulary of divided will before his *Lecture on Romans*.[59]

From 1516 to 1522, Luther expounds Romans 7 several times, the most exhaustive treatment occurring in *Against Latomus* (1521). The main thrust of his argument remains similar, but because of the Reformation controversies Luther increasingly

---

[57] Cf. WA 56, 343, 6–7: 'non tantum unius sunt personae [carnalis] mens et caro, sed etiam unius voluntatis.'

[58] See Saarinen (1994), 20–86 and Rubiglio (2002).

[59] At least in his *First Lecture on Psalms* (1513–1515): WA 55 2/1, 23, 16–19.

emphasizes the sinfulness of the righteous Christian. Because even the best Christians continue to complain like the Apostle Paul in Romans 7, it needs to be taught that some repugnancy of the flesh remains in all actions. Luther adheres straightforwardly to late Augustine, claiming that this repugnancy must be called sin. Thus a Christian is 'righteous and sinner at the same time' (*simul iustus et peccator*)—not because he or she consents to the temptations, but because the presence of this temptation is enough to qualify the state of the Christian mind as sinful. Luther can even claim that the attack of sin is greater in righteous people who have the antidote of grace.[60]

In the preparatory part of the *Heidelberg Disputation,* Luther claims that the righteous person sins even 'between' his good works. This is proved by appeal to Romans 7:19, 22. Throughout our lives the good will and the resisting bad will struggle with one another. There is never a 'total' or 'whole' will, all will remaining 'mixed' in this way.[61] For this reason, there is always some sin present, even in and between our good works. Luther claims that a person

wills the good according to the spirit, but does not do it, doing that which is contrary. This particular 'contrary' is a sort of nilling (*noluntas*) which is always also present when there is the will. With the will, good is done; with the nill, evil is done. Nilling proceeds from the flesh and willing from the spirit . . . These two are always mixed in the whole life and in our works . . . For this reason we always sin when we do good, although sometimes more, sometimes less.[62]

This passage shows firstly that Luther cannot so easily avoid the topic of contrary powers as he claims in the *Lecture on Romans.* Although willing and nilling exemplify the process of becoming spiritual, the contrary powers are portrayed here in a some-what dualistic fashion. Second, the theme of spiritual action is now presented as a universal view. All good Christians act like Paul in Romans 7. Third, Luther employs a variety of medieval concepts of will, like *voluntas mixta, voluntas–noluntas.* In the immediate context, he also uses *voluntas tota,* a concept which alludes to *voluntas non tota.* These concepts are typical of the younger Augustine of the *Confessions,* but Luther connects them with his anti-Pelagian view of permanent sinfulness.

In the *Leipzig Disputation* of 1519, the theme of sin and concupiscence was discussed between Andreas Karlstadt and Johann Eck.[63] Luther had written theses for this occasion, claiming that no one does good without sinning. In his *Resolutiones,* written after

---

[60] *Against Latomus,* LSA 2, 512, 7–10: 'fortiores sunt cogitationes malae piorum quam impiorum, non tamen polluunt, non damnant, illos vero polluunt et damnant. Cur hoc? nonne utrobique idem peccatum? Vere idem peccatum, sed pii antidotum habent.' The phrase 'idem homo est . . . iustus et peccator' appears already in the *Lecture on Romans,* WA 56, 343, 18–19. For the reception history of Luther's views one needs to see that while *Lecture on Romans* remained a manuscript, his later expositions of Romans 7 became widely circulated and discussed. The fact that Luther's exposition remained fairly stable from 1516 to 1522 need not mean that the so-called 'Reformation breakthrough' already took place before 1516; our discussion concerns the power of sin over human will, rather than the justification of sinners by faith.

[61] WA 1, 367, 2, 15–27.

[62] WA 1, 367, 18–21, 24–7.

[63] For this discussion, see Saarinen (2007), 286–8.

Leipzig, Luther explains this view in terms of Romans 7. Even the most holy apostle must admit that all his actions are contaminated by the repugnant flesh and he thus fails to achieve the desired perfect and 'full' implementation of the law. Therefore, nobody does good without sinning.[64] The interpretation of Romans 7 is thus universalized and polemically presented as a distinctive doctrine of 'righteous and sinner at the same time'.

As this doctrine has often been superficially connected with the human inability to do good in later Lutheranism, it is important to see that Luther does not regard Paul or other exemplary Christians as akratic, but strong-willed or enkratic persons. In biblical studies, the paradigm of the 'Lutheran Paul' has not seldom been taken to mean an interpretation of Romans 7 according to which exemplary Christians remain weak-willed and unable to do what they plan to do.[65]

The same perspective is presupposed in *Against Latomus* (1521), where Luther again defends the view that the imperfections of justified Christians must be called sin. In Romans 7:16, the Christian Apostle Paul wills and consents to the good, but because his existence is both carnal and spiritual, his will is not wholly good (*vult non totus*). Thus it can happen that he does not do what he wants. In this sense of involuntary and compulsory wrongdoing, the external deeds do not correspond to the good intended by the good will.[66] This does not mean, however, that the flesh dominates action. Because the description concerns the spiritual person, the spirit prevails. Even when the spirit accuses the flesh, Luther considers that the spirit finally rules over the rebellious flesh, but because of the flesh the sin remains and the spiritual person is sometimes effectively impeded from doing good.[67]

To obtain a precise view of Luther's theory of human action in these writings, we need to focus on his concepts of sin and will. In *Lecture on Romans*, Luther wants to speak of harmful desires as sin but he also retains the Augustinian vocabulary of consent. Luther does, however, want to describe as sin the harmful passions and other realities of the flesh even when no additional act of positive consent pertains to them. In the context of Rom 7:19, this aspect of sinfulness is highlighted by the Augustinian distinction between *facere* and *perficere*: a spiritual person may 'do' evil even when he does not want to 'accomplish' it.

Another similar, though not identical, Augustinian distinction employed by Luther in *Against Latomus* is that between 'ruling' sin (*peccatum regnans*, Rom. 6:12) and 'ruled' sin (*peccatum regnatum*). A ruling sin involves consent; spiritual or 'holy' people do not consent to evil, but do nevertheless suffer from ruled sin.[68] In some sense, Luther's difference from the prevailing Catholicism is nominal and exegetical: while Catholics

---

[64] WA 2, 412, 13–20.

[65] See Westerholm (2004). The essays in Schneider and Wenz (2001) treat the history of this doctrine. Hermann (1934) is a comprehensive older study. Steinmetz (1990) studies the reception of Romans 7 in the Reformation.

[66] See, e.g., LSA 2, 509, 23–8.   [67] LSA 2, 510, 38–511, 12.   [68] e.g. LSA 2, 477, 9–22.

do not call the remaining concupiscence sin, Luther wants to call it a ruled sin because he believes that Paul also calls it sin.

There is, however, a more fundamental difference. Although Luther takes over the Augustinian notion of consent and identifies the 'accomplishment' of evil through this notion, the act of consent cannot for him be the actual criterion of culpability and sin. In *Against Latomus,* Luther makes this point particularly clearly: the scholastic tradition says that concupiscence is only infirmity and punishment of sin, not a culpable act of sin. It teaches that we first commit a sin when we consent to concupiscence. For Luther, however, it is wrong to say that the act of consenting to something non-culpable brings about culpability. Such a view creates a new concept of sin: 'Plainly a new notion of sin is this: weakness is neither sin nor condemned, and yet if you consent to a thing which is neither condemned nor culpable, you sin.'[69] In Luther's own definition, sin is simply something contrary to the law of God.[70]

We have seen that the act of consenting can increase culpability: a 'ruled' sin becomes a 'ruling' sin, a 'deed' becomes an 'accomplishment'. And yet the act of consent does not for Luther provide a demarcation line for sin or moral culpability. The demarcation line stretches beyond consent to the sinful desires which can be meaningfully forbidden. As God's law forbids concupiscence ('you shall not covet'), the harmful desires are not inevitable in the same sense as, for instance, thirst or fever:

Weaknesses, penalties, and the things involved in our mortality are not subject to legal restraint, nor can they be brought within our range of choice (*in arbitrio nostro*) ... When Paul commands us not to obey certain things but to put them to death, he certainly means sins, rather than punishments, things pertaining to our mortality or weaknesses. What sort of law would this be: Do not obey ulcers, do not obey fever, do not obey hunger and thirst ... aren't all these weaknesses, penalties, and things pertaining to mortality? No, what must not be obeyed is sin.[71]

Which harmful desires belong to the category of sin and occupy the area between natural weaknesses and consented evil actions? Concupiscence is an overall theological name for the sinful passions which God forbids in the tenth commandment of the Decalogue. Romans 6:12 (Vulgate), which serves as Luther's biblical evidence at this point, likewise considers concupiscence as the essence of 'ruled' sin. Luther regards different passions as belonging to this category of sin:

sin and evil passion remain after baptism. These are openly called anger, lust, covetousness, and incontinence—names which, by universal consent and in all languages, are customarily used to designate faults and sins.[72]

This passage in *Against Latomus* is the only place in Luther's works in which the Latin term *incontinentia* is dealt with in some detail. Luther discusses 1 Cor. 7:5 (Vulgate).

---

[69] LSA 2, 478, 32–5: 'Rursum consentire ei quod peccatum et damnatum non est, peccatum erit. Nova plane ratio peccati. Infirmitas non est peccatum nec damnata. Et tamen si consentias rei nec damnatae nec culpabili, peccasti.'

[70] LSA 2, 463, 26–7, cf. Augustine, *Contra Faustum Manichaeum* 22, 27.

[71] LSA 2, 480, 19–27.   [72] LSA 2, 481, 40–482, 2.

arguing against Latomus that 'incontinence' in the phrase *ne temptet vos Satanas propter incontinentiam vestram* does not refer to weakness or penalty, but to sinful passion which resembles concupiscence or anger. He argues against Latomus with biting irony:

Latomus will arise, proving by a comprehensive demonstration [against Paul] that incontinence is not incontinence but simply a weakness and penalty. When Satan tempts the saints, he does not tempt them to incontinence, but to weakness, and if it happens that they consent to incontinence, they do not assent to sin but to a weakness and penalty, and so when they sin they will really not sin.[73]

In 1 Cor. 7:5, incontinence is a harmful state which Luther interprets as passion: married people suffer from the passion of incontinence which Satan attempts to transform into illicit actions. Given the context of marriage, Luther presupposes an Augustinian notion of continence (cf. 1.2). Incontinence is sin in the same way as concupiscence in general: it does not need consent in order to be a 'ruled' sin. If consent is given, it becomes a ruling sin.

The word *incontinentia* also appears in two other places in *Against Latomus* in this sense. Together with other harmful desires, incontinence in 1 Cor. 7:5 shows that Paul calls such desires 'sin' even in spiritual individuals.[74] The biblical concept of sin is 'everywhere absolutely the same, even though it does not everywhere have the same strength, or the same mode of acting or being acted upon . . . [Paul] uses it to refer to incontinence, evil desire, anger, etc.'[75]

There is no distinct category of incontinent actions in Luther's usage of *incontinentia*, incontinence simply being a subspecies of that sinful passion which remains active in the 'flesh'. As the demarcation line of culpability does not go with consent but with the biblical command, this passion is sinful regardless of whether the person consents to it or not.

The act of consent is nevertheless important, since it transforms a 'ruled' sin into a 'ruling' sin. In addition, the state of repugnancy which characterizes the spiritual person disappears when that person consents to the evil desire. When sin rules, there is no repugnancy between spirit and flesh and the person ceases to be spiritual. Although Luther presents these points in order to defend his exegetical view that sin necessarily remains in the faithful, his analysis has some theoretically interesting features. His point that consent to something which is not in itself culpable cannot constitute culpability is a theoretical and even philosophical argument which calls the 'commonplace Augustinian' theory of morality into question.

In order to understand this point properly one needs to see that consent can nevertheless increase the culpability of certain moral states. What Luther actually claims is that the act of consent can only make a qualitative difference, not a quantitative one, with regard to the sinfulness of a given moral state. In one sense, this view turns the Aristotelian discussion on akrasia upside down, since Aristotle's virtuous person acts with a unified mind, whereas the enkratic and akratic states are characterized by inner

---

[73] LSA 2, 478, 21–5.   [74] LSA 2, 497, 13–16.   [75] LSA 2, 509, 17–21.

tension. Because of this permanent inner tension, the Aristotelian akratês later repents. For Luther, however, the best moral state of the spiritual person in this life is the enkratic state which is characterized by the continuing repugnancy of the flesh. If a person lapses from this state through consenting to a sin, the inner tension ceases and the person acts wrongly with a unified mind.

This fall into sin does not, however, create a qualitative difference in the understanding of culpability, but only a quantitative one in that the 'ruled' sin now becomes a 'ruling' sin. A person may fall from the enkratic state into the state of wickedness, but the nature of his sin or culpability remains qualitatively similar, since even the concupiscence which is not consented to is a sin because it is against God's law. Given this, there is no theoretical room for akrasia. The closest parallel to akrasia in Luther may be those wrongdoings of the spiritual individual which are not willed or consented to (Rom 7:19), but such deeds are compulsory actions which the subject does not control. The example of the horseman who cannot master his horses exemplifies this kind of behaviour.

There is one more angle in Luther's theory which needs further elucidation. God forbids harmful desires. This command distinguishes them from inevitable natural desires. As a result of this command, the appearance of forbidden desires causes culpabilility or sinfulness. Now, if the harmful desires are not consented to, in what sense are they proper to human beings in their life and actions? It would be good to have them eradicated, but is there any technique or strategy by means of which this could be done? The active struggle between spirit and flesh pertains to not following the temptation in action, but is there any practical means of eradicating the inward evil or sin which causes this temptation?

This question is difficult and the answer may be negative. Both the accomplishment of external good (*bonum perficere*) and the eradication of internal evil desire remain beyond the scope of human will. Its consent pertains to the 'middle ground' between the external goal and the internal origins of action; that is, to that middle part of action which concerns the everyday struggle against the temptations of the flesh. If Luther has any answers regarding the eradication of sinful desires, they are not philosophical but religious or theological answers: a person should trust in God and receive the divine gifts; he or she should pray and participate in the sacramental life of the church.[76]

Luther's famous treatise *De libertate Christiana* (1520) focuses on the inner freedom of faith. He distinguishes between the 'inner man' who is free and does no works and the 'outer man' who does all kinds of works. The outer man is depicted as a servant. The working life of the servant resembles the discussion of the spiritual person who fights agains the remaining sin and cannot 'accomplish' the good by his own power, although he does not consent to evil. The inner man does not work but rests in faith. He does

---

[76] On Luther's view of emotions, affects, and passions, see Metzger (1964); Zur Mühlen (1977). For the life of faith, see Bayer (2003), 15–40, 264–87. For the mystical connections of this *vita passiva*, see Bayer (2003), 38–40 and Hamm and Leppin (2007).

not have control over externals but rules over a 'spiritual dominion' which is a 'dominion of its own liberty'.[77]

Luther's description of this spiritual dominion and inner freedom from sin is designed to be a sort of 'anti-action theory'. A person who looks at this inner sphere from the perspective of active involvement is deceived. It is only possible to receive this freedom, not to achieve it:

From these considerations any one may clearly see how a Christian man is free from all things; so that he needs no works in order to be justified and saved, but receives these gifts in abundance from faith alone. Nay, were he so foolish as to pretend to be justified, set free, saved, and made a Christian, by means of any good work, he would immediately lose faith, with all its benefits. Such folly is prettily represented in the fable where a dog, running along in the water and carrying in his mouth a real piece of meat, is deceived by the reflection of the meat in the water, and, in trying with open mouth to seize it, loses the meat and its image at the same time.[78]

As the inner freedom relies on faith, God's command regarding the inner desires can only be fulfilled in faith. Faith is trust and freedom from works, but its power also leads to the union of the soul with Christ. In the actual, active life, a person always remains a servant who works and struggles against the residual sin.[79]

In this manner Luther emphasizes that 'no external thing' contributes to the true piety and righteousness (*frommkeit, iustitia*) which constitutes the spiritual person.[80] This spiritual quest falls beyond the scope of this study. Luther is probably alluding to some traditions of patristic and medieval mysticism which connect the passivity of the spiritual life with the eradication of harmful emotions.[81] Luther repeatedly stresses that the commandment 'you shall not covet' cannot be fulfilled so that a complete 'purity of the heart' (*das Herz rein haben*) can be achieved. The battle with sinful desires continues until death. The tenth commandment is therefore not meant for malicious people (*böse Buben*) but for the most pious ones (*die Frommsten*).[82] In this sense, the commandment 'you shall not covet' is finally spiritual, rather than ethical.

Although the inner life concerns spirituality and not ethics, it is important that Luther distinguishes between those feelings which cannot be meaningfully controlled by commandment, like thirst or fever, and the harmful passions which God's commandment defines as sin. Although the latter cannot be eradicated by means of free will, the commandment concerning them is meaningful because moral perfection requires a purity of the heart, and the life of faith attempts to follow this goal.

The biblical and Augustinian background of Luther's distinction between non-sinful and sinful feelings is Romans 7:7–9, in which Paul describes the impact of the tenth commandment. If the law had not said: 'you shall not covet', Paul would not have known sin, but once he recognized the meaning of this commandment, the sin which

---

[77] Cf. Bayer (2003), 256–80.   [78] LSA 2, 282, 9–16.   [79] LSA 2, 264–6; 284–6.
[80] LSA 2, 266–7, Schwarz (1986), 192.
[81] On these traditions, see Knuuttila (2004); Hamm and Leppin (2007).
[82] WA 30/1, 176, 16–18; 178, 10–21. WA 6, 276, 10–20.

was previously dead took the opportunity from this cognitive act. In *Contra Iulianum* 2, 4, 8, Augustine applies these verses to childhood: children are not moral subjects because their sin lies dormant within them as an inchoate feeling. The power of reason and will is needed in order that feelings can become morally qualified as sinful passions. This insight is important, since it attaches a judgement to the feeling so that the agent becomes conscious of it. A cognitive passion or desire of this kind is no longer morally neutral. This means, however, that desire and consent cannot be separated in the manner of medieval 'commonplace Augustinianism', since a cognitive desire already involves self-reflecting assent having moral value. Only children can have morally neutral inchoate feelings.

In his exposition of Romans 7:7–9, Luther quotes Augustine's elaboration and undertakes a similar distinction between the inchoate natural feelings and the cognitive passions which are known to be sinful with the help of the law: 'The Law revives and sin begins to make its appearance when the Law begins to be recognized; then concupiscence which had lain quiet during infancy breaks forth and becomes manifest.'[83] Luther applies this distinction both to children and to those adults who do not know the law: 'Because the Law has not yet been given to them they have no sin. But if they knew the Law against which they are sinning . . . they doubtlessly would immediately admit their sin. Thus when the Law comes to them, sin revives for them.'[84]

In this manner, the demarcation line of culpable passions becomes clearly defined: culpable passions are those which the person recognizes as sinful. This recognition is prompted by the commandment 'you shall not covet'. Philosophically speaking, this criterion of sinfulness is not a very sharp one: all passions which the individual thinks fall under the scope of the commandment become sinful. Augustine and Luther, however, underline the cognitive nature of harmful passions, which are not merely inchoate feelings, but appear together with a judgement concerning their nature and moral value.

This status of cognitive passions is interesting, since it deviates from the medieval, 'commonplace Augustinian' understanding of desire and consent which we can find in writers such as Buridan and Usingen (1.5, 3.1), who regard desires as non-culpable until a definite act of consent regarding them appears. Romans 7:7–9, however, prompts the late Augustine to offer a reading in which many desires appear as cognitive passions connected with moral judgement. For Luther, this self-awareness is enough to qualify concupiscence as sin. The self-awareness does not mean that the person consents to the temptation presented by the passion. For Luther, the act of consent pertains to the accomplishment of action. The reason why certain desires are sinful is simply that they appear together with a judgement as cognitive passions. In this manner, Luther comes close to our 'moderated Stoic model' (1.2, 1.5), in which emotions appear as morally relevant judgements.

---

[83] WA 56, 348, 8–10.   [84] WA 56, 348, 19–22.

In *Against Latomus* Luther says in passing that inchoate feelings and natural weaknesses are not 'in our range of choice' (*in arbitrio nostro*).[85] Sinful passions are more in our range of choice than natural weaknesses in two ways: (1) a cognitive act of judgement pertains to them so that they emerge as sinful passions; (2) we are called not to consent to their temptation so that sin remains a 'ruled' sin. Sinful passions are not freely chosen in the sense that we could avoid them or eradicate them, however. Adults necessarily use reason and become aware of the law; thus they inevitably make judgements regarding their passions.

Awareness of one's own sins under the law creates a situation in which the individual understands that he cannot fulfil the law and needs grace.[86] This awareness has little bearing on akrasia or action theory in general, since the individual in this state understands himself simply as sinful, not as weak-willed or akratic. The will is not changed because of this insight; the only change in the will can be caused by God, as Luther argues in detail in *De servo arbitrio*.

The range of choice and free will became a major issue after Erasmus of Rotterdam published his criticism of Luther, *De libero arbitrio Diatribe* (1524). Luther's response, *De servo arbitrio* (1525), is an extensive work in which many different and complex topics are treated. We will leave aside Luther's theological argument according to which God's foreknowledge predetermines the events of the world.[87] Our discussion focuses on the human side of that necessity, which Luther ascribes to actions and events.

To understand Luther's view of human action in *De servo arbitrio*, it should first be noted that he reads Erasmus's definition of free decision (*liberum arbitrium*) in a maximalist manner. For Luther, free decision means the self-moving power of human will, without the aid of grace, to follow and to turn away in issues regarding salvation. This power he vehemently denies, arguing that Erasmus contradicts himself because he defends free decision but does not want to affirm such an obviously Pelagian concept. Luther often shows that Erasmus in fact teaches that divine grace is needed to turn the will towards good.[88] Luther seems to exaggerate his opponent's view.

Because of his maximalist interpretation of problematic free decision, Luther can relate more positively to some other concepts of freedom which in his view do not represent free decision. First, he affirms the so-called natural aptitude, the power 'by which a man is capable of being taken hold of by the Spirit'. Animals and plants do not have this kind of receptive capacity, which thus distinguishes humans from animals.[89] Second, Luther concedes that humans have some freedom 'in inferior things': man has

---

[85] LSA 2, 480, 20 (quoted above).

[86] On this theological theme of Lutheranism, see Peters (1981).

[87] For this topic, see Kolb (2005). For the history of the argument, see Saarinen (2001). The phrase *servum arbitrium* is taken from *Contra Iulianum*, 2, 8, 23. For other major topics in the controversy between Erasmus and Luther, see Kohls (1972); O'Rourke Boyle (1983); Tinkler (1991).

[88] WA 18, 634–5, 664–6.

[89] WA 18, 636, 16–22.

'the right to use, to do and to leave undone, according to his own free choice'. This freedom is controlled by God's omnipotence, concerning merely the choice of means in everyday life, not the fundamental direction of the will.[90] Third, Luther states that 'we are not discussing what we can do through God's working, but what we can do of ourselves'. For him, the 'new creation' is able 'to follow and cooperate'. With the help of grace, humans can do everything (*nihil non posse auxiliante dei gratia*).[91]

But even in the spiritual state there is no self-moving choice between two contrary options. Luther's peculiar way of defining necessity and volition rules out this possibility. He states that 'by "necessarily" I do not mean "compulsorily", but by the necessity of immutability'. Given the definition of necessity as immutability, Luther claims that there are no more than two theoretical cases of willing something, neither of which allows for autonomous mutability. (1) Without the Spirit of God, a person acts wrongly 'of his own accord and with a ready will' (*sponte et libenti voluntate*). Since a person cannot by his own power change the direction of this will, he does not possess free decision. Even when 'he is compelled by external force to do something different . . . the will within him remains averse'.[92]

(2) When the Spirit of God works within the individual, the will is changed by God's power. The will of the spiritual person then wills the good 'of its own accord, not from compulsion' (*sponte sua vult, non coacte*). But neither in this voluntary cooperation is there free decision, because no self-movement towards the contrary can cause a change in the direction of the will (*nullis contrariis mutari in aliud possit*). Even the use of external force cannot change the good will of the holy people.[93] In this manner, both carnal and spiritual people act willingly and cooperate, but neither group possesses a self-movement of free decision with regard to the fundamental direction of their wills.

This is the point of Luther's famous comparison: 'The human will is placed between the two like a beast of burden. If God rides it, it wills and goes where God wills . . . if Satan rides it, it wills and goes where Satan wills; nor can it choose to run to either of the two riders or to seek him out.'[94]

This comparison does not rule out voluntary behaviour or cooperation. Luther is only interested in denying the autonomous power of choosing between two contrary opposites. For the purposes of our study, we need not discuss the actual validity of Luther's argument much further.[95] It is essential to see that this argument again effectively denies the possibility of akratic behaviour. A human being cannot act against

---

[90] WA 18, 638, 4–11.
[91] WA 18, 753–4. On cooperation, see Seils (1962).
[92] WA 18, 634, 14–29.
[93] WA 18, 634, 37–635, 7.
[94] WA 18, 635, 17–21.
[95] Kolb (2005) discusses the theological points in detail. The studies available in Pesch (1985) also treat Erasmus fairly. One problem is that Luther's argument from the foreknowledge of God pleads for a stronger determinism than his description of human action presupposes.

his own judgement or will: whatever he does apart from external compulsion, he does willingly.

The description of the spiritual person given above may look slightly different from that in Luther's earlier writings. Now Luther is not particularly worried about the impurity of spiritual actions caused by the remaining repugnancy, but he is confident that Christians can do good with the help of God. When Luther discusses the various biblical verses related to the bondage of the will, he nevertheless states that Romans 7 provides strong evidence in favour of his view. Paul's description of the struggle between the spirit and the flesh proves that carnal people cannot choose contrary to the flesh. The spiritual people for their part need to struggle in order to follow the Spirit. It may sometimes happen that spiritual people cannot do what they want (*non facere possint quae vellent*).[96] The possibility of compulsory enforcement against one's own will is here affirmed in the same manner as in Luther's earlier writings. Since the battle against Erasmus concerns the two-way freedom of the will without grace, the analysis of spiritual people and their action remains only a digression in *De servo arbitrio*.

Luther's effective denial of akrasia and related phenomena is significant for the understanding of later Lutheran discussion. At the same time, his view of human action in *De servo arbitrio* remains open-ended, at least when it is not looked at from the perspective of God's foreknowledge but from that of necessity as immutability. All human action is regarded as voluntary, action being carefully distinguished from animal behaviour and natural events. People cooperate willingly in both their carnal and spiritual actions; the only restriction is that the will cannot autonomously change its fundamental direction, in particular from its natural or carnal state towards the spiritual state.

In 'inferior things', the will even possesses a two-way freedom, the extent of which is not discussed in detail in *De servo arbitrio*. One way to interpret this freedom is to understand it as pertaining to the middle part of action (step 2). The dominating passions of the human heart (step 1) and the final accomplishment of the action (step 3) are dependent on God, clearly relating to the 'superior things' relevant in the struggle between flesh and spirit. In his or her cooperation, the individual cannot change the qualitative state of his sinfulness, but through being a faithful servant in the 'inferior' choices of everyday life he or she may act in consonance with the bigger picture.

Such an interpretation of the inferior things has two advantages. It does not create any external separation between worldly and spiritual actions. It also continues Luther's earlier discussion on human consent which cannot serve as a moral criterion of sin but which may nevertheless be of some help in 'ruling' the sin. In *De servo arbitrio*, the notion of consent does not play much of a role, but Luther concedes that the free decision can to an extent produce moral and civil justice and good works.[97] These inferior things pertain neither to the final destiny of people nor to the inner state of

---

[96] WA 18, 783, 3–15.

[97] e.g. WA 18, 767, 40–2: 'Atque ut dem, liberum arbitrium per conatum suum aliquo posse promoveri, videlicet ad opera bona vel ad iustitiam legis civilis vel moralis, Ad iustitiam Dei tamen non.'

their hearts, but to their everyday behaviour. In his later ethics of state and household, Luther grants people a role as a 'secondary cause' in cooperation with God. He can also say that while the efficient and final causes of worldly events can only be understood in theology, philosophical ethics can to some extent grasp the material and formal causes of civil matters.[98]

Although *De servo arbitrio* does not change Luther's earlier view of spirit and flesh, I have treated it at some length because this work illuminates later solutions by Lutheran theologians and philosophers. Although the theological side of this work emphasizes God's rule over all actions and events, the description of human action leaves many open possibilities for later philosophical ethics. Since human action is depicted as deeply voluntary, human persons remain responsible for their actions. In civil life, free decision is affirmed to an extent. Although God rules over the habits of the heart as well as over the final goal of the will, individuals can exercise cooperation in the 'middle part' of their actions, which pertain to the particular choices of everyday life. Luther's bigger picture of 'superior things' does not leave room for akrasia, but his smaller picture of 'inferior things' may, at least in the later reflection of other Lutherans, approximate Aristotelian and other philosophical theories of action.

Luther employs only once the example of Medea found in Josse Clichtove's commentary (2.4); it occurs in his late *Lectures on Genesis* (1535–1545). As this example has become a Protestant commonplace since Melanchthon (3.3), we should note its appearance in Luther. It is, however, little more than an anecdote, which Luther tells as follows:

This is what happens to the ungodly: though they know that they are sinning and that punishment of sin is imminent, they smugly overcome their fear when their wickedness gains the upper hand. Thus in the passage before us [Gen. 11:4], the words reveal a conscience that is confused and yet smugly keeps on disregarding the punishment. Such a conscience is attributed to Medea by Ovid when she says: 'I see and applaud the better things, but I follow the worse.' And we ourselves once heard Karlstadt say at this very place [the Wittenberg lecture room], when he was conferring a doctor's degree that he knew that it was a sin to create doctors of theology, but that he was doing it nevertheless. It is no trivial sin to harden oneself against conscience and to glory in a sin willingly and knowingly.[99]

This anecdote only describes a common mode of sinning willingly and knowingly. The phrase 'confused conscience' (*conscientia perturbata*) is relatively often employed by Luther to denote a situation in which different reasons or authorities suggest different

---

[98] See Saarinen (2005); Ebeling (1982), 333–431, especially 351–3.

[99] WA 42, 416, 36–417, 5: 'Sic enim impiis accidit, etsi sciunt, se peccare et impendere peccati poenas, tamen securi perrumpunt, superante malicia, timorem. Ita hoc in loco ostendunt verba perturbatam conscientiam, et tamen secure pergentem et contemnentem poenas, qualis Medeae apud Ovidium fingitur, cum dicit, Video meliora proboque, deteriora sequor. Et nos hic aliquando audivimus Carolostadium, cum Doctores promoveret, dicentem, se scire, quod Doctores Theologiae creare esset peccatum, et tamen facere. Hoc non leve peccatum est, indurari contra conscientiam, et in peccato quasi gloriari volentes et scientes.'

courses of action.[100] This perturbation does not, however, qualify volition or cognition in any sense which would alleviate culpability in the resulting action. On the contrary, Luther seems to think that Medea and Karlstadt act in a particularly determined manner in this example.

It is difficult but not impossible to classify Luther's view of action using the categories created for the understanding of akrasia in 1.5. Luther's view of sinful passions follows the moderated Stoic model proper to late Augustine. In many other respects, Luther follows voluntarist patterns of thought: all action is voluntary, ignorance does not explain or excuse wrong actions, and the presence of higher appetitive powers distinguishes humans from animals. The framework of voluntarism is, however, programmatically stripped of its most typical claim, that of self-determination or self-movement. Regarding the issue of self-movement, Luther says that he is closer to Aristotelian scholasticism than to the voluntarist view of Erasmus.[101] At the same time, his own vocabulary stems from Buridanian voluntarism presented in the guise of his teacher, Bartholomaeus Arnoldi de Usingen. Although Luther vehemently opposes Usingen's teachings, the underlying question of contrary appetitive powers shapes his own Augustinian view of spiritual and carnal actions. Luther's view does not allow for a distinct category of akratic actions, since all sinful actions proceed from the unified mind and volition in the same way.

3.3 Lutheran Humanists: Melanchthon and Camerarius

Luther's close friend and Wittenberg colleague, Philip Melanchthon (1497–1560) was a bridge-builder who connected Luther's theological insights with the broader currents of ecclesiastical and intellectual life. After Luther's vehement criticism of Aristotle, Melanchthon reintroduced the *Nicomachean Ethics* into the curriculum of the emerging Protestant universities. But, as several recent studies have shown, Melanchthon equipped his philosophical commentaries and textbooks with a number of new theological insights.[102] Melanchthon's works were immensely popular throughout Europe in the sixteenth and seventeenth centuries, having had formative influence in the academic life far beyond the borders of Lutheranism.[103]

Melanchthon applies Luther's distinction between law and gospel in his ethical treatises, arguing that natural reason can attain the truth in the realm of law, whereas the truth of the gospel can only be grasped in revelatory theology. The natural realm is not, however, devoid of God's activity. God has implanted the so-called natural notions in humans, which enable the knowledge of virtue. The emergence of human virtue is further dependent on divine impetus or movement (*impetus, motus*),

---

[100]   e.g. WA 5, 405, 1; 603, 14–19; WA 39/2, 137, 11–12.

[101]   WA 18, 664, 2 6–665, 30.

[102]   See Frank (1995) and (2005); Kusukawa (1995); Bellucci (2005).

[103]   For Melanchthon's European influence, see, e.g., Scheible (1997); Frank et al. (2001–2002); Frank, Köpf, and Lalla (2003).

which helps decisively in the learning and exercise of moral virtue.[104] Although ethics can be learned and practised in an Aristotelian manner, Melanchthon equips ethics with a theological substructure.

Melanchthon underlines this theological foundation in his later works, for instance, the textbook *Liber de anima* (1553). He teaches that the Holy Spirit is really present in the vital spirits of human veins and nerves in a manner which enables a reorientation of knowledge and emotions. The vital spirits

> exceed the sun with their light, and the light of all the stars, and even more miraculously, in the case of the pious the divine Spirit is mixed with these spirits, which makes them shine even more brightly with the divine light, so that their knowledge of God would be even clearer, their ascent to Him stronger, and their feelings for Him more ardent. Similarly, if devils occupy the heart, they will disorient the spirits in heart and the brain with their blow; they hinder judgement and produce perceptible insanity, and drive the heart and other members to cruel acts, as when Medea killed her children or when Judas killed himself.[105]

Melanchthon here performs a theological move which is similar to Luther's distinction between spirit and flesh (3.2). The Lutheran Reformers consider that a human is possessed either by the Spirit or the evil powers. There is no self-movement in the sense of a neutral choice between good and evil, the human condition being already predetermined by the constant struggle between sin and divine intervention.

Melanchthon has sometimes been portrayed as a moderate Humanist who has a more optimistic view of the freedom of the will than Luther. The present study, however, follows the view that Melanchthon sided with Luther in the debate on free will against Erasmus.[106] As we will see below, Melanchthon differentiates his views on human freedom, but he is no Erasmian. The points with regard to which Melanchthon teaches a limited human freedom resemble Luther's affirmations. In *De servo arbitrio* Luther affirms the possibility of human cooperation after receiving grace, as well as a limited freedom regarding the 'inferior' choices of everyday life (3.2). Melanchthon makes use of these features and can thus remain in agreement with Luther.

Melanchthon lectured on EN in Wittenberg and published several commentaries and ethical textbooks.[107] He did not, however, comment on EN VII, nor do his textbooks contain any thematic discussion on akrasia. He uses the word *incontinentia* in

---

[104] For law and gospel, see Wengert (1997); Scheible (1997). Keen (1990) is a study of Melanchthon's moral thinking. On natural notions and impetus, see Frank (1995). Melanchthon's texts are available in *Corpus Reformatorum* (CR) and, to some extent, in *Studienausgabe* (MSA).

[105] CR 13, 88–9: 'sua luce superant solis et omnium stellarum lucem. Et, quod mirabilius est, his ipsis spiritibus in hominibus piis miscetur ipse divinus spiritus, et efficit magis fulgentes divina luce, ut agnitio Dei sit illustrior, et adsensio firmior, et motus sint ardentiores erga Deum. Econtra ubi diaboli occupant corda, suo adflatu turbant spiritus in corde et in cerebro, impediunt iudicia, et manifestos furores efficiunt, et impellunt corda et alia membra ad crudelissimos motus, ut, Medea interficit natos, Iudas sibi ipsi consciscit mortem.' Translation from Vainio (2008), 89, who also provides a good commentary.

[106] As argued in Wengert (1998).

[107] Listed e.g. in Frank (2005), 217. A concise list of all works by Melanchthon is provided in Scheible (1992), 386–9. Melanchthon, *Ethicae doctrinae elementa* is a new edition.

its Augustinian sense, meaning adultery or lack of sexual chastity. The best clues to Melanchthon's view of weak-willed conduct are provided in his treatment of the inner conflict between natural reason and harmful passion. Melanchthon often refers to the example of Medea, whose akratic conflict was considered to be the paradigm of akrasia in Clichtove's influential commentary (2.4).

Medea illustrates the standard conflict between natural reason and harmful passion, leading to an act against one's own better judgement. As Medea represents pre-Christian antiquity, her conflict is slightly different from the Apostle Paul's conflict between spirit and flesh, which is also significant for both Luther and Melanchthon. Medea's conflict is predominantly anthropological and philosophical, whereas Paul's conflict is spiritual and theological. Luther and Melanchthon deal with 'weakness of will' indirectly for the most part in the context of these conflicts. The Lutheran interpretation history of Aristotle's akrasia in the narrow sense begins, therefore, with Joachim Camerarius, to whom we will turn in the latter part of this chapter. At the same time, the Protestant interpretation history of akrasia is deeply dependent on Luther's and Melanchthon's formative teachings.

Among Melanchthon's writings, his theological textbook *Loci communes* and his *Liber de anima* offer the most detailed view of human action. Both works employ the example of Medea. Melanchthon's expositions and editions of classical texts can be used as supplementary material. Melanchthon lectured on Ovid's *Metamorphoses* and translated the *Medea* of Euripides into Latin.[108] While Clichtove (2.4) introduced Medea's love as an example of acting against judgement, Melanchthon also employs her rage as an illustration of the inner conflict. In the following, I will first discuss Melanchthon's view of human freedom in the various editions of his *Loci communes*,[109] and then proceed to other works in which Medea's conflict is mentioned. This method of presentation is not exhaustive, but does set out the philosophical core of Melanchthon's view regarding human weakness. His theological view of human beings is laid out more fully in his different expositions of Romans 7.[110]

In the first edition of *Loci communes* (1521), Melanchthon defends a straightforward view of human action, teaching that the passions or 'affects' (*affectus*) of the will determine human conduct. Since people cannot choose their affects, there is no free will in the sense of the possibility of acting or not acting. The cognitive powers remain servants of the will and its affects: the will rules over knowledge as a tyrant rules over the state.[111] There is some external freedom with regard to 'greeting a person or not

---

[108] CR 19, 499–654 (Ovid); CR 18, 449–90 (Euripides).

[109] In addition to CR, I quote the first edition according to Melanchthon, *Loci* 1521 *Lateinisch-Deutsch*, and the third edition (*aetas*) according to MSA. For the complicated text history of different editions, see the introductions to the CR and Scheible (1997).

[110] They include, for instance, the *Annotationes in Epist. Pauli ad Romanos* 1521–1522 (CR 15, 463–6). *Commentarii in Epist. Pauli ad Romanos* 1532 (CR 15, 642–54) and *Enarratio Epist. Pauli ad Romanos* 1556 (CR 15, 935–44).

[111] *Loci* 1521, 1, 8–19. CR 21, 86–8. Throughout this study, from Melanchthon to Spinoza, I will use 'affect' as a translation of *affectus*.

greeting him, wearing this cloth or not, eating flesh or not', but the internal affects are not in our power. The will and human heart is their source but the will cannot exercise freedom over them.[112] Even natural reason can see that the will cannot control internal affects, although the will has some freedom with regard to the external works. Finally, everything happens according to divine predestination.[113]

This straightforward view may have some terminological differences to Luther's writings from the same period, but basically it contains the same theological teaching. The individual is always ruled either by sinful passions and affects or by spiritual affects. Both the inner affects of human actions and their final goal remain determined in this manner; some freedom pertains to the 'middle part' (cf. 3.2), that is, to the actions of everyday life; but this observation does not mean that there is genuine human freedom. Like Luther, Melanchthon stresses that even the most holy and spiritual people, like Paul in Romans 7, suffer from captivity under sin.[114] Against the scholastics, Melanchthon teaches that there is no such 'new will' which could control human affects. It is true that the individual can sometimes move against the affects, but such occasional successes do not prove that the will has real control.[115] The natural powers of human beings can only cause sin.[116]

As in the case of Luther, this straightforward denial of human freedom does not leave much room for a philosophical discussion of akrasia. The second and third editions (aetates) of Loci, however, contain a differentiation of the will's powers. This differentiation allows a discussion of the inner conflict of Medea and, as its corollary, other akratic and enkratic non-spiritual acts. In the second aetas of his Loci (1535–1543), Melanchthon describes the natural reason and natural freedom in more detail. Because there is some remnant of good judgement even in sinful human beings, they can to an extent behave rationally and perform external actions which promote civil goods. In this sense, the human will can be called free and it can to some extent act in consonance with the external requirements of the law.[117]

Melanchthon adds immediately that the weakness of our nature, provoked by the devil, often overcomes this freedom. People are full of evil affects which overrule the right judgement, as is the case of Medea in Ovid's *Metamorphoses*. The devil can also cause even 'the best of men', who aim to live honestly, to fall into serious sins. In the midst of all these difficulties, one can nevertheless detect a remnant of freedom which can bring about civil righteousness.[118]

---

[112] *Loci* 1521, 1, 42–6. CR 21, 90.   [113] *Loci* 1521, 1, 66–9. CR 21, 93.
[114] *Loci* 1521, 2, 78–9. CR 21, 107.   [115] *Loci* 1521, 2, 82. CR 21, 108.
[116] *Loci* 1521, 2, 122. CR 21, 114.

[117] CR 21, 374: 'Primum igitur respondeo: cum in natura hominis reliquum sit iudicium et delectus quidam rerum, quae sunt subiectae rationi aut sensui; reliquus est etiam delectus externorum operum civilium. Quare voluntas humana potest suis viribus sine renovatione aliquo modo externa legis opera facere. Haec est libertas voluntatis, quam Philosophi recte tribuunt homini.'

[118] CR 21, 374: 'hanc ipsam libertatem efficiendae civilis iustitiae saepe vinci naturali imbecillitate, saepe impediri a Diabolo. Nam cum natura sit plena malorum affectuum, saepe obtemperant homines pravis cupiditatibus, non recto iudicio. Sicut inquit apud Poetam Medea: Video meliora proboque, deteriora

Melanchthon here develops Luther's teaching that some external freedom can be observed in actions. He also makes room to conceptualize a struggle which is not merely between spirit and flesh, but between the remnants of the natural capacities on the one hand, and sinful passions on the other. Even people without the spirit, like Medea, can witness to this struggle between reason and passion. In this sense, there can be continent and incontinent behaviour in the natural sphere of external actions which intend civil righteousness. Luther did not admit any third moral state between obdurate vice and continence (cf. 3.2), but he did affirm the limited sphere of external freedom regarding ordinary civil life. The postulate of this sphere now leads Melanchthon to the new conclusion that there can be natural instances of inner conflict. In Medea, as well as in 'the best of men', the inner conflict results in a moral state in which one acts akratically against one's better judgement. One can also, at least occasionally, remain continent. In this sense, there is room for akrasia and enkrateia in Melanchthon's theory of action.

Melanchthon emphasizes that the corruption of our nature is so horrible that we cannot achieve proper obedience to God with our own power and will. The infirmity of human powers is such that our free decision (*liberum arbitrium*) can never satisfy the requirements of God's law. God requires spiritual affects which can only be the work of the Holy Spirit.[119] At the same time, Melanchthon considers that some free will can be detected in the life of holy people. They are helped by the Spirit and their life remains imperfect, but the Spirit also renews their will so that their subsequent free acts can to an extent be ascribed to them. Pious people are not like statues, their will cooperating with the help of the Spirit.[120] This doctrine of cooperation is to some extent present in Luther's *De servo arbitrio* (3.2), but Melanchthon elaborates it to make the point that some people possess at least a partially free will. Although the second *aetas* of *Loci* remains in the footsteps of Luther, Melanchthon makes use of the opportunity provided by Luther's concessions regarding external freedom and human cooperation. Through the example of Medea, Melanchthon's discussion of external freedom becomes connected with the philosophical issue of acting against one's own better judgement.

Both Medea's case and the cases of virtuous cooperation are characterized in terms of wrestling and struggle. Melanchthon uses the image of the wrestling will: 'When the will wrestles with weakness, it nevertheless does not reject the word, but remains with the word, so that consolation follows...In this wrestling the soul must be encouraged.'[121] The topic of wrestling (*lucta*) pertains primarily to the cases of cooperation with

---

sequor. Praeterea Diabolus captivam naturam impellit ad varia flagitia etiam externa, sicut videmus summos viros, qui tamen conati sunt honeste vivere, lapsus turpissimos habere. Sed tamen inter has difficultates, utcunque reliqua est aliqua libertas efficiendae iustitiae civilis.'

[119] CR 21, 374–5.

[120] CR 21, 377.

[121] CR 21, 376: 'Quanquam autem luctatur voluntas cum infirmitate, tamen quia non abiicit verbum, sed sustentat se verbo, consequitur consolationem...In hac lucta hortandus est animus.' The metaphor of wrestling is coloured by Eph. 6:12 (Vulgate): 'conluctatio...adversus principes et potestates.'

God. Melanchthon can sometimes say, with Luther, that the wrestling will actually indicate that God is working in the person, for the impious do not feel any such struggle.[122] At the same time, the will's wrestling proves that the faithful are not statues but real agents who contribute in their acts of cooperation.[123]

Both Luther and Melanchthon assume that divine cooperation pertains to the theological situations of continence in which the person does good while also remaining reluctant. In addition, Melanchthon holds that, even in the natural sphere of civil righteousness, people sometimes bring forth externally good acts, and sometimes act against their better judgement. Although they want to do good, and at times are able to perform acts of civil justice, they are also aware of their own failures. In the second *aetas* of *Loci*, two examples of such akrasia are mentioned: Medea, who follows her love, and the best of men, who fail in their honest intentions.

The third *aetas* of *Loci* (1544–1559) discusses human freedom extensively. Melanchthon first mentions the Stoics, who deny freedom and contingency. Christians should affirm that some remnant of good judgement and freedom of the will remains in human nature in its current state, rather than believe in such determinism. People can thus perform external acts that are in accordance with the moral law. On the other hand, one should always pay attention to the magnitude of sin in discussing this matter.[124] In these passages, Melanchthon closely follows the formulations of the second *aetas*.

The example of Medea is now embedded in a longer list of cases in which people, driven by their evil affects, act against their good judgement (*contra consilium mentis*). The case of Medea proves that such people could have resisted evil passions if they had tried hard enough.[125] Biblical passages like Eph. 2:2 attest to this in claiming that the devil is at work in impious persons. Saul and Judas exemplify this demonic irrationality. Tyrannic rule and brutal warfare can also be regarded as the devil's work, contrary to reason.[126] Melanchthon comes to the conclusion that, on the one hand, the calamities of history and human experience teach that the natural rule of reason cannot produce true freedom. On the other hand, he admits that between the demonic interventions people can to some extent safeguard external morality and in this sense act freely.[127]

---

[122] CR 10, 873: 'Cumque voluntas luctatur, signum est, eam a Deo trahi. Qui vero expectant violentos raptus, ut Enthusiastae, et Stenckfeldiani loquuntur, hi manent hostes Dei, et Deum trahentem repellunt.'

[123] CR 23, 280, 436; CR 24, 387–8.

[124] CR 21, 652–4. MSA II/1, 262–5.

[125] CR 21, 655: 'Nam quia vitiosi affectus in hominibus sunt acres stimuli et magna animorum incendia, homines saepe obediunt illis contra consilium mentis, etiam cum possent se cohibere, si anniterentur, ut Medea inquit: Video meliora proboque. Deteriora sequor.' MSA II/1, 266.

[126] CR 21, 655. MSA II/1, 266–7.

[127] CR 21, 655: 'Est ingens igitur imbecillitas generis humani, ut omnium temporum historiae et quotidiana experientia docet, in qua tantum horribilium miseriarum cernitur, ut sapientes Ethnici omnes valde mirati sint, unde tantum sit in hac praestanti natura confusionum et tristissimorum casuum. Sed tamen inter haec impedimenta manet aliquis delectus, aliqua libertas in mediocriter sanis, regendi externos mores.' MSA II/1, 267.

Melanchthon discusses inner freedom and human cooperation with God in a manner which is fairly similar to the earlier editions of *Loci* as well as to Luther's views: true inner freedom is the Spirit's work, but there is also human cooperation in which the human will reacts a posteriori to the divine initiative.[128] Melanchthon now amplifies his view of the will's wrestling, which demonstates that the will is not merely passive: saints, unlike statues, continue to wrestle.[129] Various heretics, for instance the Manicheans and the Enthusiasts, claim that the faithful remain totally calm and passive, but it is not the calmness but the wrestling of the faithful which shows that the Spirit is active in them.[130] In this sense it is not their perfect virtue but their wrestling with repugnant vice which is evidence of their agency and of a degree of freedom.

Although there is some human freedom, it is often impeded. With regard to such impediments, 'there are many confused judgements, because human beings for a great deal live like drunkards without discipline, proper attention, and any exercise of faith and prayer'.[131] Three impediments prevent people from exercising their freedom, namely, the corruption of human nature, the works of the devil, and the general confusion of human life. Because of such impediments one cannot simply insist that God has left people to take their own course, as Eccl. 15:14 seems to state. People have freedom to go wrong and their will is never merely passive, since they are not statues. At the same time, they cannot produce truly good actions without the help of the Spirit.[132]

Melanchthon offers two complementary viewpoints: while people are real agents and can even see the good and avoid evil to an extent with the remnants of their natural capacities, all truly good works are finally spiritual and theological. The two viewpoints are not in full consonance with each other, since the capacity of the natural will remains unclear: does it have a natural ability to bring about good or not?[133] Melanchthon wants to have it both ways: in terms of civil righteousness, the individual can sometimes bring about external good, but in a theological sense the human will always needs the help of the Spirit in order to act well.

We cannot press Melanchthon's remarks into a system which could settle this question in a philosophically consistent manner, but we may note that he discusses

---

[128] CR 21, 655–6, 660, 664. MSA II/1, 266–7, 273, 278–9.

[129] CR 21, 658: 'Haec sunt perspicua, si in veris doloribus, in vera invocatione experiamur, qualis sit lucta voluntatis, quae si se haberet ut statua, nullum prorsus certamen, nulla lucta, nulli angores essent in sanctis. Cum autem sit certamen ingens et difficile, voluntas non est otiosa.' MSA II/1, 271.

[130] CR 21, 658–9. MSA II/1, 271–2.

[131] CR 21, 662: 'Sed ideo de hac quaestione confusiora sunt iudicia, quia homines magna ex parte tanquam ebrii sine disciplina, sine diligentia, sine ullis exercitiis fidei et invocationis vivunt.' MSA II/1, 276.

[132] CR 21, 662–3. MSA II/1, 276–8.

[133] For Melanchthon, 'natural' is a divine gift of creation and in this sense theologically conditioned; see Frank (1995). But 'natural' also means something in the realm of the law, in distinction from the gospel, the Spirit, and the salvific acts of God. In this second sense, 'natural' refers to philosophical truths which can be discussed with the inventory of reason. The will and reason of Medea and other non-Christians act 'naturally' in this sense and should be so explained.

the remaining natural powers of the will in some more detail than Luther. Melanchthon claims in the second and third editions of *Loci* that there may be a natural conflict
between reason and evil desire. Often, as in the case of Medea, this conflict leads to
akratic actions, but Melanchthon also admits that people can sometimes exercise their
imperfect freedom to produce externally good actions. If Luther tacitly denied the
category of akrasia for theological reasons (3.2), Melanchthon reintroduces the philosophical category of acting against one's better judgement.

The image of the 'wrestling will' is significant for several reasons. It develops the
older ideas of 'struggle' and 'contrary appetites' which are prominent for Luther but
derive from his predecessors (cf. 2.4, 3.1). The theme of wrestling continues to be
relevant for later Protestant authors (3.4, 4.3). For Melanchthon, wrestling involves a
spiritual component and therefore confirms theological truths. The natural conflict
between the remnants of reason and evil affects is not called wrestling in this sense. The
akratic actions of Medea, Saul, Judas, and 'the best of men' occur when their reason is
prevented by the impediments of weakness and demonic power. Melanchthon does
not explain the emergence of akrasia in philosophical detail, but it is nevertheless
important that his *Loci* reintroduces the non-spiritual and philosophical problem of
inner conflict.

In his other works, Melanchthon uses the example of Medea fairly often, relating it
both to Medea's conflict between her fatherland and Jason (Ovid's *Metamorphoses*), and
to her killing of her children. One of the most revealing quotes occurs in *Liber de anima*,
in which Melanchthon speaks of the discrepancy between cognitive and appetitive
parts:

But here we realize and deplore our infirmity: the will and heart can shamefully overrule the
judgement of cognitive power, as Medea says: I see the better and approve it, but follow
the worse. The will of Roman gladiators receives the blows against the judgement of mind.
For the will can resist the right judgement. It also happens that the demons move the hearts
so that the minds become furious and the judgement of the cognitive part is obscured...
Because of such events it cannot be said that the natural light would be extinct in these
people or, even less, in other healthy persons. But the demons move the nature deserted by
God violently.[134]

Melanchthon here reinterprets Luther's anthropology. There is no neutral realm which
natural reason could occupy, since people are always controlled by either God or the
devil. There is, however, the natural cognitive power which can produce good
judgements. The demonic powers exercise their influence through the will, or the

[134] CR 13, 141: 'Sed hic agnoscamus et deploremus infirmitatem nostram, quod etiam contra iudicium in
potentia cognoscente, ruunt voluntas et cor in tetra scelera, ut inquit Medea. Video meliora proboque, deteriora
sequor. Voluntas in Romanis gladiatorum caedes recepit, contra iudicium mentis. Potest enim voluntas
repugnare recto iudicio. Accedit huc etiam, quod diaboli et corda impellunt, et mentibus inserunt furores, ut
etiam caligo in parte cognoscente iudicium obruat... Nec propter talia facta lux naturalis in his ipsis, ac multo
minus in aliis sanis extincta est. Sed diaboli violenter impellunt desertam a Deo naturam.' MSA III, 330.

appetitive part, and can thus impede the exercise of good judgement. In *Liber de anima*, Melanchthon also illustrates this state of affairs by a reference to Medea's killing of her children.[135] The affect overrules the judgement and becomes the efficient cause of action, but there also remains a cognitive component which can produce judgements. Because of this component, people are involved in a real psychological or mental conflict: they have the light of reason, and they are also responsible for the eventual cooperation of their will. In this sense, their own mental powers interact with the external power of God or the demons.

Medea exemplifies a person who is not obdurately evil but commits evil acts episodically or occasionally. As she 'sees the better', she has the natural light of reason but, because she is not a Christian, she does not have the Spirit. Thus she illustrates the philosophical phenomenon of akrasia in a standard manner. Although Melanchthon does not provide an elaborate philosophical explanation of this phenomenon, he clearly acknowledges it by referring to Medea in various contexts. His final explanation of akrasia is theological: sin and the devil impede weak nature from doing good. This explanation employs a voluntarist theory of action in which the appetitive and voluntary powers are distinct from the cognitive power and the will can overcome reason. Akrasia can thus occur in a fairly clear-eyed manner. Melanchthon's voluntarism nevertheless also presupposes that the natural light of reason remains weak in the human condition; since reason is the highest power, it should remain fairly weak in order to be overcome by lower powers.

In his *Exposition of the Nicene Creed* (1557), Melanchthon again admits that the natural powers of non-Christians can occasionally produce externally good acts and be free in this limited sense, but they are often impeded by the devil and the weakness of nature. Medea's words prove that this is the case.[136] Philosophers wonder how such weakness is possible and how we can achieve virtue. In Paul's theology, the externally good acts are called the 'works of the law'. People can command their will and external conduct in such acts, although the deepest affects of their heart remain sinful.[137] Melanchthon thus concedes that there is some natural enkrateia or continence.

---

[135] CR 13, 89 (quoted above). This example also occurs in a textbook by Melanchthon's pupil Johannes Velcurio, *In philosophiae naturalis* (1537), 66–7.

[136] CR 23, 542: 'Quanquam autem hanc externam disciplinam, id est, gubernationem locomotivae, ne fiant externa facta contra Legem, humanae vires etiam in non renatis aliquo modo efficere possunt, tamen simul sciendum est, hanc libertatem duabus causis saepe impediri insidiis Diaboli, et imbecillitate nostrae naturae, qua fit, ut saepe homines contra iudicium mentis impulsi affectibus ruant in scelera, sicut Medea inquit: Video meliora proboque, deteriora sequor.'

[137] CR 23, 542: 'Miratur Philosophia, unde sit tanta infirmitas in homine, ut affectus tanto impetu repugnent notitiis recta iubentibus: quaerit igitur, quid sit virtus, et an virtutem humana diligentia assumere possit, sicut pictores, musici, artes suas assumunt exercitiis. Paulus disciplinam nominat opera Legis, id est, actiones externas, quae fiunt locomotiva sciente aut frenante externa membra, et regitur locomotiva cogitatione et imperio voluntatis, etiamsi cor habet contrarios affectus.'

Melanchthon's *Postilla* (printed 1594), a collection of his biblical expositions, contains a passage in which he points out the importance of making a proper distinction between cognitive and appetitive powers. Even non-Christians can possess the natural light of reason as a divine gift but, as the example of Medea shows, this light is often overcome by raging appetitive powers.[138] In an *Exposition of Hesiod's Works and Days* (1532), Melanchthon says that Pandora's box contains the harmful passions. As the example of Medea shows, since a person cannot control these passions even if he or she knows them to be harmful, one should not provoke the passions and keep the box closed.[139]

Melanchthon deals with Medea's love fairly extensively in his *Commentary on Ovid's Metamorphoses* (1554). He underlines the great power of love, a major affect which can distract cognitive powers.[140] In her conflict, Medea understands that her love turns her mind away from reason, love recommending one thing, reason another. She also understands that a clear mind should resist love, but she cannot. Thus she wrestles with herself and succumbs to her passion reluctantly. She is forced to obey her love.[141] Using phraseology which is common to many discussions of akrasia (e.g. *invita, non ignoro, luctor mecum*), Melanchthon portrays a conflict between reason and desire. Although he does not refine his conceptual analysis, his dualistic concept of soul and the clear-eyed nature of akrasia are again evident. Melanchthons's various expositions of *Metamorphoses* 7, 20–21 thus repeat and illustrate the theory of action outlined in *Loci* and *Liber de anima*.

We saw in 1.2 that 'Medea's akrasia' can refer to Medea's love, as in Ovid's *Metamorphoses* 7, 20–21, or to her rage, as in Euripides's *Medea* 1078–1079. It is significant for the reception history of these classical texts that Melanchthon is very familiar with both. His Latin translation of Euripides's *Medea* was published in 1558; in this translation, the crucial lines are translated 'Et intelligo, qualia sint ea mala, quae molior; Sed ira est praestantior meis consiliis'.[142] (I know what evil I propose to do, but anger overrules my deliberations). The translation does not contain a commentary, but Melanchthon occasionally refers to this example in his other works. We have already discussed his reference in *Liber de anima*.

Melanchthon employs the example of Medea's rage in his biblical expositions several times. In their fury, people like Medea and Cain lack the good affects (*storgai*) and benevolence which are God's gift. When this benevolence is lacking, Satan can enter

---

[138] CR 24, 355.

[139] CR 18, 199.

[140] CR 19, 568–9.

[141] CR 19, 569: 'Haec est summa disputationis, quae periphrasi explicari possit vel hoc modo: Nescio, quis motus rationi non obtemperans verset animum meum; certe quantum intelligo, amor est. Cur enim parentis iussa mihi displicent? cur Iasoni metuo? Atqui castae mentis est resistere amori. Fateor; sed qui possum? Equidem luctor mecum atque invita huic perturbationi animi succumbo; aliud enim amor, aliud ratio suadet. Ac quamquam non ignoro affectum amoris esse pessimum consultorem: tamen illi obtemperare cogor.'

[142] CR 18, 481.

the hearts of furious people,[143] provoking a fury which vexes the mind and runs contrary to all natural condition. Medea's killing of her children is an example of such fury.[144] She follows the demonic impulse.[145] The theological dynamics of Medea's fury is thus similar to the dynamics of her love. In both, the appetitive part becomes occupied by evil powers so that the will does not listen to the voice of reason but follows the harmful passion.

Melanchthon's deliberations regarding the problem of acting against one's own better judgement remain theological: the will can overcome reason when evil powers control it, making use of the infirmity of human nature and impeding the use of reason. At the same time, akratic actions remain voluntary and clear-eyed, as the example of Medea shows. Melanchthon's significance for our topic lies primarily in his ability to transmit Luther's theological views in a form which could be received in ethics and the theory of action. As we shall see with regard to later authors like Calvin (4.1) and Daneau (4.3), this transmission sometimes provided a theological substructure to ethics and the theory of action.

In spite of this theological predominance, Melanchthon's discussion provides room for a more philosophical treatment of akrasia. He affirms the potential for natural reason to seek the good and even to attain it in external actions. Because of our continuing infirmity, our actions often fail but, precisely for this reason, both incontinence and continence are real possibilities which should be discussed in ethics. Melanchthon does not provide any deeply philosophical explanation of these phenomena. Philosophically, he can be labelled as a voluntarist. He presupposes a strong dualism between cognitive and appetitive powers, underlining on many occasions that this dualism should be kept in mind when human action is discussed. He therefore displays some features of 'commonplace Platonism' in the sense of our typology (1.5), but it may be more adequate to label him as a strongly voluntarist Aristotelian who employs Aristotle's EN and De anima in his textbooks, adapting the Aristotelian learning to meet the requirements of Lutheran theology.

At the same time, one needs to add that 'voluntarism' is a somewhat misleading label, since Melanchthon also believes that the human mind is primarily possessed either by God or the demonic powers. The will directs action, but this will is free only in the limited sense of cooperation with the primary power in question. Melanchthon is, however, a voluntarist in the sense that he is fairly close to the Aristotelianism of Henry of Ghent (1.4) and John Mair (2.5), believing that the will finally rules the mind. These voluntarist features become more systematically applied to Aristotle's akrasia in the commentary by Melanchthon's student and colleague Joachim Camerarius.

Camerarius (1500–1574) was one of Melanchton's most prominent pupils. He reorganized the universities of Tübingen and Leipzig and published widely in the fields of classical philology and history. His extensive *Explicatio librorum Ethicorum ad*

---

[143] CR 15, 839.   [144] CR 25, 576.   [145] CR 14, 360.

Nicomachum appeared in Frankfurt in 1570 and was reprinted there in 1578 and 1583. It contains a new translation and an elaborate commentary, which often focuses on various matters of Greek language. In its philological erudition, the work can be compared with Pier Vettori's commentary published in 1584.[146] We will, however, turn our attention to the philosophical side of Camerarius's commentary. The author claims that he prefers to clarify the issues instead of merely elaborating on the words;[147] some philosophical sophistication can thus be expected.

In addition to EN VII, Camerarius discusses akrasia in the preface to his commentary. As this preface deals with the differences between the Aristotelian and Stoic psychologies of human action and distinguishes Christian theology from ethics, it also clarifies the general approach of the author. Camerarius points out that his discussion on ethics proceeds from human reason, which needs to be kept distinct from theological truths. It is very dangerous to confuse human and divine matters in a discussion regarding ethics.[148]

Like Melanchthon, Camerarius holds, however, that this does not imply any conflict between reason and theology. Because the human mind is the image of God, it is useful to study it in many ways and to learn the virtues and human precepts regarding good conduct. The philosophical study of human nature and condition is a helpful preparation for the study of theology. At the same time, the study of ethics does not show the way to salvation and final blessedness; philosophers like Socrates can only offer shadows of the truth available in the church.[149] In practice, the distinction between philosophy and theology means that Camerarius expounds his text merely in a philosophical and philological manner, an approach which distinguishes him from Melanchthon.

A major part of the preface is devoted to the issue of distinguishing among various powers and faculties of the mind. Camerarius adheres to Plato and, in particular, Aristotle in claiming that the different impulses of the mind presuppose different faculties. Like the body, the mind has various faculties which we can experience.[150] Camerarius mentions the rational, animal, and vegetative soul, and the division between the irascible and the concupiscible soul. He criticizes the Stoics for their lack of sufficient distinctions.[151] When the mind is pulled in different directions

---

[146] Kunkler (2000) offers an overview of Camerarius. I am using the 1578 edition of *Explicatio*. On Vettori, see Lines (2002), 238–46. Lines (2002), 240–1 complains of Vettori's lack of philosophical interest; in this respect Camerarius fares better.

[147] *Explicatio*, 17: 'Quae omnia re declarari quam verbis praedicari malo.'

[148] *Explicatio*, 13–14: 'Religio enim coelestis et divina res est, et ideo explicari doctrina huius, humana et terrena cognitione atque scientia non potest. Separanda itaque longissimo intervallo sunt divina et humana omnia, quorumque confusione nihil fieri possit deterius, neque perniciosius.'

[149] *Explicatio*, 14–16; cf. Kraye (1988), 314.

[150] *Explicatio*, 4: 'Utque corpus ipsum quoque non est unum et simplex...sic in animo experimur esse diversas facultates et incitationes.' I often translate *animus* as 'mind', following Camerarius's equation *animus-mens-nous* in distinction to *anima*; see *Explicatio*, 23–4.

[151] *Explicatio*, 4–6. As we remarked in 3.1, the doctrine of a real distinction between the faculties of the soul may also have Ockhamistic origins. For Ockham's view, see Adams (1987), 654–69 and Hirvonen (2004).

simultaneously, disparate causes must be assumed for its various tendencies. The same faculty does not struggle (*non pugnat*) with itself, and the motion towards contrary opposites cannot emerge in one faculty alone.[152]

According to Camerarius, the Stoics are very confused on this point, for they teach that there is only one power at work within the mind's judgement, producing hidden and sudden changes so that the judgement swiftly changes between true and false. The Stoics call this process, and the resulting false assent, the perturbation of opinion.[153] Camerarius points out that such states of perturbation and changing judgement must be analysed with great care; he mentions the case of Medea as an example of such a conflict.[154] Unlike the Stoics, Camerarius argues that the activities of mind, reason, and judgement represent one power, whereas the passions, affects, and emotions represent another.[155] Here he clearly follows Melanchthon.

Reason does not display passions, which are altogether another thing (*alia res*). Reason cannot struggle with itself; it is rather the case that the passions cause corruption (*corripitur*) or errors (*defertur*) in the practical mind (*nous praktikos*).[156] To explain why the mind can follow the passions instead of reason, Camerarius introduces the doctrine of free will:

There is in the human being a free and self-regulating power which we call the will. It can always turn to both parts of the soul. If this power joins with the animal part of the human being, turning away from reason, then it cannot deliberate on anything well, nor think rightly, nor investigate the matter in an uncorrupted manner.[157]

Because the human mind has all these different parts and powers, we should not interpret its dynamics in Stoic terms as passions which emerge as false judgements of reason.[158] The power of good reason remains even at that moment of struggle in which the will turns to the harmful passion and follows it. The mind can be compared to a prodigal son: although the son follows his passions, he can remember and even

---

[152] *Explicatio*, 6: 'Cum enim constet, ad diversa animum saepe eodem tempore impelli, et contentionem atque certamen in homine existere, quid agat aut omittat, quo pacto se hac vel illa re gerat, ex quo dubitatione animi conturbantur... in hac distractione animi, et contrariis istis motionibus, diversas causas inesse oportet. Non enim unum et idem secum pugnat, neque in uno unquam contrarii simul motus reperiuntur.'

[153] *Explicatio*, 7: 'Hoc loco maxime conturbati Stoici, unam vim esse suspicati sunt in homine iudicii atque rationis, id est, *tou logou*, mutabilem illam quidem occulto et subito, ita ut animadversionem fallat, ad retinendum verum, et assentiendum falso, et hanc ipsam esse opinionis perturbationem.'

[154] *Explicatio*, 7–8.

[155] *Explicatio*, 8: 'non esse eandem vim et effectionem eius quae ratio et consilium et mens et iudicium nominatur, et aliarum affectionum animi, ut metus, libidinis, spei, cupiditatum omnium, et quaecunque aliae sunt commotiones, quas Graeci *pathê* vocant.'

[156] *Explicatio*, 8.

[157] *Explicatio*, 8: 'Est autem in homine quaedam libera et plane sui iuris, quam voluntatem nominamus. Ea in utranque partem potest omnia. Quod si patitur haec vis allici sese ad eam partem quae est animalis in homine, et recedit a ratione, tum nihil neque consuli laudabiliter, neque recte cogitari, neque decerni incorrupte solet.'

[158] *Explicatio*, 8–9.

praise the goodness of his parents. The good judgement of reason remains alive even when the person has consented to the passions.[159]

To illustrate this situation, Camerarius quotes Xenophon's *Cyropaedia*, in which Araspas claims to have two souls or minds (*animus*). One and the same soul cannot be both willing and nilling, both honest and evil. Camerarius adds that Xenophon is not literally speaking of two souls, but of different affects and teachings.[160] An illness can often prevent the use of reason; similarly, strong affects and a stubborn will can prevent the adequate application of right reason. The harmful affects can corrupt the reason so that the will and the passions can have their way.[161]

Thus Camerarius outlines a psychology which is both Aristotelian and voluntarist. The soul has the faculties which the Aristotelian tradition has ascribed to it. The rational faculty is really distinct (*alia res*) from the seat of the affects. Passions are not false judgements, as the Stoics claim, but represent the powers of the animal soul. The human will can choose between the different powers. Although Camerarius rejects the cognitive theory of emotions as put forward by the Stoics, his own description of the human condition in terms of harmful passions has some Neo-Stoic elements. Camerarius often points out that the discipline of ethics is for moral education—an education that moderates passions and inner conflicts, and allows the individual to act according to his or her reason.[162] This ideal of moral progress connects his discussion with Neo-Stoicism.

After presenting his basic psychology, Camerarius asks the standard question regarding akrasia in the preface:

It should also be asked, when mind and reason exercise the role of principal part, which the Greeks as mentioned call the *hêgemonikon*, how can it be that harmful passions nevertheless dominate the human being so strongly that he cannot make use of his principal part?[163]

The answer is straightforward: this is the fault of the evil will which deviates from reason and perturbs everything. The passions are in the service of this evil power: they

---

[159] *Explicatio*, 9: 'Non abest tum quidem vis et acrimonia rationis, quippe eidem insitae et innatae animo. Sed voluntas cupiditatem malam adiuvans et stabiliens, non sinit parere hanc rationi, et ipsius rationis acumine callide abutitur, ad scelera aut flagitia, quemadmodum partis bonis parentum luxuriosi filii. Manet tamen nihilominus quemadmodum laus diligentiae paternae, quae rem quesiverat, ita rationis sententia, de rectis et pravis, id est virtute et vitiis, et de officio ac culpa, seu faciendis et fugiendis, quorum illa laus, haec vituperatio sequitur, decernente iudicio veritatis.'

[160] *Explicatio*, 10, quoting Xenophon, *Cyropaedia* 6, 41: 'I see now that we have two souls.'

[161] *Explicatio*, 10–11: 'Quemadmodum autem morbus rationis usum saepe impedit, atque etiam pervertit, ita vehementia effraenatarum affectionum, et pertinacia voluntatis, rectam rationem suo munere fungi in animo non patitur... de aliis perturbationibus, quae sunt vitiosae affectiones animi, similiter omnia commemorari possunt. Quae cum in rationem, ut ita dicam, sese insinuarunt, vel illam potius attrahendo corripuerunt, confirmata voluntate ad scelus vel flagitium.'

[162] *Explicatio*, 10, 12–13, 15.

[163] *Explicatio*, 11: 'Quaeri autem etiam solet, cum mens et ratio in homine principatum teneat, quod Graeci *hêgemonikon* (ut diximus) nominarunt, quo pacto fiat ut in homine interdum vitiosae affectiones sic dominentur, ut rationis imperium et principatus nihil proficere possint.'

are alienated from the truths of good education and become agitated so that the person 'sees the better and approves it, but follows the worse'.[164]

This conflict does not concern obdurately evil people, but rather those in whom right reason emerges but is not followed. Aristotle calls these people akratic and this phenomenon akrasia; Camerarius deviates from the standard Latin translation *incontinentia* and translates akrasia as *impotentia*.[165] Whereas the obdurately evil people do not hesitate in doing evil, 'in the akratic people the true reason does not rest oppressed or overcome, but quarrels and struggles with the harmful passions'.[166]

In this manner, akrasia is characterized by the free and evil decision of the will. This decision does not, however, extinguish right reason, which continues to struggle against the passions. In his preface, Camerarius continues the tradition of 'struggle' and 'contrary tendencies' as the essential characteristics of akrasia. Unlike Luther, however, he teaches that the struggle continues even after the consent to evil. Like the medieval voluntarists, Camerarius affirms the Aristotelian divisions of the soul and considers the will to be finally responsible for human action. In many ways, this voluntarism resembles the views of Henry of Ghent and the Franciscans (1.4), as well as John Mair (2.5) and, of course, Melanchthon. His account of the relative autonomy of the animal soul resembles Ockham's psychology.

Unlike the medieval voluntarists, Camerarius does not regard the will as the rational appetite or the highest potency of the soul. This place is reserved for the intellectual faculties. Camerarius discusses the will in its interplay with affects and passions. Later in his preface, he teaches that the will exists in close connection with the irrational passions. At the same time, while *voluntas* does not mean primarily a desire or drive, the concept of will depicts the instance of choosing among alternatives.[167] While the scholastics understood the will to be the rational appetite, Melanchthon and Camerarius locate the will in the realm of affects and passions in distinction from the cognitive soul.

Because of this inherent non-rationality or even irrationality, Camerarius's understanding of human will deviates from traditional voluntarism and approaches later,

---

[164] *Explicatio*, 11: 'hanc esse culpam voluntatis pravae, quae a ratione detorta, omnia perturbat, neque quisquam ia recte et ordine geripatitur. Inserviunt autem huic affectiones, per se alienae ab omni honestate et decore, et neglecta veritate educationis liberalis, redditae intractabiliores et ferociores, ut videns aliquis et probans meliora, deteriora tamen sequatur.' Cf. Ovid, *Metam.* 7, 20–1.

[165] *Explicatio*, 11–12: 'Hoc non tam apparet in iis qui . . . improbi et vitiosi vocantur . . . quam in illis quos appellat Aristoteles *akrateis*. Malum hoc, id est *akrasian*, quae impotentia est, ab altero vitio *tas kakias* distinguens.' He often also uses 'impotentia animi'.

[166] *Explicatio*, 12: 'Nam improbi illi . . . non . . . hesitant in facinoribus malis . . . cum in iis qui impotentes perhibentur, non prorsus oppressa neque victa iaceat vera ratio, sed cum pravitate cupiditatum adhuc quasi controversetur et pugnet.'

[167] *Explicatio*, 21–2: 'Est autem in animo hominis etiam altera quaedam seu natura sive affectio, quae a Graecis *alogos* dicitur, a Latinis bruta: non quod rationis capax neque sit, et esse omnino nequeat, sed quod per se expers rationis, interdum ad laudem et decus inservire rationi, interdum ad vitia et turpitudinem deferri soleat. In his maxime valet et conspicitur ea vis quae Voluntas dicitur, cuius est electio, id est *prohairesis*, unum alteri praeponens et aliquid sumens, aliquid reiiciens.'

modern concepts of free will. The will decides over actions while it remains allied with the irrational powers of the soul. In keeping with this psychology, Camerarius's view of akrasia approaches 'deliberate irrationality': akratic people retain their right reason even during the wrong action which they have deliberately chosen of their own will (cf. 1.5). The powerful role attributed to education is compatible with this view, since educated people have moderated their affects and are therefore more likely to refrain from irrational choices, although they remain capable of performing them.

While the preface to Camerarius's commentary gives a systematic overview of his psychology, his exposition of EN VII remains somewhat fragmentary and is often dominated by the details of the Greek language. In some places, however, he remains true to his maxim of expounding the issues rather than words.[168] The philological erudition of Camerarius is sometimes relevant for philosophy. At the beginning of EN VII, 2, he argues with the help of Xenophon's *Memorabilia* that Socrates did not finally deny the existence of akrasia. He also points out that, although the Stoics regarded all passions as evil, there are also good passions (*eupathês*).[169]

The classical problem of akrasia is outlined in EN VII, 2 as follows:

How is it said that the akratic person ignores the best alternative? She knows and sees, but does not follow nor persevere, according to Medea's confession which we quoted elsewhere. And the comical complaint of the youngster: being prudent, knowing, living, and seeing I am ruined; I do not know what I am doing, and other similar sayings. A fine picture of this tension and struggle is given in Plato's *Phaedros*, the horses and charioteer. Examples of lovers are given in the comedies. Everyone experiences this more or less in everyday life, so that no more needs to be said.[170]

In this description the picture of struggle dominates, whereas the motif of ignorance is almost completely absent. The clear-eyed character of akratic struggle is strongly stressed.

The answer to this query is given in the exposition of EN VII, 3. In keeping with earlier interpreters, Camerarius focuses on the syllogistic structure of akratic reasoning. He first describes the nature of the general proposition as knowledge pertaining to the nature of things. The particular facts become associated with this general knowledge as, for instance, the proper name is ascribed to a human being.[171] Knowledge concerning generalities can, however, err in its estimation of the particular facts. For Camerarius, this is no small matter, since he claims that it is the primary reason for confusion among

---

[168] *Explicatio*, 17 (quoted above).

[169] *Explicatio*, 316. Dorion (2003) is a new study of akrasia in Xenophon coming to similar conclusions.

[170] *Explicatio*, 317: 'Quomodo igitur dicetur ignorari ab impotente quid sit optimum? Qui intelligit et videt, sed non sequitur neque tenet, secundum Medeae confessionem quam alibi retulimus, et indignationem comici adolescentis, Prudens, sciens, vivus vidensque pereo, nec quid agam, scio, et similia alia. Contentionis autem et pugnae istius imago venusta extat in Phaedro Platonis, equorum et aurigae, et exemplis amantum in Comoediis declaratur, et unusquisque plus minusve experitur in cotidiana vita, ut hac de re plura dici necesse non sit.'

[171] *Explicatio*, 325: 'Est autem notitia generalis, qua seipsum aliquid complectitur, nihil aliud quam cognitio suae naturae, quam comitari singularem etiam notitiam necesse est, ut, qui se esse hominem scit et animantem, scit nimirum se esse Calliam.'

human beings and even 'the cause of all evil'.[172] Such a statement exemplifies the author's humanistic style of exaggerating the subject matter rather than aiming at philosophical precision. The statement is nevertheless highly significant, as the examples show.

A physician knows what kind of medicine it is proper to give when the patient has fever, but it is extremely difficult to give the right amount at the right time. Therefore one often fails to heal, as the medical knowledge concerning particulars is not certain.[173] Other examples include political leadership, in which even wise men often fail, and the composition of literary texts which contain errors.[174] Camerarius adds that errors concerning life and conduct are due to bad habits, incorrect judgement, and evil will. Life could be conducted successfully, if only we had clear and perfect knowledge regarding these matters.[175]

As the examples show, Camerarius holds that the life of all humans is characterized by the uncertainty which gives rise to errors, not simply pointing out accidental errors in the estimation of particulars. Even experts like physicians err in their particular actions. Camerarius points out that when 'knowledge' is discussed in the context of akrasia, Aristotle does not speak of scientific knowledge in the strict sense, but of cognition or apprehension.[176] Such practical knowledge is constituted in the practical syllogism:

The discussion [on akrasia] focuses on the claim that the propositions regarding the particulars do not always correspond to the universal knowledge. For the particulars are neither certain nor immutable. When they are led away from the true universal, something erroneous is stated. When such a case pertains to the actions being deliberated on (as now indicated by the appellative *poiêtikón*), the act of stating or discerning something also comprises the action itself.[177]

In other words, small errors in the formulation of the particular propositions of the practical syllogism lead to misguided actions. As actions concern particulars, one can possess the right universal knowledge and nevertheless act wrongly.

---

[172] *Explicatio*, 325: 'Sed generalis cognitio negotii, in singulis rebus errare et falli potest et solet. Nam hac inscitia vita hominum inprimis conturbatur. Et est haec causa omnium malorum et infelicitatis atque miseriae humanae universae, quae peccatis et delictis commovetur et incitatur.'

[173] *Explicatio*, 325: 'Medicus quispiam scit in febri certa danda esse aegroto quae refrigerent et sint humida, sed in iis temperandis et adhibendis, quorum frigus et humor conveniens sit, et talem febrim corrigat, scientia similiter certa non est. Unde et peccatur saepe, et est diligentiae atque artis eximiae felix curatio.'

[174] *Explicatio*, 325–6.

[175] *Explicatio*, 326: 'Quam absurdae autem rationes vitae ineuntur, et quantum delinquitur? Sive more seu etiam iudicio perverso et prava voluntate. Quod si esset hac etiam in parte liquida et efficax scientia, omnia nimirum fierent laudabiliter et recte in praeclarissima officii custodia.'

[176] *Explicatio*, 326: 'In mentione autem scientiae hoc loco, non utitur nomine autor significatione exquisita atque peculiari, sed de cognitione seu notitia quacunque. Quae enim vera sit scientia, id est *epistêmê*, et cuius rei hoc non nomen proprium, supra est demonstratum.' The distinction *scientia–cognitio* already occurs in Albert the Great; see Saarinen (1994), 105.

[177] *Explicatio*, 326: 'Summa autem hoc disputationis haec est, non respondere ubique sententias de singulis generali scientiae. Illae enim non sunt certae neque immutabiles. Itaque cum ab hac detorquentur, perperam statuitur aliquid. In iis autem quorum finis est operis elaboratio (quae nunc indicantur *poiêtikón* appellatione communi) decernere seu statuere, ipsam actionem complectitur.'

Although this view in some sense comes close to the so-called Aristotelian model 1a (see 1.5), Camerarius does not ascribe error primarily to ignorance either here or in his preceding discussion, but rather stresses that the realm of particulars is so uncertain and mutable that even experts, like the physician or the political leader, often err in their estimation of a particular situation. This emphasis on uncertainty resembles John Buridan's discussion of akrasia (1.5). Camerarius regards practical knowledge by its very nature as uncertain and concerned with particulars so that it cannot reach the certainty of 'scientific knowledge' (epistêmê, scientia) and the possibility of akrasia remains.

Camerarius uses these syllogistic observations to explain the emergence of akratic reasoning. He also uses three examples, of which the first and second deal with Medea. In the first example of Ovid's Metamorphoses, Medea knows that the love for the fatherland and for one's parents is to be preferred. Her passion for Jason does not extinguish this truth, but she does not allow it to enlighten her mind, and her will pushes her to stay with Jason.[178] This description reveals some of Camerarius's central ideas. Akrasia is primarily caused by the will. It does not extinguish knowledge concerning general truths, but, as conflict situations are characterized by mutability and uncertainty, the person may choose akratically.

Immediately after this example, Camerarius quotes the lines from Euripides's Medea, 'I know what evil I propose to do, but anger rules my deliberations' as his second example.[179] As we have seen in 1.2, the discussion on 'Stoic akrasia' revolves around this quote. Melanchthon reintroduces Medea's rage into the discussion of inner conflicts; Camerarius employs these crucial lines of Euripides in his discussion on EN VII. He only briefly remarks that anger rules Medea's deliberation, leading her to affirm the most disastrous deed. The use of the verb affirmo again underlines the voluntary nature of Medea's decision. His third example concerns the drunk who acts wrongly, knowing that his deed is harmful. The drunkard focuses on his short-term pleasure.[180]

The three examples receive the same explanation:

The [akratic] argument goes as follows: this desire is harmful. Harmful things are to be avoided. Therefore, one should not be seized by this desire. But covetousness carries the person away, so that he is ordered by this last proposition concerning perception: this is pleasant and joyful. Therefore I enjoy the present pleasure. The person does not want to hear or follow the knowledge-based truth which argues that such deeds are wicked and blameworthy. In the

---

[178] Explicatio, 326: 'Iam quomodo istae rationes in impotente animo pervertantur, videamus. Verum est, patriam et parentes omnibus esse debere carissimos, sed Medea capitur externi amore. Haec cupiditas non illa quidem extinguit veritatem scientiae de patriae caritate et parentum amore, sed non sinit quasi elucere neque esse efficacem, et voluntatem ad Iasonem conservandum impellit.'

[179] Explicatio, 326: 'Et ipsa apud Euripidem ait [Greek quote from Euripides, Medea 1078–9, cf. 1.2, English translation above]. Vinci dicit consilia sua iracundia, quam quidem esse hominibus perniciossimam affirmat.'

[180] Explicatio, 326: 'Turpis est et nocens res ebrietas. Sed inter epulas animus exhilaratur, et contra sententiam veram prolabitur ad id quod scit dedecus habere et detrimentum.'

same manner one can explain other cases in which one acts against true knowledge and right reason.[181]

This explanation in some way follows the Aristotelian model 1a in claiming that the correct minor premise or 'last proposition' is ignored in the akratic action, although the person is aware of general truths. At the same time, Camerarius continues to employ non-Aristotelian features which strongly colour his explanation. The voluntary character of the wrong decision is again highlighted in the phrase 'does not want (neque . . . admittit) to hear or follow'. Moreover, when this explanation pertains to the two non-Aristotelian examples of Medea, it pleads for a clear-eyed akrasia which proceeds with full awareness of the wrongness of one's akratic decision.

Other important and likewise non-Aristotelian features are given by the preceding observations, which stress that the frequent errors in particulars are 'the cause of all evil' and that the knowledge regarding particulars often remains uncertain. Camerarius returns to this general perspective as the last point of his discussion regarding the cause of akrasia. He remarks that

> if we want to admit the truth, the mind turns away from true and right in all errors, sins, and crimes. This is the impulse of wickedness. But when that person is concerned whom Aristotle calls akratic without qualifications, the philosopher wants to show that this only happens with greater tension and is more clearly visible.[182]

When this is read together with the statement that errors in particulars are 'the cause of all evil', we obtain a general description of error, sin, and crime as a process in which the mind turns away from the true good and follows the harmful impulses. This process is voluntary, but it is also made possible by the state of affairs that particular facts remain uncertain and changeable.

In this general framework, akrasia represents a special case in which the mind is fairly well aware of the available options. Because of this awareness of the conflicting options, it remains mired in a state of tension and struggle. While it is true that the akratic person neglects or even ignores some particulars in his actual decision, the akratês is also much more aware of the particular options than the wicked person who simply commits a sin or crime. In this sense, it is the increased awareness of conflicting options which is characteristic of akrasia, not ignorance.

In sum, Camerarius's view of akrasia is fairly close to the voluntarist branch of late scholasticism. He distinguishes among the different faculties of the soul in Ockhamist

---

[181] *Explicatio*, 326: 'Estque argumentatio talis: Voluptas ista mala est. Malum est vitandum. Cavendum igitur ne capiamur illa voluptate. Sed cupiditas alio rapit, et orditur ab eo quod ultimum est atque sub sensus cadit: Hoc suave et iucundum est. Ergo fruar suavitate praesente. Neque illa quae scientiae veritas de turpitudine et damno argumentatur, admittit vel audiendo vel sequendo. Similiter de aliis quae contra veram scientiam et rectam rationem committuntur, explicari res potest.'

[182] *Explicatio*, 327: 'Nam, si verum fateri volumus, in omnibus erroribus peccatisque et delictis, animus a vero et recto detorquetur. Quae est pravitatis impulsio. Sed in eo quem simpliciter impotentem vocat Aristoteles, hoc fieri quasi maiore cum contentione et esse evidentius, intelligi vult.'

fashion. He shares the voluntarism of Henry of Ghent and John Mair, but his closest scholastic ally is probably John Buridan, who also emphasizes the uncertain nature of moral deliberation. Camerarius does not, however, reach the scholastic precision of Mair or Buridan. He wants to retain the plurality of psychological concepts available in the Aristotelian tradition; he also employs the figure of the practical syllogism in his analysis of akrasia. His use of the Aristotelian tradition nevertheless remains fragmentary, as he finally supports strong voluntarism and wants to affirm the clear-eyed akrasia of Medea. His competent and critical portrayal of Stoicism is remarkable.

Finally, Camerarius's voluntarism is in some sense even stronger than the rational action theory of John Buridan and the scholastic voluntarists. Melanchthon's pupil already approaches the modern view of 'deliberate irrationality' in terms of our typology in 1.5. Both Melanchthon and Camerarius situate the will in the realm of affect and distinguish this appetitive realm from the rational and cognitive soul. The will is responsible for its choice but, since the nature of the will itself is not inherently rational, its choice can be both deliberate and irrational.

3.4 Lutheran Aristotelians: Golius and Heider

The late sixteenth and early seventeenth centuries in Germany are often characterized in terms of Protestant Orthodoxy. Various disputes concerning the right understanding of Christian faith were settled in favour of the emerging system of confessional dogmatics. One philosophically relevant feature of this period was the re-emergence of Aristotelianism, which offered a systematic account of the received body of learning that could be employed in the service of orthodoxy.[183]

The Lutheran teaching of ethics during this period has been insufficiently studied. While we do possess new studies on ethics in early Calvinism and in the Catholic Reform,[184] the Lutheran textbooks of moral philosophy have not received the attention they deserve. In the early seventeenth century, Lutheranism was not only a remarkable political power, but the Lutheran universities also exercised a strong educational influence beyond the confessional borders. A typical example of this influence was the *Epitome doctrinae moralis* of Theophilus Golius (1528–1600).

A professor of moral philosophy in Strasbourg, Golius wrote Greek and Latin grammars and textbooks on three Aristotelian branches of practical philosophy.[185] His textbook on moral doctrine was published posthumously in Strasbourg in 1615 and reprinted in Frankfurt (1617), Strasbourg (1621), Cambridge (1634), and London (1662).[186] Golius's work was also used at Harvard, the first university of the New World.[187] The *Epitome*

---

[183] For the general features of orthodoxy, see Petersen (1921); Sparn (1976); Muller (1987–2003).

[184] In addition to Strohm (1996) and Lines (2002), see Kraye (1998) and Kraye and Saarinen (2005), with further literature.

[185] *Epitome doctrinae politicae*, Strasbourg 1606; *Epitome doctrinae oeconomiae*, Strasbourg 1622.

[186] Lohr (1977), 702–3. Additions from 'Early English Books Online' database, http://eebo.chadwyck.com

[187] Fiering (1981), 67–76; Hoeveler (2007), 38.

doctrinae moralis is arranged according to the books and chapters of EN, and we will quote it accordingly. Golius proceeds by presenting a great variety of very short and unnumbered questions relating to each chapter of Aristotle's text. He often quotes Greek expressions, but does not discuss philology. Golius uses the traditional Latin translations of Aristotle's terms.

Unlike the medieval scholastics, Golius does not advance different arguments regarding his questions, being content to give a concise magisterial answer to each question. This style reveals a systematic interest in Aristotle while also echoing the pedagogical humanism of Melanchthon and the Strasbourg reformers.[188] Although Golius's *Epitome doctrinae moralis* was influential in the English-speaking world and is occasionally referred to in the scholarship,[189] it has not been studied in detail.

Golius follows the vocabulary of Daneau (4.3) in calling continence and incontinence, endurance and softness, the imperfect habits. In his introductory question to EN VII, 1, he defines the imperfect habits as follows:

> Why are continence and endurance, as well as their opposites, called imperfect habits? Because, as there is no struggle between reason and appetite in the perfect habits—they are fully dominated by either reason or the appetite—so in the imperfect habits there is struggle between reason and appetite. And if reason overcomes in the realm of desires, it is called continence; if in the realm of sufferings, endurance. But if appetite overcomes in desires, it is called incontinence; if in sufferings, softness.[190]

Golius continues the long tradition depicting the akratic situation in terms of 'struggle' (*pugna*). Like Camerarius (3.3), he assumes that the struggle takes place between the different parts of the soul.

Golius gives a definition of continence and incontinence in EN VII, 1:

> Continence is a virtue with the help of which the harmful desires and inordinate affects are reluctantly subordinated under the command of reason so that they cannot commit sin. Incontinence is a vice which pushes the harmful desires and affects to commit sin contrary to the judgement of our right reason. This happens in some way reluctantly and unwillingly.[191]

This definition connects the long Augustinian tradition of 'reluctant' (*invitus*) actions to akrasia. Golius evidently wants to hand over the received body of learning in a

---

[188]   Among his Strasbourg teachers and colleagues, the pedagogian Jean Sturm (1507–1589) is the most famous.

[189]   e.g. Denzer (1972); Fiering (1981); Kraye (1988), 304–20.

[190]   *Epitome doctrinae moralis*, 254: 'Quare continentia et tolerantia, earumque contraria, dicuntur imperfecti habitus? Quia sicut in perfectis habitibus nulla est pugna inter rationem et appetitum, sic vel ratio, vel appetitus plene dominatur; ita in imperfectis habitibus existit pugna inter rationem et appetitum. Et si ratio vincit in voluptatibus, dicitur continentia, si in doloribus, tolerantia. Si vero appetitus vincit in voluptatibus, vocatur incontinentia; si in doloribus, mollicies.'

[191]   *Epitome doctrinae moralis*, 255–6: 'Continentia est virtus, qua pravae cupiditates, et inordinati affectus rectae rationis imperio inviti subiiciuntur, et a peccando abstrahuntur . . . Incontinentia est vitium, quo contra rectae rationis iudicium, a pravis cupiditatibus et affectibus, aliquo modo inviti et nolentes ad peccandum pertrahimur.'

systematic fashion. At the end of EN VII, 1 he gives the traditional list (cf. 2.2) of six questions to be asked in the context of akrasia.[192]

The third question, that is, the classical problem of akrasia, is formulated in two ways: 'Does the incontinent person commit wicked actions knowingly?', or 'Does the incontinent person act differently from what he knows should be done?'.[193] A preliminary answer is given in EN VII, 2. Socrates wanted to deny the existence of akrasia because knowledge cannot be overcome by affects, but experience proves the occurrence of akrasia. Many people act differently from what they know to be better, as Medea does. The nature of such akrasia is explained in EN VII, 3 in more detail.[194]

All aspects of this answer are available, for instance, in Clichtove (2.4), Zwinger (4.2), and Camerarius (3.3). In his extensive series of questions relating to EN VII, 3, Golius first claims that the incontinent person knows 'to an extent' (partim) and ignores 'to an extent'. The akratês can have habitual knowledge but he does not actually use this knowledge. In terms of the practical syllogism, it can further be said that the akratês has the major proposition but not the minor proposition. This distinction is illustrated by an example that is also found in Camerarius: a person may know generally that medicine alleviates fever, but he does not know whether this or that herb provides help in this particular case of fever.[195] For Camerarius, this kind of ignorance regarding particulars is at stake in all human errors and proves that even experts frequently err (cf. 3.3). Golius does not say this, but his use of the example is symptomatic of his allegiance to Camerarius.

The agent may not use his or her knowledge for three different reasons. Akratic actions can, first, be caused by the vehement perturbations of the soul; second, they sometimes have corporeal causes. The same distinction is made with regard to akrasia in Zwinger's commentary (4.2). Third, Golius counts actions compelled by an external force as pertaining to the agent's failure to use knowledge.[196] In addition to these traditional teachings, Golius asks whether other causes can be sought. He replies that

Aristotle also takes the cause of this phenomenon from nature, that is, from the natural discrepancy between reason and appetite which more or less always oppose one another. For when the reason recommends the honest way, which is laborious and troublesome, the appetite turns to the alternatives which appear nice and pleasant to the senses, although they are in many ways harmful. Thus it happens that these two, reason and appetite, do not judge and conclude similarly regarding the acceptance of an action. Thus the mind of the incontinent person is torn

---

[192] Epitome doctrinae moralis, 256–7.

[193] Epitome moralis doctrinae, 256: 'Utrum incontinens sciens agat ea, quae sunt mala? Vel, utrum incontinens aliter agat, quam scit esse agendum?'

[194] Epitome doctrinae moralis, 258: 'Socrates quidem videtur statuere, neminem posse contra scientiam suam aliquid agere: propterea quod scientia sit adeo firmus habitus, ut non possit facile a cupiditatibus, aut aliis affectibus vinci. Sed tamen ipsa experientia testatur, multos homines intedum aliter agere, quam sciunt esse agendum. Imo illud ipsum quoque fateri, quemadmodum Medea apud Ovid lib. 7 conqueritur. Video, inquit, meliora, proboque, deteriora sequitur. Sed de hac quaestione plenius in sequenti cap. explicabitur.'

[195] Epitome doctrinae moralis, 260–1.

[196] Epitome doctrinae moralis, 262.

between different parts, so that he to an extent sins knowingly and willingly, insofar as he follows the appetite. But to an extent he sins from ignorance and unwillingly, insofar as the appetite violently drags the reluctant reason.[197]

In this passage, Golius regards Aristotle's psychology as dualistic in the sense of commonplace Platonism (1.1). When Aristotle considers the cause of akrasia with reference to the 'facts of nature', he says that the syllogistic analysis shows in which sense appetite and right reason are contrary to one another (EN 1147a24–1147b5). Golius ascribes universal significance to these remarks, claiming that reason and appetite 'more or less always' (*fere semper*) oppose one another. This claim is reminiscent of Piccolomini (2.6), Zwinger (4.2), and, in particular, Camerarius (3.3), all of whom emphasize the dualistic struggle between reason and appetite. Like Zwinger, Golius says that the appetite 'judges' and even 'concludes' in a quasi-rational fashion. Like Camerarius, Golius sees the discrepancy as a basic fact of the human condition.

Golius affirms Aristotle's doctrine (EN 1147b3–5) that animals are not akratic, as they are only led by their appetite.[198] Although akratic people are likewise led by their appetite, their akrasia is, unlike animal behaviour, also due to their reason. To explain in what sense this is the case, Golius introduces an example which illustrates Aristotle's 'facts of nature' syllogistically. In his view, the natural discrepancy between reason and appetite was already apparent in the biblical paradise. To obey God's command was pious and honest; but Satan tempted Adam and Eve to choose that which is beautiful and pleasant. Adam and Eve had, therefore, two different practical syllogisms in their minds, one related to reason, another to the appetite. Because they paid primary attention to their appetite, Adam and Eve followed the conclusion of the wrong syllogism, as if forgetting (*quasi obliti*) the correct syllogism. They were nevertheless led knowingly and willingly to the act of sin.[199]

The so-called 'Adam's akrasia' introduced by Henry of Ghent (1.4) underlines the voluntary and clear-eyed nature of akratic decisions. As Adam and Eve were not yet plagued by the punishments of the Fall, their decision was not due to concupiscence or

---

[197] *Epitome doctrinae moralis*, 262: 'Aristoteles huius rei causam etiam sumit ex ipsa natura, hoc est, ex naturali dissidio, quod est inter rationem et appetitum, quae fere semper sibi mutuo adversantur. Nam cum ratio suadet ea, quae sunt honesta, coniuncta tamen cum labore et molestia, appetitus autem fertur ad ea, quae sensibus sunt grata et iucunda, plerunque tamen turpia. Inde fit, ut non eodem modo haec duo, ratio et appetitus de actione aliqua suscipienda iudicent et concludant et sic animum incontinentis in diversas partes rapiant, ut partim sciens et volens peccet, quatenus obsequitur appetitui, partim vero ignorans et non volens, quatenus appetitus rationem invitam violenter secum pertrahit.'

[198] *Epitome doctrinae moralis*, 263.

[199] *Epitome doctrinae moralis*, 263: 'Manifestum huius rei exemplum conspicitur in peccato primorum parentum, in quorum animis duo contrarii syllogismi concurrebant. Nam recte rationis talis erat syllogismus. Mandato Dei parere, est pium et honestum. Sed abstinere a fructibus arboris vetitae, est mandatum Dei. Ergo ab his fructibus est abstinendum. Contra vero, appetitus, sive Satan sic argumentabatur: Deo similem fieri, est pulchrum et iucundum. Sed si de arbore scientiae boni et mali comederitis, efficiemini Deo similes. Ergo debetis istud facere. Utrumque syllogismum probe tenebant primi parentes Adam et Eva, sed quia appetitui suo magis auscultabant, quam mandato Dei, ideo quasi obliti prioris syllogismi, arripuerunt conclusionem alterius syllogismi, et sic inducti sunt scientes et volentes ad peccandum.'

ignorance. At the same time, this example makes the concept of 'natural discrepancy' quite strong, since Golius holds that even in the original state of sinlessness, humanity could prefer to follow their appetitive powers instead of their reason. Although the appetite is represented by Satan, Adam and Eve also 'preferred to follow their own appetite' (*appetitui suo magis auscultabant*). Given this, the struggle between reason and appetite does not simply represent the struggle with sin or harmful passions, but is embedded in the twofold constitution of humanity. In paradise, there was already a real distinction between reason and appetite in the soul. This view is 'commonplace Platonist' and voluntarist-Ockhamist at the same time, thus resembling the psychology of Camerarius.

In explaining the 'natural discrepancy' and 'Adam's akrasia' Golius goes beyond Aristotle and approaches many other sixteenth-century interpreters, in particular Camerarius. In the next questions of EN VII, 3, Golius again offers fairly Aristotelian views: the akratês is like the sleeper or the drunk whose state resembles ignorance. The akratic person knows clearly before and after his or her action, but during this action he or she does not fully possess the relevant knowledge. Likewise, Adam knew well the divine command before and after eating from the tree; but in the act of eating the command was forgotten (*obliviscebatur*).[200]

When Socrates claims that no one can act against knowledge, this claim is valid only with regard to theoretical matters. Where human action is concerned, one needs to take the particular and singular facts into account. This knowledge relates to perceptions and practical matters, and our knowledge concerning these is not so firm that it cannot be violated. Practical knowledge is not 'scientific' in the strict sense of Aristotle's theoretical knowledge, but remains an apprehension of the particulars.[201] This final remark of EN VII, 3 again connects Golius with Camerarius. Both underline the lack of certainty or firmness with regard to particular facts. This feature has informed the discussion of akrasia since John Buridan (1.5), but Camerarius and Golius emphasize this point beyond Buridan, claiming that since the particular facts are already in themselves coloured by uncertainty, practical knowledge cannot achieve the firmness of Aristotelian *scientia*. Given this, the possibility of acting akratically always remains an option. While the scholastic Aristotelians believe that firm knowledge concerning particulars can be achieved, the Lutheran Aristotelians tend to deny this.

Golius's distinction between theoretical and practical knowledge quoted above implies the view that certainty can only be achieved with regard to theoretical knowledge. What Golius calls 'practical knowledge' represents an apprehensive

[200] *Epitome doctrinae moralis*, 264.

[201] *Epitome doctrinae moralis*, 265–6: 'Quomodo igitur intelligenda est Socratis sententia, qua dixit, neminem posse contra suam scientiam peccare, atque ideo nullam esse incontinentiam? Haec sententia Socratis videtur solum intelligenda esse de vera et proprie dicta scientia, quae est principiorum, et universalium conclusionum, quae ex principiis, et necessariis propositionibus per demonstrationem sunt effectae. Talis scientia non refertur ad actionem, sed in sola contemplatione et cognitione rerum acquiescit, ideo nominatur *epistêmê theôrêtikê*. Quod vero ad propositiones particulares et singulares attinet, quae sunt de rebus agendis, earum noticia non dicitur proprie scientia sed *doksa aisthêtikê, kai epistêmê praktikê*. Haec non ita firma est, ut contra eam nemo possit agere.'

knowledge (*notitia*) that does not reach the level of proper *scientia*. Here Golius again follows Camerarius. Given this, akrasia is not merely an exception prompted by confusing circumstances, the circumstances of human action remaining themselves uncertain. In its own peculiar way, the case of Adam can be employed as proof of this view: although Adam and Eve had optimal circumstances and immaculate cognitive powers, the discrepancy available in their very nature was sufficient to prompt lack of firmness, forgetting, and akratic action. Although Golius in many respects returns to Aristotle and summarizes his points in a scholastic fashion, the underlying themes of continuous struggle and remaining uncertainty give his views a strongly non-Aristotelian twist. As the soul is naturally dualistic, inner struggle and remaining uncertainty cannot be avoided.

When Golius discusses the relationship between intemperance and incontinence in EN VII, 7–10, he again underlines the clarity of akratic judgement and the uncertainty of the akratic situation. The incontinent person has a good choice and sound judgement; he simply acts against them.[202] At the same time, the incontinent person does not sin with 'full will' (*plena voluntate*),[203] acting 'willingly' (*sponte*), following his harmful passions.[204] Such willingness does not, however, make him wicked, because he does not act with proper deliberation. The perturbation of the soul pushes him to the sinful action contrary to his opinion and will.[205] These considerations are relatively Aristotelian and even Thomist, but they also outline a situation which is characterized by a permanent discrepancy between different options and a lack of certainty concerning concrete actions.

The Reformation thinkers developed at least two argumentative strategies which increased the relative importance of the 'imperfect' habits of continence and incontinence. The first strategy, exemplified by Luther (3.2) and Daneau (4.3), argues that humans cannot achieve true virtue in this life. Continence remains the best option available and ethics should therefore pay special attention to the situations of lasting repugnancy and struggle. The second strategy, exemplified by Camerarius (3.3) and Golius, argues that practical knowledge can never obtain the full certainty which could rule out akrasia. Because the struggle between reason and appetite continues and conflicting particular options are always available, akrasia remains a real possibility. While the second strategy affirms free will, the first tends to deny it. Both strategies employ the idea of continuous struggle between right reason and harmful desires.

---

[202] *Epitome doctrinae moralis*, 275: 'incontinens vero peccat *para tón prohairesin*, praeter suum propositum ... In incontinente autem est adhuc sanum iudicium ... Incontinens ... habet enim adhuc rationem salvam et integram.'

[203] *Epitome doctrinae moralis*, 276.

[204] *Epitome doctrinae moralis*, 279.

[205] *Epitome doctrinae moralis*, 280: 'Quoniam dicis innocentem sponte peccare: videtur ne tibi esse improbus? Minime. Quia non peccat consulto, aut insidiose vel fraudulenter, sed tantum ex animi quadam perturbatione, qua praeter opinionem et voluntatem suam, subito ad peccandum abripitur.'

One of the most prominent moral philosophers of early Lutheranism was Wolfgang Heider (1558–1626), professor of ethics and politics in Jena from 1587. His massive *Philosophiae moralis systema* appeared in Jena 1628 and was reprinted there in 1629, 1634, and 1646. This thousand-page work is accompanied by a textbook of politics of equal size, *Philosophiae politicae systema* (Jena 1628). As the University of Jena was a prominent centre of Lutheran orthodoxy, Heider was an influential philosopher of his times. Neither his work nor his influence has, however, been studied in detail.[206]

Heider's work is a 'system', that is, a textbook in which the material is presented in an order which deviates from Aristotle's text and aims at pedagogical and thematic clarity. Earlier examples of this kind are Piccolomini's *Universa philosophia de moribus* (2.6) and, in particular, Keckermann's *Systema ethicae* (4.4). The three main chapters of the present study all conclude with a textbook that is 'systematic', leaving behind the older genre of commentary, and thus marking the end of Renaissance and Reformation Aristotelianism. In the literary genre of 'system', a given subject matter is organized according to those precepts and rules which are proper for correct explanation.[207]

Heider's chapter on 'Continence and Toleration'[208] is a fairly autonomous presentation of its subject matter; the broader concerns of his 'system' do not play any role in it. Within the systematic division of virtues, continence and toleration belong to the class of imperfect virtues. The perfect virtues are distinguished from the imperfect ones as follows:

Between the perfect habits or virtues and proper vices on the one hand and these [the imperfect habits] on the other, the difference is this: in the perfect habits either reason or appetite prevails, while in the imperfect habits there always remains *symmachia* or wrestling and struggle between reason and appetite.[209]

This distinction follows Daneau (4.3) and Golius, as well as much of the earlier tradition. Continence is defined by Heider as 'an imperfect disposition or virtue which moderates the covetous desires so that the appetite obeys right reason while remaining repugnant'.[210] Incontinence is 'an imperfect disposition or vice which surrenders to the covetous desires so that right reason argues against this but is overcome by the appetite'.[211]

Heider distinguishes among four senses in which the individual can be called incontinent. Incontinence in the first and proper sense of the term pertains to the

---

[206] See Lohr (1977), 716. For instance, Garber and Ayers (1998) does not pay any attention to Heider.

[207] On the seventheenth-century genre of system, see e.g. Lohr (1988), 634–5; Schmitt (1988).

[208] Heider, *Philosophiae moralis systema*, 812–31. I use the 1628 edition.

[209] *Philosophiae moralis systema*, 812: 'Inter perfectos enim habitus seu virtutes, et vitia proprie dicta, et has inter dispositiones hoc est discriminis: in illis vel ratio vel appetitus plane dominantur, in his rationis et appetitus *symmachia*, seu lucta quaedam et pugna semper est reliqua.'

[210] *Philosophiae moralis systema*, 812: 'Continentia est dispositio seu virtus imperfecta, quae cupiditates voluptatum moderatur, repugnante quidem appetitu, sed tamen rectae rationi succumbente.'

[211] *Philosophiae moralis systema*, 813: 'Incontinentia est dispositio seu vitium imperfectum, quod cupiditatibus voluptatum succumbit, contradicente quidem recta ratione, sed tamen appetitui cedente.'

impossibility of controlling the necessary bodily desires, such as covetousness. As anger can to a large extent be controlled by reason, it does not properly belong to this first meaning of incontinence. Second, some desires are natural, whereas others are contrary to nature. The latter do not properly pertain to akrasia. Third, one can distinguish between weak and precipitate akrasia. Fourth, as continence and incontinence pertain to all virtues and vices as an imperfect stage, they can be distinguished according to the number of virtues.[212]

All these distinctions are traditional. Heider quotes Aristotle's EN in three first distinctions; with regard to the fourth distinction, he refers to Piccolomini's *De moribus* (2.6). It is evident from his discussion that weak akrasia pertaining to those desires which are 'necessary' in the sense of inevitability represents the standard and proper mode of incontinence. The very definition of akrasia as imperfect vice is conditioned by the underlying circumstance that the appetite remains in a state of struggle with reason, thus inevitably causing harmful desires.

The main part of Heider's discussion regarding akrasia is organized around the traditional six opinions and questions which appear in most commentaries on EN VII, 2 (cf. 2.2). The third question, which expresses the classical problem of akrasia, is formulated in the following somewhat clumsy manner: 'Does the incontinent person act knowingly in his wicked action, spurred by certain perturbations of the mind? And the continent individual, knowing that the covetous desires are harmful, does not follow them, but acts according to right reason.'[213]

In his treatment of the third question, Heider first discusses the opinion of Socrates, quoting Piccolomini. Like Piccolomini, he also points out that this is supported by Plato. Nobody sins willingly. People act for the sake of goodness and, since they choose the greater good instead of the lesser good, there is no akrasia.[214] Contrary to this view, Aristotle points out that the existence of akrasia is proved by experience. Most people know that what they are doing is wrong. They also feel a painful wrestling between reason and appetite, as the example of Medea shows.[215] Such examples elegantly show the struggle between reason and appetite. People who in this state of discrepancy perform disgraceful acts nevertheless strongly advise their children and friends not to follow them. This example is again taken from Piccolomini.[216] Heider

---

[212] *Philosophiae moralis systema*, 814–17.

[213] *Philosophiae moralis systema*, 817: 'An incontinens sciens agat ea, quae mala, animi quadam perturbatione incitatus. Continens autem sciens, vitiosas esse cupiditates, non obsequatur, sed rationi rectae morem gerat.'

[214] *Philosophiae moralis systema*, 821–2.

[215] *Philosophiae moralis systema*, 822: 'Aristoteles vero Incontinentem scientem agere per ipsam demonstrat experientiam, quae testatur, maximam hominum partem ea facere, quae sciunt, esse mala et rationis appetitusque luctam sentire gravissimam. Vid 7 Metam. de Medea.' Heider here also gives the examples of Althea, Biblida, and Myrrha from *Metam.* 8–10.

[216] *Philosophiae moralis systema*, 822: 'Quibus in locis elegantissime describitur rationis et appetitus *zygomachia*. Quin hoc ipsum in se dissidium plurimi fatentur et deplorant, suisque cupiditatibus obsecuturi latebras quaerunt, liberos ac amicos iisdem a flagitiis, quibus dediti sunt, ardenter dehortantur.' Piccolomini, *De moribus*, 253.

further points out that it would be stupid to argue contrary to experience in this matter, as the Bible also demonstrates this in Romans 7:15–23 and Gal. 5:17.[217]

As the Augustinian and early Protestant tradition (3.2, 4.1) clearly takes Romans 7 to exemplify continence rather than akrasia, the last remark is somewhat careless. Perhaps Heider only wants to say that the Bible at least proves the existence of continence. In this context, Heider also puts the traditional argument that, since opinions are as firm as knowledge, one cannot hold that the incontinent person only violates his or her opinion.[218] In any case, Heider wants to show that there is akrasia and that it is fairly clear-eyed, as the examples of Medea and Romans 7 show.

Heider has built into his treatment of the 'third question' two additional subsidiary questions, the first of which is formulated as: 'In what sense does the incontinent sin contrary to his knowledge?'[219] This question contains his most elaborate account of akrasia. Heider undertakes four distinctions with regard to the 'knowledge' present in the akratês. First, one should distinguish between three periods: before the action, during the action, and after the action.[220] The akratic person knows well before and after his or her action, but during the action, that is, for a certain period, resembles the ignorant person, because the violent and harmful perturbations have oppressed right reason.[221] This answer is traditional; one may note that Heider does not say 'ignorant' but 'resembles the ignorant' (ignoranti similis).

The second distinction is the Aristotelian distinction between having and using knowledge (EN 1146b30–35).[222] Philosophically most interesting are the third and the fourth distinctions, in which Heider interprets Aristotle's text in the manner of Camerarius and Golius. The third distinction prevails between universal and particular propositions. Heider further underlines Aristotle's distinction (EN 1147a1–9) between two kinds of universals; that is, universal in itself (e.g. dry food is good for every man) and universal in physical objects or as related to the actions (whether this food is such and such). The latter class is closely related to the particulars, Heider claiming that it 'barely differs' from the particulars.[223] The person who knows in the sense of this latter class can hardly be ignorant of the relevant particular facts.

[217] *Philosophiae moralis systema*, 822.

[218] *Philosophiae moralis systema*, 822.

[219] *Philosophiae moralis systema*, 823: 'Quomodo incontinens contra scientiam peccat?'

[220] *Philosophiae moralis systema*, 823: 'In actionibus incontinentis tria tempora consideranda veniunt. Praeteritum ante factum; praesens quod in facto; futurum quod post factum.'

[221] *Philosophiae moralis systema*, 824: 'Ante factum et post factum non est dubium, quin rectae rationis judicio probe norit incontinens, quid bonum sit aut malum, quid honestum aut turpe, quid faciendum aut omittendum . . . In ipso facto, cui tamen non punctum aut momentum satis est, sed justum temporis spacium, ignoranti similis est incontinens, adeo perturbationis vitiosis et violentis recta ratio opprimitur.'

[222] *Philosophiae moralis systema*, 823.

[223] *Philosophiae moralis systema*, 823: 'Duo sunt genera propositionum (quibus utimur in disciplinis practicis, sine quibus nulla deliberatio suscipi potest): quaedam universales . . . quaedam particulares . . . ad quas pertinet actio . . . Ibidem universale iterum duplex: vel *katholou eph heautou*, universale in se et in intellectu, ut si quis sciat, omni homini sicca prodesse; vel *peri tou pragmatou*, in re, quod extra intellectum in rebus ipsis inest, et parum differt ab ipsis particularibus. Et hoc qui norit, is particularia haut nescire poterit, ut si quis cognitum

Although the third distinction is Aristotelian, its impact becomes clearer when the fourth distinction is spelled out. This is that 'knowledge is of two kinds: first, *kyriôs epistêmê*, which is a certain apprehension achieved by demonstration, second, *mê kyriôs epistêmê*, which collects the contingent facts of perception and experience; for this reason it is called *aisthêtikê*'.[224] This distinction is also relevant to Camerarius and Golius. For them, as for Heider, certain and immutable knowledge is only concerned with the first class of universals. The most relevant facts concerning action are, however, universals of the second class and particular facts. These inevitably remain connected with perception and experience and lack absolute certainty.

Given these distinctions, Heider can conclude his discussion on akrasia by showing how the akratic knowledge involves some ignorance:

They say the same [i.e., that the akratês resembles the ignorant person] who claim that incontinence [!] possesses the habitual knowledge and the first act, but not the use and the second act. Likewise that the incontinent person has no free knowlege but a bound and prevented knowledge, so that he resembles the sleeper, the obsessed, and the drunkard, Aristotle EN VII, 3. Likewise those who say that he knows *ta katholou*, the universals in themselves, but does not know *ta kath' hekasta* [the singulars, particulars] and cannot apply them to the universals.[225]

Although akratic people can utter demonstrations and good propositions which prove that they have retained the knowledge regarding the middle part or theoretical part of their deliberation, they nevertheless behave like people possessed by anger or love, or like children who do not really understand what they say, or like actors who recite their lines without actually approving them. Akratic people either do not attend to what they say or do not put it into practice.[226]

This explanation of akrasia is in many ways closer to Aristotle's own intentions than the interpretations put forward by Camerarius, Golius, and Piccolomini. Heider wants to show that Aristotle ascribes the possibility of akrasia to the ignorance of the particular facts. Clear-eyed akrasia is not possible. At the same time, however, Heider also continues along the relatively new path of Camerarius and Golius: we do not achieve

habeat, qui sint homines, quae sicca, quod fieri non potest, nisi sciamus, quod hic, quod ille, quod iste sit homo, quod hoc, quod illud, quod istud sit siccum.'

[224] *Philosophiae moralis systema*, 824: 'Scientiae duplex est: 1. vel *kyriôs epistêmê*, quae est certa notitia per demonstrationem acquisita. 2. vel *mê kyriôs epistêmê*, quae contingentium sensu et experientia collecta; unde quidem *aisthêtikê* appellatur.'

[225] *Philosophiae moralis systema*, 824: 'Idem dicunt, qui incontinentiam ajunt habere scientiae habitum et actum primum, sed usum et actum secundum non habere. Idem, qui scientiae habitum non liberum, sed ligatum et impeditum esse tradunt in Incontinente, qui similis dormienti, curioso et vinolento. Aristoteles lib. 7 Ethic. cap. 3. Idem, qui dicunt, ipsum scire *ta katholou*, universalia in seipsis, sed *ta kath' hekasta*, non scire, nec ad illa, quae universalia sunt, applicare posse.' On actus primus–secundus, see 2.2.

[226] *Philosophiae moralis systema*, 824: 'Quamvis autem incontinentes saepe rationes firmas et bonas sententias asserant in medium, quae scientiam in ipsis salvam et integram esse, dum ajunt, arguere videntur; tamen id eadem fit ratione, qua 1. irati et amantes demonstrationes et versus Empedoclis recitant, quibus tamen non obsequuntur. 2. qua pueri orationem quidem connectunt et legunt, sed antequam adolescant, non intelligunt, 3. histriones multa pronunciant, non tamen ex animo, sed ficte et simulate. Eundem ad modum incontinentes vel non attentiunt ad ea, quae loquuntur, aut iis morem non gerunt.'

a precise practical knowledge regarding particularities; since we are always in a situation of struggle between reason and appetite, akrasia remains a real possibility for most, if not all people.

The examples of Medea and Romans 7 underline the clear-eyed nature of akrasia, whereas the closer analysis emphasizes the role of ignorance. Although these two trends are not reconciled with each other, Heider is content with saying that

> knowledge in the true and proper sense, if it is prominent, cannot be overcome by perturbation; in this sense Socrates is right in saying that no one can sin against one's own knowledge. Knowledge regarding *aisthêtikê* [sense perception] can easily be weakened and shattered.[227]

Because Heider holds that practical knowledge is always related to the senses which experience the conflict between reason and appetite, practical knowledge is uncertain and, as a result, the door to akrasia remains open. In this sense, Heider proceeds along the new path of Camerarius and Golius.

This feature is even more strongly present in the second part of his third question: 'Where does incontinence come from?'[228] Like Golius, Heider understands Aristotle's remark on the 'facts of nature' (EN 1147a24–b5) in the straightforward sense of discrepancy and struggle:

> Aristotle here says that the natural cause of incontinence is the discrepancy between reason and appetite. Reason recommends the good and the honest, but they are connected with labour, difficulties, and many troubles. Appetite is drawn to that which is pleasant and agreeable, although in many ways harmful and dangerous. The incontinent person is led in both directions; and since the passions are stronger and reason weaker, reason finally surrenders to passions in the same way as the stubborn horse leads the rider or the strong wind overcomes the skill of the sailor. In this manner the incontinent individual sins knowingly and ignorantly; we have already examined how this needs to be understood.[229]

The two examples given in this quote do not concur well with the Aristotelian examples given above. The horseman and the sailor are not ignorant in the same sense as the drunkard or the children. They are fully aware of what they should do, but they lack the skill and the strength to do it. The example of the horseman probably comes from Luther.

---

[227] *Philosophiae moralis systema*, 825: 'Scientia vera et proprie dicta, si praesto sit, a perturbatione vinci non potest, et hoc sensu verum est illud Socratis: qui neminem contra scientiam suam peccare posse dicebat. Scientia *aisthêtikê* a cupiditatibus facile labefactatur et convellitur.'

[228] *Philosophiae moralis systema*, 825: 'Unde incontinentia?'

[229] *Philosophiae moralis systema*, 825: 'Aristoteles ibidem incontinentiae naturalem causam esse ait, dissidium rationis et appetitus. Ratio suadet ea, quae bona sunt et honesta, sed cum labore, difficultatibus et molestiis plerumque conjuncta. Appetitus fertur ad illa, quae sensibus grata sunt et jucunda, sed ut plurimum turpia et perniciosa. Huc igitur et illuc trahitur incontinens, sed quia vehementiores sunt cupiditates, et ratio languidior, haec tandem illis succumbit non aliter, quam refractarius equus sessorem excutit, aut ventorum impetus superat artem gubernatoris. Et ita quidem sciens peccat incontinens et ignorans, quod qua ratione sit accipiendum, jam ante diximus.'

Heider further illustrates the cause of akrasia with the example of akratic alcoholism. The incontinent person's appetite pushes him towards drinking while his reason argues that shameful things are to be avoided and that this is shameful. The appetite formulates an opposing syllogism, according to which pleasant things should be enjoyed and this is pleasant. The akratic person knows the right universal premise, but he may doubt the particular premise, for instance, thinking that other people get drunk without shame, or he may simply be blinded by his strong desire so that he neglects the relevant particulars and follows the desire. This is what the statement that the incontinent does not know the particulars and cannot apply them to the universals means.[230]

This example again fits well the Aristotelian scheme of temporary ignorance, although it differs from the horseman and sailor examples. Heider's main interest is, however, to emphasize the continuing discrepancy between reason and appetite as the 'natural cause' of akrasia. This natural cause may result in powerlessness or temporary ignorance, but the examples are united in the underlying fact of struggle between reason and appetite. Heider adds that some illnesses and temperaments of the body may also cause similar weakening of reason. He also holds, like Golius, that compulsion by force can be counted among the causes of akrasia.[231]

Heider concludes the second subsidiary question, as well as his entire third question, with a theological remark:

Finally, if it is asked where this discrepancy between reason and appetite comes from, all philosophy remains silent. But the Holy Scripture teaches that this *ataxia* as well as other genres of wickedness and all this vanity to which nature is subjected [Romans 8:20] has its origin nowhere else than in sin. On this matter theologians say more.[232]

This final remark, of course, represents the voice of Martin Luther who (3.2) understood the human condition so strongly in terms of struggle and the discrepancy between God's spirit and sinful flesh. After Melanchthon, this struggle and discrepancy was treated philosophically and identified with Aristotle's discussion on the 'natural cause' of akrasia (EN 1147a24–b5) but, as Heider points out, the deeper truth of this struggle needs to be understood theologically. In this sense, Luther's 'first strategy' of explaining continence and sin is compatible with Camerarius's 'second strategy' of explaining akrasia in terms of struggle and uncertainty.

---

[230] *Philosophiae moralis systema*, 825: 'Exempli gratia: si ad ebrietatem propendeat incontinens, ei recta ratio prohibet, sed appetitus suadet. Rationis rectae argumentum hoc est: Noxia fugienda; Ebrietas noxia; Ebrietas fugienda. Contra, excipit appetitus: Rebus jucundis fruendum; Ebrietate nihil jucundius; Ergo fruendum illa. Jam incontinens in rectae rationis syllogismo propositionem universalem, quam majorem vocamus, probe novit esse veram. Assumtionem autem vel in dubium vocat, eorum exemplis, qui sine noxa inebriantur, vel suis occoecatus cupiditatibus se ponit, negligit, abjicit, oblivioni tradit, et ita contrarium ejus, quod effecerat recta ratio, concludit. Et hoc illud ipsum est, quod supra diximus: Incontinentem particularia nescire, et ad haec ipsa universalia non applicare.'

[231] *Philosophiae moralis systema*, 825–6.

[232] *Philosophiae moralis systema*, 826: 'At vero, si quaeratur, unde sit illud rationis et appetitus dissidium, omnis Philosophia conticescit. Sacrae vero literae docent, et hanc *ataxian* et alia malorum genera, et totam hanc vanitatem, cui natura subjecta, non aliunde quam a peccato originem trahere, qua de re Theologi plura.'

Like Golius, Heider attempts to set out an Aristotelian understanding of akrasia. However, this attempt remains strongly coloured by the underlying structure of the discrepancy between reason and appetite. Golius and, in particular, Camerarius, argue that different faculties and powers of the soul need to be presupposed to avoid the problems of Stoicism; this differentiation of mental powers is understood to represent Aristotelianism. At the same time, the approach of Camerarius, Golius, and Heider proceeds beyond ancient and medieval Aristotelianism in claiming that the struggle and wrestling between reason and appetite is a universal phenomenon which leaves all consideration of particular actions more or less uncertain.

Heider may be more moderate than Camerarius and Golius. He does not say in the manner of Camerarius (3.3) that such uncertainty is 'the cause of all evil', nor does he claim, in the manner of Golius, that Adam and Eve suffered from this discrepancy. Instead, Heider wants to have it both ways: akrasia is due to the negligence of particulars, but it is also clear-eyed powerless behaviour which resembles the sailor's sailing before the storm, Paul's introspection in Romans 7, or Medea's falling in love. Because of this integration of different traditions and examples, Heider's discussion remains somewhat incoherent. He focuses on the struggle between reason and appetite; but the impact of this struggle is sometimes described as clear-eyed powerlessness, and sometimes as Aristotelian ignorance of the particulars.

We will summarize the outcome of each chapter in more detail in 5.1. Here we have only pointed out some interconnected aspects of Lutheran discussion. The last such aspect is the great relevance of sense perception for Camerarius, Golius, and Heider. The Protestant Orthodoxy was not a particularly innovative current in philosophy, but it immediately precedes the prominent period of Descartes, Spinoza, and Leibniz (5.3). Camerarius affirms voluntarism, claiming that a variety of options remain available in the consideration of particular actions, as they are related to the uncertain grasp of our perceptions. Golius and Heider likewise claim that practical knowledge represents *aisthêtikê*, the perceptual component of knowledge. Although these Lutheran thinkers can hardly be regarded as empiricists, their emphasis on sense perception as the necessary basis of practical knowledge is worthy of attention. They all interpret Aristotle as saying that akrasia is proved by experience (EN 1145b27) and they see this experience confirmed in the continuing struggle between reason and appetite. Because the agents almost always perceive conflicting particular options among which they must choose, they remain uncertain. This experience, the perception of conflict and remaining uncertainty, becomes the 'natural cause' of akrasia.

4

The Calvinist Reformation

4.1 John Calvin: Sin and Akrasia

John Calvin (1509–1564) shares Martin Luther's appreciation of late Augustine (cf. 3.2). He regards the harmful desires as impulses against God and therefore already sinful in themselves.[1] Like Luther, Calvin holds that Christians are righteous and sinners at the same time.[2] Because Calvin is an erudite and a systematic thinker, he is concerned with the relationship of this new view to the broader tradition of theology and philosophy. In many works, in particular his *Institutio Christianae religionis*, he discusses the Aristotelian and Stoic traditions. Unlike Luther, Calvin makes explicit reference to the Aristotelian problem of akrasia. Because Calvin has more systematic rigour than Melanchthon and because his most important references to akrasia already appear in the 1539 and 1543 editions of *Institutio*, he can be called the first Protestant author who consistently applies Luther's insights to the Aristotelian issue of weakness of will.

My exposition of Calvin's view of akrasia proceeds from the final edition of *Institutio* (1559), which carefully outlines the systematic context of harmful passions and sinfulness. As Calvin's views first appeared in the earlier editions (in particular, 1539 and 1543), I will indicate in the footnotes the first occurrence of the passage quoted. After describing the position of *Institutio*, we will briefly look at Calvin's commentaries on Romans and First Corinthians.

Calvin's discussion on akrasia and related phenomena in the *Institutio* is embedded in the larger issue of knowledge regarding God and God's will.[3] Calvin distinguishes among three aspects of what he calls 'spiritual insight' (*perspicentia spiritualis*); that is, the understanding that human reason can obtain regarding the final ends of humanity. The two first aspects concern knowing God and God's salvific will; for Calvin, people are completely blind with regard to these. The third aspect concerns knowing 'how to

---

[1] *Institutio* (1559), 3, 3, 10–13. I refer to the paragraphs of the 1559 edition and to the page numbers of the English edition ICR (here: 602–6). I also indicate the earliest occurrence of the quote (in the 1539 and 1543 editions of *Institutio*). Whenever relevant, the page numbers of the *Corpus Reformatorum* edition (CO) are also given. Biblical expositions are quoted according to Calvin's *Commentaries* (2005). Introductory information on Calvin is found in deGreef (1989); McKim (2004). On Calvin's ethics, see Sauer (1997).

[2] e.g. *Institutio* (1559), 3, 3, 12 (ICR, 604–5).

[3] For these larger issues, see e.g. Pitkin (1999) and Helm (2004).

frame our lives according to the rule of his law'.[4] In *Institutio* 2, 2, 22–25, Calvin discusses this third aspect, while *Institutio* 2, 2, 26–27 applies the results of this discussion to the human will.

Calvin admits that the human mind seems 'more acute' with respect to right conduct than with respect to knowing God, as witnessed by Romans 2:14–15, as well as by the phenomenon of natural law, which is said to instruct all humans in the right standard of conduct. It is important for Calvin that all human beings, Christians and non-Christians alike, as Romans 2:14–15 points out, possess conscience which gives instruction on right conduct. This knowledge should be understood as the sinful consciousness of human beings, rather than as the possibility of controlling their actual behaviour. Although people try to ignore their capacity for judging between good and evil, they are constantly reminded of their faults, and are thus aware of the innate judging capacity of conscience. For Calvin, therefore, 'the purpose of natural law ... is to render man inexcusable'.[5] This view is taken from Luther: it is the so-called *usus theologicus* of the law, the use which evokes the feeling of guilt and sinfulness but does not give the power to control one's own conduct. It also resembles John Mair's view of conscience (2.5), which keeps warning the incontinent person.

For Calvin, the constant presence of the capacity to judge between good and evil raises the problem which Plato discusses in *Protagoras* (cf. 1.1). In order to overcome this capacity, something needs to be ignored; thus sinful deeds proceed from ignorance, and the awareness of them would only emerge afterwards. Calvin considers that the human mind is not so corrupted that it could deliberately and permanently ignore the good. The mind exercises its capacity of judgement by opening its eyes at least 'at times' (*aliquando*). Although the sinner tries to evade his inner power of judgement, he is continually drawn back to the recognition of the true nature of his actions. Therefore it cannot be said that human beings only sin from ignorance.[6]

Calvin is prepared to ascribe some significant role to ignorance, although it cannot explain everything. He has a high regard for moral knowledge, a regard which leads him close to the Socratic position, since a person possessing this knowledge cannot simply act against it and some ignorance needs to be taken into account. The presence of moral judgement and conscience leads to a quasi-intellectualist dilemma: without the capacity of judgement between good and evil, people could not bear the whole responsibility for their sins; but if this capacity were effective always and with regard to everything, people would not be such grave sinners as they in fact are. To resolve this issue, Calvin steers a middle course which stems from the medieval commentaries on EN:

---

[4] *Inst.* 2, 2, 18 (=1539); ICR, 277; CO 2, 200: 'formandae secundum legis regulam vitae rationem.'

[5] *Inst.* 2, 2, 22 (=1539); ICR, 281–2. For this activity of conscience, see also *Inst.* 3, 2, 20, and 22 (=1539).

[6] *Inst.* 2, 2, 22 (=1539); ICR, 282; CO 2, 204: 'Qua ratione videtur impulsus fuisse Plato, ut existimaret non peccari nisi ignorantia. Id quidem ab eo convenienter dictum foret, si humana hypocrisis tantum in tegendis vitiis proficeret, ut mens non sibi male conscia esset coram Deo. Sed quum subterfugiens peccator impressum sibi boni et mali iudicium, illuc identidem retrahatur, nec connivere ita permittatur, quin cogatur, velit nolit, aliquando aperire oculos: falso dicitur, ipsum ignorantia sola peccare.'

Themistius more correctly teaches that the intellect is very rarely deceived in general definition or in the essence of the thing; but that it is illusory when it goes farther, that is, applies the principle to particular cases. In reply to the general question, every man will affirm that murder is evil. But he who is plotting the death of an enemy contemplates murder as something good. The adulterer will condemn adultery in general, but will privately flatter himself in his own adultery. Herein is man's ignorance: when he comes to a particular case, he forgets the general principle that he has just laid down.[7]

Although Calvin quotes Themistius in a humanistic manner here instead of scholastic authors, the explanation is Aristotelian (cf. EN 1147a1–b5, 1.1) and can be found in all medieval commentaries on the EN. Knowledge of universal facts cannot be overcome by lower faculties. At the same time, the knowledge regarding universals does not prompt action. The particular facts do not express proper knowledge and can be ignored in a particular situation. The person who acts against better universal judgement puts the particular under another principle, which allows him to deliberate on the sinful action 'as something good' (tanquam de re bona deliberat). This is the scholastic view of acting wrongly under some aspect of goodness (sub ratione boni) so that the person has two competing practical syllogisms in his mind (cf. 1.3–1.4). Under the wrong general principle, the harmful aspects of the particular fact remain ignored.

Given this, Calvin's view of acting against better judgement represents the typical Aristotelian-Thomist model (1a of our typology in 1.5). Calvin is not, however, willing to hold that all instances of sinning are due to partial ignorance. There are also some cases of clear-eyed wrongdoing, as we learn from the case of Medea:

Themistius' rule, however, is not without exception. Sometimes the shamefulness of evil-doing presses upon the conscience so that one, imposing upon himself no false image of the good, knowingly and willingly rushes headlong into wickedness. Out of such a disposition of mind come statements like this: 'I see what is better and approve it, but I follow the worse.' To my mind Aristotle has made a very keen distinction between incontinence and intemperance: where incontinence reigns, he says, the disturbed mental state or passion so deprives the mind of particular knowledge that it cannot mark the evil in its own misdeed, which it generally discerns in like instances; when the perturbation subsides, repentance straightway returns. Intemperance, however, is not extinguished or shattered by the awareness of sin, but on the contrary, stubbornly persists in choosing its habitual evil.[8]

---

[7] Inst. 2, 2, 23 (=1539); ICR, 282; CO 2, 204: 'Verius Themistius, qui intellectum in definitione universali, seu rei essentia, rarissime falli docet; hallucinationem esse quum ultra progreditur, nempe quum ad hypothesin descendit. Homicidium esse malum, si in genere quaeratur, nemo erit qui non affirmet; qui autem conspirat in mortem inimici, tanquam de re bona deliberat. Adulterium in genere damnabit adulter; in suo privatim sibi blandietur. Haec est ignorantia, dum homo, ubi ad hypothesin ventum est, eius regulae obliviscitur, quam in thesi nuper constituerat.' Cf. Themistius, On Aristotle's On the Soul, 6.

[8] Inst. 2, 2, 23 (=1539); ICR, 282–3; CO 2, 204: 'Quanquam ne istud quidem est perpetuum. Sic enim interdum flagitii turpitudo conscientiam urget, ut non sibi imponens sub falsa boni imagine, sed sciens ot volens, in malum ruat. Ex quo affectu prodeunt istae voces: video meliora, proboque; deteriora sequor. Quare mihi scitissime Aristoteles incontinentiam et intemperantiam videtur distinxisse. Ubi incontinentia regnat, dicit per affectum perturbatum seu pathos particularem notitiam menti eripi, ne malum observet in suo facinore, quod generaliter in similibus cernit; ubi deferbuit perturbatio, poenitentiam exemplo succedere.

This passage is a remarkable one in many respects; Calvin is aware of the Aristotelian discussion of akrasia and connects it with his own discussion on moral conduct. Like Luther, Melanchthon, and Camerarius, he also employs the example of Medea which was available in the commentary by Clichtove. In Calvin's view, Medea is not imagining some false good (*sub falsa boni*) which would cause partial ignorance and justify her wrong action. Instead, she rushes into wickedness *sciens* and *volens*, while her conscience judges that this is wrong.

For Calvin, Medea therefore serves as an example of intemperance rather than incontinence. This is somewhat odd, because Aristotle as well as the Aristotelian tradition holds that the intemperate 'is unconscious of itself' (EN 1150b36). In other words, there is no twofold inclination or divided will in the mind of the intemperate person: he or she simply wills and chooses evil. In a non-Aristotelian manner, Calvin thinks that the conscience of the intemperate person is active but is pressed or 'urged' so that the intemperate individual persists in her evil choice and in that sense acts 'willingly'. Thus, for Calvin, Medea exemplifies the situation in which the person follows the habitual vice in spite of the judgement of conscience. The 'awareness of sin' is thus not lost in the intemperate person.

As for Luther (cf. the end of 3.2), Medea's case is for Calvin a conflict of conscience. The conscience is a universal psychological reality (*Inst.* 2, 2, 22; 3, 2, 20–22) which evokes the awareness of sins in all people. Thus even wicked wrongdoers cannot remain 'unconscious of themselves' in the Aristotelian sense, since their conscience witnesses the depravity of their action. Calvin's example of the intemperate Medea resembles compulsive behaviour in that although Medea intellectually recognizes the depravity of her action, she cannot stop her prevailing habitual choice of evil. This feature bears an interesting resemblance to the Stoic example of 'the runner who cannot stop running' (cf. 1.2). So, although Medea's behaviour is voluntary, it also expresses a sort of compulsion, further evidencing the discrepancy between intellect and will, a feature of Calvin's thought to which we will return below.

Incontinence is characterized in this passage as ignorance of the particular facts relating to a particular action. Calvin's interpretation of akrasia follows the Aristotelian-Thomist model 1a. His strong concept of conscience works in agreement with this model, akrasia being caused by the perturbations which obscure the right evaluation of particulars, and repentance beginning immediately after the passion has evaporated. As we have seen, Calvin takes the intellectualist view of Plato in *Protagoras* very seriously.

This strongly intellectualist theory of knowledge and action is differentiated in the following passages (*Institutio* 2, 2, 24–25). The innate ability of conscience works a posteriori: people know the universal judgement well enough. They cannot excuse

---

Intemperantiam autem non exstingui aut frangi peccati sensu, sed contra obstinate in suscepta mali electione persistere.' Although the English translation (ICR, 283) gives the latter part as a quote from Aristotle, it is not; it is a paraphrase which combines different passages of EN (1146b20–23; 1147a1–18; 1150b29–30, 36) with Calvin's own ideas.

their sin by appealing to ignorance, but they do not know the truth in individual and particular instances. With regard to the moral precepts of the Decalogue, people do not know naturally the principal points of the First Table. They have more understanding of the commandments of the Second Table, but even with regard to these, the philosophers 'take no account of the evil desires that gently tickle the mind (*placide titillant animum*)'.[9] Thus the understanding is darkened even more strongly than the philosophers assume.

At the same time, Calvin criticizes the voluntarist views which ascribe deliberate consent to all sin:

Just as we deservedly censured Plato above because he imputed all sins to ignorance, so also ought we to repudiate the opinion of those who suppose that there is deliberate malice and depravity in all sins. For we know all too well by experience how often we fall despite our good intention. Our reason is overwhelmed by so many forms of deception, is subject to so many errors, dashes against so many obstacles, is caught in so many difficulties, that it is far from directing us aright.[10]

This argument proceeds from the overload of deceptive impressions, resembling Petrarch's argument (2.1). Like Petrarch, Calvin calls Augustine as a witness to show that the 'grace of illumination' is needed in order to see things truthfully (*Institutio* 2, 2, 25). For Calvin, however, illumination and the Holy Spirit are primarily needed for the sake of our defective knowledge. The intellectualist argument serves a purpose which is similar to Luther's definition of sin (3.2): people are not sinful because free will chooses wrongly, but rather because the natural state is one of deception, error, and ignorance. Errors and ignorance make people sinful even when there is only good intention and no deliberate malice. In an original manner, Calvin connects his intellectualist emphasis with the insights of Luther. The incontinent person who does not choose evil but acts in some sense *sub ratione boni* is thus no less sinful than other sinners.

The concluding passages (*Institutio* 2, 2, 26–27) treat the will in its connection with the knowledge of the good. Although Calvin is intellectualist in his view of sin and the innate capacity for judgement, he is voluntarist in his action theory insofar as he considers that choice belongs to the sphere of the will rather than that of the understanding.[11] Calvin is no voluntarist, however, in the sense that he regards free will as the ruler of the soul. On the contrary, Calvin teaches that the human being seeks good in the manner of animals. He has only a natural desire for good but no free will:

---

[9] *Inst.* 2, 2, 24 (=1539); ICR, 283–4; CO 2, 204–5.

[10] *Inst.* 2, 2, 25 (=1539); ICR, 284; CO 2, 205: 'Quare, ut supra merito reprehensus est Plato quod omnia peccata ignorantiae imputavit, ita et eorum est repudianda opinio qui consultam malitiam et pravitatem in omnibus peccatis intercedere tradunt. Nimium enim experimur quoties labamur cum bona nostra intentione. Tot obruitur hallucinationum formis nostra ratio, tot erroribus est obnoxia, in tot impedimenta impingit, tot angustiis irretitur, ut plurimum a certa directione absit.'

[11] *Inst.* 2, 2, 26 (=1539); ICR, 286; CO 2, 207: 'Examinanda nunc voluntas, in qua praecipue arbitrii libertas vertitur. Quandoquidem magis huius esse electionem, quam intellectus, ante visum est.' Cf. *Inst.* 2, 2, 4.

like an animal he follows the inclination of his nature, without reason, without deliberation. Therefore, whether or not man is impelled to seek after good by an impulse of nature has no bearing upon freedom of the will. This instead is required: that he discern good by right reason; that knowing it he choose it; that having chosen he follow it . . . To sum up, much as man desires to follow what is good, still he does not follow it.[12]

Calvin wants to show that the Holy Spirit is always needed for the effective following of what is good. In doing this, he adumbrates an exposition of Romans 7 which is basically similar to Luther's understanding. Calvin joins Augustine and Luther in maintaing that the speaker of Romans 7 is *Paulus Christianus* in his spiritual struggle. The good will of the Apostle comes from his regeneration in the Spirit. The natural man is only flesh which has no impulse towards the good:

Yet if we hold the view that men have, apart from grace, some impulses (however puny) towards good, what shall we reply to the Apostle who even denies that we are capable of conceiving anything (2. Cor. 3:5) . . . For even if believers sometimes ask that their hearts be conformed to obedience to God's law . . . yet we must also note that this desire to pray comes from God.[13]

This dichotomy between the spirit and the flesh is similar to Luther's view that the flesh follows the impulses of nature while the spirit is led by God, so that there is no human freedom of self-movement or self-decision. Calvin therefore concludes, quoting Augustine, that all good things come from God and evil things from man's own nature (*Institutio* 2, 2, 27).

From a philosophical point of view, there is a discrepancy between Calvin's relative appreciation of the intellectual powers and his view of the total depravity of the human will. Calvin's aims are theological; that is, he wants to affirm a strongly anti-Pelagian view of will but also to establish the responsibility of human beings. The powers of intellect and conscience endow people with judgement concerning good and evil, but this judgement does not prompt action since there is no corresponding power of movement and action. Although the human being differs from animals insofar as the intellective powers of reason are concerned (*Institutio* 2, 2, 12), humans do not differ from animals which follow their natural inclinations in their active pursuit of goals (*Institutio* 2, 2, 26). This discrepancy between being rational and being without free choice allows Calvin to affirm both the responsibility and the powerlessness needed for an orthodox Protestant theology.

In his discussion on the sinfulness of the believers (*Institutio* 3, 3, 10–13), Calvin again mentions the relationship between incontinence and intemperance. Like Luther, he teaches that the mere presence of harmful desires qualifies the individual as sinful. And because all human actions are disordered, there is no real difference in the moral character of intemperance and incontinence:

---

[12] *Inst.* 2, 2, 26 (=1539); ICR, 286.
[13] *Inst.* 2, 2, 27 (=1539); ICR, 288.

Now, all man's faculties are, on account of the depravity of nature, so vitiated and corrupted that in all his actions persistent disorder and intemperance emerge. Because these appetitive forces cannot be separated from incontinence of the same kind, we contend that they are vicious. Or, if you would have the matter summed up in fewer words, we teach that all human desires are evil, and charge them with sin.[14]

Although Calvin, in *Institutio* 2, 2, 23, approves Aristotle's distinction between intemperance and incontinence, the distinction is only relevant insofar as it points out the two different dynamics of sinful actions. The culpability or viciousness of intemperance and incontinence is similar, because both stem from the harmful desires which dominate corrupted nature. Because Calvin follows Luther in locating culpability not in the act of consent or choice, but in the underlying desires, he draws the logical conclusion that intemperance and incontinence stem from the same source and are thus sinful in the same way.

The difference between Luther and Calvin pertains to their different view of the intellect. While Calvin acknowledges that many sins are due to ignorance of particulars and that even willful wrongdoers possess a conscience, Luther's straightforward action theory does not allow for this kind of divided mind with regard to sinful acts. For Luther, the enkratic mode of good actions exemplifies the only kind of divided will (cf. 3.2).

It is important to see that for Calvin, as well as for Luther, the imperfections of corrupted nature concern non-Christians and Christians alike. Like Luther, Calvin wants to show in this context (*Institutio* 3, 3, 13) that Augustine teaches the sinfulness of believers. For Calvin, 'all desires of the flesh are sins' and 'the law of sin still remains in the saints'.[15] Therefore, 'the saints are as yet so bound by that disease of concupiscence that they cannot withstand being at times tickled and incited either to lust or to avarice or to ambition'. Thus 'in the saints ... there is always sin'.[16] Although strong-willed moral conduct is possible, it is entirely God's work and the saints remain sinners in the sense that their corporeal existence is contaminated by harmful desires.

In philosophical terms, this means that the struggle with harmful desires is a universal phenomenon of all human beings. Moreover, people cannot control their actual conduct by means of their reason or will, because the higher part cannot control either the natural inclinations or the persistent disorder of emotions. The intellect can to some extent comprehend this situation, although it is also subject to error. This understanding brings about a sense of responsibility, but only in the form of *sensus peccati*, an awareness concerning the wrongdoings of the individual. The intellectual awareness regarding the knowledge of good and evil has no corrective power.

---

[14] *Inst.* 3, 3, 12 (=1543); ICR, 604; CO 2, 442: 'Iam vero quum ob naturae pravitatem omnes facultates adeo vitiatae sint ac corruptae, ut in omnibus actionibus emineat perpetua *ataxia* et intemperies, quia ab eiusmodi incontinentia separari nequeunt appetitiones, ideo vitiosas esse contendimus. Aut (si paucioribus verbis summam habere libet) omnes hominum cupiditates malas esse docemus, et peccati reas peragimus.'

[15] *Inst.* 3, 3, 11–12 (= 1543); ICR, 604–5.

[16] *Inst.* 3, 3, 10 (=1543); ICR, 602–3.

Calvin uses the word *incontinentia* in its Augustinian sense; that is, as referring to the lack of sexual chastity, outside of *Institutio*. This meaning is for the most part conditioned by 1 Cor. 7:5; the Christian understanding of this verse makes marriage a 'remedy for incontinence' (*remedium incontinentiae*). We will, however, leave aside most texts dealing with incontinence in this sense, since they are beyond the scope of this study.[17]

Calvin's *Commentary on Romans* is, however, a text which is relevant for our history of akrasia. Calvin again uses the example of Medea in his exposition of Romans 7:16. His interpretation is influential for the Protestant understanding of inner division within the soul. Calvin employs the term *incontinentia* in this text on the problems of marriage in a manner which exemplifies the Augustinian use of the word.

In Romans 7:16 (Vulgate), Paul says that if he does what he does not want to do, he consents to the law. For Luther, this verse attested to inner repugnancy: Paul wants to do good in a perfect manner, but manages to do good only in an imperfect way. Because both Calvin and Luther follow the late Augustine in holding that the speaker is the Christian or the spiritual person, they need to understand Paul's inner conflict in a manner which differs from the inner conflicts of those beyond the realm of grace or spirit. Calvin accomplishes this by comparing Paul to Medea as follows:

> But if what I do not will, I do, I consent to the law, etc.; that is, 'When my heart acquiesces in the law, and is delighted with its righteousness (which certainly is the case when it hates the transgression of it), it then perceives and acknowledges the goodness of the law, so that we are fully convinced, experience itself being our teacher, that no evil ought to be imputed to the law; nay, that it would be salutary for men, were it to meet with upright and pure hearts.' But this consent is not to be understood to be the same as what we have heard exists in the ungodly, who have expressed words of this kind, 'I see better things and approve of them; I follow the worse.' Again, 'What is hurtful I follow; I shun what I believe would be profitable.' For these people act under a constraint when they subscribe to the righteousness of God, as their will is wholly alienated from it, but the godly man consents to the law with the real and most cheerful desire of his heart; for he wishes nothing more than to mount up to heaven.[18]

This passage elucidates the discussion on Medea undertaken in the *Institutio*. A person without grace remains in the state in which the discrepancy between reason and will makes her behaviour in some respects compulsive. Medea 'subscribes' to the right moral conduct by way of lip service or empty recognition: this knowledge does not direct action,

---

[17] See, for instance, CO 7, 670; 8, 74; 10, 260, and Calvin's commentary on 1 Cor. discussed below.

[18] CO 49, 131: 'Si vero quod nolo facio, consentio legi. Id est, dum cor meum in lege acquiescit et oblectatur eius iustitia (quod certe fit ubi transgressionem odio habet), in eo sentit ac fatetur legis bonitatem. ut satis vel experientia docente convincamur, legi nihil mali esse imputandum: imo salutarem hominibus eam fore, si in recta puraque corda incideret. Hic autem consensus non est accipiendus qualem audimus in impiis. quorum sunt voces: Video meliora, proboque, deteriora sequor. Item: Quae nocitura, sequar: fugiam, quae profore credam. [Horatius, *Epist.* 1, 8, 11] Illi enim coacti faciunt, quod subscribunt in Dei iustitiam, a qua sunt alioqui prorsus aliena voluntate: at pius serio quoque et promptissimi pectoris desiderio consentit: quia nihil mallet quam in coelum evolare.' See also Steinmetz (1990).

her will remaining on the habitual track of wrongdoing. Thus she acts under constraint (*coactus*) and her behaviour resembles the Stoic example of the 'runner who cannot stop running' (cf. 1.2). The discrepancy between intellect and will remains radical.

The spiritual person, in this case the Apostle Paul, directs his will appropriately, consenting to the law. It is not his will that causes the problematic action, this action simply happening in spite of the good consent which stems from the heart. It may be that Paul's and Medea's actions look similar when viewed from the outside, because both behave against what they believe to be the best option. But Medea's will remains fixed to wrongdoing, whereas Paul's will consents to the good and the non-willed carnal imperfections simply overcome his will and intellect.

The difference may not look philosophically very convincing or deep, since it does not explain why Paul nevertheless misses the best option. To understand this, we should look at Calvin's exposition of the following verses. In Calvin's view, Paul first underlines (7:17) how far he has been alienated from his flesh, which still may display its imperfections. In the next verse, Calvin employs Luther's argument: Paul wants to do good in a pure and perfect manner, but 'the work really done did not correspond to his will; for the flesh hindered him from doing perfectly what he did'. In this sense he cannot 'accomplish' (*perficere*, 7:18) his good will.[19]

In a similar vein, Paul's doing evil (7:19) does not mean external sins but, because the saints are so self-conscious of the remaining harmful desires, they hold that even their 'best works are always stained with some blots of sin' and thus cannot bring about the perfection they want and desire.[20] Like Luther, Calvin teaches that the inner division pertains to the 'pious'; that is, Christians who aim to be enkratic in their struggle with the flesh:

Here [Rom 7:22–3] then you see what sort of division there is in pious souls, from which arises that contest between the spirit and the flesh, which Augustine in some place elegantly calls the Christian wrestling. The law calls man to the rule of righteousness; iniquity, which is, as it were, the tyrannical law of Satan, instigates him to wickedness: the Spirit leads him to render obedience to the divine law; the flesh draws him back to what is of an opposite character. Man, thus impelled by contrary desires, is now in a manner a twofold being; but as the Spirit ought to possess the sovereignty, he deems and judges himself to be especially on that side. Paul says that he was bound a captive by his flesh for this reason, because as he was still tempted and incited by evil lusts, he deemed this a coercion with respect to the spiritual desire, which was wholly opposed to them.[21]

---

[19] CO 49, 131–2.
[20] CO 49, 132.
[21] CO 49, 133: 'Hic ergo vides qualis sit in piis animis divisio, ex qua oritur illa concertatio spiritus et carnis, quam Augustinus alicubi eleganter vocat luctam christianam. Lex Dei ad iustitiae rectitudinem hominem vocat: iniquitas, quae est velut lex tyrannica Satanae, ad nequitiam instigat. Ad divinae legis obedientiam fert spiritus: caro in contrariam partem retrahit. Homo ita variis voluntatibus distractus iam quodammodo duplex est: sed quoniam principatum debet tenere spiritus, illa praecipue sese parte censet ac aestimat. Ideo Paulus ait, se captivum a carne sua vinciri: quia, quod titillatur adhuc pravis concupiscentiis et commovetur, id coactio est respectu spiritualis desiderii, quod prorsus resistit.'

We can still see some traces of the scholastic discussion regarding the 'contrary appetitive powers' (3.1, 3.2) at work in Calvin's understanding of Romans 7. Like Luther, Calvin regards the divided soul as characteristic of pious, rather than impious, persons. Even the most pious, like Paul, remain to an extent captive of their harmful desires. Calvin here admits that this captivity is also a sort of compulsion (*coactio*), but the compulsion does not concern the inner life of the spiritual desire. Extending this view, it could be said that whereas the dynamic part of Medea's soul, her desire and will, remained constrained by habitual wrongdoing, Paul's captivity only means that he is surrounded and tempted by harmful desires while his prevailing desire nevertheless remains spiritual.

More important than the plausibility of this explanation is the general observation that Calvin pays systematic attention to the different traditions of divided will. He is aware of the scholastic explanation regarding the ignorance of particular facts and ascribes to it a significant role in understanding sinful actions. He takes over Luther's and Augustine's analysis of Romans 7 and compares it to the division of mind in the example of Medea. Unlike Clichtove (2.4), he regards Medea as an example of intemperance rather than incontinence, and places this example in the category of compulsive actions in which the individual conscience remains aware of what is happening. In the comparison of Medea and Paul as two instances of divided mind, Calvin also employs the scholastic discussion concerning the contrary appetitive powers. The different Augustinian and Aristotelian traditions are thus united in Calvin's systematic treatment of the problem of weakness of will.

If we look at Calvin's position on akrasia with respect to the earlier tradition, it is clear that he follows Luther in his doctrine of sinfulness. At the same time, his discussion on akrasia and intemperance follows the intellectualist tradition of Thomism in which the akratic mode of wrongdoing is characterized by the temporary ignorance of particular facts (our model 1a in 1.5). Calvin's view of conscience and permanent sinfulness colour this Thomist idea in a new way, but Calvin's emphasis on ignorance nevertheless distinguishes him from Luther. At the same time, Calvin is only a 'semi-intellectualist' in the sense that he repudiates the intellectualism of Plato and Socrates, arguing that sometimes one may act against one's better judgement in the clear-eyed manner of Medea.

One possible source of this semi-intellectualist view may be John Mair's commentary.[22] In his discussion on akrasia, Mair ascribes the causes of sinning partially to ignorance, and partially to willful wrongdoing in a somewhat similar manner (see 2.5). Calvin's reference to Themistius's commentary on *De anima* is not very informative; this commentary was frequently used in late medieval and early modern psychology and, as noted above, Calvin's point was already made by Aristotle in EN.[23]

[22] Although Calvin was not directly taught by Mair, as Ganoczy (1966) argues against Reuter (1963), a literary relationship or dependence on common tradition cannot be ruled out.
[23] Themistius, *On Aristotle's On the Soul* is a new English translation with historical information. Early Latin printings (Venice 1499 and 1534) of Themistius were available in Calvin's times.

In addition to this general summary, we can briefly look at a text in which Calvin discusses incontinence in its Augustinian sense of chastity. In his exposition of 1 Cor. 7:1–2, Calvin introduces the traditional view of marriage as a remedy for incontinence. Although the first purpose of marriage and sexual life is procreation, the weakness of the flesh (*incontinentia*) is also helped by the institution of marriage, in which sexuality can be practised with one's own spouse.[24] In 1 Cor. 7:5 (Vulgate), the word *incontinentia* appears as the weakness which Satan employs in the temptation. Calvin briefly returns to the topic of the remedy for incontinence in the context of 1 Cor. 7:11, allowing and even recommending the use of this remedy.[25]

In the context of 1 Cor. 10:6, Calvin uses the term *incontinentia* in a somewhat broader sense, referring to the general phenomenon of 'desiring evil'. Some transgressions reported in the Bible are here used as typological examples of incontinence. People who follow concupiscence and exceed God's commands are incontinent and incur divine punishment.[26] These occurrences of *incontinentia* do not contain any conceptual analysis. They demonstrate the continuing use of the Augustinian meaning of the term. The broader use in 1 Cor. 10 is motivated by the twofold occurrence of the verb *concupisco* in the Vulgate text, which draws attention to sexual lust.

The presence of harmful desire provides a connecting link between the Aristotelian and the Christian understanding of *incontinentia*. Because the Protestant interpreters regard the mere presence of concupiscence as culpable sin, they tend to focus on the role of harmful desires more strongly than the earlier authors. For this reason, the non-philosophical use of *incontinentia* in the context of marriage and sexuality may nevertheless have some bearing on the more conceptual discussions.

4.2 Ramism and Humanism: Zwinger and van Giffen

As the Calvinist Reformation spread over Europe, from Switzerland to Hungary, the Netherlands, Great Britain, and the New World, it was in many ways more international and complex than its Lutheran counterpart. Many different approaches can be observed in the field of ethics. The earliest teaching of ethics in Calvinist academies was influenced by the Humanist approach of Philip Melanchthon,[27] whose pupil Andreas Hyperius published one of the first Reformed commentaries on the *Nicomachean Ethics* in 1553. Petrus Vermigli's commentary on the three first books of EN appeared in 1563. Whereas Hyperius expounds the EN in a fairly non-theological manner,

---

[24] CO 49, 401–2.

[25] CO 49, 410–11.

[26] CO 49, 457: 'Dominus hac incontinentia offensus gravem plagam populo inflixit. Unde vocatus fuit locus sepulcra concupiscentiae: quod illic sepelierunt, qui a Domino percussi fuerant. Hoc exemplo testatus est Dominus quantum oderit cupiditates, quae ex fastidio donorum suorum et nostra incontinentia proveniunt: malum enim et illicitum merito censetur quidquid modum a Deo praescriptum excedit.'

[27] Sinnema (1993); Strohm (1996), 93–5.

Vermigli compares Aristotle with the biblical truth.[28] Another follower of Melanchthon was Victorinus Strigellus, whose commentary on EN was published in 1572.[29]

Later Calvinist discussions on akrasia are characterized by two different perspectives:
on the one hand, many Calvinists are devoted Humanists who wish to clarify the
philosophical issues using new methodologies and pedagogical-rhetorical skills. On the
other hand, ethics becomes increasingly drawn to the sphere of theology, so that a
distinct 'Christian ethics' emerges. In this section, we focus on Theodor Zwinger and
Hubert van Giffen, two scholars whose work was influenced by Humanism and, in the
case of Zwinger, by so-called Ramism, a new method of analysis developed by Petrus
Ramus.[30] The next section (4.3) is devoted to the emergence of Christian ethics in the
work of Lambert Daneau.

Zwinger and van Giffen regard ethics as a discipline taught in the faculty of arts.
Their understanding of moral philosophy continues the tradition of Renaissance
Aristotelianism in many ways. At the same time, the new method of Ramism had
the reputation of being a thoroughly anti-Aristotelian alternative to the traditional
logic. Ramus himself and many of his adherents propagated the use of analytical tables
as a new philosophical approach.[31] This may have been an exaggeration, since Ramism
basically offers a new method of dividing and presenting the thematic issues by using
elaborate tables. It was entirely possible, as we shall see in the case of Zwinger, to
present the Aristotelian views using this new method.

Theodor Zwinger (1533–1588), who taught medicine and ethics in Basel, is best
known for his *Theatrum vitae humanae* (1565), an encyclopedic work of universal
history. His commentary on EN (1566)[32] is innovative in its consistent use of the
Ramistic method. In its subtitle, the commentary claims to be a counterpart to the
encyclopedia: whereas *Theatrum* treats human life from the viewpoint of historical
examples, this work teaches the philosophical precepts related to human life.[33] In his
preface, Zwinger underlines his indebtedness to the method of Ramus. With the help
of Ramus, Zwinger can expound 'Aristotle with Aristotle'; that is, without leaning on
diverse schools.[34]

Zwinger's discussion on akrasia in EN VII is long and elaborate. He frequently uses
Greek terms, but his discussion is not philological. Although he displays considerable

---

[28] Sinnema (1993); Strohm (1996), 94–5.

[29] Sinnema (1993), 17–8; Lohr (1982), 177–8.

[30] On Petrus Ramus and his method, see Copenhaver and Schmitt (2002), 230–40.

[31] Cf. Copenhaver and Schmitt (2002), 230–2.

[32] Full title: *Aristotelis Stagiritae de moribus ad Nicomachum libri decem: tabulis perpetuis, quae Commentariorum loco esse quaeant, explicati et illustrati.* Basel 1566.

[33] Subtitle: *Ut quorum in THEATRO vitae humanae habituum EXEMPLA historica describuntur, eorundem in his libris PRAECEPTA philosophica, summa facilitate et perspicuitate tradita cognoscantur.*

[34] *De moribus*, 23: 'Illud ego non obscure fateor, ex praelectionibus simul atque scriptis Talaei, maxime vero Petri Rami (quem preceptoris loco et colui olim, et nunc quoque veneor) id boni me consecutum . . . Rameum tamen illud alta manebat mente repostum, ex Aristotele Aristotelem declarari, praecepta ad usum revocari debere.' Talaeus is Omer Talon (1595–1652). The Reformation theologians aimed at interpreting 'Scripture by Scripture'.

philosophical sophistication on the issues, he does not approach akrasia in the problem-orientated manner of the scholastics. His approach is didactic and pedagogical, elucidating the various meanings of terms and arguments through the use of Ramistic tables. At the same time, Zwinger's debt to scholasticism is evident at the beginning of EN VII. Like Acciaiuoli (2.2) and most other Renaissance authors, Zwinger begins the discussion on akrasia by reporting the six opinions and the order in which Aristotle discusses them.[35]

Concerning the third opinion, 'How does the person who acts wrongly and incontinently act knowingly?',[36] Zwinger distinguishes between Aristotle's approval and refutation of the Socratic view. Socrates denies the existence of akrasia because nothing can be stronger than knowledge, but Aristotle holds that the existence of akrasia is proved by experience: 'We see clearly in everyday life that there are incontinent people. They "see the better and approve it, but follow the worse". In seeing the better they are led by reason; in getting involved with the worse, they are preoccupied with vehement desires.'[37]

The incontinent people know the good both before and after their akratic action. They are not simply ignorant, but know what is to be done and preferred. Because of the powerlessness of their soul (*impotentia animi*) they fall away from the right course of action and follow the worse.[38] As in other Renaissance commentaries, this short deliberation on the 'third opinion' does not yet give a full answer to the issue, but it is discussed in more detail in the context of EN VII, 3.

Although Zwinger's method of exposition is new, its content is traditional in many ways. He does not merely expound 'Aristotle with Aristotle' but adds, for instance, the words of Medea, which had already been employed by Clichtove (2.4) and several other interpreters. Another closely related non-Aristotelian topic is Zwinger's frequent use of the term *pugna*—'struggle'—throughout EN VII. The continent person is one who overcomes the bad desires in his or her struggle, whereas the temperate person is not occupied with this *pugna*.[39] When Zwinger begins his exposition of the crucial issues of EN VII, 3, he characterizes the akratês as a person in whom 'reason and appetite struggle with one another; reason says one thing, the appetite follows another'.[40]

The straightforward use of the picture of the struggle between reason and appetite colours Zwinger's analysis of Aristotle's text. We remarked in the context of Clichtove (2.4; cf. also 1.2 and 2.2) that the motif of struggle and the example of Medea can be understood either in terms of Stoicism or 'commonplace Platonism'. We will return to these alternatives after our analysis of Zwinger's position.

---

[35] *De moribus*, 204 (the order), 204–7 (discussion of all six).

[36] *De moribus*, 204: 'Quo modo sciens quis se male agere, male et incontinenter agat?'

[37] *De moribus*, 204: 'Videmus enim in quotidiana vita manifeste, incontinentes quosdam esse, qui videant meliora probentque, deteriora sequantur. Scientes igitur meliora, rationis ductu, deteriora amplectuntur, vehementia cupiditatis praeoccupati.' The quote is Medea's dictum in Ovid, *Metam.* 7, 20–1.

[38] *De moribus*, 204.

[39] *De moribus*, 206.

[40] *De moribus*, 209 (caput V in Zwinger's counting): 'In incontinente enim ratio et appetitus inter se pugnant: aliud ratio dictat, aliud sequitur appetitus.'

The akratic person not only acts against opinion, but contrary to some kind of knowledge. Zwinger first discusses the ways in which akratic knowledge may be defective from the viewpoint of pure knowledge: that is, without respect for the passions and desires. On this view, the akratic person can know something but not use this knowledge, or he can know the universal truths without knowing the particular facts. At the end of this basically Aristotelian discussion, Zwinger makes the non-Aristotelian remark that when reason and appetite conflict, the 'use' of knowledge can be understood as the input of one's free will. If the individual does not 'want to use' knowledge, he or she is drawn by the appetite.[41] In this sense, the individual can also be morally responsible for his surrender to the harmful desires since it lies within his free will to use reason.

Zwinger's main interest in explaining akrasia is, however, directed to the interplay between reason and appetite; he never returns to the issue of free will in his discussion on akrasia.[42] True to his Ramist strategy of creating elaborate distinctions, Zwinger distinguishes between two 'causes' which, taken together, make akrasia possible. According to the 'first cause', harmful desire prevents knowledge from proceeding to the right action. This can happen in sleep, drunkenness, and insanity. Perhaps because Zwinger is also a physician, he discusses various cases of madness as being related to bodily changes,[43] but the perturbations can also affect the soul:

The affect can move the person forcefully so that the judgement of reason is obscured. This can happen with regard to the anger-related perturbations (emerging from anger), but also with regard to the perturbations related to concupiscence (emerging from venereal appetite). These desires manifestly affect the external body of some people (so that one can read their faces like a mirror of the soul). When the inner organs of the mind suffer, the mind itself seems to suffer.[44]

In addition to the corporeal and soul-related impediments, Zwinger identifies a third strategy for the perturbations to prevent the mind from acting in accordance with knowledge. This third way pertains to cases in which the person is aware of the facts here and now but the perturbation prevents the effective application of this knowledge. Examples of this kind include children and actors who say the right things but do not behave in accordance with them. In this manner, akratic people can quote poets

---

[41] De moribus, 210. Cf in particular: 'cur non utatur scientia. Quae quidem differentiae eo in loco recensentur, quoniam appetitus cum ratione confertur. Nisi tu velis ... hic liberum intelligi, qui sponte sua volensque, non utatur scientia; illic vero coactum, intercedente nimirum vehemente appetitu.' And further down on p. 210: 'Et superius quidem solam rationem considerabamus, quatenus libera quis voluntate scientia utitur vel non utitur.'

[42] Cf. John Mair (2.5) and John Case (4.4), who also insert an unconnected remark on free will into their discussion on akrasia. This may have been a sort of aftermath of the 'Parisian articles', which Mair explicitly mentions.

[43] See De moribus, 211.

[44] De moribus, 211: 'Affectus enim vehementer hominem ita commovet, ut rationis iudicium videatur obscurare. Apparet hoc in perturbationibus animae irascibilis (ex ira scilicet) praeterea etiam ipsius concu-piscibilis (ex appetitu venereo) quae manifeste in quibusdam corpus immutant exterius (id quod ex facie tanquam animi speculo videre licet) et interius etiam mentis organis laesis mentem ipsam videntur laedere.'

without acting accordingly.[45] Although these examples come from Aristotle and earlier commentators (2.2), it is important to see that Zwinger's basic aim is non-Aristotelian. While Aristotle holds, like Socrates, that nothing can be stronger than knowledge, Zwinger shows that reason can be effectively impeded from pursuing the good in many different ways. In particular, the various perturbations of the soul prevent people from acting rationally, although their reason remains sound.

Zwinger's different explanations and classifications proceed from the straightforward and consistent underlying premise of the struggle between reason and appetite. As Zwinger does not return to the discussion on free will, he is not primarily a voluntarist. He rather believes that the strong lower parts of the mind can impede a weak higher part in many different ways. The free will argument quoted above is simply intended to support the overall view of a basic struggle (*pugna*) between reason and appetite.

The various impediments do not produce many different genres of akrasia. The seemingly different genres created in the discussion concerning the 'first cause' only exemplify the various ways in which right reason is impeded from pursuing the good. The presence of an impediment does not yet explain why the akratês pursues the wrong alternative. To explain this, a 'second cause' needs to be added. The second cause responds to the question of how the akratic mind is changed to the contrary. Given this, akrasia emerges as the combination of its first and second cause.

In Zwinger's elaborate discussion of the 'second cause', the harmful desire affects reasoning so that it is changed towards the contrary (*mutatur in contrariam*).[46] This change occurs within the logical dynamics of the practical syllogism. For Zwinger, the syllogism generates a disposition which in theoretical matters pertains to cognition, while in practical matters it tends towards action. When the conclusion of a practical syllogism is dictated, its conclusion is followed by action. The disposition is thus a readiness to follow the conclusion in action.[47]

This description of the practical syllogism distinguishes between the verbal conclusion and the action proceeding from it. Zwinger may follow some earlier adherents of this view (Burley, Acciaiuoli, 1.3, 2.2) but his main aim is to highlight the underlying conflict between reason and appetite. In the akratic situation of the 'second cause', Zwinger defines his point of departure as follows: 'A struggle between reason and appetite emerges, reason concluding one way, appetite another. Both employ a mode of reasoning: reason truthfully, appetite in a false manner. We can understand this

---

[45] *De moribus*, 211: 'quantum scilicet ad praesens negocium pertinet. Incontinens scit sese male agere, et rationem habet integram. Illa tamen impeditur a vehementi appetitu, ne possit veritatem persequi... Quemadmodum pueri verba quidem connectunt, nondum tamen quid ea sibi velint intelligunt... Incontinentes verba quidem proferunt... ut puta versus Euripidis... Quemadmodum histriones personati eorum voces, quorum personas gerunt, loquuntur.'

[46] *De moribus*, 211–12.

[47] *De moribus*, 211: 'syllogisticam dispositionem, in qua ex universali et particulari praemissis conclusio infertur: eaque rursus vel in Theoricis, theorica est, hoc est, ad cognitionem solam pertinet... Practicis... practica est, quoniam ad actionem tendit, ut scilicet id quod conclusio dictavit, re ipsa praestetur. Est enim *diôksis* in iis quibus bonum est propositum.'

when we investigate the matter further.'[48] If the conclusion of the practical syllogism is a dictate of the reason which only tends towards action, rather than being itself the action, the conflict between reason and appetite can easily emerge, because it is a struggle between words and tendencies. Zwinger says here in a Stoic manner that the appetitive desire already expresses reasoning and its conclusion.

Zwinger divides the struggle into two dynamics: while the material dynamic occurs between reason and the senses, the formal dynamic can be described with the help of two syllogistic structures, one representing reason, the other the appetitive powers. Zwinger's description of the two syllogisms is in itself traditional. The appetitive powers offer the following syllogistic reasoning: everything pleasant is to be pursued; everything sweet is pleasant; thus everything sweet is to be pursued; this is sweet; thus this is to be pursued. The right reason offers the following practical syllogism: nothing sweet is to be tasted; this is sweet; thus this is not to be tasted.[49]

During the akratic action, the false reasoning obscures (offuscat) the right reason. This change to the contrary can occur because the two major premises 'nothing sweet is to be tasted' and 'everything sweet is pleasant' are not directly contrary to one another since both may be true. They are only contrary by accident; that is, with regard to the particular facts expressed by the minor premises. Given this, the akratic person in some way sins 'under the influence of reason' (EN 1147b1–2).[50]

The syllogistic aspect of this explanation follows Aristotelian model 1a: the akratês retains the right major premise but is deceived in the estimation of particulars. The overall dynamics of Zwinger's explanation is, however, non-Aristotelian. Because the practical syllogism only brings about a tendency to act, the different judgements can coexist and struggle with one another. In this basic struggle between reason and appetite, the appetitive powers of the lower part may overcome the higher part. They need syllogistic forms in order to do this and, within the limits of these forms, 'reason concludes one way, appetite another'. They remain contrary tendencies, however, neither of these 'conclusions' representing the action.

Zwinger summarizes his discussion on akrasia as follows. The harmful desire prevents the reason from pursuing the good (first cause) and replaces the right syllogistic reasoning with its own pleasure-seeking reasoning (second cause) so that the akratic action can proceed. Given this, the akratic person knows the universal premise but does not follow it. Blinded by the appetitive powers, the akratês follows the appetitive power, which offers another universal proposition leading to the wrong

---

[48] *De moribus*, 212: 'Pugna oritur inter rationem et appetitum; et illa quidem uno modo concludit, hic vero altero. Utrobique ratiocinatio est, sed illi vera, hic falsa. Quam ut intelligamus, observare debemus tum.'

[49] *De moribus*, 212.

[50] *De moribus*, 212: 'Peccat cum ratione quodam modo, et opinione. Non modo quia recta ratio impeditur (ut paulo ante monuimus) verum etiam quoniam appetitus ipse falsa quadam ratiocinatione veram offuscat . . . Opinio porro ista verae opinioni sive ratiocinationi contraria per se non est. Neque enim propositiones universales inter se pugnant: Nullum dulce esse gustandum, et: Omne dulce esse iucundum. Sunt enim verae ambae . . . Per accidens est [opinio falsa verae opinioni contraria].' For the different syllogisms, see 1.3 and 2.5. For the interpretation of EN 1147 b1–2, see also van Giffen below.

syllogism.[51] The akratic person can be said to possess the particular proposition, but not in a perfect manner. Thus he knows the relevant particular facts only imperfectly.[52] Socrates is right in holding that nobody can act against perfect knowledge; the akratic persons know the good in some way, but not perfectly.[53]

This summary is Aristotelian in the sense of our model 1a. Zwinger not only interprets 'Aristotle with Aristotle', but embeds his explanation into the broader framework of struggle between reason and appetite. This doctrine is non-Aristotelian in its emphasis on the strong perturbations which can impede and even replace right reason in many different ways. Although Zwinger briefly mentions free will, his discussion for the most part only revolves around the basic struggle between reason and appetite.

Further evidence of the impact of this broader framework can be obtained from the passages in which the akratic choice and the relationship between akrasia and intemperance are discussed. When it is said that akrasia occurs contrary to good choice (cf. EN 1152 a13–18), this means for Zwinger that the akratic person possesses the dictate of right reason but does not follow it in his action, because he is overcome by passion.[54] Here we see again that the propositional conclusion of the practical syllogism can be distinguished from action and that the powerful lower part of the soul may overcome the weak higher part.

In this context, Zwinger also says directly that the appetitive part overcomes reason in the akratic person.[55] A little later, he concludes that 'the incontinent person is well endowed with good and sound judgement; he knows that these desires are not to be followed, but the vehement passion overcomes him'.[56] He further concludes that 'the incontinent person does not do [the good] but merely knows what is to be done. His appetite overcomes his reason.'[57] 'In the incontinent person appetite struggles with right reason; reason is not corrupted but impeded by the appetite.'[58] 'In the incontinent person, less than the greater part of the human being endures with the right reason.'[59]

All these statements approach the 'clear-eyed akrasia' exemplified by Medea's words. In our discussion on Clichtove's commentary (2.4), we have already discussed

---

[51] De moribus, 213: 'ratione universali cognoscere, quod mala sit et fugienda, tamen non sequi rationem rectae imperantem, sed appetitum; atque adeo ab appetitu excaecatum, propositionem universalem aliam a ratione sumere, et ex vitiosa connexione paralogizôn.'

[52] De moribus, 213: 'Hoc modo incontinens dicitur habere particularem propositionem: hoc est, scire, non quidem perfecta scientia, sed imperfecta.'

[53] De moribus, 213.

[54] De moribus, 228: 'Incontinentia para prohairesin est . . . Est enim in incontinente recta ratio, quae quid sit agendum dictat. Rationi tamen non obsequitur in agendo, quoniam appetitus vehementia superatur.'

[55] De moribus, 228: 'Est igitur malus incontinens, quia ab appetitu rationem superari patitur.'

[56] De moribus, 230: 'Incontinens integro et sano iudicio praeditus, scit voluptates istas non esse persequendas, vincitur tamen a vehementi cupiditate.'

[57] De moribus, 231: 'Incontinens vero non facit, sed scit tantum quid faciendum sit. Appetitus enim rationem superat.'

[58] De moribus, 220: 'Incontinentia vero pugnam habet appetitus cum recta ratione, neque corrupta est ratio, sed ab appetitu tantum impedita.'

[59] De moribus, 232: 'Incontinens: minus quam maxima pars hominum in recta permanet ratione.'

briefly whether 'Medea's akrasia' exemplifies Stoic or 'commonplace Platonic' influences. This discussion is difficult in many respects, mainly because the example of Medea was originally Stoic but had been employed in a 'commonplace Platonist' fashion at least since Galen (1.2). As our typological inventory of akrasia (Table 1.1) makes a clear distinction between Stoic and commonplace Platonist models, we have concluded in our earlier discussions relating to the motif of 'struggle' (e.g. 2.2, 2.4) that they exemplify the commonplace Platonist model of akrasia rather than the Stoic.

The case of Zwinger, however, needs to be weighed carefully for both historical and philosophical reasons. New historical studies underline the impact of Neo-Stoicism in early Calvinist ethics. In his study of Lambert Daneau, Christoph Strohm considers that the 'Stoic motif of struggle' (*stoischer Kampfgedanke*) was an important background idea for Calvinist Neo-Stoicism, that the 'perturbations of the soul' remained the basic problem to be confronted by the Neo-Stoics, and that the basic human condition was characterized as 'struggle' in this current of thought.[60] As we have seen, all these are highly significant for Zwinger, making him a historical representative of Neo-Stoicism, irrespective of what his explanatory model of akrasia is to be called.

It can also be argued that Zwinger's analysis of the struggle differs from earlier commentators, in particular Acciaiuoli and Clichtove. In his syllogistic analysis of the 'second cause', Zwinger attributes the appetitive power with an elaborate capacity of formulating syllogisms and drawing conclusions which emerge as judgements. This view understands the perturbations of the soul as strongly cognitive powers which express reasoning and conclusions. Given this, Zwinger's view approaches the Stoic view of cognitive emotions. While the 'commonplace Platonism' treats harmful desires as the lower part of the soul, Zwinger regards appetite as a power which performs acts of reasoning and draws conclusions which deviate from right reason.

The Aristotelian commentators also extensively reconstruct the 'wrong' practical syllogism and discuss the contrary powers prompted by the two syllogisms. Augustine's and Albert the Great's treatments of the 'two wills' and 'contrary acceptances' are continued in the late medieval and Renaissance commentaries, which speak of two syllogisms (1.3, 2.2), but these earlier traditions do not equip the perturbations with a capacity for reasoning. Zwinger is aware of the new features of his view when, after stating that the appetite employs a mode of reasoning, he concludes that: 'Although the appetitive power cannot in itself perform the act of reasoning, it seems to perform this act by accident. When some reason complies with the appetitive power, it can neglect the proper reasoning when the waves of desire push it forward.'[61]

Because of his strongly cognitive view of desire, we may label Zwinger's position as a kind of Neo-Stoicism in which a cognitive and judgement-related account of desire is

---

[60] Strohm (1996), 79–158.

[61] *De moribus*, 212: 'Etsi enim appetitus ipse per se ratiocinari nequit, per accidens tamen ratiocinari videtur: quoniam ratio appetitui obsecundans, exactam ratiocinationem negligit, cum fluctibus cupiditatis abripiatur.'

presupposed. In terms of our classification (1.5), the 'moderated Stoic model' may give an approximation: the akratês, both powerless and fairly well aware of his own state and his akratic perturbation, involves some kind of judgement and assent. At the same time, Zwinger in many respects continues the earlier tradition of 'struggle' between reason and desire, a motif which can also be connected with our 'commonplace Platonism' model. Because of these features, Zwinger deviates from the Aristotelian paradigm, although he claims to explain 'Aristotle with Aristotle'.

Hubert van Giffen, or Obertus Giphanius, (1534–1604) taught ethics and jurisprudence at the Protestant academies of Strasbourg and Altdorf. In his younger days, van Giffen was a 'resolute Calvinist',[62] but he converted to Catholicism in 1590 and became a professor of law in Ingolstadt. Van Giffen was 'an outstanding figure in humanist philology, philosophy and jurisprudence'[63] in his own time, but his ethics has not received much attention in contemporary scholarship. The seventh book of his *Commentarii in X libros Ethicorum,* published posthumously in Frankfurt in 1608, is based on van Giffen's lectures delivered in Altdorf before his conversion.[64]

The printed commentary expounds Aristotle's text passage by passage without using questions. Excerpts from the Greek text of EN indicate the relevant passage so that we can see very precisely to which line of Aristotle van Giffen refers. Although van Giffen makes some philological remarks, his main interest remains the philosophical understanding of Aristotle. He can discuss, for instance, the positions of Cicero and Stoicism in a humanist manner,[65] but does not use any Ramistic analytical tools. His style and method of exposition resembles that of Camerarius (3.3), although Giffen is less nuanced. Both Camerarius and van Giffen translate akrasia as *impotentia,* thus differing from all other authors in our study.[66] Like Zwinger, van Giffen remains entirely within philosophical ethics, not becoming involved in theological or confessional matters.

Like so many other commentators, van Giffen begins his discussion of akrasia by listing the six traditional opinions and questions related to them.[67] The third opinion, the classical problem of akrasia, is formulated as follows:

the incontinent person is one who, as Medea says in Ovid, sees the better, knows that doing this is wrong, but nevertheless acts wrongly, overcome by perturbation. Contrary to this, the continent person is one who, knowing that covetous desires are harmful, does not yield to them but follows reason.[68]

---

[62] Ridderikhoff (1992), 78. Some biographical information on van Giffen is given on pp. 76–8; see further Lohr (1977), 701.

[63] Brett (2002), 31.

[64] For this information, see Lohr (1977), 701.

[65] In *Ethicorum,* 538–9.

[66] Van Giffen has some other linguistic peculiarities as well: he often calls premise *sumptio* (e.g. *In Ethicorum,* 538: 'ex praemissis seu sumptionibus') and can use *imprudens* in the sense of 'ignorant'.

[67] In *Ethicorum,* 532. The six opinions are spelled out in 2.2.

[68] In *Ethicorum,* 532: 'Praeterea impotens ille dicitur, qui, ut inquit Medea apud Ovidium, videt quidem meliora, scit ea, quae agat esse mala, sed agat tamen perturbatione victus. Contra vero continens is, qui cum

In this manner, van Giffen defines akrasia as a fairly clear-eyed violation of right reason. Given this, one can expect van Giffen not to be very sympathetic to the intellectualistic arguments of Plato and Socrates.

In his comments on EN VII, 2 van Giffen explains the position of Socrates extensively, pointing out that if the incontinent individual is considered to be ignorant, he can to a large extent be exonerated from his culpability. In this context, van Giffen says that Aristotle in EN 1145b27–31 refutes the Socratic position. Unlike many Lutheran interpreters (3.3–3.4), van Giffen does not say that the Socratic position is refuted by experience, but refers to Aristotle's point that the incontinent person knows the right before and after his action.[69]

The philosophical discussion on Aristotle's position with regard to akratic knowledge takes place in EN VII, 3. Van Giffen states his aim clearly: 'In this whole disputation Plato and Socrates are completely refuted. As shown above, they claim that nobody acts against what he or she knows to be right. Therefore they consider that the incontinent person does not have knowledge.'[70] The disputation also serves two other important purposes:

This disputation is useful for the purpose of seeing in what sense the incontinent individual can be held culpable. For if he sins because of ignorance, he deserves to be excused. Another useful aspect of this disputation is that it shows us the struggle between reason and covetousness. The Apostle Paul reminds us of this struggle, as Plutarch also does elegantly in his booklet on moral virtue; Plato compares this struggle with the chariot which is drawn in different directions against the charioteer.[71]

Like Zwinger, Daneau (4.3), and the Lutheran expositors (3.3–3.4), van Giffen underlines the situation of inner struggle as the background of akrasia. Like Luther, he sees Romans 7 as an image of this paradigmatic struggle. Although van Giffen refutes intellectualist Platonism, he can affirm the so-called 'commonplace Platonism' (1.1, 1.5) which distinguishes between the various parts of the soul. The refutation of Socratic Platonism is not, however, as categorical as these passages seem to be saying. Van Giffen considers that EN 1147a1–b18 actually says that the incontinent individual knows to an extent (*partim*) and remains ignorant to an extent. Aristotle here undertakes three distinctions with regard to akratic knowledge.[72]

---

sciat, cupiditates esse malas, iis non patet, sed rationi potius.' The example of Medea is also used on p. 591 (in EN VII, 9).

[69] *In Ethicorum*, 533–5.

[70] *In Ethicorum*, 543: 'Refellitur autem tota hac disputatione maxime Plato aut Socrates, qui, ut supra dictum, neminem existimavit facere contra, atque sciret faciundum, et proinde impotentis nullam esse scientiam.'

[71] *In Ethicorum*, 543: 'Usus autem huius disputationis in eo cernitur, ut cognoscatur, quae culpa impotenti sit tribuenda, nam per imprudentiam si peccaret, excusationem mereretur. Alter huius disputationis usus in eo est, quod nobis ob oculos ponat pugnam rationis et cupiditatem, cuius pugnae meminit et apostolus Paulus, et pulcherrimo in libello de virtute morali Plutarchus, quam Plato comparat quadrigis adversus aurigam in diversas partes intendentibus.'

[72] *In Ethicorum*, 544: 'serio hic adversus Platonem docere orditur, quae impotentis sit vel scientia vel inscientia. Cuius disputationis summa est, impotentem facere impotenter, partim scientem, partim ignoran-

The first distinction obtains between having knowledge and using this knowledge. It is possible to have knowledge without actually using it and in this sense to act against knowledge. This kind of habitual knowledge resembles the presence of reason in a person who is asleep.[73] For van Giffen, Aristotle's third distinction (EN 1147a10–23) is a subspecies of the first one: the third distinction is between the free use of knowledge and the situation in which knowledge remains 'bound' and 'impeded' (*constrictum et impeditum*). Passions like love or anger impede the use of knowledge like the states of drunkenness and sleep.[74]

The second distinction (EN 1147a1–9) takes place between the universal and the particular premise of the syllogism. Actions are considered as particulars, being thus connected with the particular premise of the practical syllogism. When the person has both premises of the practical syllogism but does not use the particular premise, it is possible to act against knowledge.[75] Thus a physician may know that hellebore cures disease, but he does not know which plant hellebore is. Similarly, an akratic person knows what kinds of actions are wrong, but he does not know whether this particular action belongs to those kinds.[76] Van Giffen also subsumes Aristotle's distinction between universals 'in themselves' and 'in the object' (EN 1147a4–7) under the second distinction,[77] which he summarizes by saying that the incontinent person knows the universals but cannot apply them to the particulars which connect it with proper action; in this sense he is ignorant.[78]

This explanation follows the tradition of Renaissance Aristotelianism; the biggest difference may be that van Giffen claims to have completely refuted Plato and Socrates, although he grants that the incontinent person is in some way ignorant. Van Giffen briefly discusses Aristotle's three examples (EN 1147a18–23) of the drunk quoting Empedocles, the children who recite words without understanding, and the actors on the stage. People in these examples claim to know, but their words are without the voice of reason (*sine mente sonum*). They do not represent true knowledge.[79]

In spite of this concession to the Socratic position, van Giffen holds that the distinctions between having and using knowledge and between universal and particular knowledge in their peculiar manner refute the intellectualist doctrine of Socrates and

---

tem. Dici posse, eum nunc scientem, nunc ignorantem facere, dissimili ratione, et adhibita distinctione scientiae. Adfert igitur tres distinctiones Aristoteles.'

[73] *In Ethicorum*, 544–5.

[74] *In Ethicorum*, 546.

[75] *In Ethicorum*, 545: 'Ex duabus syllogismi sumptionibus, qui utramque quidem habet, singulari tamen non utitur, is adversus scientiam facere dici potest. Nam ut recte Aristoteles, *prakta . . . ta kath' hekasta*, id: actiones sunt rerum singularum. Quare qui singulari sumptione non utitur, qui inquam adversus hanc facit, is in rebus agendis adversus scientiam facere dicitur.'

[76] *In Ethicorum*, 545.

[77] *In Ethicorum*, 545–6.

[78] *In Ethicorum*, 546: 'Summa est, impotentem scire universa, et rursus nescire illa quidem rebus non accommodata, id est, vere universa; haec rebus applicata, quae sunt res ipsae singulae, et hoc est, quod modo dictum impotentem syllogismi practici propositionem maiorem quidem scire, assumptionem ignorare posse.'

[79] *In Ethicorum*, 547.

Plato. The next passage (EN 1147a24–b5), which refers to the facts of nature, or physics, shows from another angle how the akratês acts against his own knowledge and conscience.[80] For van Giffen, this passage concerns physics because it deals with the various parts of the human soul and their dynamics. The two relevant parts are reason and covetousness, or appetite, and their mutual conflict, which takes place in the incontinent person.[81]

Aristotle's reference to the 'facts of nature' (EN 1147a24) means for van Giffen that incontinence needs to be understood in terms of struggle between the two parts of the soul, reason and appetite. The image of the chariot and its charioteer illuminates this situtation. The appetitive powers are like a flood or storm which rages contrary to the controlling reason.[82] After explaining the difference between theoretical and practical syllogism and explaining that, when practical and productive opinion is concerned, the soul must immediately act,[83] van Giffen proceeds to say that the syllogistic examples of EN 1147 a29–b5 concern the struggle between reason and appetite, thus illustrating the situation of the akratês.[84]

Van Giffen's analysis of the syllogistic examples is fairly traditional as such. Right reason puts forward the major premise: 'Nothing sweet ought to be tasted', whereas the appetitive power holds that 'Everything sweet is pleasant' and all pleasure is to be followed. The incontinent person knows both major premises, but neither of them prompts action, since action is related to particulars.[85] The relevant minor premise is: 'This is sweet'. With regard to this, reason and appetite conflict, because this minor premise can be operative under both major premises. Right reason forbids tasting sweets, but the appetite persuades the agent to pursue pleasure.[86] The incontinent

---

[80] In Ethicorum, 547: 'Sententia Platonis, eiusque conclusio lacerat: Nemo scientia praeditus contra eam facit. Ergo nec impotens. Verum Aristoteles antecedens refellit, adhuc duabus potissimum actionibus analyticis, nam illa, cum de scientiae habitu et usu, si de sumptionibus universa et singulari analytica seu dialectica esse videntur. Hoc autem loco Physice idem refellit, et docet, quemadmodum impotens contra conscientiam seu scientiam faciat.'

[81] In Ethicorum, 547: 'Nam animum hominis hoc loco pertractat penitus, eiusque partes, ratio et cupiditas, quemadmodum impotente confligant, luculenter ostendit. Sic accipiendum puto verbum *physikôs* [1147a24], quod confirmat verbum infra in finem capituli, *ton physiologian* [1147b8], quicquid dicant alii. Est igitur haec tractatio physica, quatenus animae partium conflictum attingit, ad mores tamen, ut pote ad actiones impotentium accommodata.'

[82] In Ethicorum, 547–8: 'Est autem insignis hic locus de pugna partium animae, rationis et cupiditatum inter se, quam, ut supra initio dictum, Plato quadrigis, ut cupiditatibus in diversum nitentibus, et aurigae tanquam rationi comparare solet. Nam ut poeta: Fertur equis auriga, nec audit currus habenas [Virgil, Georgica, 1, 514]. Ut, inquam, ibi poeta, ita et impotentem auferunt cupiditates, nequicquam reclamante ratione. Alii, ut est apud Plutarch. Nam eam comparare solent, cui moderetur quidem gubernator tanquam ratio, sed undique saeviant fluctus et venti, tanquam cupiditates.'

[83] In Ethicorum, 548–9, EN 1147a25–29.

[84] In Ethicorum, 549: 'Hoc tandem loco [EN 1147a20ff.] pugna cupiditatum et rationis explicatur, et quae modo communiter, hic proprie ad impotentem accommodantur.'

[85] In Ethicorum, 549: 'Ponatur igitur opinio universa: nullum dulce esse gustandum ex recta ratione. Ponatur et altera: omne dulce esse iucundum. Utramque novit impotens. Verum neutra ad agendum est idonea, etiam singulari est opus.'

[86] In Ethicorum, 549: 'Fit igitur ista: hoc autem est dulce. Hic iam confligunt ratio et cupiditates. Nam ratio, cuius universa opinio fuerat, nullum dulce gustandum, suadet et hoc non gustandum, sed fugiendum. At

knows the right major premise but, in proceeding to action, he does not allow (*non admittit*) the relevant minor premise to enter under the right major premise. For this reason, the relevant particular fact is considered under the wrong major premise.[87]

Van Giffen is not, however, entirely satisfied with this traditional interpretation and wants to understand it from the particular perspective of a struggle between two different parts of the soul. In the context of EN 1147b1–2, he discusses extensively the sense in which the akratês is said to behave incontinently but nevertheless under the influence of some reason (*cum ratione*). Reason cannot be in conflict with itself, but an opinion concerning singulars can be called *ratio*. Such 'reason' can conflict with the right reason. In this case, the harmful desire pushes this singular reason into a struggle with right reason.[88] Van Giffen intends to make an anti-Stoic point which resembles the considerations of Camerarius (3.3): akratic behaviour is not caused by the swift changes in one reason, but the underlying struggle must concern two different powers, one being rational and the other non-rational.

This aim leads van Giffen to point out that the real nature of the struggle is not found in the discrepancy between the two syllogisms, both of which represent reason. The real conflict takes place between reason and appetite or covetousness. Although the appetitive power can lure reason to consider false syllogisms, it operates mainly through the minor premises which immediately concern covetousness and action:

Reason, or the minor premise in itself, does not conflict with the major premise. But covetousness comes, perturbs the right syllogism, and replaces it with another. Its singular proposition and minor premise are not subsumed as if by the reason. Covetousness offers the false or alien minor proposition. Covetousness is thus itself the cause of this reason's erring in the minor premise and conflicting with the prior right syllogism. It is generally said that there are two major propositions: nothing shameful ought to be followed, etc., everything sweet ought to be followed, etc. But these two do not struggle with one another; we are not concerned with that struggle. We are concerned with the struggle of the minor premise, that is, covetousness, not with a struggle between two propositions. We are concerned with the battle between the major premise which stems from right reason and the minor premise which stems from covetousness.[89]

---

cupiditas contra, quia omnia iucunda persequenda constituit, hoc autem dulce iucundum esse sentiat, continuo id quoque persequendum esse suadet.'

[87] *In Ethicorum*, 549: 'Impotens igitur novit quidem nullas turpes voluptates esse persequendas, sed ad agendum cum accedere debet, minorem propositionem non admittit suadente cupiditate, et proinde aliam quoque maiorem facit.'

[88] *In Ethicorum*, 550: 'Aristoteles . . . rationem quidem rationi non repugnante ait per se, sed ex eventu, nempe, quia accidit ut cupiditas assit et concurrat cum opinione singulari seu ratione, eamque secum trahat, et quodammodo universae repugnare cogat. Singularis igitur opinio, id ratio, universae non repugnat per se, sed ex eventu, id est, ob cupiditatis concursum.'

[89] *In Ethicorum*, 550–1: 'Ratio, seu minor per se considerata, non repugnaret maiori, sed cupiditas venit perturbans rectum syllogismum, et constituit loco recti alium. Singularis propositio et minor non subsumunt ut a ratione. Cupiditas substituit falsam seu alienam minorem propositionem. Ipsa cupiditas in ipsa est causa, ut ipsa ratio in minore peccet, et repugnet priori. Vulgo dicunt, duae sunt majores propositiones, nullum turpe persequendum, etc., omnia dulcia persequenda, etc. Illi non repugnant inter se, de illa pugna non

Van Giffen wants to show that even the seemingly rational component of akratic action is only quasi-rational since akratic reasoning is fundamentally prompted by the appetite, which can affect reason's consideration of particular facts. Van Giffen says that this dynamic is treated in Aristotle's *Prior Analytics,* in which the distinction between having knowledge and using it is discussed in detail. It is shown that knowledge in use may conflict with habitual knowledge. He also remarks that the commentators do not usually discuss this point.[90]

It may be true to say that the earlier commentators do not normally interpret the distinction between having knowledge and using it in terms of a simple discrepancy between reason and appetitive power. Van Giffen thinks here that the minor premise which is actually used represents the appetitive power which struggles with right reason. At the same time, van Giffen's overall theme of struggle is very common in the tradition. The Lutheran interpreters in particular connect this struggle with the primacy of sense perception when actions are discussed (3.3–3.4). Van Giffen's view of the primacy of the minor premise in the struggle closely resembles this view, which was spelled out in his time in the commentary by Camerarius.

Camerarius is led to this emphasis by the need to avoid the Stoic position in which mental conflicts are due to the swift changes of the one reason. For both Camerarius and van Giffen, it is important to stress that reason cannot conflict with itself: the different syllogisms may illustrate the conflict, but the real dynamic occurs between reason and non-rational appetite. These two faculties of the soul are really distinct from one another. The appetitive powers can overcome reason because action is so closely related to our perception of particulars. While Camerarius relates this knowledge to sense perception and experience, van Giffen approaches the 'primacy of particulars' from his viewpoint of natural causes or 'physics'. This viewpoint is also prominent in later Lutheran commentaries (3.4).

The last remarks concerning EN VII, 3 are again fairly traditional. After the analysis of natural causes, van Giffen says that the incontinent person goes wrong knowing to an extent and being ignorant to an extent. He knows the universals and is ignorant with regard to the particulars. The cause of this ignorance is covetousness.[91] The akratic state resembles the states of sleep and drunkenness.[92] Van Giffen further concedes that Plato and Socrates are not completely wrong, but their doctrine can be modified so

---

agitur. Sed de pugna minoris, hoc est, cupiditatis, non de duarum propositionum pugna agitur. Sed de maioris, ex recta ratione, et minoris ex cupiditate.'

[90] *In Ethicorum,* 551: 'Caeterum accuratior de pugnantia scientiae et rationis inter se (interpretes praetereunt omnia) explicatio videatur apud. Arist. lib. 2 prior Analyt. ca. 21 ubi multa ad hunc locum accommodata. Hinc omnia scientia vel habitu, vel usu. Haec divisio ibi quoque affertur: scientia quae est usu interdum repugnat scientiae, quae est habitu. Habitus scientiae repugnat cum actu. Uno verbo magnam et longam disputationem attingit Aristoteles saepe. De his, quae hic tractantur, altum apud scriptorem silentium.'

[91] *In Ethicorum,* 551: 'Ex prioribus perspicuum est, impotentem, partim scientia, partim ignorantia peccare: scientem quidem universam opinionem, ignorantiam singularis... Perspicuum denique et hoc ignorantiae eius causam esse cupiditatem.'

[92] *In Ethicorum,* 551–2.

that it does not remain absurd. The Socratic position can be reformulated as follows: 'The incontinent individual does not decide to act against the universal, but against the particular (which is corrupted by the passions, and not the universal, as explained above, and repeated here). Therefore he does not act against knowledge.'[93]

Hubert van Giffen appears to be an eclectic interpreter of Aristotle. Like the medieval and Renaissance Aristotelians, he considers that the akratês is ignorant of particular facts. The underlying, 'natural' cause of akrasia resides, however, in the struggle between reason and appetitive power. This emphasis on struggle connects him with the Reformed tradition of Zwinger and Daneau, but also with the Lutheran tradition of Camerarius. Although van Giffen does not mention any contemporaries by name, he follows Camerarius on many significant issues of his commentary. They both avoid Stoic positions and affirm a 'commonplace Platonist' understanding of the parts of the soul. They focus on the 'primacy of particulars': akrasia is possible because action is concerned with particulars. They affirm a relatively clear-eyed and voluntarist view of akrasia by holding that the akratês 'does not allow' (non admittit) the proper hearing of right reason.

In his analysis of the dynamics of 'covetousness', van Giffen differs from Zwinger, who is closer to the cognitive view of emotions put forward by the Stoics. Van Giffen emphasizes that the dynamics of appetite must differ from the dynamics of reason. The difference between Zwinger and van Giffen is subtle and needs to be seen in the broader context of their many common features regarding the general nature of 'struggle' (pugna). Van Giffen's careful analysis of this struggle may nevertheless be original: unlike the Lutherans (3.3–3.4), he does not explain the akratic state of mind by referring to the uncertainties of experience and sense perception. Instead, van Giffen argues that the appetitive power can overcome right reason by introducing and determining the particulars under consideration in a quasi-rational fashion in which the singular premise appears 'with reason'. Although both van Giffen and the Lutherans focus on this 'primacy of particulars', they do so in slightly different ways.

Van Giffen's relationship to Socratic intellectualism remains inconsistent. He claims that Aristotle wants to refute the position of Socrates and Plato, but he also concedes that Socrates is right in many ways and that the akratês remains ignorant to an extent. At the same time he also wants to affirm the clear-eyed struggle between reason and appetite. The difficulties related to this inconsistency connect his exposition with many others, in particular Francesco Piccolomini's (2.6) and Wolfgang Heider's (3.4).

4.3 Lambert Daneau's Christian Ethics

Martin Luther worked out a radically Augustinian alternative to medieval and Renaissance anthropology. In Luther's view, people without grace remain sinners who cannot even try

---

[93] In Ethicorum, 552–3: 'Impotens non tam contra universam, quam contra singularem facit sumptionem (ea namque est, qua torquetur cupiditatibus, non universa, ut supra explicatum, et hic iteratur). Ergo contra scientiam facere non videtur.'

to be good. Christians who have received the Spirit strive for goodness, but even the best Christians remain enkratic; that is, they continue to be plagued by the harmful desires so that their good works remain imperfect. They are sinners, because the presence of harmful desire is the criterion of sinfulness. Perfect virtue can only be attained after death (3.2).

Philip Melanchthon accepted and reinterpreted Luther's doctrine but did not provide any deeply philosophical foundation for it (3.3). Although Calvin discussed akrasia briefly in his *Institutes*, he was primarily a theologian and no moral philosopher (4.1). The early Protestant commentaries on EN by Camerarius and Zwinger were philosophically ambitious but did not discuss Luther's views in detail (3.3, 4.2). In these different ways, the first wave of Protestant writings on ethics connected Luther's insights with the prevailing traditions of moral philosophy only to some extent.

The theological and philosophical elements of early Protestantism were, however, brought together in the voluminous work of Lambert Daneau, *Ethices Christianae libri tres*. The precise nature of Daneau's ethics has been discussed in recent scholarship. According to Donald Sinnema, in spite of his Christian premises Daneau attempts to compose a philosophical ethics.[94] Christoph Strohm's extensive study distinguishes between the influence of Aristotelian and Stoic philosophical traditions, Daneau's legal background, and his theological 'fundamental decisions'. Strohm comes to the conclusion that Daneau's work is fundamentally theological, being primarily dependent on Calvin.[95]

Lambert Daneau (1530–1595) studied philosophy and law in Orléans and Paris, and theology in Geneva. He taught theology in Geneva from 1572 to 1583, working as pastor during the rest of his life. He was a prolific author, who published a theological dogmatics and a commentary on Lombard's *Sentences*. In addition to his Christian ethics, he also published a Christian physics, a Christian politics, and even a Christian geography, as well as a great number of other major and minor works. The Calvinist Reformation wanted to achieve a comprehensive reformation of life in all areas of culture and learning; Daneau's books express this spirit of reforming the received learning from a distinctive Christian perspective.[96]

The spirit of reform did not prove equally fruitful in all fields, but in ethics it was able to change the paradigm in many respects. *Ethices Christianae* first appeared in Geneva 1577; it was reprinted without changes at least eight times until 1640.[97] In the late sixteenth and early seventeenth centuries a new discipline of moral theology or theological ethics emerged both in Catholicism and Protestantism, Lambert Daneau contributing significantly to this development.[98] As our discussion is limited to the

---

[94] Sinnema (1993), 23.

[95] Strohm (1996), 525–8.

[96] On Daneau's life and work, see Strohm (1996), 11–20; a thorough bibliography is given on pp. 670–6.

[97] Strohm (1996), 672. I quote according to the 1583 edition. As far as I can judge, the page (folio) numbers change between the editions, but the text and the chapter numbering remain the same.

[98] For the emergence of theological ethics and practical theology, see Sinnema (1993), 20–3; Strohm (1996), 16–20 and Saarinen (forthcoming). See also the end of this chapter.

issue of akrasia, we can only take a stance on this historical development insofar as Daneau's discussion of continence and incontinence is symptomatic of it.

The three books of Daneau's ethics proceed from three different points of departure. The first book deals with the principles and causes of human actions, virtues, and vices as they appear in the philosophical tradition. The second book is an exposition of the Ten Commandments which express God's law. The third book combines the insights of books one and two, showing how the different virtues and vices look when discussed from the theological perspective of the Decalogue.[99] Daneau's work is no commentary, but a textbook which is divided into thematic chapters. The chapter headings are sometimes treated in the text like questions, but as a rule Daneau discusses his subject matter freely.

The discussion on continence and incontinence takes place towards the end of the first book, that is, in chapter 23; the context of chapters 20–22 and chapter 24 is also relevant for the understanding of this theme. Daneau does not return to *enkrateia* and akrasia in book three; an obvious reason being that in book one he does not regard these two moral states as particular virtues but, as will be shown below in more detail, as a foundational stage (*genus, gradus*) relevant for many different particular virtues. Books two and three also contain an abundance of legal and theological material which has no direct relevance for the theory of action.

After briefly discussing the concept of virtue and its possible divisions in book 1, chapter 20, Daneau introduces Aristotle's threefold division of virtue as it appears in EN VII. He then treats the heroic virtue in chapter 21, taking five pages, the human virtue as *habitus* in chapter 22 (seven pages), and the imperfect virtue, or continence and incontinence, in chapter 23 (eighteen pages). The last chapter 24 (thirteen pages) of the first book lays out another threefold division of virtue, that which exists between 'philosophical', 'scholastic', and 'Christian' virtue.

Why does Daneau discuss virtue only briefly but continence and incontinence so extensively? This question needs to be addressed properly before investigating continence and incontinence in detail. At the beginning of chapter 22, Daneau divides human virtue into two fundamental stages. He refers to the Stoics, who teach that the wise can operate at the stage of perfect virtue or duty, whereas common people practise the middle level of virtue. His source for this distinction is Cicero.[100] Daneau interprets these stages in terms of his Christian theology: the first describes a person who is so completely spiritual that all affects which go contrary to the Holy Spirit and virtue have been extinguished. The second and lower stage depicts a person in whom the Spirit dwells, but who still has the harmful passions which struggle against virtue. The life of

---

[99] For this structure, see Sinnema (1993), 23; Strohm (1996), 396.

[100] *Ethices Christianae*, 99v: 'Quemadmodum autem Stoici duo genera officiorum constituunt, unum perfectum, illi *katorthôma* dicunt, quod in solum sapientem cadit, alterum autem medium et commune, *kathêkon meson* illi, quod in communi hominum vita versatur. Sic nos humanae huius virtutis duos quosdam gradus distingui oportere dicimus.' See Cicero, *De officiis*, 1, 3, 8 and *De finibus* 1, 15, and Strohm (1996), 136–7.

such a person can be characterized as 'wrestling and struggle' (*lucta, pugna*). When this person tries to be virtuous, he or she experiences the resistance (*repugnantia*) of harmful passions.[101]

The first and higher stage is called perfect virtue; it is the subject of chapter 22. The second and lower stage, called the imperfect virtue, *enkrateia* or continence, is discussed in chapter 23.[102] Daneau points out that the philosophers usually focus on perfect virtue, but they have not realized, as the church father Lactantius shows, how the harmful passions overcome even people aiming at good.[103] In his discussion of virtue and continence, Daneau often quotes Augustine and Lactantius to point out the rule of sin and to underline the perpetual struggle between virtue and vice.[104] This strategy leads him to his fundamental and far-reaching claim that no human being can achieve perfect virtue: 'No one can reach this [excellent stage] because the power and tinder of sin are active in us, even in the most perfect, as the Bible teaches in Romans 7.'[105] Even the Apostle Paul could not achieve perfect virtue in this life.

We already saw with regard to Martin Luther (3.2) and John Calvin (4.1) that this was the preferred Protestant interpretation of Romans 7 and of sin. But while Luther and Calvin do not relate this discussion to Aristotle's *enkrateia* and akrasia in detail, Daneau does accomplish this step. Because of the continuing rule of sin, the stage of imperfect virtue and vice, continence and incontinence, becomes the only possible forum in which to practise virtue in this life. Daneau is categorical in his denial of pure virtue:

Therefore this virtue called *heksis* is so absolute that it has never been found in any mortal human being (excepting in some sense in Christ); it is not found now nor will be in the future as long as this condition of the world and its things last, whatever the profane philosophers may claim regarding this. For sin inhabits our flesh so strongly.[106]

Given this, it is understandable that perfect virtue is treated very briefly in chapter 22: Daneau uses most of his seven pages in this chapter to deny the existence of pure virtue. In keeping with this assumption, the discussion on continence and incontinence needs

---

[101] *Ethices Christianae*, 99v–100r: 'Aut enim eo usque progressa esse statuitur vis illa contentioque animi nostri a Spiritu Sancto indita, ut omnem affectionis virtuti contrariae impetum extinxerit in nobis. Aut non est progressa eo usque, sed in eo tantum gradu totus conatus animi nostri (qui et ipse a Deo nobis infusus est) subsistit, ut in agendo bono opere, luctam adhuc et pugnam cum repugnante et adversante virtuti impetu et affectu sustineamus.'

[102] *Ethices Christianae*, 100r: 'Prior igitur ille gradus, humana quidem, sed perfecta virtus appellatur. Posterior autem, imperfecta. Prior ille vocatur, definiturque esse *hexis*, id est, habitus. Posteriori autem ignobiliori et illaudabiliori nomine *enkrateia* tantum, id est, continentia dicitur.'

[103] *Ethices Christianae*, 100v–101r.

[104] On Daneau's use of church fathers, see Strohm (1996) who remarks (pp. 59–60) that Lactantius is referred to sixty times in Daneau's *Ethics*, often to justify the Stoic or Ciceronian stance in moral philosophy.

[105] *Ethices Christianae*, 101r.

[106] *Ethices Christianae*, 101r–v: 'Ergo huiusmodi tamquam absoluta haec virtus est, quae *hexis* appellatur, ut in nullo mortali homine (uno modo excepto Christo) unquam vel fuerit, vel sit, vel etiam futura sit, quandiu hic rerum et mundi status durabit, quicquid contra Philosophi prophani rixose contendant. Nam in carne hac nostra tam alte habitat peccatum.'

more space, since it covers the whole range of ethical striving in this life. The definition of imperfect virtue in terms of 'struggle' and 'wrestling' means that all virtuous human life consists of struggle. The recurring motif of *pugna* which derives from Plato, Augustine, and Albert the Great is expanded in Daneau's Christian ethics into a universally valid situation of moral reflection.[107]

Like Luther and Calvin, Daneau teaches that although the virtue remains imperfect in this life, vice can be perfect or complete.[108] The fact of struggle characterizes the life of all morally conscious people, whereas many vicious people do not struggle. Since Daneau has denied the possibility of extinguishing the opposite vices, he also needs to take some stance towards the traditional problem of 'simultaneous contrary opposites' as his last point of chapter 22 (cf. 3.1, 3.2). In his view, the contrary opposites of vice and virtue can simultaneously coexist in the same subject when one of these, that is, virtue, comes from outside. This external goodness cannot, however, fully eradicate the vice which inheres in the nature of sinful humanity.[109]

Before entering the discussion on imperfect virtue in chapter 23, something should be said concerning chapter 24, which reflects on the distinction between philosophical and Christian virtue. This is not a quantitative but a methodological distinction. The philosophical and scholastic conceptions of virtue proceed from reason, whereas discussing Christian virtue means paying constant attention to the activity of God's spirit in people. Although the first book of *Ethices Christianae* focuses on philosophical ethics, the philosophical and scholastic virtues have already been evaluated from the definitive Christian perspective there. Thus all three books practise Christian ethics; the object of this Christian reflection in the first book is philosophical ethics.

Philosophical ethics does not understand the struggle between reason and appetitive powers properly. Philosophers claim that this struggle can be successfully mastered through the repeated practice of good actions, but they do not grasp the real cause of appetitive powers, that is, sin; their view also wrongly ascribes the merit of good actions to people, not to God.[110] Only Christian ethics can see that people without God

---

[107] In addition to Augustine's *invitus facere* (1.2) and Albert's *contrariae acceptiones* (1.5), the older roots of this tradition comprise the Neoplatonic distinction between *virtutes purgatoriae* (purifying virtues) and *virtutes animi purgati* (pure virtues), which is relevant in Scholasticism since Albert the Great; see Müller (2001), 192–7. In Daneau's exposition of the Ten Commandments, the Tenth Commandment ('you shall not covet') is 'the hidden center of the Decalogue'; so Strohm (1996), 415 because it focuses on this struggle.

[108] *Ethices Christianae*, 102v: 'Quod quandiu inhabitat in illis [homines] virtus, perfecta esse non potest. Potest autem vitium, quia tanta labes atque corruptio nostrae naturae supervenit.'

[109] *Ethices Christianae*, 102v: 'Contraria autem ea demum circa idem inesse possunt, et nata sunt, quorum alterum nobis non inhaeret natura. Quum enim eorum alterum inest natura, extrudi omnino non potest.' Like Luther (3.2), Daneau here distinguishes himself from such dualistic (Ockhamistic) psychology, in which a real distinction within the soul is assumed. The good impulse in the struggle comes from outside.

[110] *Ethices Christianae*, 114v: 'Sed quum iidem [philosophi] animadverterent pugnam rationis cum voluntate, nec tamen eius causam intelligerent, nec originem, senserunt definieruntque illam tolli assidua bene agendi consuetudine, adeo ut repetitas illas actiones dicerent, tandem in nobis gignere *hexin* bene agendi, et omnino subiectum rectae rationi, parentemque appetitum hac via posse comparari. Hominem autem ipsum honestarum actionum authorem, non autem Deum constituunt.'

cannot do any good. When God's Spirit has renewed them, they can cooperate with the Spirit. Even then, they cannot achieve perfect virtue in this life. Their Christian virtue remains an enkratic state in which the subjects are not in autonomous control of their actions.[111] In this manner, Daneau embeds the basic theological doctrines of the Reformation (cf. 3.2, 4.1) into his ethics.

Having made these preliminary observations we can proceed to Daneau's analysis of continence and incontinence in chapter 23. The chapter heading, 'On the imperfect human virtue, called *enkrateia*, and its opposite vice' underlines the character of this virtue from the outset. Although this is the last thematic chapter of the first book, the stage of virtue described in it does not proceed to the final victory over harmful desires, but continues to wrestle with them.[112] Continence is by its very nature a 'wrestling virtue' (*virtus luctans*), because this virtue continues to wrestle with vices and harmful desires.[113]

As human actions in this life belong to the spheres of vice and imperfect virtue, continence represents the ultimate virtue available in this life; given this, it is understandable that it is treated as the last item of book one. The virtue of *enkrateia* is a middle state between perfectly virtuous and vicious people, resembling the lukewarm state between hot and cold.[114] Daneau reflects on the continuing struggle between virtue and vice, arguing that one of these opposing forces must finally prevail.[115] In many things, however, one can observe that two contrary powers are both active, remaining mixed with one another so that neither of them perfectly overcomes the other.[116] This

can also take place in the mind, as when because of nature something cannot become more perfect in us, it is a middle state even in the most perfect and best people, and is called a state in which the participation of virtue and vice, that is, spirit and flesh, and a kind of cohabitation or mixture of the two, remains balanced.[117]

---

[111] *Ethices Christianae*, 116r: 'Nam ante innovationem nostram ipsi per nos non magis bene vel velle vel agere possumus, quam volare. Sed ubi Dei Spiritus sese cordibus et affectibus nostris insinuavit, eosque dirigit, et inflectit, tum incipimus bene velle et agere; quamquam et hae actiones nostrae honestae sunt semper infinitis modis imperfectae. Itaque quae in nobis virtutes esse dicuntur, eae non sunt *hexeis*, sed tantum *enkrateias*, id est, non plene perfecteque voluntatis nostrae Dei mandato, et rectae rationi subiectae.'

[112] *Ethices Christianae*, 103r: 'Restat autem, ut de eo virtutis humanae gradu, in quo imperfecta virtus perspicitur, neque pervenit ad summum illud culmen et victoriae fastigium, per quam omnis cum vitiosis affectibus lucta in nobis sopita est.'

[113] *Ethices Christianae*, 103r: 'Illa [virtus] vero *enkrateia* dicitur, vulgo Latinis Continentia (fortasse melius, atque ad praesentem quaestionem accommodatius, si Luctantem virtutem dicere placuerit).'

[114] *Ethices Christianae*, 103r–v: 'Est igitur hic medius quidam status inter eos, qui perfecte virtutem assequuti sunt, et eos, qui omnino ac plane vitio ses dediderunt…Nam medius quidam hominum status est, in quo neque perfectae virtuti neque consummato vitio adhuc locus est, quemadmodum inter calidum et frigidum est medius quidam tepor.'

[115] *Ethices Christianae*, 103v–104r.

[116] *Ethices Christianae*, 104r: 'sed potest in multis rerum generibus is status observari, in quo fit utriusque contrarii participatio quaedam, et commixtio, adeo ut neutrum quidem illic vere et perfecte insit; sed utrunque ex parte, et cum quodam temperamento cernatur.'

[117] *Ethices Christianae*, 104r–v: 'Sic in animis ipsis idem evenit, ut quoniam naturae huius ratio quiddam in nobis perfectius ferre non potest, sit medius tantum etiam perfectissimorum et optimorum virorum, qui dicuntur status, qui virtutis et vitii, id est, spiritus et carnis participatione, et quadam cohabitatione adhuc mistus est, et temperatus.'

This description of *enkrateia* is reminiscent of Martin Luther's analysis of the interplay between spirit and flesh, as well as of Luther's view of the Apostle Paul, who is an optimal moral agent but who nevertheless remains a sinner because of continuing repugnancy (3.2). Daneau presents the theological counter-argument that God wants either hot or cold, not lukewarm Christians (Rev. 3:16). He responds that Christians should be as hot as their natural condition allows, but some imperfection nevertheless always remains in this life.[118]

Given this, continence can be defined as a state in which the individual has a sincere will so that she is not only wrestling with vices in a carnal manner but is aided by the Holy Spirit and so can overcome vice.[119] Analogically,

when the bad will of the mind overcomes the virtue and the desire to act rightly, this state is called *akrateia*. In this state, virtue fights and struggles with vice, and vice with virtue. We then clearly perceive as if two persons and two wills were active in us.[120]

These definitions of continence and incontinence are remarkable in that they combine so many traditions. First, Aristotle's akrasia becomes connected with the Augustinian tradition of two wills. Second, both are embedded in the Lutheran and Calvinist doctrine of sin, according to which all people suffer from sinful desires and can therefore only achieve continence in this life. Finally, the motif of wrestling and struggle resembles the Platonic and Stoic images of the conflict between reason and desire.

The basic definitions are also spelled out using two examples:

When the virtue and the holy desire to do good, which the Spirit of God gives, prevail in this wrestling, the will remaining repugnant, it is called continence. Such is the case of Jacob wrestling with the angel. But when our harmful desire overcomes reason, it is called incontinence. Such is the case of Medea in Ovid: 'I see the better and approve it, but follow the worse.'[121]

In this quote, the theme of remaining repugnancy is mentioned; it is also important that the role of the Holy Spirit is emphasized. According to Luther's and Calvin's doctrine of justification by faith, all good works by Christians remain the sole merit of God's grace. When people are able to bring about some good work, such action exemplifies an enkratic state in which the will remains to an extent repugnant and the virtue imperfect.

---

[118] *Ethices Christianae*, 104v.

[119] *Ethices Christianae*, 104v: 'Ac quidem quum ea virtus, atque honesta voluntas ita in nobis est, ut cum foeda carnis libidine et cupiditate non tantum luctetur, sed etiam vi Spiritus Dei in nobis agentis vincat, et superet, is status animi *enkrateia*, quemadmodum antea saepe diximus, appellatur.'

[120] *Ethices Christianae*, 104v: 'Quum autem prava animi voluntas superat contrarium virtutis et bene agendi desiderium, quod restat in nobis, vi peccati regnantis, *akrateia* dicitur, in quo certe statu dimicatio et certamen virtutis cum vitio, et vitii cum virtute cernitur, sentiturque manifestissime, quasi homines duo, duaeque voluntates in nobis sentiantur, atque habitent.'

[121] *Ethices Christianae*, 105r: 'Quum in ea lucta vincit virtus, et sanctum illud bene agendi desiderium, quod dat Dei Spiritus, repugnantem voluntatem, dicitur Continentia, quale quid cernitur in Iacobo cum Angelo colluctantem. Quum autem a turpi affectu nostro vincitur ratio, appellatur Incontinentia, quale quid etiam cernitur in illa Ovidii Medea: video meliora, proboque, deteriora sequor.'

The example of Medea is not spelled out in detail. Daneau teaches that while the continent person continues to have contrary tendencies, the simply vicious person possesses only an evil tendency. He further departs from Luther and agrees with Calvin in admitting that the will remains divided not only in enkratic actions but also in akratic ones. In the broader framework of the Reformation, however, Daneau follows Luther's insights in stressing the class of enkratic people as the paradigm of exemplary behaviour. Daneau is not particularly interested in the classical problem of akrasia; that is, how one can act against one's own better judgement. Given the strong view of sin, it is obvious that any sinner can do that; the question is rather whether a person who behaves wrongly can possess good judgement. To answer this question, Daneau undertakes further theological distinctions which characterize akratic action.

Daneau refines his discussion by introducing the Calvinist division between the true Christians who predestined to salvation, the so-called elect (*electi*), and others who are denied salvation, the non-elect (*reprobi*). Now, continence and incontinence can be defined as the dispositions of the mind in its wrestling between vice and virtue. This wrestling takes place among the elect, because the Holy Spirit has regenerated them to fight vice.[122] Many non-elect do not participate in such struggles because their vice prevails without any inclination towards the contrary. Some non-elect people do, however, experience a similar wrestling. When the harmful desire emerges in them and finally overcomes them, they nevertheless can oppose it with the power of their conscience, reason, and sense of honesty.[123]

These akratic people

have not renounced their sense of conscience. Because they are non-elect, however, they do not possess the renewing Spirit of God, and their conscience wrestles alone, bravely resisting the harmful passions; but their conscience is overcome by the harmful passions. These people can retain their sound mind and produce better fruits more easily [than the vicious].[124]

This quote is followed by a long passage from EN VII, 8 in which Aristotle compares the akratic and the intemperate person. Daneau concludes that the stage (*gradus*) of incontinence can be distinguished from intemperance. The intemperate people do not wrestle with vice, but remain completely overcome by sin.[125]

---

[122] *Ethices Christianae*, 105r-v: 'Nos tamen hic non tam scrupulose verbis istis [Aristotle in EN VII, scholastic discussion of continence as sexual chastity] inhaeremus, quum commodior appellatio nobis iam non succurrat, nisi Colluctationem virtutis et vitii hanc animi nostri habitudinem fortasse nominemus. Versatur vero haec, atque inest hoc certamen in Dei electis, et illius Spiritu vere renatis hominibus, ac iis quidem omnibus.'

[123] *Ethices Christianae*, 105v: 'In reprobis autem et hypocritis etiam, qui externe Christi nomen profitentur, nullis proprie inest, etsi tamen in quibusdam inest. Inesse in illis videtur, in quibus, quanquam vitiosi affectus et appetitus insurgunt, servent, et tandem vincunt, sese tamen illis conscientiae vis, et rationis atque honestatis cogitatio fortiter opponit.'

[124] *Ethices Christianae*, 105v: 'Itaque sensum conscientiae illi non exuerunt, Dei autem Spiritum, quia sunt reprobi, eos renovantem nullo modo habet, sed retinent tantum luctam conscientiae vitiosae libidini vehementer resistentis, quae tamen a libidine ipsorum vitiosa vincitur. Atque iidem possunt ad sanam mentem, atque meliorem frugem facilius revocari.'

[125] *Ethices Christianae*, 105v–106r.

Daneau also holds that the harmful desire begets sin and 'diverts us away from the right reason which we know'. This does not happen to the elect, because their conscience is aided by the 'seeds of true holiness', which resist the evil desire of concupiscence.[126] This does not mean, however, that the elect are always successful in their wrestling. It only means that they do not sin with their 'full will' (*tota voluntate*), because some part of them is already renewed, so that the true knowledge and the spiritual 'seeds' remain active.[127] In this sense, the elect can sometimes lapse into akrasia, although they cannot fall into the simple vice characterized by the complete absence of wrestling or struggle.

Although Daneau's discussion pertains to the 'philosophical' part of his ethics, it strongly expresses his theological views. *Enkrateia* and akrasia are prominent topics for Daneau because they exemplify the 'wrestling virtue'. This is the state of the elect and, in addition, of some honest non-elect who can ascend from vice to akrasia, although not to genuine *enkrateia* because they lack the renewing Spirit. Proceeding from this perspective, Daneau can say that

Not the human mind as such, but the human mind already renewed can be capable of this virtue which we call continence and the wrestling virtue. Only this kind of virtue can exist in our worthless person so that we can be its seat and subject (as the schoolmen say).[128]

In keeping with this, Daneau concludes that the non-elect can only display the 'shadows' of continence and wrestling, not possess true continence.[129]

The elect, for their part, can achieve continence, but they may also lapse into akrasia. The spiritual part of their will nevertheless continues wrestling.[130] Most non-elect simply live in sin, but some few may be guided by their conscience towards wrestling with vice. Without the Spirit, they may achieve akrasia or even a 'shadow' of continence, though true continence is only possible for the elect. As a rule, the situation of wrestling characterizes the life of the elect. Daneau thus combines the Aristotelian discussion with the insights of Luther and, in particular, Calvin.

In Daneau's model, *enkrateia* may be more interesting than akrasia, since *enkrateia* becomes the prevailing paradigm of earthly virtue. But akrasia is also significant because

---

[126] *Ethices Christianae*, 106r: 'Cupiditas enim, cui nimium indulgemus, concipit et parit peccatum, et nos a recta ratione, quam scimus, abducit. Id quod electis Dei non accidit... manent tamen in iisdem verae sanctitatis... semina... atque vitio pravaeque concupiscentiae in nobis repugnant.'

[127] *Ethices Christianae*, 106r: 'Itaque electi Dei nunquam tota voluntate, quemadmodum reprobi, peccant, etsi tamen nonnunquam in suis peccatis electi indormiunt, et diutissime torpent. Quae autem pars in Dei renatis verae cognitionis Dei, veraeque sanctitatis semina a Dei Spiritu immissa habet, Spiritus appellatur.'

[128] *Ethices Christianae*, 107r: 'Ergo non animus hominis per se, sed animus hominis iam renovatus huius gradus virtutis, quem Continentiam et Luctam appellamus, quique solus in nobis hic degentibus esse potest, est capax, illiusque sedes, et (ut loquuntur in scholis) verum subiectum.'

[129] *Ethices Christianae*, 107r: 'Ex quo fit ut in caeteris hominibus, qui hoc Dei beneficio carent, non insit vera continentia, sed verae tantum continentiae et luctae umbra quaedam.'

[130] Daneau here leans towards the so-called 'perseverance of the saints', a Calvinist theological doctrine according to which all elect finally prevail, though they may temporarily lapse into sin. Cf. Calvin, *Inst.* 3, 24, 6–11; ICR, 971–8.

it exemplifies the kind of struggle which occurs among some elect and some non-elect. In some sense, akrasia is the only moral state of which both the elect and the non-elect are capable. Daneau is not directly interested in the classical philosophical problem of whether the akratês sins knowingly, and his answers to this issue remain fragmentary. His emphasis on conscience[131] and his use of the example of Medea suggest a fairly clear-eyed akrasia. On the other hand, the state of wrestling always exemplifies a mixed state of imperfection in which the mind does not achieve full clarity. The gift of God is not simply a power of acting, but also a state of perfect clarity which the human mind does not naturally possess.[132] In this sense, akrasia is accompanied by a less than full clarity of mind. Generally speaking, however, Daneau's model of akrasia is not Aristotelian but either commonplace Platonic or Stoic.

The latter part of Daneau's treatment of continence in book 1, chapter 23 is devoted to the 'object' of this virtue. The object of *enkrateia* is twofold: continence pertains to actions as well as to desires and passions.[133] In this context, Daneau discusses the Stoic opinions concerning passions extensively. He refutes the Stoic programme of eradicating all emotions. Jesus Christ was an example of positive emotions. The voice of God in the Bible commands us to moderate and rule our emotions instead of eradicating them. Moreover, some emotions, for instance those of self-preservation and loving one's spouse, are wholly positive. When continence and incontinence are discussed, one has to pay attention to this diversity and sometimes seek a proper mean between the extremes.[134]

With regard to the daily wrestling with the passions, Daneau gives general advice which relates to Luther's and Calvin's theological premises. We can never obtain perfect virtue in this life, but constantly have the possibility of becoming better or worse. It often happens that the good thoughts of the holy ones seem to have completely disappeared (*submersus, periit*), but these thoughts and the voice of conscience return after wrong action. It can also happen that one does good without any strong inclination to do so. Such examples show that human nature is variable and our wrestling can occur in manifold ways. Even among the elect and holy ones, some are closer to perfection, while others remain close to vice.[135]

This observed plurality prompts Daneau to present another opinion against the Stoics: while the Stoics generally believe that all virtues are connected, the Christian truth shows that this is not the case. All virtues are connected with the Spirit of Christ dwelling in the elect and are in that sense related to each other. As they remain diverse

---

[131] For Daneau's doctrine of conscience, see Strohm (1996), 485–520. I agree with Strohm (pp. 498–502) that Daneau's notion of *conscientia* displays a proximity to *recta ratio*, joining him with both Cicero and Calvin, who stress the subject's continuous self-awareness regarding good and evil.

[132] e.g. *Ethices Christianae*, 106 v: 'Hoc donum Dei, vel hic Spiritus in renatis est . . . in cognoscenda Dei veritate lux intelligentiae nostrae pura et certa, quam nulla mens humana per se consequi potest.'

[133] *Ethices Christianae*, 107 r. Here Daneau employs the terms *affectus*, *horme*, and *pathe* synonymously.

[134] *Ethices Christianae*, 108v–109v.

[135] *Ethices Christianae*, 110r–v.

and, in different ways, imperfect, they are not connected with one another in the manner of Stoic teaching. In the state of imperfection, some virtues often progress while others remain neglected.[136]

The progress of some virtues is related to the emotions accompanying them:

The pleasure and pain which we feel in the practice of virtue or vice is strongly indicative of their progress and perfection. Those who enjoy the most in doing good progress the most. Those who rejoice only slightly know that they have progressed only slightly in the pursuit of virtue and true renewal. Those who enjoy doing evil the most are more gravely incontinent.[137]

Although this quote can be read as a pedagogical reminder, it also elucidates Daneau's view of emotion. In spite of his criticism of the Stoics, Daneau approximates the cognitive view of emotions: like the Stoics, he thinks that the appearance of emotion reveals some deeper state of the human mind.

Daneau further holds that the person who wants to make progress in virtue should pay attention to such indicative signs. In the pursuit of virtue, the affects of the soul emerge and grow, following repeated practice.[138] When this exercise is aided by the Holy Spirit, the repeated practice may grow into a virtue of continence. For instance, one can practise self-humiliation, and this preparation of the mind may evoke the virtue of humility.[139] Although Daneau does not refine this discussion philosophically, he leans towards a view in which the cognitive, affective, and voluntary components of the mind are tightly interwoven. The training of one of them affects others so that the progress of virtue requires a unification of mental powers. Although the different virtues are not connected as such, the mind that generates them should act in an integrated manner. This kind of 'unity of mind' or *totus homo* view was not uncommon during the Reformation; it can also be interpreted as a Neo-Stoic feature.[140]

Given this, the 'wrestling' which is so important for Daneau's grasp of continence and incontinence is not in the first place a 'commonplace Platonic' conflict between reason and desire. It rather resembles the Stoic idea of emotions as cognitive judgements which can be modified and educated through the consistent use of other mental powers. The emotions with which people aiming at true virtue, that is, the elect, continue to wrestle, are remnants of the sinful flesh, as Luther and Calvin have pointed

---

[136] *Ethices Christianae*, 110v–111r.

[137] *Ethices Christianae*, 111r: 'Magnum autem nostri in alterutro, vel virtute vel vitio nimirum, progressus et profectus indicium est, dolor et voluptas, quam in agendo capimus. Nam qui bene agendo plurimum delectantur, plurimum profecerunt. Qui vero leviter gaudent, parum se adhuc in virtutis et verae reformationis studio progressos esse agnoscant. Qui male agendo plurimum laetantur, illi in maiori incontinentiae gradu.'

[138] *Ethices Christianae*, 111r–v.

[139] *Ethices Christianae*, 111v: 'quaedam ... animi praeparationes, quae ab ipso virtutum gradu, quem consequi possumus, differunt, ex quibus praeparationibus paulatim progredientibus, Dei Spiritu propellente, nascitur, et gignitur postea iste gradus continentiae, quem adipiscimur. Exempli gratia, prius in nobis est humiliatio, quam ista humilitas.'

[140] For the Stoic background in general, see Sorabji (2000); Kusukawa (1995), 88–90 discusses the *totus homo* view in the Reformation.

out. But for Daneau, they are also indicators of the state of the soul, and in this sense cognitive judgements which can be re-educated. An akratic person who feels great pleasure and repents only a little afterwards is in a much worse state than another akratês who only feels a slight pleasure and has great pangs of conscience afterwards. In this sense, the emotions are symptomatic of the deeper state of the mind in a manner which can be called Neo-Stoic, rather than Platonist or Aristotelian.

In sum, Lambert Daneau presents a highly original analysis of *enkrateia* and akrasia, which connects the theology of Luther and Calvin with Aristotelian and Neo-Stoic views. *Enkrateia* and akrasia have a universal significance because sinful humankind cannot attain any higher level of virtue. Moral progress is always conducted in terms of 'wrestling virtue'; that is, as a struggle against harmful perturbations. A successful struggle is only possible for the elect and takes place under the guidance of the Holy Spirit. Thus Daneau practises theological ethics and is critical of traditional moral philosophy. At the same time, however, he leans towards some Neo-Stoic features: he regards emotions as indicative of the deeper state of the soul, he considers akrasia to be a result of simultaneous cohabitation of different judgements, and he can also plead for progress through unification of mental powers. While such features relate him to Zwinger (4.2), Daneau's most original contributions are not philosophical but pertain to his theological elaboration of *enkrateia* and akrasia.

This outcome of our analysis prompts some comments on the earlier studies by Sinnema and Strohm. First, Daneau's textbook can properly be called 'theological ethics', being radically different from the philosophical ethics of the Renaissance as well as from the works of Camerarius and Zwinger. It is probably the first of its kind. Although medieval ethics and Renaissance ethics were sometimes conditioned by theological doctrines, such as those spelled out in the Parisian articles of 1277, the massive role of doctrinal theology clearly distinguishes Daneau's textbook from the earlier academic work on ethics. For these reasons one cannot hold, as Sinnema does, that *Ethices Christianae* is nevertheless a philosophical ethics.

Second, Strohm has, in his extensive study, carefully investigated the various background factors relevant to Daneau's work. I can agree with most of his findings, but want to make some minor qualifications. Strohm considers that the distinction between perfect and imperfect virtue, or *habitus* and *enkrateia*, 'has no background in Aristotle but is rooted in Stoicism'.[141] This is not the case; Daneau's extensive discussion in book 1, chapters 20–24 are an original contribution to the Aristotelian discussion on akrasia. It is rather the case that the 'Stoic' background of the distinction in Cicero is only a springboard from which Daneau launches his own Christian paradigm.

Strohm has seen the interplay between the Aristotelian and Stoic influences in an illuminating and helpful manner. I would not, however, call the 'idea of struggle' (*Kampfgedanke*) in itself a merely 'Stoic' feature. The conflict between reason and

---

[141]   Strohm (1996), 111.

appetite is also well known in the Platonic and Aristotelian traditions. My own criterion of 'Stoicism' employed in this book is a narrower one: namely, a cognitive view of emotions in which passions are understood in terms of assented judgements. This criterion allows sharper distinctions among the various Platonic, Augustinian, and Stoic images of struggle. But Strohm is right in holding that the loose concept of *Stoarenaissance* captures the intellectual climate of early Calvinism in many ways. The language of 'perturbations', 'wrestling', and 'progress' belongs to this broader context.[142]

Strohm sees Daneau's ethics in close relationship to Calvin, but he often considers that Luther's views were very different from Daneau's. He regards Luther as a 'relational' and Daneau as a 'substance-based' (*substanzhaft*) thinker; in Strohm's view, Luther's doctrine of the 'bondage of the will' loses its theocentric focus in Daneau's work.[143] My study has emphasized the strong lines of continuation, not only between Calvin and Daneau, but also between Luther and Daneau. The fundamental view of the human condition which even in the best cases can, with the help of God, achieve the state of *enkrateia*, is common to Luther and Daneau. This doctrine shapes their concept of the powerless human will in a similar way. Daneau's view of Christ and the Holy Spirit as the fundamental subject of good works has many resemblances to Luther and Melanchthon.[144]

4.4 Textbook and System: Case and Keckermann

As we have seen in 4.1–4.3, the approaches to ethics in the Calvinist Reformation vary considerably. Luther's and Calvin's theological insights are carried forward by Lambert Daneau. Theodor Zwinger and Hubert van Giffen represent the extensive humanist learning which does not, at least on the surface, involve itself with theological questions. In spite of these huge differences in approach, two topics unite these authors. The first is the concept of 'struggle' or 'wrestling' (*pugna, lucta*). The human condition is universally conceived in terms of struggle between reason and appetite, or, theologically speaking, between spirit and flesh.

Another common denominator is the relative importance of 'imperfect' virtues in ethics. In the theological approach of Calvin and Daneau, true virtue cannot be fully achieved in this life, since everyone remains a sinner. Thus imperfect virtues like continence are the best we can hope for. Although the philosophical textbooks are not equally pessimistic with regard to moral progress and can deal extensively with virtues, the philosophers also develop a new and extensive interest in the imperfect virtues or 'half-virtues'. The second of these topics is a corollary of the first: since reason and appetite remain in conflict, the imperfect virtues represent the intermediate victories of reason while the struggle still continues.

---

[142] Cf. Strohm (1996), 116–58.
[143] Strohm (1996), 445; 472.
[144] For the history of this doctrine in the Reformation, see Vainio (2008).

Although theological matters are not directly discussed in philosophical commentaries, these two topics are closely connected with the theological insights of Luther and Calvin. The theme of struggle is as such a 'commonplace Platonist' feature which was relevant to some extent before the Reformation (2.2, 2.4), but the Protestant doctrine of remaining sin gives it a new prominence. Thus the philosophical commentaries of early Protestantism indirectly reflect the influence of theological doctrines. The basic motif of struggle is illustrated by the non-Aristotelian picture of Medea, who claims to practise clear-eyed akrasia. This example, introduced by Clichtove (2.4), becomes like a stone in Aristotle's shoe: it does not fit into the framework of EN but, once introduced, can no longer be taken out.

We have already seen in 2.6 and 3.4 that towards the end of the sixteenth century the commentaries were increasingly replaced by textbooks and 'systems' of ethics. Francesco Piccolomini and Wolfgang Heider produced extensive ethical systems which elaborate the moral doctrine comprehensively. Towards the end of the Reformation period it became more common, however, to write brief textbooks which summarize the basic points to be learned by students. Such textbooks may lack the philosophical depth of bigger volumes, but they were widely disseminated and very influential. We will focus on two concise textbooks written by John Case and Bartholomaeus Keckermann. While Case summarizes the old-fashioned but still vital Aristotelianism of his times, Keckermann's textbook crystallizes the outcome of Protestant discussions.

John Case (Johannes Casus, 1546–1600) worked at the University of Oxford. Although an Anglican, he uses Thomas Aquinas and many other medieval scholastics, as well as Donato Acciaiuoli and Lefèvre d'Étaples in his works. Case continues the tradition of Renaissance Aristotelianism and Humanism; although he experienced the ecclesiastical turbulence of England, his moral philosophy is not deeply affected by the confessional divides. Case is an important figure in the history of ethics because of the wide circulation of his textbooks: 'except for a few school texts, his books were more often reprinted than any other British works of philosophy of the sixteenth century'.[145]

Case's *Speculum moralium quaestionum* (1585) is a commentary on EN consisting of a brief exposition and questions. The questions are accompanied by seemingly Ramistic conceptual divisions *(distinctiones)*; they are, however, much less exhaustive than Zwinger's elaborate tables. Case is above all a Humanist Aristotelian, but his work is also influenced by the new methods and styles relevant for a textbook. After the first printing in Oxford in 1585, the *Speculum* was reprinted in Frankfurt eight times between 1589 and 1625 and in Oxford again in 1596.[146] Like Piccolomini's *Universa philosophia de moribus* (2.6), Case's textbook was thus widely used in the Protestant universities of continental Europe.

---

[145] So Copenhaver and Schmitt (2002), 123. For Case and his historical context, see ibid. 122–6 and, in particular, Schmitt (1983a).

[146] Lohr (1975), 706. I quote from Dana Sutton's internet edition of the 1585 text (Latin and English translation). Case's text is organized into Aristotle's book and chapter (caput) numbers; within each chapter the paragraphs are numbered.

One of the reasons for the popularity of *Speculum* may have been that it is a very concise textbook. Immediately before his discussion on akrasia in EN VII, 2, Case remarks that his aim is to 'pursue great brevity'. His comments on EN VII, 2 consist of six extremely brief questions which more or less follow the traditional list of Aristotle's six common opinions (cf. 2.2). The only earlier commentator mentioned in the context of akrasia is Walter Burley.[147]

The first question asks 'whether the incontinent man knows what he is doing is evil'. Case first points out that two things should be considered with regard to akrasia, namely, the power of mind with which the akratês knows that what he does is evil, and the attack of passion which weakens (*hebescit*) the power of mind or reason so that the akratic person is led to criminal deeds.[148] This dichotomy resembles the basic conflict of Zwinger's commentary and, more generally, all those earlier commentators who use Medea as an example. Unlike his predecessors, however, Case avoids calling the interplay between the two powers a struggle.

The question is settled by mentioning two objections and two responses. The objections proceed from the Socratic position that all sin happens out of ignorance. The responses state that the akratic person sins knowingly, although he is affected by passion and does not know without qualifications (*simpliciter*). He is ignorant with regard to (*ex parte*) his passion, but not with regard to his mind.[149] This brief statement does not say much; it merely employs the standard 'commonplace Platonic' view (1.1, 1.5) in emphasizing the dichotomy between reason and passion and the clear-eyed nature of akrasia.

The exposition of EN VII, 3 is brief; its overall title is 'Does the habit of knowledge exist in the incontinent man?',[150] and therefore continues the discussion started in the question mentioned above. Case first gives an exposition, in which he argues that Aristotle's view differs from Socrates. Aristotle

teaches that the knowing man can be taken in two ways, either for the man who possesses knowledge or for the man who employs it...so men who have lost self-control and the

---

[147] *Speculum*, VII, 2, 1–4. Q1: see next note; q2: 'Utrum prudentia in incontinente concupiscentiae resistat? q3: An idem sit continens et temperans, idemque incontinens et intemperans? q4: An continens semper prudens, incontinens semper imprudens dicatur? q5: An intemperans sit deterior incontinente? q6: An continentia et incontinentia in omnibus omnium virtutum moralium obiectis versentur?' Burley is mentioned once in q5 as saying that Aristotle in EN VII, 2 only investigates the issues and gives his own proofs later. Case, too, repeats most of the q1–6 in his exposition EN VII, 2–10.

[148] *Speculum*, VII, 2, 1: 'An incontinens sciat id esse malum quod agit. Duo in homine incontinente considerari debent: [1] Vis mentis, et sic scit malum esse quod aliquando agit; habet enim scientiam in habitu sed non in usu. [2] Impetus affectus, et sic vis mentis et rationis hebescit, ipseque incontinens furentius ad scelus designandum rapitur.' Here and in the following, the numbers in brackets elucidate the Ramistic 'divisions'.

[149] *Speculum*, VII, 2, 1: 'Oppositio: Nemo contra scientiam, ut ait Socrates in textu, trahitur: ergo idem sciens et incontinens esse non potest. Responsio: Non simpliciter sciens, sed potius affectu aestuans scienter ruit. Oppositio: Omnes ignorantes peccamus: ergo incontinens. Antecedens in primo capite tertii libri. Responsio: Verum est ex parte affectus, non mentis.'

[150] *Speculum*, VII, 3, 1: 'An habitus scientiae sit in incontinente?'

perturbed retain an idle habit of knowledge, but understand its use little if at all as long as they are in their madness.[151]

In a similar manner, the akratic person goes wrong in the estimation of particulars:

Furthermore, just as many men correctly demonstrate and understand a universal who carelessly go wrong in particular; so, for example, incontinent men know that drunkenness and lechery are harmful, but, boiling with perturbation, pursue this cup, because it is sweet . . . So he who either ignores or fails to weigh a particular manifestation, although he may understand the universal, is nevertheless capable of sinning in action.[152]

Case sets out a conventional Aristotelian explanation of akrasia. The emphasis on strong perturbations and the general claim that the akratic person sins knowingly relate him to some extent to the commonplace Platonic and quasi-Stoic views of Clichtove and Zwinger, but basically Case defends ordinary Aristotelianism. This explanation is also summarized in terms of a table.[153]

Some brief objections elucidate this position. The first and second objections proceed from a Socratic perspective, claiming that the incontinent person cannot have knowledge (1) because knowledge is a virtue and the akratês is not virtuous; and (2) because he is like a drunkard or sleeper who do not possess knowledge. The response states briefly that a 'mental virtue' can coexist with akrasia and that the sleeper and the drunkard retain habitual knowledge. The third objection takes a different perspective, claiming (3) that the akratês knows even the particular facts. The response states, however, that the akratês 'knows them confusedly, not distinctly'. Even when the akratic person recites the words of the minor premise, he or she is nevertheless under the influence of perturbations.[154]

Case thus steers a middle course between Socratic intellectualism and clear-eyed akrasia. His explanation remains compatible with Aristotelian model 1a. Some quasi-Stoic features can be observed in the emphasis on perturbations, but Case does not refine his discussion on perturbations in the manner of Zwinger.

---

[151] *Speculum*, VII, 3, 1: 'docetque scientem sumi duobus modis, aut pro illo qui scientiam habet aut pro illo qui utitur . . . impotentes et perturbati otiosum habitum scientiae tenent, usum vero dum insaniunt parum aut non omnino intelligunt.'

[152] *Speculum*, VII, 3, 1: 'Praeterea, ut multi universale recte demonstrant et sciunt qui parum attenti in particulari errant, ita incontinentes (verbi causa) sciunt ebrietatem et veneritatem nocere, qui tamen perturbatione aestuantes hoc poculum, quia est dulce . . . persequuntur. Qui ergo particularem enunciationem aut ignorarit aut non perpenderit, is licet universalem norit agendo tamen peccare poterit.'

[153] *Speculum*, VII, 3, 2: 'Scientia consideratur vel in [1] Habitu, qui est aut de [a] Universis, et sic incontinens sciens dicitur. [b] Singulis, et sic incontinens sciens non agit. [2] Actu, qui est aut [c] liber et immunis, ut in caste viventibus. [d] Astrictus perturbationi, ut est in perniciosis.'

[154] *Speculum*, VII; 3, 2: 'Oppositio: Scientia est virtus: ergo non est in incontinente. Responsio: Ratio non valet, quia est virtus mentis. Oppositio: Incontinens dormienti, vinolenti et insano assimilatur: sed isti scientiam non habent; ergo nec incontinens. Responsio: Isti non habent usum, sed habitum tenere possunt. Oppositio: Incontinens novit hoc poculum inebriare, et hanc venerem nocere; ergo non recte dicitur in textu quod universalia sciat et particularia ignoret. Responsio: Confuse non distincte novit. Mussitat enim secum hoc poculum quidem inebriare, sed vehementius perturbatus solum quam suave sit hoc poculum considerat, aliudque non cogitat quamdiu durat perturbatio.'

After giving this explanation, however, Case adds a completely non-Aristotelian question:

Is it necessary that the will always does that which intellect has concluded? [Response] It is not necessary that the will always comply with the concluding intellect, because of [1] the freedom it has in willing and nilling, [2] the dignity which it possesses in attracting the intellect itself to its own object.[155]

This question is not explained further. It resembles John Mair's voluntaristic remarks pertaining to the Parisian articles of 1277. As we have seen, some earlier authors, most notably Buridan and Mair (1.5, 2.5; see also Camerarius and Zwinger, 3.3, 4.2) attempt to make the Aristotelian view of human action compatible with the idea of free will. Case evidently wants to continue this tradition but, as he does not discuss this compatibility any further, one cannot draw precise conclusions with regard to his overall view of akrasia. Perhaps Case simply wants to retain the character of a concise textbook: prominent views which occur in the tradition are mentioned but not discussed further.

Case discusses chapters 4–10 of EN VII in the same, concise manner. The distinction between incontinence and intemperance is treated at some length; Case points out that while intemperance is a *habitus*, incontinence is an affect (*affectus*).[156] The notion of affect is defined very broadly, since Case can also say that wickedness is counted among affects (*malicia inter affectus definitur*).[157] Akratic persons are like sleepers where the use of reason is concerned; they are like madmen when their affect is considered.[158] In discussing akrasia, Case often employs the concepts of *perturbatio, affectus*, and *voluptas*, which link him with the Neo-Stoic concern for the education and eradication of harmful desires. On the other hand, he does not speak of 'struggle' in the manner of Zwinger or Piccolomini. Case's actual explanation of akrasia in EN VII, 2–3 remains fairly Aristotelian in the sense of our model 1a.

Case is thus closer to Thomas Aquinas than his Catholic counterpart Piccolomini. It is noteworthy that these two authors were extensively used in Protestant universities, as the number of reprints produced in Frankfurt shows. One needs to remember, however, that during the days of Zwinger, Case, and Piccolomini, the discipline of ethics had not yet become genuinely confessional. Views could be accepted across confessional borders.

---

[155] *Speculum*, VII, 3, 2: 'Utrum necessario id agat semper voluntas quod intellectus concluserit? Non est necesse ut concludenti intellectui voluntas obtemperet, propter [1] Libertatem quam habet in volendo et nolendo. [2] Dignitatem quam tenet in ipso intellectu ad suum obiectum pertrahendo.' For [2], cf. Thomas Aquinas, *De veritate* q22 a11 r: 'Perfectio autem et dignitas intellectus in hoc consistit quod species rei intellectae in ipso intellectu consistit; cum secundum hoc intelligat actu, in quo eius dignitas tota consideratur. Nobilitas autem voluntatis et actus eius consistit ex hoc quod anima ordinatur ad rem aliquam nobilem, secundum esse quod res illa habet in seipsa.'

[156] *Speculum*, VII, 7, 2.

[157] *Speculum*, VII, 8, 2.

[158] *Speculum*, VII, 10, 1.

Bartholomaeus Keckermann (1571–1609), whose textbooks were widely used among the Protestant Aristotelians, taught biblical languages and philosophy in Heidelberg and Danzig. His *Systema ethicae* appeared in London in 1607 and was reprinted in Hanau in 1610 and 1613, as well as in his *Opera omnia* in Geneva in 1614. Many textbooks by Keckermann carry the title *Systema*.[159] As we already noted with regard to Heider (3.4), a 'system' is a literary genre in which the subject matter is organized pedagogically so that the relevant teachings appear as a logical system of precepts and rules.[160]

The precepts pertain to the definitions and distributions of the subject matter. In ethics, Keckermann calls his rules 'canons'. Rules and canons are conclusions and theorems which lay out the doctrine to be discussed.[161] *Systema ethicae* is a concise textbook which formulates several hundred canons, which are often only briefly discussed. The work is divided into three books: the introduction and the first book discuss the basic concepts and divisions; the second book discusses the virtues, while the third deals with the imperfect virtues.[162] The treatment of virtues is much longer than the discussion on imperfect virtues; in this sense, Keckermann does not share Daneau's views regarding the impossibility of virtue in this life. It is nevertheless noteworthy that the imperfect virtues need a separate book.

The imperfect vices are discussed in the context of imperfect virtues. Four canons in Keckermann's textbook pertain to continence and another ten canons to akrasia.[163] In addition, some unnumbered 'general canons' are pronounced on the general nature of continence.[164] These are, in turn, closely linked to the general canons which describe the difference between perfect and imperfect virtues.[165] The first such canon at the beginning of third book says that

the perfect virtue is a firm and placid quality which does not easily disappear unless together with life itself. The imperfect virtue is, first, at least a kind of passion, and, second, some kind of impression or disposition of the will and emotions. It easily disappears in certain people and it readily changes to its opposite.[166]

While the perfect virtue dominates the appetite, the imperfect virtue does not employ the full will and thus it cannot control the whole appetite. The perfect virtue is

---

[159] e.g. *Systema logicae*, Hanau 1600; *Systema rhetoricae*, Hanau 1608. For Keckermann's career, see Lohr (1977), 738–40; Garber and Ayers (1998), 1439–40; Muller (1984); Copenhaver and Schmitt (2002), 73–4.

[160] For Keckermann's method, see Lohr (1988), 632–7; Kraye (1998), 1285.

[161] Lohr (1988), 634.

[162] In addition to *continentia*, the imperfect virtues of the third book include *pudor, verecundia, sympathia, immunitas ab invidia et a suspicione, tolerantia, amicitia imperfecta*.

[163] *Systema ethicae*, 242–7. I use the London 1607 edition.

[164] *Systema ethicae*, 240–1.

[165] *Systema ethicae*, 224–5.

[166] *Systema ethicae*, 224: 'Virtus perfecta est firma et constans qualitas, quae non facile nisi cum vitam ipsam desint. Virtus autem imperfecta primo est saltem passio quaedam, et deinde ex passione levis aliqua impressio sive dispositio voluntatis et affectuum, quae subinde desinit in certis hominibus, et facile mutatur in contrarium.'

achieved by long practice, but the imperfect virtue may be a natural disposition, or may have emerged from a superficial imitation of some examples.[167]

Keckermann does not name his sources, but the canons follow the tradition of many interpreters, including Daneau, Piccolomini, and Golius. Among the imperfect virtues, continence and endurance are virtues connected with the power of reason. These virtues 'are called imperfect virtues because, as in perfect virtues appetite is mostly subjected to right reason, so it is in these imperfect virtues, although there is a great wrestling between right reason and appetite'.[168] The theme of wrestling reflects the tradition of Zwinger, Daneau, and several others; Keckermann explains this canon with reference to Piccolomini. Aristotle distinguishes between perfect and imperfect virtues in EN VII, 1. The perfect virtues do not contain any struggle (*pugna*) between reason and appetite, but the imperfect virtues are characterized by wrestling and struggle. Because of this Piccolomini calls them half-virtues.[169]

Generally speaking, continence refers to all imperfect virtues of this kind; but in the narrower sense, continence means a successful struggle with anger or with various kinds of covetous desires.[170] The imperfect vice of incontinence pertains to cases in which harmful desires, in particular those of gluttony and sexual desire, draw the person to wrong action in some sense reluctantly.[171] Akrasia thus belongs to the context in which reason and appetite wrestle with one another.

Employing this general context, Keckermann can state eight canons regarding incontinence. After number eight, he formulates another two. The first four canons are particularly relevant for the classical problem of acting against knowledge. The first canon states the basic solution of Aristotle's problem in EN VII, 3: 'The incontinent person acts knowingly to an extent and remains ignorant to an extent. He acts knowingly insofar as he knows generally that wrong actions are to be avoided. He remains ignorant insofar as he does not apply this general knowledge to his own action.'[172] In his

---

[167] *Systema ethicae*, 224: 'Virtus perfecta plene domat appetitum moralem. Virtus autem imperfecta nondum plene habet voluntatem et appetitum domitum.Virtus perfecta praeceptis et longa exercitatione acquiritur. Virtus autem imperfecta magis per naturam inest, aut leviusculo saltem usu possidetur, vel uno et altero exemplo, ac imitatione imprimitur.'

[168] *Systema ethicae*, 240: 'Dicuntur hae virtutes imperfectae propterea, quia sicut in perfectis virtutibus appetitus magis subiectus est rectae rationi, ita in his virtutibus imperfectis, adhuc magna est lucta inter rectam rationem et appetitum.'

[169] *Systema ethicae*, 240–1: 'Aristoteles dicto libro, c. 1 facit distinctionem inter virtutes perfectas et imperfectas, quod nempe virtutes perfectae non habeant pugnam rectae rationis et appetitus, imperfectae autem virtutes adhuc contineant luctam et pugnam, ratione cuius luctae, sunt semivirtutes, ut Picolom. appellat.'

[170] *Systema ethicae*, 241: 'Continentia vel generalius accipitur, vel specialius. Generalius accepta, est concertatio quaedam virtutis cum vitio, sic tamen, ut virtus vincat... Specialis continentia est virtus imperfecta, per quam luctamur cum ira, cum cupiditate cibi, potus, veneris. Item cum cupiditate sermonis et locomotivae, et sic luctamur, ut tamen virtus superior sit.'

[171] *Systema ethicae*, 243: 'opponitur incontinentia, qua tum affectibus aliis, tum inprimis in gula et venere modum qui excedit, ita ut a pravis cupiditatibus quodammodo invitus ad peccandum pertrahatur.'

[172] *Systema ethicae*, 243: '[Canon 1] Incontinens partim sciens agit, partim ignorans. Sciens agit, quatenus in genere novit turpe fugiendum. Ignorans agit, quatenus generalem istam notitiam non applicat ad suam actionem.'

brief commentary on this canon, Keckermann mentions that Aristotle uses the third chapter of EN VII in discussing this problem. The whole matter can, however, be reduced to the one distinction which prevails between knowing something in a generic or general manner (*in genere*) and knowing with regard to the particular kind of action *(in specie)*.[173]

This is a very brief summary of the basic Aristotelian model 1a of akrasia (see 1.5). The second canon and its explanation colours this summary with the overarching idea of struggle:

> The incontinent person does not apply his general knowledge to the particular kind because of the repugnancy of appetite and reason and because of the perturbations of soul. In EN VII, 3 Aristotle also asks how it can happen that, when the incontinent person knows generally, he cannot apply this knowledge to the particular kind. He responds that this happens because of the perturbations of soul; they impede the mind so that it cannot relate the general to the particular kind.[174]

The second canon and its explanation summarize the Protestant discussion which has so persistently revolved around the idea of struggle. As we have seen (3.3–3.4, 4.2), the interpreters regard this struggle as the 'natural cause' of akrasia. The motif of struggle can be combined with Aristotle's discussion regarding the 'facts of nature' (EN 1147a24–b5) in this manner.

The third canon outlines the traditional view regarding different temporal moments: before and after the action the akratês knows clearly and therefore repents later; but during the action her mind is perturbed so that she cannot use the knowledge she has. Given the brevity of the canons, the third canon is interesting in that it spells out the distinction between having and using knowledge. Furthermore, Keckermann says here, like Camerarius and van Giffen, that the incontinent individual has 'allowed' (*admissum*) his wrong action. In all three, the use of the verb *admitto* underlines the voluntary nature of akrasia.[175]

Possibly the most interesting feature of canon three is its illustration with the help of Adam's akrasia: 'These three times can be noted in Adam's first sin which was due to incontinence. For before eating he had all knowledge; when he was eating some oblivion occurred; after eating he remembered and was penitent.'[176] This remark is not

---

[173] *Systema ethicae*, 243: 'Totum caput 3 lib. 7 Aristoteles consumit in ista quaestione: an incontinens agat sciens vel ignorans. Sed tota res ista distinctione expeditur, quod incontinens sciat quidem in genere, quid sit faciendum, in specie autem non applicet ad suam actionem, id quod in genere novit.'

[174] *Systema ethicae*, 243–4: '[Canon 2] Incontinens id, quod in genere novit, non applicat in specie, propter repugnantiam appetitus et rationis, et propter animi perturbationes. [Explanation] Aristoteles dicto cap. 3 etiam disputat, quomodo fieri possit, ut cum incontinens sciat generalia, non applicet ea ad speciem, et respondet hoc fieri, ob animi perturbationes, quibus impeditur mens, ne possit genus ad speciem contrahere.'

[175] *Systema ethicae*, 244: 'Circa incontinentem igitur tria tempora sunt consideranda. 1. est, quod praecedit eius actionem, et tunc omnino praeditus est scientia honesti tam generali quam speciali. Alterum tempus est in ipsa actione incontinentis; tunc enim est similis ignoranti, quia animus est perturbatus pravis affectibus, ita ut non possit uti eam scientiam quam habet. Tertium tempus est post actionem sive post peccatum admissum; tum enim incontinens redit ad notitiam, quam ante habebat, ita ut incipiat eum facti poenitere.'

[176] *Systema ethicae*, 244: 'Ita in primo peccati Adami, quod fuit incontinentia, tria ista tempora notari possunt. Nam ante comestionem fuit plena scientia; in comestione autem fuit obliterata; post comestionem recollecta et cum poenitentia coniuncta.'

explained further. As we have seen in the cases of Henry of Ghent (1.4) and Wolfgang Heider (3.4), Adam's akrasia is a somewhat puzzling case. Christian theology normally regarded concupiscence as the punishment of the first sin; thus Adam in paradise did not have the same kind of harmful desires as later sinners. On the other hand, Heider, and probably Keckermann as well, think that the natural discrepancy between reason and appetite is enough in itself to confuse Adam in his ideal state. The use of this example in Protestant textbooks thus underlines the natural givenness of the confusing discrepancy between reason and appetite.

The fourth canon repeats the traditional doctrine that the akratês nevertheless uses some kind of reason in the akratic action.[177] Canon eight and its two corollaries briefly discuss the voluntary and involuntary aspects of akrasia. Here Keckermann first states that the perturbations of the soul push the akratês into sinning 'as if against his will' (*quasi praeter voluntatem suam*). Such partially involuntary action is more excusable in the case of precipitate akrasia, in which the passions are stronger and no time for thinking remains.[178] The standard 'weak' akrasia (*infirmitas*) leaves more time for consideration and inner struggle. In weak akrasia, the agent only surrenders to the passions after considerable resistance. This means that weak akrasia is more culpable, since the agent has had time and opportunity to equip himself against passions.[179] In this manner, the agent is responsible for his or her weak akrasia. At the same time, weak akrasia is difficult to cure, because it relates to the agent's very nature.[180]

Like most other themes of Keckermann's treatment of akrasia, these last points are traditional and occur in Aristotle's text (as in EN 1150b19–28). Keckermann's discussion is not philosophically deep, but it crystallizes the two topics mentioned at the beginning of this chapter which unite most moral thinkers of the late sixteenth century. First, they see akrasia as the natural result of the underlying struggle between reason and appetite. Second, they ascribe great importance to the so-called 'imperfect virtues' which exemplify the good behaviour within the limits of this struggle.

Most Reformation authors see these two topics as fundamentally Aristotelian, but their textual background in the EN is thin. They do not attain the same relative importance in medieval commentaries. The historical background of these two topics in the Reformation period can be located in the 'commonplace Platonism', which seeks to understand the human soul in terms of a discrepancy between reason and appetitive powers. At the same time, this struggle is connected with Luther's and Calvin's theological insights concerning the remaining sinfulness of all humans. A third

---

[177] *Systema ethicae*, 244. This is why animals cannot be akratic, EN 1147b3–5. See also 4.2 (van Giffen).

[178] *Systema ethicae*, 246.

[179] *Systema ethicae*, 246: 'Infirmitas est incontinentia, quam quis affectibus et cupiditatibus pravis aliquandiu resistens, tandem succumbit, et cupiditatibus suis quasi victus ad peccandum seducitur . . . Infirmitas magis est reprehendenda quam precipitantia, quia infirmitas habet spatium et moram sese sese muniendi adversus cupiditates et affectus pravos.'

[180] *Systema ethicae*, 246: 'Infirmitas minus est sanabilis quam praecipitantia, quia aliquo modo per naturae vitium inest; naturalia autem difficulter mutantur.'

background may be the Neo-Stoic trends of the late sixteenth century. Several authors, in particular Camerarius (3.3) and van Giffen (4.2), think that the doctrine of different parts of the soul should be defended against the Stoic view of the unity of soul or mind. For these writers, the existence of akrasia proves that the Stoics are wrong at this point. At the same time, however, the increased tendency to interpret the human condition in terms of continuing struggle against the perturbations of the soul employs features that resemble Neo-Stoicism.

5

Conclusions and Epilogue

5.1 Akrasia from 1360 to 1630

We have seen in chapters 2–4 that the problem of acting against one's own better judgement was a much-discussed philosophical and theological issue during the Renaissance and the Reformation. Both Aristotle's akrasia and Augustine's problem of the divided and powerless will continue to present a challenge. Medieval solutions are defended and refined; new interpretations of old texts as well as new psychological issues emerge. We can conclude that the view quoted in the Introduction, according to which neither the concept nor the problem of 'weakness of will' was a relevant issue following the medieval period, is completely unfounded.

In the Introduction to the present study it was claimed that the problem of akrasia was a source of lively debates and significant innovations during the Renaissance and the Reformation. It was further claimed that the study of these debates and innovations sheds light on the general understanding of the human condition during the formative period between medieval times and early modernity (1360–1630). In the following, I will first present a brief overview of the most important debates and innovations, bringing together the different threads that make the larger picture. Second, I will discuss the broader significance of these results for the history of ideas. To illustrate this broader significance, the study concludes (5.2, 5.3) with a brief presentation of some prominent early modern authors in whose works the problem of weakness of will plays a role.

Aristotelian intellectualism, as formulated in the medieval commentaries of Thomas Aquinas and Walter Burley, remains a dominant current of the fifteenth-century discussion of akrasia. John Versor offers a systematic account of the Thomistic understanding of akrasia. Virgilius Wellendorffer and Donato Acciaiuoli defend Thomistic positions, but they also often adhere to Burley's work on crucial issues regarding weakness of will. Acciaiuoli and Wellendorffer are sympathetic to Burley's suggestion that the conclusion of the practical syllogism is not action, but a propositional opinion which remains ignored in akratic conduct. Acciaiuoli and Wellendorffer step beyond Thomism in claiming that the akratic person can know both premises of the practical syllogism and nevertheless ignore its conclusion.

Although the Renaissance writers use new translations, they are often content with Thomist philosophical and theological positions which they explain in elegant, non-scholastic Latin, Donato Acciaiuoli being a typical example. Jacques Lefèvre d'Étaples, whose work on Aristotelian ethics has often been seen as a turning point from Scholasticism to Humanism, also exemplifies this strategy insofar as akrasia is concerned. His brief discussion of weakness of will is similar to Aquinas and Versor and does not offer new philosophical viewpoints. More original is the influential commentary of his pupil, Josse Clichtove, who emphasizes the inner struggle between reason and desire in a 'commonplace Platonist' manner (for this and other models of akrasia mentioned below, see the end of 1.5). Clichtove introduces the example of Medea's inner conflict, a prominent new illustration employed by most later commentators on akrasia.

The influence of late medieval voluntarism is apparent in Petrarch's reflection on the Augustinian problem of the divided will. The puzzling end of his *Secretum* has often been understood as a farewell to scholasticism. We have argued, however, that Francesco's final inability to follow Augustine's path of continence at the end of *Secretum* remains in keeping with Henry of Ghent's late scholastic voluntarism. A sinful person cannot simply return to the past instance of wrong choice, since his or her desires can no longer be eradicated. Thus Francesco must remain in this state of disorder. This view opposes Augustine's *Confessions*, but it does allude to the permanent rule of desires, a view expressed in Augustine's *Contra Iulianum* and later put forward programmatically by Luther and Calvin.

Petrarch's work did not have an immediate reception history in the discussion on akrasia, but it remains a prominent example of fourteenth-century voluntarism. In the universities, various voluntarist positions are defended by Bartholomaeus Arnoldi de Usingen and John Mair at the turn of the sixteenth century. Usingen adheres to John Buridan's moderate voluntarism, which builds upon the so-called 'commonplace Augustinian' (1.2, 1.5) view of human action. On this view, the Augustinian interplay between inevitable desire and free consent is transformed into a rationalist theory of human deliberation and action. For Usingen, the Buridanistic theory proves the 'free decision' of the will in its act of consent, as well as representing the 'Catholic way of speaking' of human action.

In his commentary on EN, Mair presents a refined version of Buridan's theory. He affirms the intellectualist preconditions of Aristotelianism and Thomism, according to which nothing can be stronger than knowledge, but he also defends free will, adhering to the voluntarism of the Parisian articles of 1277. To combine intellectualism and voluntarism, Mair investigates how the words *est faciendum* need to be understood in the practical syllogism. He claims that akratic agents can have simultaneous contrary judgements so that they keep the phrase *non est faciendum* in mind as a moral judgement on the one hand, while on the other they actually follow the phrase *est faciendum*, which appears to them as an effective indicative. With the help of this semantic duality of the syllogistic phrases, Mair can hold that one can voluntarily act against one's own better judgement. Mair's elaborate solution also shows how the old controversies between intellectualist Thomists and voluntarist Augustinians continue to be relevant in the early sixteenth century.

The emergence of Platonism in the second part of the fifteenth century has left traces in the commentaries. The view of continuous struggle (*pugna*) between reason and desire is an obvious example of this development. Although this struggle plays some role in the medieval Aristotelian discussion of akrasia, its relative importance increases in Acciaiuoli's commentary, in which it is applied to the conflict between the right and wrong practical syllogisms. For Usingen and his Erfurt colleagues, the so-called simultaneous contrary appetites become a much-discussed problem, since they cause repugnancy (*repugnantia*) in continent and incontinent actions. In their treatment of the contrary appetitive powers, the Erfurt thinkers incline towards an Ockhamist real distinction between the sensitive and the rational parts of the soul. In Clichtove's Humanist commentary, the motif of struggle appears in a 'commonplace Platonist' fashion, making the inner struggle between reason and desire the main psychological background of akrasia.

The various discussions of the Renaissance are summarized in Francesco Piccolomini's extensive textbook on ethics. This book is, however, a harmonization of different traditions rather than a philosophical system. Piccolomini knows that Plato defends strict intellectualism and denies akrasia in the *Protagoras*. Piccolomini prefers Aristotle's affirmation of akrasia, but in so doing he develops a view which is heavily dominated by the continuous struggle between reason and sensual perturbations. Referring to Medea's conflict as a paradigm of akrasia, he considers that human actions remain mixed and are characterized by the struggle in which the akratic person chooses voluntarily, although not irrationally, among available options. This explanation of akrasia is close to a 'commonplace Platonism' in which the higher and lower parts of the soul remain in conflict.

Although Luther and Melanchthon do not explicitly comment on Aristotle's akrasia, their writings on the will's inability to do good continue the earlier Augustinian discussion. They are heavily opposed to the voluntarist scholasticism of their predecessors; for Luther and, in particular, Calvin, the true theology of permanent sinfulness and the will's inability needs to remain faithful to the anti-Pelagian texts of Augustine. Augustine's late anti-Pelagian writings are thus programmatically played off against the 'commonplace Augustinian' theory of free consent. The theme of struggle takes on a new role in Luther, Melanchthon, and Calvin since the Pauline conflict between spirit and flesh (Romans 7) concerns everyone. The spirit does not represent human reason, but is a power emanating from outside. At the same time, there is no perfect virtue in human beings which could completely extinguish the harmful desires of the flesh.

Martin Luther interprets this human condition to mean that an individual is either a hardened sinner or a person experiencing the struggle. Everyone is thus either obdurately vicious or, with the help of the spirit, remains continent in their struggle. If they lapse in this struggle, they fall back into the vicious state. Given this, akrasia does not emerge for Luther as a distinct third possibility. Melanchthon affirms both the wrestling (*lucta*) between the spirit and the flesh, and the inner conflict between natural reason and harmful passions. The inner conflict can bring about continent and incontinent moral states. Melanchthon often uses the conflict of Medea as an example of acting against one's own better judgement.

Melanchthon's anthropology is close to late medieval voluntarism, but for him the will is not a particularly noble faculty. Since the will is distinct from the cognitive power and allied with passions, its decisions need not reflect cognitive rationality. As the will remains occupied by either God or the devil in its theological wrestling, the inherent freedom of the will does not play much role in action. Melanchthon's anthropology receives a new philosophical prominence in the commentary on EN by his pupil Joachim Camerarius. Camerarius leaves the theological side of this anthropology undiscussed and interprets the inner conflict in philosophical terms. He employs Buridan's view of the final uncertainty of moral knowledge in order to conclude that the will can freely choose among the available options. As the passions can immediately please the will and thus qualify among the options to be chosen, Camerarius subscribes to a particularly strong version of voluntarism. In spite of Luther's criticism of Usingen and other scholastics, one can therefore identify a continuing line of voluntarism which goes from Henry of Ghent and Buridan to Melanchthon and Camerarius.

The line from Buridan to Camerarius is also interesting in its emphasis on moral uncertainty. Camerarius emphasizes the Aristotelian views that action is concerned with particulars and sense perception, and that our knowledge regarding these remains imperfect. The perceptual and uncertain nature of moral knowledge is also emphasized in later Lutheran ethical works by Theophilus Golius and Wolfgang Heider. Golius reintroduces the old example used by Henry of Ghent, namely the case of Adam as the paradigm of voluntary and clear-eyed wrongdoing. Since our knowledge after Adam is perturbed by passions and our moral knowledge remains perceptual and uncertain, our will chooses akratically among conflicting options. Both Golius and Heider employ the Greek term *aisthêtikê* to characterize the perceptual nature of moral knowledge. Heider emphasizes that since this knowledge can easily be weakened and shattered, akrasia remains a real possibility. Golius and Heider regard the discrepancy (*dissidium*) between reason and appetite as constituting the anthropological background to this uncertainty and confusion, in which respect they approach the dualistic psychology of Ockhamism and 'commonplace Platonism'.

One way of describing the early Lutheran emphasis on uncertainty and confusion regarding moral truths is to call it 'epistemic pessimism', because of which the early Lutheran expositors of akrasia contribute to the increase in emphasis on perceptual knowledge in early modern thought. Our study has not investigated this matter further, but we have explicated the theological roots of this trend. Because Luther and Melanchthon stress the remaining sin and deny the possibility of achieving perfect virtue in this life, the human condition is basically a struggle in which the cognitive powers remain distracted and human knowledge uncertain. Because it is difficult to attain true knowledge, the agent needs to focus his or her mind on the uncertain evidence with particular care.

Luther's radically theological anthropology is accepted in Calvinism even more completely than in Lutheranism. Calvin emphasizes the remaining sinfulness and the spiritual struggle. Calvin's *Institutes* contains a thematic passage on Aristotle's akrasia in which he connects akrasia with ignorance of particular facts. Calvin also holds that there are instances of clear-eyed acting against one's own better judgement, as in the case of Medea. Calvin stresses the voluntary nature of akrasia and teaches that the conscience of wrongdoers nevertheless remains alive. Similar points, expressed by Calvin's teacher John Mair, also resemble the Stoic example of 'the runner who cannot stop running' as the paradigm of akrasia.

The issue of Neo-Stoicism is relevant for most Calvinist authors. Although they do not want to be Neo-Stoics, their strong emphasis on perturbations of the soul and the soul's wrestling with them has some Neo-Stoic features. Among the Calvinists, Theodor Zwinger may be closest to Neo-Stoicism. He emphasizes the struggle between reason and passion, and considers that the perturbations of the soul are fundamentally cognitive, expressing reasoning, conclusions, and judgements. This 'cognitive theory of emotions' allies him with Neo-Stoic views. At the same time, Zwinger is a highly eclectic author who employs Ramistic methods and claims to be Aristotelian. Because he presents the inner conflict in syllogistic terms and claims that both the right and the wrong practical syllogism yield propositional conclusions, he resembles the intellectualism of Walter Burley at times.

Lambert Daneau may be the author who most consistently turns Luther's theological insights into an ethical system. Because of the continuing struggle between the spirit and the flesh, we only achieve continence, not pure virtue. Moral consideration should therefore focus on the 'wrestling virtue' (*virtus luctans*) which experiences the resistance of the flesh. For this reason, continence and incontinence receive a prominent place in Daneau's theological ethics. Daneau also applies Calvin's view of predestination in his discussion: the genuinely continent people are the elect who can persevere in their struggle with carnal passions. Among the non-elect, one can distinguish the akratic people who retain their conscience and are thus aware of their wrongdoings. In the natural realm, they are morally better than the obdurately vicious people. Daneau's highly original interpretation of continence and incontinence contains some Neo-Stoic elements; for instance, he regards the emotions as symptomatic of the soul's state and, in that sense, as cognitive judgements. He also considers that the soul or mind is fundamentally one.

Hubert van Giffen, John Case, and Bartholomaeus Keckermann remain closer to Aristotle. Van Giffen and Case defend the intellectualist view of Aristotle and Aquinas that the akratês remains ignorant of the minor premise of the practical syllogism. While Case remains on the intellectualist track of Aquinas and Versor, van Giffen is an eclectic Aristotelian who emphasizes the continuous struggle between reason and harmful desires. He mentions ignorance as the cause of akrasia, but holds, nevertheless, that the akratês has consciously allowed his misguided action. Van Giffen's position resembles the harmonization of Piccolomini. Keckermann likewise emphasizes the inner conflict and struggle between reason and appetite. Although Keckermann admits that the akratês is in some sense ignorant, he likewise emphasizes the voluntary nature of akrasia. In this respect, van Giffen and Keckermann follow the voluntarism of Camerarius.

In both Lutheranism and Calvinism we can observe the difference between theological and philosophical viewpoints. Theology dominates the work of Luther, Melanchthon, Calvin, and Daneau; philosophical discussion has primary importance for Camerarius, Golius, Heider, Zwinger, van Giffen, Case, and Keckermann. But the distinction is by no means clear: Reformation theology has deeply influenced most commentators, although this influence is not always explicit. Camerarius, for instance, applies the theological anthropology of Melanchthon, an influence reflected in the work of van Giffen and Keckermann. The philosophical tradition also has its impact on theology: Luther and Calvin are well informed of scholastic philosophy and construct their theological doctrines as critical responses to scholasticism. In this process, their vocabulary remains shaped by the late medieval *via moderna*.

In spite of all this interaction, we may observe a differentiation of theological ethics as a discipline which slowly departs from philosophy. Daneau is a programmatic example of this development, but the two disciplines do not become consistently separated in our sources. During the period covered by our study, that is, from 1360 to 1630, it is therefore necessary to treat philosophical and theological source texts as complementary discussions of the same phenomenon.

At the end of 1.5, a brief inventory of the explanatory models of akrasia was presented in terms of a table. One way to summarize the discussion on akrasia from Petrarch to Keckermann and Heider is to subsume each under the typology created in that inventory. This needs to be done with proper care. Although the following groupings to some extent indicate the currents of different reception processes, the inventory does not provide a full account of the interpretation history.

No one subscribes to the pure intellectualism of Socrates and Plato in *Protagoras*, but very many sixteenth-century interpreters incline towards 'commonplace Platonism', according to which akrasia can be explained as the occasional outcome of the permanent conflict between reason and harmful desires. Josse Clichtove and Francesco Piccolomini exemplify this tendency particularly well. Because the concept of struggle or wrestling (*pugna, lucta*) becomes prominent in the Reformation, the explanations of akrasia undertaken by Golius, Heider, Zwinger, van Giffen, and Keckermann contain elements of commonplace Platonism. The theological authors who describe a similar struggle between flesh and spirit in Pauline terms influence this discussion in their own way.

The Aristotelian and Thomist model 1a, according to which the minor premise of the practical syllogism is ignored in akrasia, remains popular throughout the fifteenth and sixteenth centuries. John Versor, Jacques Lefèvre d'Étaples, and John Case typically represent this model. Elements of it are apparent in many authors, such as Acciaiuoli, Wellendorffer, Calvin, Mair, Heider, and Keckermann. Walter Burley's Aristotelian model 2, according to which the propositional conclusion is ignored, is supported by Donato Acciaiuoli and Virgilius Wellendorffer. Some elements of it are present in Zwinger.

The Stoic-Augustinian models constitute a heterogeneous group. All probably aim at being Augustinian and do not want to be seen as Stoics. In terms of our inventory, no one supports the strictly Stoic theory of emotions as assented judgements, although Zwinger has some leanings towards this position. In 1.2 and 1.5 we have argued that the so-called 'moderated Stoic position' holds that harmful emotions are already sin and qualify the moral state of the agent before his or her subsequent consent. This is the view of Luther, Melanchthon, Calvin, and Daneau; they also regard it as the genuine view of Augustine. Although they are not Stoics, their interpretations of akrasia exhibit Stoic features; for instance, that there is no akrasia (Luther), that the dynamics of akrasia resemble the runner who cannot stop running (Calvin), or that no one is truly virtuous because all progressing individuals remain in struggle (Luther, Daneau).

The so-called 'commonplace Augustinian' model, which considers inevitable desires as morally indifferent and ascribes moral value to the agent's free consent, occurs in our study in connection with John Buridan's action theory. For Buridan, the choice of the will occurs as free consent in a situation of many uncertain alternatives. Akrasia takes place as the wrong choice is this situation. This view of human action is supported by Bartholomaeus Arnoldi de Usingen, and also by John Mair, who further refines the syllogistic features of this view. Elements of Buridanism can be found in Camerarius, Golius, and Heider, all of whom emphasize the uncertain nature of moral knowledge as the background to akrasia. In doing this, they also lean towards voluntarism.

Voluntarist authors in our study include Petrarch and Philip Melanchthon, who also deviate from medieval voluntarism in important respects, since they teach that the will finally cannot exercise its freedom to overcome all obstacles. Some voluntarist features are included in the action theories of Mair, van Giffen, and Keckermann. 'Adam's akrasia', a voluntarist view according to which the choice of free will after Adam becomes limited due to the punishment of sin, is relevant for Petrarch, Golius, and Keckermann. The most extreme variant of voluntarism, that is, 'deliberate irrationality', is not as such defended by anyone, but the conceptual roots of this possibility begin to be available in Camerarius. Both Melanchthon and Camerarius detach the power of the will from the cognitive-rational faculty and associate it strongly with passions or affections. In denying the freedom of the will, Melanchthon also strips the will of its rationality. Camerarius uses Melanchthon's anthropology, but ascribes more freedom to the human will without, however, restoring its inherent rationality.

With necessary caution, we can thus fill in Table 5.1 as follows (see next page).

It is essential to see the manifold character of this interpretation history and not to press it into too simple a narrative. Both the Renaissance and the Reformation are characterized by a great variety of approaches. Although the relative importance of theology may be stronger in the Reformation period, it is also essential to see the philosophical background of Lutheran and Calvinist authors. And, vice versa, the

Table 5.1. Models of akrasia: a brief inventory (revisited)

Platonic models. Distinctive feature: reason vs desire (but no syllogism, no assent)
– Socratic-Platonic model: intellectualist action theory, no one goes wrong willingly
– commonplace Platonism: tripartite soul, strong lower part may overcome small higher part, therefore desire sometimes overcomes reason (Clichtove, Piccolomini; also Golius, Heider, Zwinger, van Giffen, Keckermann)

Aristotelian models. Distinctive feature: the practical syllogism
– 1a: the minor premise is ignored in akrasia (Versor, Lefèvre d'Étaples, Case; also Acciaiuoli, Wellendorffer, Calvin, Mair, Heider, Keckermann)
– 1b: when the premises are not properly connected, akrasia can occur
– 2: in akrasia, the propositional conclusion is reached but not followed (Acciaiuoli, Wellendorffer; also Zwinger)

Stoic-Augustinian models. Distinctive feature: the concept of assent/consent/free will
– strictly Stoic model: emotions are assented judgements, no real distinction between desire and consent (Zwinger?)
– moderated Stoic model: emotions are preliminary judgements, later assents play a role (Luther, Melanchthon, Calvin, Daneau)
– commonplace Augustinian model: a clear distinction between inevitable desires and free consent; the judgemental nature of desires remains in the background while merit and sin are consequential to the consent
– Buridanism: rational decision-making within the commonplace Augustinian model (Usingen, Mair; also Camerarius, Golius, Heider)
– voluntarism: the self-determining will as the supreme ruler; the will represents the most noble part of the soul (Petrarch, Melanchthon; also Mair, van Giffen, Keckermann)
– Adam's akrasia: the will chooses freely without interference of emotions; passions and ignorance only emerge afterwards, as the consequence (punishment) of misguided choice (Petrarch, Golius, Keckermann)
– deliberate irrationality: the will chooses freely; the will does not represent the rational soul or the most noble part of the soul (Camerarius?)

Renaissance was also a religious and even theological movement. Authors like Petrarch and Acciaiuoli very consciously aim at reinterpreting theologians like Augustine and Thomas Aquinas.

While affirming all this variety, we should nevertheless ask whether there is any red thread or *leitmotif* which goes through this interpretation history. A significant long-term transformation process concerns the treatment of the 'two syllogisms' of the akratês which in the medieval discussion were regarded as competing with one another in akratic deliberation. Medieval Aristotelianism understood these contrary alternatives primarily in terms of syllogistic deliberation. The dynamic side of this deliberation was not completely absent, since Albert the Great speaks of 'contrary acceptances' and Buridan of 'double inclination'. Aquinas employs the concept of *repugnantia* to highlight the opposing force of concupiscence.

As a whole, however, the late medieval scholastics do not use the vocabulary of 'struggle' (*pugna*) in the way it begins to be used after Acciaiuoli and Clichtove.

Although the Renaissance authors continue to employ syllogistic structures, they understand the akratic conflict primarily as a dynamic conflict between the competing powers of reason and desire. An important intermediate step in this process of transformation is the reflection on 'simultaneous contrary appetitive powers', which is a major issue for Wellendorffer, Usingen, Luther, and Mair. These powers appear as judgements and propositions within a syllogistic structure, but they also express the fundamental psychological dynamics of the human soul.

After the days of Luther and Mair, the inner conflict of the human condition is primarily expressed through examples, among which Medea's conflict is by far the most prominent. Melanchthon introduces the concept of 'wrestling' (*lucta*) as another major concept highlighting the inner struggle. Theologically speaking, struggle and wrestling exemplify the Pauline conflict between the spirit and the flesh. In this conflict, the flesh stands for the harmful passions, in particular concupiscence, while the spirit is a divine power coming from outside. In the emerging Protestant theological anthropology, pure virtue is unattainable in this life. The Christian is 'justified and a sinner at the same time': he or she remains involved in the struggle and can achieve continence with the help of the Spirit, but not perfect virtue.

This theological grounding of human wrestling and inner struggle ascribes a new prominence to the concepts of continence and incontinence. As Lambert Daneau argues, theological ethics under the premises of Protestant anthropology should focus on the imperfect virtue of continence, because it is the highest realistic goal of moral wrestling. At the same time, the concepts of struggle and wrestling also increasingly permeate the philosophical commentaries on Aristotle and other textbooks on ethics. Aristotle's akrasia is no longer interpreted as a syllogistical problem but as the actual inner conflict of an individual person. The non-Aristotelian example of Medea is discussed as the paradigmatic case of this akrasia. Syllogistic discussion is for the most part replaced by a dynamic psychology of inner faculties and their powers. The changing vocabulary shows this transformation process: two syllogisms, double inclination, contrary appetitive powers, repugnancy, struggle, and wrestling.

Although this development is motivated on the Protestant side by the theological ideas of permanent sinfulness and continuing struggle between spirit and flesh, it also occurs in the Renaissance Catholic texts. Francesco Piccolomini's extensive discussion of 'half-virtues' teaches how the continent person has to live 'with struggle' (*cum pugna*). In addition to continence, the power of endurance (*tolerantia*) belongs to the realm of half-virtues. One corollary of this development is, therefore, that both Protestant and Catholic textbooks on ethics begin to discuss the half-virtues in great detail. Although this discussion is formally located in the seventh book of EN, the treatment of half-virtues exceeds the limits of Aristotle's ethics. Because moral life and the development of virtue are increasingly treated in terms of continuous inner struggle and wrestling with oneself, continence and incontinence remain important in early modern ethical discourse.

In sum, the present study has made visible some important traditions which contributed to the portrayal of the human condition as a continuous struggle. The Protestant view of Christian existence as that of being justified and sinner at the same time was connected with these traditions in significant ways. The human condition was no longer predominantly characterized as being either virtuous or wicked. Instead, the human being aiming at the good remains half-virtuous and continues to wrestle with his or her conflicting inner powers. While the emerging Protestant theology emphasized the problematic nature of remaining sin, in a parallel manner the early modern ethics increasingly began to outline human moral life as continuous wrestling and human character as permanently half-virtuous.

The mental conflict of human beings is also a prominent theme of modernity. When Eugène Delacroix portrayed the inner struggle in his *Médée Furieuse* (1838), his contemporaries regarded this painting as radical and even scandalous. At the same time, however, Delacroix remains committed to the early modern patterns: the shadow over Medea's eyes and the ambivalence of her bodily movements visualize the long literary tradition of weakness of will and mental conflict.

This feature of early modern ethics has its roots, as we have seen, in the discussions during the Renaissance and the Reformation. The impact of these discussions on the formative ideas of modernity has not been investigated in detail. The present study cannot undertake this investigation, but we will discuss in an illustrative manner what kind of impact may be at stake. We will first look at William Shakespeare's play *Troilus and Cressida* (5.2), and then turn our attention to the remarks on akrasia in the works of three prominent early modern philosophers, Descartes, Spinoza, and Leibniz (5.3). Although we cannot present an exhaustive study of these major figures, a brief look at some prominent texts indicates the relevance of Renaissance and Reformation discussions for them.

5.2 Epilogue I: Shakespeare's *Troilus and Cressida*

People who display half-virtues and remain caught in their inner struggle have an obvious dramatic appeal. Although it is notoriously difficult to prove connections between academic and literary texts, in some cases the available evidence is illuminating. Scholars have observed that William Shakespeare (1564–1616) plays with various themes of Aristotle's *Nicomachean Ethics* (EN) in his *Troilus and Cressida* (TC). Shakespeare alludes to Aristotle's distinctions between voluntary and involuntary, as well as to the themes of choice and virtue.[1] In addition to these scholarly observations, it can be argued that Shakespeare employs three of his main characters, that is, Hector, Troilus, and Cressida, to display different variants of half-virtue and akrasia.

---

[1] Elton (1997). See also Elton (2000). Palmer (1982), 311–20 has listed the parallels between EN and *Troilus and Cressida*. I am using the orthography and line numbering of *The Norton Shakespeare (based on the Oxford Edition)* (1997).

The Trojan war hero Hector pleads for the use of reason and is inclined to have peace with the Greeks. Troilus, his younger brother, is a determined person who has no doubts about the pursuit of what he considers to be virtuous. To Hector's Aristotelian mind, his brother's precipitate conduct represents the rule of desires:

Paris and Troilus, you have both said well,
And on the cause and question now in hand
Have glossed but superficially—not much
Unlike young men, whom Aristotle thought
Unfit to hear moral philosophy.
The reasons you allege do more conduce
To the hot passion of distempered blood
Than to make up a free determination
'Twixt right and wrong (TC 2, 2, 162–170)

In TC 2, 2 Hector and Paris talk with other Trojans about the proper use of reason. Scholars have already noted that this discussion employs a variety of Aristotelian features.[2] For Hector,

modest doubt is called
The beacon of the wise, the tent that searches
To th' bottom of the worst. (TC 2, 2, 14–16)

Hector's careful rationality does not mean, however, that he does not experience inner conflict. His ability to use reason makes him see the different viewpoints simultaneously, and so his actions remain somewhat impeded by his continuing doubts. For instance, when Hector and the Greek warrior Ajax enter into a single combat, Aeneas remarks beforehand that Hector cannot fight effectively because Ajax is his relative:

This Ajax is half made of Hector's blood,
In love whereof half Hector stays at home.
Half heart, half hand, half Hector comes to seek
This blended knight, half Trojan and half Greek. (TC 4, 6, 85–88)

When the duel takes place, Aeneas is proved right. Hector only fights for a while and then refuses to continue, because he cannot harm his relative:

The obligation of our blood forbids
A gory emulation 'twixt us twain.
Were thy commixtion Greek and Trojan so
That thou couldst say 'This hand is Grecian all,
And this is Trojan; the sinews of this leg
All Greek, and this all Troy; my mother's blood
Runs on the dexter cheek, and this sinister

---

[2] For these, see in particular Elton (1997) and Bloom (2000), 90–4. Adamson (1987), 115–65 has paid some attention to the inner conflict, or 'changeful potency' (TC 4, 5, 97; see below).

Bounds in my father's', by Jove multipotent
Thou shouldst not bear from me a Greekish member
Wherein my sword had not impressure made (TC 4, 7, 7–15).

Shakespeare portrays the inner conflict in this remarkable picture of the mixed object of the will. Hector's action remains half-hearted because of the inner conflict caused by disparate rational viewpoints.

Troilus, on the other hand, does not let such considerations impede his actions. Ulysses praises Troilus because of his single-minded determination:

His heart and hand both open and both free.
For what he has he gives; what thinks he shows;
Yet gives he not till judgement guide his bounty,
Nor dignifies an impure thought with breath.
Manly as Hector but more dangerous (TC 4, 6, 103–107)

Shakespeare's text illustrates the different appearance of the inner conflict. Hector thinks that Troilus is led by passion, but in the eyes of other warriors it is Hector who remains hampered by the inner conflict, whereas his younger brother Troilus can act with determination.

Hector is the most sympathetic hero of the play, because he pleads for peace and can understand both parties. But precisely these virtues lead him to his tragic fate. In his final combat with Achilles, Hector first gains the upper hand but grants Achilles a pause to recover (TC 5, 6). When the battle is over, Hector lays down his arms and rests. In this situation Achilles and his men find him unarmed and cruelly kill him (TC 5, 9). Troilus, however, fights with determination to the bitter end. When he hears of Hector's death, he swears to haunt the coward Achilles 'like a wicked conscience' (TC 5, 11, 28).

Hector and Troilus illustrate the problems of courage, determination, and anger. In Aristotle's ethics, young people are hampered by their passions, but the case of Hector shows how the rational hero also remains hampered by the variety of available reasons. Hector's conflict does not primarily occur between reason and passion, but between different reasons. His method of taking into account the 'modest doubt' to some extent resembles the treatment of contrary simultaneous reasons in Buridan's theory of action. But, as Shakespeare employs the traditional problems of inner conflict for dramatic purposes, we should not claim that the playwright is promoting some specific philosophical view of human action. Shakespeare uses his sources playfully, making dramatic use of half-virtues.

The bride of Troilus, Cressida, exemplifies akratic conduct with regard to the varying passions of love. During their first love scene, Troilus and Cressida exchange lines which playfully allude to the academic concepts of action theory:

Cressida: Blind fear, that seeing reason leads, finds safer footing than blind reason, stumbling without fear. To fear the worst oft cures the worse

Troilus: This is the monstruosity in love, lady—that the will is infinite and the execution confined; that the desire is boundless and the act a slave to limit. (TC 3, 2, 66–77).

While Troilus repeatedly claims how his love is sincere and straight, Cressida expresses hesitations which illustrate her divided self:

I was won, my lord,
With the first glance that ever—pardon me:
If I confess much, you will play the tyrant.
I love you now, but till now not so much
But I might master it. In faith, I lie:
My thoughts were like unbridled children, grown
Too headstrong for their mother. (TC 3, 2, 106–112)

I have a kind of self resides with you—
But an unkind self, that itself will leave
To be another's fool. Where is my wit? I would be gone. (TC 3, 2, 135–137)

In spite of her reservations, Cressida remains with Troilus overnight. Next morning she hears that she will be handed over from Troy to her father Calchas, who has betrayed the Trojans and now sides with the Greeks (TC 4, 2). Cressida confesses her love for Troilus and he asks her to be faithful and strong against temptation. His vocabulary reflects the theological view of the devil as the agent behind akratic actions:

Troilus: There lurks a still and dumb-discoursive devil
That tempts most cunningly. But be not tempted.
Cressida: Do you think I will?
Troilus: No, but something may be done that we will not:
And sometimes we are devils to ourselves,
When we will tempt the frailty of our powers,
Presuming on their changeful potency. (TC 4, 5, 91–97)

The words of Troilus portray an akratic situation in which the inner conflict prompts action against one's own better judgement. Troilus fears that Cressida will behave like Medea, who knows the better but follows the worse.

The fears of Troilus are later proved right. Among the Greeks, Cressida begins to flirt with Diomedes:

Cressida: Now, my sweet guardian. Hark, a word with you . . .
Diomedes: Will you remember?
Cressida: Remember! Yes.
Diomedes: Nay, but do then,
And let your mind be coupled with your words. (TC 5, 2, 8–15)

With Diomedes, Cressida again expresses her coquettish hesitations, saying that she cannot follow him. But when Diomedes sets out to leave, Cressida changes her mind:

Diomedes: Fo, fo! Adieu; you palter.
Cressida: In faith, I do not. Come hither once again . . .
Diomedes: But will you then?
Cressida: In faith, I will, la. Never trust me else. (TC 5, 2, 47–57)

In her concluding monologue, Cressida summarizes her inner struggle with words that bear a resemblance to Medea's conflict:

Troilus, farewell. One eye yet looks on thee,
But with my heart the other eye doth see.
Ah, poor our sex! This fault in us I find,
The error of our eye directs our mind.
What error leads must err. O then conclude:
Minds swayed by eyes are full of turpitude. (TC 5, 2, 107–112)

Cressida finally sends a letter to Troilus. We are not informed of its content, but after reading the letter, Troilus, who already knows of his bride's lack of faithfulness, laments the discrepancy between her words and deeds:

Words, words, mere words, no matter from the heart.
Th' effect doth operate another way.
Go, wind, to wind: there turn and change together.
My love with words and errors still she feeds,
But edifies another with her deeds. (TC 5, 3, 109–114)

Given that Shakespeare employs themes from EN throughout the play, it is reasonable to assume that the inner conflicts of Hector and Cressida are inspired by the akratic situations which are described at length in the sixteenth-century commentaries on EN. The evidence in the texts quoted above is not sufficient to determine whether Shakespeare had some particular commentaries in mind. It is safer to say that he is creatively alluding to the commonplaces which repeatedly occur in ethical textbooks. Cressida's case is in many ways close to the sixteenth-century discussions regarding Medea in Ovid's *Metamorphoses* 7. The ethical textbooks teach that a woman under the influence of love is easily torn in a conflict between words and deeds, being drawn to her actions against her better judgement.

The case of Hector is more complex, as it reflects a conflict within the rational mind. Shakespeare shows that a prudent person does not necessarily act with determination and that the virtues of pity and non-violence can be turned against the agent. Hector's deliberation resembles the careful considerations of Buridan's action theory in which the agent acts with an awareness of conflicting evidence and different primary inclinations. Buridan does not draw the conclusion that careful deliberation weakens the strength of subsequent action, but Shakespeare plays with this possibility.

As Shakespeare makes playful allusions without wishing to write a philosophical treatise, we need to be careful in interpreting his texts. I have argued that *Troilus and Cressida* consciously employs the academic treatment of akrasia and inner struggle which is found in the commentaries on EN, as well as in other ethical textbooks. He uses the Aristotelian discussions for dramatic purposes; that is, to make Hector, Cressida, and Troilus act as individuals within the complex matrix of inner tensions, between hesitation and determination, or between reason and desire.

The characters of Shakespeare's play do not act as moral paradigms, but as individuals. The ethical textbooks provide some raw material for their personalities, but fundamentally Hector, Cressida, and Troilus are unique characters in a drama. Their deliberation and action is based on a dynamic moral psychology which varies between different agents and their unique situations. This emphasis on individual psychology allies Shakespeare with modernity. But at the same time he makes use of the interpretative tradition of Aristotelian ethics.

5.3 Epilogue II: Descartes, Spinoza, and Leibniz

Several studies have already focused on akrasia in the writings of Descartes, Spinoza, and Leibniz; and scholars have noted that all three philosophers employ Medea's 'I see the better and approve it, but follow the worse' as a convenient illustration of weakness of will.[3] The background of Medea's akrasia in Renaissance and Reformation thought has not, however, been explored.[4] In the following I will briefly comment on the three great philosophers' view of akrasia in the light of my own findings. I cannot, however, outline their philosophical theories in the comprehensive manner they would deserve.

René Descartes (1596–1650) quotes Medea's akrasia in a letter (1637) to Father Mersenne, who suspects him of Pelagianism. Descartes responds that he follows the ordinary teaching, according to which

the will does not turn to evil, unless the intellect represents it to the will under some aspect of goodness. Whence the saying, 'every sinner is ignorant', such that if the understanding never represents anything as good to the will when it is not so, the will could not fail in its choice. But the understanding often represents to it different things at the same time; whence the saying 'I see the better and approve it', which only concerns feeble spirits.[5]

This quote in many ways follows the traditional scholastic views of akrasia (1.3–1.5) The weak or feeble spirits can be called akratic in the sense that they see some aspects of the better alternative but cannot follow it firmly and consistently. McCarthy has studied Descartes's use of the expression 'feeble spirits', coming to the conclusion that 'from his first publication to his last, Descartes maintains that "vice ordinarily comes from ignorance"'. Because of this intellectualism, Descartes does not allow for clear-eyed akrasia, although the kind of weakness which is due to the motions of the spirits remains a problem for him. For Descartes, some of these motions have an evil foundation and prompt moral weakness.[6]

---

[3] Descartes: Ong-Van-Cung (2003); Alanen (2003), 208–58; McCarthy (2008). Spinoza: Savile (2003); Koivuniemi (2008). Leibniz: Vailati (1990); Davidson (2005); Roinila (2007).

[4] With the exception of McCarthy (2008), 178, who uses Saarinen (2006).

[5] AT 1, 366. Translation from McCarthy (2008), 177–8; translation of Latin phrases (within quotation marks) by myself. Cf. Ong-Van-Cung (2003), 735–6.

[6] McCarthy (2008), 208–9.

Several scholars have focused their attention on Descartes's two letters to Mesland in 1644 and 1645. In the first, Descartes claims that the light of the intellect prompts the will to desire and act, but it is possible to turn the mind to other reasons so that it suspends or even changes its judgement concerning action.[7] The second letter seems to promote a more voluntaristic view, since it speaks of the will as 'a positive faculty of determining oneself to one or the other of two contraries, that is to say, to purse or avoid, to affirm or deny'. Descartes further says that 'it is always open to us to hold back from pursuing a clearly known good . . . provided we consider it a good thing to demonstrate our freedom by so doing'.[8]

Without entering into the extensive debate concerning the mutual compatibility of the two letters[9] and their relationship to the letter of 1637, we can remark that all three texts resemble the views of Buridan (1.5) and Mair (2.5). Buridan considered that the freedom of the will largely consisted in its ability to suspend the final judgement. Buridan further taught that one can act against one's own better judgement in situations of uncertainty in which some reasons support both of the contrary alternatives. Thus for the feeble spirit, 'different things' are represented to the will 'at the same time', as the letter of 1637 suggests. Ong-Van-Cung has argued that the weak and 'feeble' minds are for Descartes characterized by a lack of clarity and determination. Because of the imperfect nature of their judgement, they can postpone their good action and act against their better judgement.[10]

This interpretation resembles Buridan's theory of postponement as well as Mair's view of the so-called 'mixed actions', which for Mair exemplify akratic conduct. In a mixed action, different things appear under different aspects of goodness; thus the will remains mixed. The seemingly voluntarist letter of 1645 in fact exemplifies this situation: while there is a clearly known good, the agent also considers it a good thing to demonstrate his or her freedom of postponement. Given this, Descartes can combine his intellectualism with free will in a manner which resembles the compatibilist positions of Buridan and Mair. His doctrine of the motion of the spirits also links him with Melanchthon (3.3).

Baruch Spinoza (1632–1677) quotes Medea's words twice in the fourth book of his *Ethics* (1677). The title of this book is 'On Human Bondage, or the Powers of the Affects'. In its preface he says that the individual's

lack of power to moderate and restrain the affects I call Bondage. For the man who is subject to affects is under the control, not of himself, but of fortune, in whose power he so greatly is that often, though he sees the better for himself, he is still forced to follow the worse.[11]

---

[7] AT 4, 116; Alanen (2003), 242. Ong-Van-Cung (2003), 736–7.

[8] AT 4, 173; Alanen (2003), 230.

[9] See Ong-Van-Cung (2003), 734–43; Alanen (2003), 240–6.

[10] Ong-Van-Cung (2003), 736–9.

[11] *Ethica*, IV Praef. (G, 205). I am for the most part using Bennett's (2008) internet translation, which renders the scholastic terms in a particularly precise manner.

Words like 'bondage' and 'affect' were extensively used in ethical textbooks at least since Melanchthon (3.3), but Spinoza's programme is highly original, as he claims that the knowledge of good and evil is nothing but 'an affect of pleasure or unpleasure of which we are conscious'.[12]

The overall project of Spinoza is to explain psychological phenomena in a naturalist fashion. The essence of the human being consists for him in the power of *conatus*, in the striving to persevere. The affects are changes in this power.[13] 'Contrary affects' are those that drive the person in contrary directions at the same time. They are not naturally contrary, but only accidentally, that is, regarding a particular situation.[14] A stronger contrary affect can overcome a weaker affect; this is the only way to restrain or to remove an affect.[15] Because the changes of affect require a contrary power, the doctrine of simultaneous contrary powers or affects has great theoretical importance for Spinoza.

As knowledge is represented through the affect, the traditional conflict between reason and desire appears for Spinoza in terms of contrary affects, which appear within the matrix of the following rules:

14. True knowledge of good and evil cannot restrain any affect through the truth that it contains, but only through its strength as an affect.
15. A desire arising from true knowledge of good and evil is not made invulnerable by its coming from that source. On the contrary it can be extinguished or restrained by many other desires arising from other affects by which we are tormented.
16. A desire arising from knowledge of good and evil, when the knowledge concerns the future, can quite easily be restrained or extinguished by a desire for things that are attractive now.
17. A desire arising from a true knowledge of good and evil, when it emerges from contingent things, can be restrained much more easily by a desire for things that are present.[16]

This naturalist analysis of knowledge denies the intellectualist axiom that knowledge is by its essence stronger than the appetitive desires. In a conflict situation, true knowledge can easily be overcome by other, contrary affects which plead for present attractions.

The second mention of Medea's akrasia occurs in the note that follows proposition 17:

With this I believe I have shown why men are moved more by opinion than by true reason, and why the true knowledge of good and evil creates disturbances of the mind, and often yields to low desires of all kinds. Hence the words of the poet, 'I see and approve the better; I follow the worse'.[17]

---

[12] *Ethica*, IV prop. 8 (G, 215).
[13] For this basic terminology of Spinoza, see e.g. Shirley (1982); Nadler (2008).
[14] *Ethica*, IV def 5 (G, 209–10).
[15] *Ethica*, IV prop. 7 (G, 214).
[16] *Ethica*, IV props 14–17 (G, 219–21).
[17] *Ethica*, IV, note on props 14–17 (G, 221).

Spinoza's explanation of akrasia is relatively simple: because knowledge does not necessarily generate an affect which is stronger than the contrary affects to do otherwise, akrasia can occur.[18] This explanation resembles our model of 'commonplace Platonism', but Spinoza's naturalist approach to knowledge differs from older theories so radically that it may not be adequate to label it in this manner.

It is nevertheless interesting that the topic of contrary affects, a *leitmotif* (cf. 5.1) of our study, has such a great significance in Spinoza's theory of action. In keeping with this, Spinoza uses the words denoting a struggle or fight between contrary powers fairly often in *Ethics IV*.[19] For instance, he teaches that hate can be overcome not by hate, but by the contrary affect of love: 'If you try to avenge wrongs by hating in return, you'll live a miserable life indeed. Whereas if you devote yourself to battling against hate with love, you'll have a fight that you can take pleasure in.'[20] The traditional theme of *pugna* is transformed into a comprehensive mastery of affects in Spinoza's ethics.

The recent studies by Savile and Koivuniemi have refined the analysis of Spinoza's account of Medea. Savile has, among other things, observed that Medea's better option lies in the future, while the worse option for her is in the present. This concurs with Spinoza's proposition 16. Koivuniemi concludes that Medea's love is blameworthy because it appears to be obsessive and therefore contrary to reason.[21] While these observations are illuminating, one also needs to see that Spinoza is not really interpreting Ovid but using Medea's example as a standard shorthand to signal that a traditional problem has now been addressed.

The quotations by G. W. Leibniz (1646–1716) of *Metam.* 7, 20–21 have been systematically studied by Davidson. Leibniz uses these quotations several times. In his early *Confessio Philosophi* (1672/3), Leibniz holds in an intellectualist manner that Medea's words cannot be taken literally. She actually considers that pleasure is the greater good and does not follow the worse. Leibniz here confuses Medea's love with her rage:

Theologian: But what will you say to the well-known expression 'I see the better and approve it, but I follow the worse'.

Philosopher: What? Just this—if it is not correctly understood, it is absurd. Medea, whose words those are, as written by Ovid, meant this by them. She saw the injustice of her deed when she slaughtered her own children, but nevertheless the pleasure of revenge prevailed as if it were a greater good than the wicked deed was evil.[22]

This basically intellectualist view remains Leibniz's position. In his later works, however, Leibniz admits that the apparent pleasure may cause something which is not

---

[18] For a fuller discussion, see Della Rocca (1996).

[19] *Ethica*, IV: *pugna*: prop. 59 corollary (G, 262); *repugnantia*: note on prop. 18 (G, 222); *repugnare*: props 51, 58, note on prop. 37, proof of prop. 48 (G, 248, 253, 236, 246); *pugnare* and *expugnare*: note on prop. 46 (G, 245).

[20] *Ethica*, IV, note on prop. 46 (G, 245).

[21] Savile (2003), 772–4; Koivuniemi (2008), 227–35.

[22] Leibniz, *Confessio philosophi*, 72–3. Cf. Davidson (2005), 237.

merely an erroneous preference but conduct which resembles akrasia. In *Theodicy* (1710) Leibniz writes:

These words which Ovid ascribes to Medea, 'I see the better and approve it, but follow the worse', imply that the morally good is mastered by the agreeably good which makes more impression on souls when they are disturbed by passions.[23]

He employs this argument in *Theodicy* to say that free will chooses in accordance with goodness; in this sense, he remains on the intellectualist path. Leibniz develops his view in his *Nouvaux Essais* (1704) in order to respond to John Locke's doctrine of 'uneasiness', as outlined in his *An Essay Concerning Human Understanding*.[24]

Locke uses this doctrine to show how a person can act against his better judgement, quoting Ovid's Medea in this context. For Locke, uneasiness is an affective and habitual power which can determine the will even contrary to the dictates of reason.[25] Leibniz argues against Locke that the agent is motivated by what he or she believes to be the greater good. Leibniz nevertheless admits that there is something like unconscious disquiet which can confuse the mind. Deliberation contains a multitude of 'imperceptible little urges which keep us constantly in suspense'. They cause disquiet which accompanies the pursuit of the greater good.[26]

In order to choose the right, the agent must have a clear sense of all aspects related to the particular case. In akratic action, some of this sensitivity is lacking:

If we prefer the worse it is because we have a sense of the good it contains but not of the evil it contains or of the good which exists in the opposite side... The finest moral precepts and the best prudential rules in the world have weight only in a soul which is as sensitive to them as to what opposes them.[27]

Although Leibniz continues to defend the intellectualist cause in *Nouvaux Essais*, he admits that akratic agents can deceive themselves:

It is a daily occurrence for men to act against what they know; they conceal it from themselves by turning their thoughts aside, so as to follow their passions. Otherwise we would not find people eating and drinking what they know will make them ill or even kill them.[28]

Scholars have interpreted this view as 'weak intellectualism'[29] or as 'two-dimensional'[30] intellectualism. A person generally pursues the greater good which he or she knows, but

---

[23] *Théodicée*, §154; cf. §297. Translation: *Theodicy*, 220.

[24] For this, see Vailati (1990) and Roinila (2007), 213–29.

[25] Locke, *Essay*, 2, 21, 35. Locke also uses the example of drunkard—not, however, like Aristotle (EN 1147b12) but like Camerarius (focus on short-time pleasure; see also the use of this example in Melanchthon and Heider, 3.3–3.4). For Locke's view of uneasiness and akrasia, see Vailati (1990) and Glauser (2003).

[26] *Nouveaux Essais*, 2,20, 6–10. Vailati (1990), 217–18; Roinila (2007), 213–29.

[27] *Nouveaux Essais*, 2, 21, 31 Translation from Vailati (1990), 220.

[28] *Nouveaux Essais*, 1, 2, 11. Translation from Roinila (2007), 216.

[29] Davidson (2005), 250–1.

[30] Vailati (1990), 221.

the immediate sense perceptions of the present may confuse this general course so that the agent acts akratically. Although the dimension of proper knowledge is in order, the perceptual knowledge of the immediate particulars can become confused, the 'little urges' of disquiet contributing to this state of affairs. Scholars have argued that Leibniz's view resembles that of Thomas Aquinas.[31]

It is also important to see another tradition, namely that which runs from Buridan through the Lutheran commentators. In this tradition, moral knowledge typically remains uncertain or confused and sense perception becomes the crucial effective cause of action (3.3–3.4, 5.1). Like Buridan and others in this tradition, Leibniz advises the agents to postpone their decisions in order to obtain sufficient sensitivity regarding the matter in question.[32]

In the discussion with Locke, Leibniz proceeds from the premise that the multitude of perceptions prompts disquiet and even confusion, as we have seen. Although knowledge generally pursues the greater good in an intellectualist fashion, the immediate surroundings of the moral agent remain conditioned by what appears to be good for the agent *prima facie*, here and now. We saw in 3.3 that Joachim Camerarius considered the small errors in immediate particulars to be 'the cause of all evil'. Although Leibniz is less voluntarist than Melanchthon and Camerarius, the careful attention he pays to the confusing elements of deliberation and the small errors of perception continues this Lutheran tradition.

Although we have highlighted the connections between Descartes, Spinoza, and Leibniz and the ethical traditions of the Renaissance and the Reformation, we can also see that the three early modern classics employ traditional themes to suit their own philosophical purposes. These new interests promote new ways of understanding moral psychology. Spinoza's naturalism and the development towards empiricism in Descartes, Leibniz, and Locke are new trends, but the new currents of early modern thought build upon the often invisible background of the Renaissance and the Reformation. The present study has attempted to make this background more visible and more explicit.

---

[31] See Davidson (2005), 250, 252.
[32] *Nouveaux Essais*, 2, 21, 47. Vailati (1990), 225.

Sources and Literature

Ancient, Medieval, and Early Modern Sources

Abelard, Peter, *Sic et non*, ed. Blanche Boyer and Richard McKeon (Chicago: The University of Chicago Press, 1976–1977).

Albert the Great, *Opera omnia*, ed. A. Borgnet. Vol. 7: *Ethicorum libri X* [Ethica II] (Paris: Vivés, 1891).

——, *Opera omnia, curavit Institutum Alberti Magni Coloniense*. Vol. 14: *Super Ethica commentum et quaestiones* [Ethica I]. Vol. 25/1: *De natura boni*. Vol. 28: *De bono* (Münster: Aschendorff, 1951–1987).

Aristoteles latinus, ed. L. Minio-Paluello, G. Verbere. Vol. 26, 1–3: *Ethica Nicomachea,* ed. R. A. Gauthier (Leiden: Brill, 1972–1974).

Aristotle, *Ethica Nicomachea*. Latin translation of Johannes Argyropoulos. Included in Donato Acciaiuoli, *Expositio* (1565) and Lefèvre d'Étaples, *Tres Conversiones* (1497).

Aristotle in Twenty-Three Volumes. Loeb Classical Library (Cambridge, Mass.: Harvard University Press, 1973).

Aristotle, *The Complete Works*, vols 1–2, ed. Jonathan Barnes (Princeton: Princeton University Press, 1985).

Augustine, *Opera omnia. Patrologia latina*, vols 32–47. [PL] Vol. 34: *De sermone Domini in monte*. Vols 36–37: *Enarrationes in Psalmos*. Vol. 44: *Contra Iulianum*. Vol. 45: *Contra Iulianum opus imperfectum*. (Paris: Lutetiae Parisiorum, 1844–1864).

——, *Opera omnia*. Corpus Scriptorum Ecclesiasticorum Latinorum. [CSEL]. Vol. 25/1: *Contra Faustum manichaeum*. Vol. 33: *Confessiones*. Vol. 36: *Retractationes*. Vol. 41: *De continentia*. Vol. 42: *De nuptiis et concupiscentia*. Vol. 60: *De spiritu et litera*. Vol. 84: *Expositio quarundam propositionum ex epistula Apostoli ad Romanos*. Vol. 85.1: *Contra Iulianum opus imperfectum 1–3*. (Wien: Tempsky, 1865–).

——, *Commentary on the Lord's Sermon on the Mount*, trans. D. J. Havanagh (Washington: The Catholic University of America Press, 1951).

——, *The Spirit and the Letter*, trans. J. Burnaby, in Augustine, *Later Works* (Philadelphia: The Westminster Press 1955), 182–250.

——, *Confessions*, trans. V. J. Bourke (Washington: The Catholic University of America Press, 1966).

Bede, Adam, *Ecclesiastical History of the English People*, ed. B. Colgrave and R. A. B. Mynors (Oxford: Clarendon Press, 1991).

Boethias, *Theological Tractates. The Consolation of Philosophy*. Loeb Classical Library (Cambridge, Mass: Harvard University Press, 1973).

Buridan, John, *Questiones super decem libros Ethicorum* (Paris, 1513). Reprint (Frankfurt: Minerva, 1968).

——, *Quaestiones super decem libros Ethicorum Aristotelis ad Nicomachum* (Oxford, 1637). [See also Pironet (2001) in Modern Literature]

Burley, Walter, *Expositio super decem libros Ethicorum Aristotelis* (Venice, 1521).

Calvin, John, *Ioannis Calvini opera quae supersunt omnia*, vol. 1–59, in *Corpus Reformatorum*, vols 29–87. [CO] Vol. 2: *Institutio christianae religionis (1559)*. Vol. 7: *Vera ecclesiae reformandae ratio*.

Vol. 8: *De scandalis*. Vol. 10: *Epistolae*. Vol. 49: *Commentarius in epistolam Pauli ad Romanos; Commentarius in epistolam Pauli ad Corinthios I*. (Braunschweig: Schwetschke, 1863–1900).

Calvin, John, *Calvin's Commentaries in 22 Volumes* (Grand Rapids: Baker, 2005).

——, *Institutes of the Christian Religion*, vols 1–2, ed. John T. McNeill (Louisville: Westminster John Knox Press, 2006). [ICR]

Camerarius, Joachim, *Explicatio librorum Ethicorum ad Nicomachum* (Frankfurt, 1578).

Case, John, *Speculum moralium quaestionum* (Oxford, 1585). Digital edition and translation of this print by Dana F. Sutton (2003) at www.philological.bham.ac.uk/speculum

Cicero, *On Duties* [De officiis]. Loeb Classical Library (Cambridge, Mass.: Harvard University Press, 1913).

——, *On Ends* [De finibus]. Loeb Classical Library (Cambridge, Mass.: Harvard University Press, 1914).

Clichtove, Josse, *Dogma moralium philosophorum* (Strasbourg, 1512).

—— and Lefèvre d'Étaples, Jacques, *Artificialis introductio in X libros ethicorum, elucidate commentariis Clichtovaei* (Paris, 1514).

Daneau, Lambert, *Ethices Christianae libri tres* (Geneva, 1583).

Descartes, René, *Oeuvres de Descartes*, ed. Charles Adam and Paul Tannery, 12 vols (Paris: Vrin, 1964–1976). [AT]

Donato Acciaiuoli, *Expositio super libros Ethicorum Aristotelis* (Venice, 1565).

Epictetus, *Discourses. Fragments. The Encheiridion*, vols 1–2. Loeb Classical Library (Cambridge, Mass.: Harvard University Press, 1925, 1928).

Erasmus von Rotterdam, *De libero arbitrio diatribe sive collatio*, in Erasmus, *Ausgewählte Schriften*, 4 (Darmstadt: Wissenschaftliche Buchgesellschaft, 1969).

Euripides, *Cyclops, Alcestis, Medea*. Loeb Classical Library (Cambridge, Mass.: Harvard University Press, 1994).

Ficino, Marsilio, *Commentary on Plato's Symposium on Love*, trans. Sears Jayne (Dallas: Spring Publications, 1985).

Galen, *De placitis Hippocratis et Platonis*, ed. P. de Lacy (Berlin: Akademie-Verlag, 1978–1984).

Giffen, Hubert van, *Commentarii in X libros Ethicorum* (Frankfurt, 1608).

Golius, Theophilus, *Epitome doctrinae politicae* (Strasbourg, 1606).

——, *Epitome doctrinae moralis* (Strasbourg, 1615).

——, *Epitome doctrinae oeconomiae* (Strasbourg, 1622).

Heider, Wolfgang, *Philosophiae moralis systema* (Jena, 1628).

——, *Philosophiae politicae systema* (Jena, 1628).

Henry of Ghent, *Quodlibeta*, ed. J. Badius (Paris, 1518). Reprint (Leuven: Bibliothéque S.J., 1961).

——, *Opera omnia*, ed. R. Macken et al. (Leuven: Leuven University Press, 1979–).

Horatius, *Satires. Epistles. The Art of Poetry*. Loeb Classical Library (Cambridge, Mass.: Harvard University Press, 1926).

Keckermann, Bartholomaeus, *Systema logicae* (Hanau, 1600).

——, *Systema ethicae* (London, 1607).

——, *Systema rhetoricae* (Hanau, 1608).

Lambin, Denys, *In libros De moribus ad Nicomachum annotationes* (Venice, 1558).

Lefèvre d'Étaples, Jacques, *X librorum moralium Aristotelis tres conversiones* (Paris, 1497 and Paris, 1505).

——, Jacques and Clichtove, Josse, *Artificialis introductio in X libros ethicorum, elucidate commentariis Clichtovaei* (Paris, 1514).

Leibniz, G. W., *Die philosophischen Schriften*, ed. C. I. Gerhardt, Vol. 6: *Essais de Theodicée*. (Berlin: Weidmann 1875–1890).

——, *Sämtliche Schriften und Briefe*, ed. Deutsche Akademie der Wissenschaften, Series 6, vol. 6: *Nouveaux essais sur l'entendement humain.* (Berlin: Akademie-Verlag 1923–).

——, *Theodicy*, trans. E. M. Huggard (New Haven: Yale University Press, 1975).

——, *Confessio Philosophi. Papers Concerning the Problem of Evil, 1671–1678*, ed. Robert C. Sleigh (New Haven: Yale University Press, 2005).

Locke, John, *An Essay Concerning Human Understanding*, ed. Peter H. Nidditch (Oxford: Clarendon Press, 1975).

Lombard, Peter, *Sententiae in IV libris distinctae.* (GrottaFerrata: Collegium St Bonaventurae, 1971–1981).

Long, A. A. and Sedley, D. N. *The Hellenistic Philosopher 1–2* (Cambridge: Cambridge University Press, 1987). [Long. sedley]

Luther, Martin, *D. Martin Luthers Werke. Kritische Gesamtausgabe.* [WA] Vol. 1: *Disputatio Heidelbergae habita.* Vol. 2: *Disputatio Iohannis Eccii et Martini Lutheri Lipsiae habita.* Vol. 5: *Operationes in Psalmos.* Vol. 6: *Von den guten Werken.* Vol. 9: *Luthers Randbemerkungen zu den Sentenzen des Petrus Lombardus.* Vol.18: *De servo arbitrio.* Vol. 30/1: *Der grosse Katechismus.* Vol. 39/2: *Die Promotionsdisputation von Joachim Mörlin.* Vols 42–4: *Genesisvorlesung.* Vol. 55: *Dictata super Psalterium.* Vol. 56: *Römerbriefvorlesung. Briefwechsel* [WABr], vol. 1. (Weimar: Böhlau 1883–2009).

——, *Luther's Works.* American Edition (Philadelphia: Fortress, 1955–1986).

——, *Studienausgabe*, Vol. 2: *De libertate Christiana; Rationis Latomianae confutatio.* (Berlin: Evangelische Verlagsanstalt, 1979–1999). [LSA].

Lutrea, Johannes de, *Exercitium librorum de anima* (Erfurt, 1482).

Mair, John, *Ethica Aristotelis Peripateticorum principis, Cum Ioannes Maioris Theologi Parisiensi Commentariis* (Paris, 1530).

Melanchthon, Philip, *Opera quae supersunt omnia.* Corpus reformatorum [CR], vols 1–28. Vol. 10: *Orationes Philippi Melanthonis.* Vol. 13: *Liber de anima.* Vol. 14: *Annotationes in Evangelia.* Vol. 15: *Annotationes in Epist. Pauli ad Romanos; Commentarii in Epist. Pauli ad Romanos; Enarratio Epist. Pauli ad Romanos.* Vol. 18: *Enarratio Hesiodei poematis inscripti opera et dies; Interpretatio medeae Euripidis.* Vol. 19: *Enarratio Metamorphoseon Ovidii.* Vol 21: *Loci communes: prima aetas; secunda aetas; tertia aetas.* Vol. 23: *Enarratio symboli Niceni; Explicatio symboli Niceni.* Vols 24–25: *Postillae Melanthonianae.* (Halle-Braunschweig: Schwetschke, 1834–1860).

——, *Werke in Auswahl* Vol. II: *Loci communes.* (Gütersloh: Gütersloher Verlagshaus, 1951–1975). [Studienausgabe, MSA].

——, *Loci communes 1521: Lateinisch-deutsch* (Gütersloh: Gütersloher Verlagshaus, 1993).

——, *Ethicae doctrinae elementa. Lateinisch-deutsch* (Stuttgart: Frommann-holzboog, 2008).

Origen, *De principiis libri IV*, ed. H. Görgemanns and H. Karpp (Darmstadt: Wissenschaftliche Buchgesellschaft, 1976).

Ovid, *Metamorphoses*, vols 1–2. Loeb Classical Library (Cambridge, Mass.: Harvard University Press, 1916).

Petrarch, *On His Own Ignorance and That of Many Others*, in Ernst Cassirer et al. (eds), *The Renaissance Philosophy of Man* (Chicago: Chicago University Press, 1948), 49–133.

Petrarch, *Secretum*, in G. Martellotti et al. (eds), *Prose*, vol. 7 (Milan: Riccardo Riccardi, 1955), 21–215.

——, *De remediis utriusque fortunae*, in *Vita di Francesco Petrarca*, digital text collection at http://tuttotempolibero.altervista.org/poesia/trecento/francescopetrarca.html. Also in *Francesco Petrarcae Opera quae extant omnia* (Basel, 1554). Reprint (Ridgewood: Gregg Press, 1965).

——, *Opere latine* 1–2. ed. A. Bufano (Torino: Unione tipografico-editrice torinese, 1987).

——, *Petrarch's Secretum with Introduction, Notes, and Critical Anthology*, ed. Davy A. Carozza and H. James Shey (New York: Peter Lang, 1989).

——, *Petrarch's Remedies for Fortune Fair and Foul*, ed. C. H. Rawski, vols 1–5 (Bloomington: Indiana University Press, 1991).

Petrus Tartaretus, *Expositio in sex priores Aristotelis libros Moralium* (Paris, 1496).

Piccolomini, Francesco, *Universa philosophia de moribus* (Frankfurt, 1595).

Plato, *Laches; Protagoras; Meno; Euthydemus. Republic 1–2*. Loeb Classical Library (Cambridge, Mass.: Harvard University Press, 1924, 1930–1935).

——, *The Collected Dialogues*, ed. Edith Hamilton and Huntington Cairns (Princeton: Princeton University Press, 1994).

Plutarch, *Moralia*, vols 1–15. Loeb Classical Library (Cambridge, Mass.; Harvard University Press, 1927–1969).

Richard of Mediavilla, *Super quatuor libros Sententiarum* (Brixiae, 1591). Reprint (Frankfurt: Minerva, 1963).

Shakespeare, William, *The Norton Shakespeare (based on the Oxford Edition)* (New York: Norton, 1997).

Spinoza, Baruch, *Opera* 1–4, ed. C. Gebhardt. Vol. 2: *Ethica Ordine Geometrico Demonstrata*. Reprint (Heidelberg: C. Winter, 1972). [G]

——, *Ethics Demonstrated in Geometrical Order*, trans. J. Bennett. Digital edition (2008) at http://www.earlymoderntexts.com/sp.html

Staupitz, Johannes, *Sämtliche Schriften: Abhandlungen, Predigten, Zeugnisse*. Vol. 1: Tübinger Predigten [Sermons]. Vol. 2. Abhandlungen [De predestinatione] (Berlin: de Gruyter, 1979, 1987).

Stobaeus, *Anthologium*, ed. C. Wachsmuth and O. Hense (Berlin: Weidmann, 1958).

Stoicorum veterum fragmenta 1–4, ed. Hans von Arnim (Leipzig: Teubner, 1903–1905).

Themistius, *On Aristotle's On the Soul*, trans. Robert B. Todd (Ithaca: Cornell University Press, 1996).

Thomas Aquinas, *Opera omnia*, ed. Leonina. Vols 4–12: *Summa theologiae*. Vol. 23: *De malo*. Vol. 47, 1–2: *Sententia libri Ethicorum* (Vatican: Vatican Polyglot Press, 1888–1982).

Trutfetter, Jodocus, *Summa in totam physicen* (Erfurt, 1514).

Usingen, Bartholomaeus Arnoldi de, *Parvulus philosophie naturalis* (Leipzig, 1499).

——, *Compendium naturalis philosophie* (Erfurt, 1507).

——, *Exercitium de anima* (Erfurt, 1507).

Velcurio, Johannes, *In philosophiae naturalis partem omnium praestantissam, hoc est Aristotelis de Anima libros, epitome longe doctissima* (Basel, 1537).

Vermigli, Petrus, *In I–III libros Ethicorum commentarius* (Zürich, 1563).

Versor, John, *Quaestiones super libros ethicorum Aristotelis* (Cologne, 1494). Reprint (Frankfurt: Minerva, 1967).

Vettori, Pier, *Commentarii in X libros Aristotelis De moribus ad Nicomachum* (Florence, 1584).

Walter of Bruges, *Quaestiones disputatae*, ed. E. Longpré (Leuven, 1928).

Wellendorffer, Virgilius, *Moralogium ex Aristotelis ethicorum libris* (Leipzig, 1509).

Xenophon, *Cyropaedia*, vols 1–2. Loeb Classical Library (Cambridge, Mass.: Harvard University Press, 1914, 1921).

——, *Memorabilia and Oeconomicus. Symposium and Apology*. Loeb Classical Library (Cambridge, Mass.: Harvard University Press, 1923).

Zwinger, Theodor, *Theatrum vitae humanae* (Basel, 1565).

——, *Aristotelis Stagiritae de moribus ad Nicomachum libri decem, tabulis perpetuis, quae Commentariorum loco esse quaeant, explicati et illustrati* (Basel, 1566).

Modern Literature

Adams, Marilyn McCord, *William Ockham 1–2* (Notre Dame: University of Notre Dame Press, 1987).

Adamson, Jane, *Troilus and Cressida* (Brighton: Harvester Press, 1987).

Alanen, Lilli, *Descartes's Concept of Mind* (Cambridge, Mass.: Harvard University Press, 2003).

Bayer, Oswald, *Martin Luthers Theologie* (Tübingen: Mohr Siebeck, 2003).

Bellucci, Dino, 'Natural Philosophy and Ethics in Melanchthon', in Kraye and Saarinen (2005), 235–54.

Bianchi, Luca, 'Un commento "umanistico" ad Aristotele. L'Expositio super libros Ethicorum di Donato Acciaiuoli', *Rinascimento* 30 (1990), 25–55.

Bloom, Allan David, *Shakespeare on Love and Friendship* (Chicago: University of Chicago Press, 2000).

Bobonich, Christoph, 'Plato on Akrasia and Knowing Your Own Mind', in Bobonich and Destrée (2007), 41–60.

—— and Destrée, Pierre (eds), *Akrasia in Greek Philosophy. From Socrates to Plotinus* (Leiden: Brill, 2007).

Bradley, Denis J. M., 'Thomas Aquinas on Weakness of the Will', in Hoffmann (2008), 82–114.

Brecht, Martin, *Martin Luther 1–3* (Minneapolis: Augsburg Fortress, 1993–1999).

Brett, Annabel, 'Natural Right and Civil Community: The Civil Philosophy of Hugo Grotius', *The Historical Journal* 45 (2002), 31–51.

Broadie, Alexander, *The Circle of John Mair* (Oxford: Oxford University Press, 1987).

——, *The Tradition of Scottish Philosophy* (Edinburgh: T&T Clark, 1990).

Bultmann, Christoph, Leppin, Volker, and Lindner, Andreas (eds), *Luther und das monastische Erbe* (Tübingen: Mohr Siebeck, 2007).

Burger, Christoph, 'Der Augustinschüler gegen die modernen Pelagianer: Das auxilium speciale Dei in der Gnadenlehre Gregors von Rimini', in Heiko Oberman (ed.), *Gregor von Rimini: Werk und Wirkung bis zur Reformation* (Berlin: de Gruyter, 1981), 195–240.

Burnell, Peter, 'Concupiscence', in A.D. Fitzgerald (1999), 224–7.

Carozza, D. A., 'Petrarchan Studies and the Secretum', in Carozza and Shey (1989), 3–8.

—— and Shey, H. J. (eds), *Petrarch's Secretum with Introduction, Notes, and Critical Anthology* (Frankfurt: Peter Lang, 1989).

Chappell, T. D. J., *Aristotle and Augustine on Freedom. Two Theories of Freedom, Voluntary Action, and Akrasia* (New York: St. Martin's Press, 1995).

Charles, David, *Aristotle's Philosophy of Action* (London: Duckworth, 1984).

Charles, David, 'Aristotle's Weak Akrates: What Does Her Ignorance Consist In?', in Bobonich and Destrée (2007), 193–214.

Charlton, William, *Weakness of Will: A Philosophical Introduction* (Oxford: Blackwell, 1988).

Colish, Marcia L., *The Stoic Tradition from Antiquity to the Early Middle Ages I–II* (Leiden: Brill, 1985).

Collijn, Isak, 'Magister Virgilius Wellendorffer i Leipzig och hans svenska förbindelser', in *Nordisk tidskrift för bok- och biblioteksväsen* 21 (1934), 101–12.

Copenhaver, Brian P. and Schmitt, Charles B., *Renaissance Philosophy* (Oxford: Oxford University Press, 2002).

Courcelle, Pierre, 'Petrarch, St. Augustine, and the Augustinians of the XIV Century', in Carozza and Shey (1989), 217–25.

Courtenay, William J., *Schools and Scholars in Fourteenth-Century England* (Princeton: Princeton University Press, 1987).

Dahl, N.O., *Practical Reason, Aristotle and Weakness of the Will* (Minneapolis: University of Minnesota Press, 1984).

Davidson, Donald, 'How is Weakness of the Will Possible?', in J. Feinberg (ed.), *Moral Concepts* (Oxford: Oxford University Press, 1969), 93–113.

Davidson, Jack D., 'Video meliora proboque, deteriora sequor: Leibniz on the Intellectual Source of Sin', in D. Rutherford and J.A. Cover (eds), *Leibniz: Nature and Freedom* (Oxford: Oxford University Press, 2005), 234–54.

deGreef, Wulfert, *The Writings of John Calvin: An Introductory Guide* (Grand Rapids: Baker, 1989).

Della Rocca, Michael, *Representation and the Mind–Body Problem in Spinoza* (Oxford: Oxford University Press, 1996).

Denzer, Horst, *Moralphilosophie und Naturrecht bei Samuel Pufendorf* (München: Beck, 1972).

Denzinger, Heinrich and Hünermann, Peter (eds), *Enchiridion Symbolorum Definitionum et Declarationum de Rebus Fidei et Morum*. 37th ed. (Freiburg: Herder, 1991)

Dieter, Theodor, *Der junge Luther und Aristoteles* (Berlin: de Gruyter, 2001).

Dihle, Albrecht, *The Theory of Will in Classical Antiquity* (Berkeley: University of California Press, 1982).

Dillon, John M., 'Medea among the philosophers', in J. J. Clauss and S. I. Johnston (eds), *Medea: Essays on Medea in Myth, Literature, and Philosophy* (Princeton: Princeton University Press, 1997), 211–18.

Doig, James C., *Aquinas's Philosophical Commentary on the Ethics: A Historical Perspective* (Dordrecht: Kluwer, 2001).

Dorion, Louis-André, 'Akrasia et enkrateia dans les Mémorables de Xénophon', *Dialogue: Canadian Philosophical Review* 42 (2003), 645–72.

Dorter, Kenneth, 'Weakness of Will in Plato's Republic', in Hoffmann (2008), 1–21.

Ebbesen, Sten, *Den danske filosofins historie. Bind 2: Dansk filosofi i renaessancen 1537–1700* (Copenhagen: Gyldendal, 2003).

Ebeling, Gerhard, *Lutherstudien II/2: Disputatio de homine* (Tübingen: Mohr Siebeck, 1982).

Elton, W. R., 'Aristotle's Nicomachean Ethics and Shakespeare's Troilus and Cressida', *Journal of the History of Ideas* 58 (1997), 331–7.

——, *Shakespeare's 'Troilus and Cressida' and the Inns of Court Revels* (Aldershot: Ashgate, 2000).

Engberg-Pedersen, Troels, 'The Reception of Graeco-Roman Culture in the New Testament: The Case of Romans 7.7–25' in: M. Müller and H. Tronier (eds), *The New Testament as Reception* (Sheffield: Sheffield University Press, 2002), 32–57.

Fidora, Alexander, 'Die Behandlung der Unbeherrschtheit in der *Summa Alexandrinorum*', in Hoffmann, Müller, and Perkams (2006), 173–96.

Fiering, Norman, *Moral Philosophy at Harvard* (Chapel Hill: University of North Carolina Press, 1981).

Fitzgerald, A. D. (ed.), *Augustine through the Ages* (Grand Rapids: Eerdmans, 1999).

Frank, Günter, *Die theologische Philosophie Philipp Melanchthons* (Leipzig: St. Benno, 1995).

——, 'The Reason of Acting: Melanchthon's Concept of Practical Philosophy and the Question of the Unity and Consistency of His Philosophy', in Kraye and Saarinen (2005), 217–33.

—— et al. (eds), *Melanchthon und Europa. Bd 1: Skandinavien und Mitteleuropa. Bd. 2: Westeuropa* (Stuttgart: Thorbecke, 2001–2002).

——, Köpf, Ulrich, and Lalla, Sebastian (eds), *Melanchthon und die Neuzeit* (Stuttgart: Frommann-Holzboog, 2003).

Ganoczy, Alexandre, *Le Jeune Calvin* (Wiesbaden: Franz Steiner, 1966).

Garber, Daniel and Ayers, Michael (eds), *The Cambridge History of Seventeenth-Century Philosophy 1–2* (Cambridge: Cambridge University Press, 1998).

Gauthier, R. A., 'Praefatio' in *Thomas Aquinas, Sententia libri Ethicorum*. Editio Leonina, Vol. 47/1 (Civitas Vaticana: Polyglot Press, 1969).

—— with Jolif, J. Y., *Aristote: l'Ethique a Nicomaque*. 2nd ed. (Louvain: Publications Universitaires de Louvain, 1970).

Gill, Christopher, 'Did Chrysippus Understand Medea?', *Phronesis* 28 (1983), 136–49.

Glauser, Richard, 'Thinking and Willing in Locke's Theory of Human Freedom', *Dialogue: Canadian Philosophical Review* 42 (2003), 695–724.

Gomes, Gabriel, *Foundations of Ethics in Walter Burleigh's Commentary on Aristotle's Nicomachean Ethics*. Ph.D Diss. (Columbia: Columbia University, 1973).

Gosling, Justin, *Weakness of the Will* (London: Routledge, 1990).

Gourinat, Jean-Baptiste, 'Akrasia and Enkrateia in Ancient Stoicism: Minor Vice and Minor Virtue?', in Bobonich and Destrée (2007), 215–48.

Graver, Margaret R., *Stoicism and Emotion* (Chicago: Chicago University Press, 2007).

Grcic, Joseph, 'Aristotle on the Akratic's Knowledge', *Phronesis* 47 (2002), 336–58.

Hadot, Pierre, *Philosophy as a Way of Life* (Oxford: Blackwell, 1995).

——, *What Is Ancient Philosophy?* (Cambridge, MA: Harvard University Press, 2002).

Hamm, Berndt, 'Naher Zorn und nahe Gnade: Luthers frühe Klosterjahre als Beginn seiner reformatorischen Neuorientierung', in Bultmann, Leppin, and Lindner (2007), 111–52.

—— and Leppin, Volker, *Gottes Nähe unmittelbar erfahren. Mystik im Mittelalter und bei Martin Luther* (Tübingen: Mohr Siebeck, 2007).

Hardie, W. F. R., *Aristotle's Ethical Theory*. 2nd ed. (Oxford: Oxford University Press, 1980).

Helm, Paul, *John Calvin's Ideas* (Oxford: Oxford University Press, 2004).

Hermann, Rudolf, *Luthers These 'Gerecht und Sünder zugleich'* (Gütersloh: Gütersloher Verlagshaus, 1934).

Hill, Thomas E., 'Kant on Weakness of Will', in Hoffmann (2008), 210–30.

Hintikka, Jaakko, 'Aristotle's Incontinent Logician', *Ajatus* 37 (1978), 48–65.

Hintikka, Jaakko, 'Was Leibniz's Deity an Akrates?', in S. Knuuttila (ed.), *Modern Modalities* (Dordrecht: Kluwer, 1988), 81–108.

Hirvonen, Vesa, *Passions in William Ockham's Philosophical Psychology* (Dordrecht: Kluwer, 2004).

Hissette, Roland, *Enquête sur les 219 articles condamnes à Paris le 7 Mars 1277* (Louvain: Publications Universitaires de Louvain, 1977).

Hoeveler, J. David, *Creating the American Mind: Intellect and Politics in the Colonial Colleges* (New York: Rowman & Littlefield, 2007).

Hoffmann, Tobias, 'Aquinas on the Moral Progress of the Weak Willed', in Hoffmann, Müller, and Perkams (2006), 221–48.

—— (ed.), *Weakness of Will from Plato to the Present* (Washington DC: The Catholic University of America Press, 2008).

——, Müller, Jörn, and Perkams, Matthias (eds), *Das Problem der Willensschwäche in der mittelalterlichen Philosophie (The Problem of Weakness of Will in Medieval Philosophy)* (Leuven: Peeters, 2006).

Hommel, Hildebrecht, 'Das 7. Kapitel des Römerbriefs im Lichte antiker Überlieferung', in Hommel, *Sebasmata. Studien zur antiken Religionsgeschichte und zum frühen Christentum, Band II* (Tübingen: Mohr Siebeck, 1984), 141–73.

Hügli, Anton, 'Willensschwäche', in *Historisches Wörterbuch der Philosophie*, Band 12 (2004), 800–9.

Irwin, Terence H., 'Will, Responsibility, and Ignorance: Aristotelian Accounts of Incontinence', in Hoffmann, Müller, and Perkams (2006), 39–58.

Kärkkäinen, Pekka, 'Theology, Philosophy and Immortality of Soul in the Late Via Moderna of Erfurt', *Vivarium* 43 (2005), 337–60.

Keen, Ralph, *The Moral World of Philip Melanchthon*. Ph.D Diss. (Chicago: Chicago Divinity School, 1990).

Kent, Bonnie, *Aristotle and the Franciscans: Gerald Odonis' Commentary on the Nicomachean Ethics.* Ph.D Diss. (Columbia: Columbia University, 1984).

——, 'Transitory Vice: Thomas Aquinas on Incontinence', *Journal of the History of Philosophy* 27 (1989), 199–223.

——, *Virtues of the Will: The Transformation of Ethics in the Late Thirteenth Century* (Washington D. C.: The Catholic University of America Press, 1995).

Kessler, Eckhart, 'Introducing Aristotle to the Sixteenth Century: The Lefèvre Enterprise', in C. Blackwell and S. Kusukawa (eds), *Philosophy in the Sixteenth and Seventeenth Centuries: Conversations with Aristotle* (Aldershot: Ashgate, 1999), 1–21.

Knuuttila, Simo, *Emotions in Ancient and Medieval Philosophy* (Oxford: Clarendon Press, 2004).

Kobusch, Theo, 'Willensschwäche und Selbstbestimmung des Willens: Zur Kritik am abendländischen Intellektualismus bei Heinrich von Gent und in der franziskanischen Philosophie', in Hoffmann, Müller, and Perkams (2006), 249–64.

Kohls, Ernst Wilhelm, *Luther oder Erasmus. Luthers Theologie in der Auseinandersetzung mit Erasmus.* Bd. 1–2 (Basel: Friedrich Reinhardt, 1972).

Koivuniemi, Minna, *Towards Hilaritas: A Study of the Mind–Body Union, the Passions and the Mastery of the Passions in Descartes and Spinoza* (Uppsala: Uppsala Universitet, 2008).

Kolb, Robert, *Bound Choice, Election, and Wittenberg Theological Method: From Martin Luther to the Formula of Concord* (Grand Rapids: Eerdmans, 2005).

Kraye, Jill, 'Moral Philosophy', in Schmitt and Skinner (1988), 303–86.

——, 'Renaissance Commentaries on the Nicomachean Ethics', in O. Weijers (ed.), *Vocabulary of Teaching and Research Between Middle Ages and Renaissance* (Turnhout: Brepols, 1995), 96–117.

——, 'Conceptions of Moral Philosophy', in Garber and Ayers (1998), 1279–316.

—— and Saarinen, Risto (eds), *Moral Philosophy on the Threshold of Modernity* (Dordrecht: Springer, 2005).

Krieger, Gerhard, *Der Begriff der praktischen Vernunft nach Johannes Buridanus* (Münster: Aschendorff, 1986).

Kunkler, Stephan, *Zwischen Humanismus und Reformation: Der Humanist Joachim Camerarius (1500–1574) im Wechselspiel von pädagogischem Pathos und theologischem Ethos* (Hildesheim: Georg Olms, 2000).

Kusukawa, Sachiko, *The Transformation of Natural Philosophy. The Case of Philip Melanchthon* (Cambridge: Cambridge University Press, 1995).

Lagerlund, Henrik, 'Buridan's Theory of Free Choice and Its Influence' in Henrik Lagerlund and Mikko Yrjönsuuri (eds), *Emotions and Choice from Boethius to Descartes* (Dordrecht: Kluwer, 2002), 173–204.

Lalla, Sebastian, *Secundum viam modernam. Ontologischer Nominalismus bei Bartholomäus Arnoldi von Usingen* (Würzburg: Königshausen & Neumann, 2003).

Lerner, Ralph and Mahdi, Muhsin (eds), *Medieval Political Philosophy*. 6th printing (Ithaca: Cornell University Press, 1989).

Lichtenberger, Hermann, *Das Ich Adams und das Ich der Menschheit. Studien zum Menschenbild in Römer 7* (Tübingen: Mohr Siebeck, 2004).

Lines, David A., *Aristotle's Ethics in the Italian Renaissance (ca. 1300–1650). The Universities and the Problem of Moral Education* (Leiden: Brill, 2002).

——, 'Sources and Authorities for Moral Philosophy in the Italian Renaissance: Thomas Aquinas and Jean Buridan on Aristotle's Ethics', in Kraye and Saarinen (2005), 7–30.

Lohr, Charles H., 'Medieval Latin Aristotle Commentaries: Authors Johannes de Kanthi–Myngodus', *Traditio* 27 (1971), 251–351.

——, 'Renaissance Latin Aristotle Commentaries: Authors C', *Renaissance Quarterly* 28 (1975), 689–741.

——, 'Renaissance Latin Aristotle Commentaries: Authors D-F', *Renaissance Quarterly* 29 (1976), 714–45.

——, 'Renaissance Latin Aristotle Commentaries: Authors G-K', *Renaissance Quarterly* 30 (1977), 681–741.

——, 'Renaissance Latin Aristotle Commentaries: Authors So-Z', *Renaissance Quarterly* 35 (1982), 164–256.

——, 'Metaphysics', in Schmitt and Skinner (1988), 537–638.

McCarthy, John, 'Descartes's Feeble Spirits', in Hoffmann (2008), 175–209.

McKim, Donald (ed.), *The Cambridge Companion to John Calvin* (Cambridge: Cambridge University Press, 2004).

Markschies, Christoph, 'Taufe und Concupiscentia bei Augustinus', in Schneider und Wenz (2001), 92–108.

Mele, Alfred R., *Irrationality. An Essay on Akrasia, Self-Deception, and Self-Control* (Oxford: Oxford University Press, 1987).

Metzger, Günther, *Gelebter Glaube: Die Formierung reformatorischen Denkens in Luthers erster Psalmenvorlesung, dargestellt am Begriff des Affekts* (Göttingen: Vandenhoeck & Ruprecht, 1964).

Moss, Ann, *Renaissance Truth and the Latin Language Turn* (Oxford: Oxford University Press, 2003).

Müller, Jörn, *Natürliche Moral und philosophische Ethik bei Albertus Magnus* (Münster: Aschendorff, 2001).

——, 'Agere contra conscientiam. The Relationship between Weakness of the Will and Conscience in Albert the Great', in M.C. Pacheco and J.F. Meirinhos (eds), *Intellect and Imagination in Medieval Philosophy* (Turnhout: Brepols, 2006), 1303–15.

——, 'Willensschwäche im Voluntarismus? Das Beispiel Heinrichs von Gent', *Archiv für Geschichte der Philosophie* 89 (2007), 1–29.

——, *Willensschwäche im Denken der Antike und des Mittelalters. Eine Problemgeschichte von Sokrates bis Johannes Duns Scotus* (Leuven: Leuven University Press, 2009).

Muller, Richard A., 'Vera philosophia cum sacra theologia nusquam pugnat: Keckermann on Philosophy, Theology and the Problem of Double Truth', *Sixteenth-Century Journal* 15 (1984), 341–65.

——, *Post-Reformation Reformed Dogmatics 1–4* Grand Rapids: Baker Academic, 1987–2003).

Nadler, Steven, 'Baruch Spinoza' in *Stanford Encyclopedia of Philosophy* (2008), http://plato.stanford.edu/

Nisula, Timo, *Augustine and the Functions of Concupiscence*. Ph. D Diss. (Helsinki: University of Helsinki, 2010).

Nussbaum, Martha, *The Therapy of Desire: Theory and Practice in Hellenistic Ethics* (Princeton: Princeton University Press, 1994).

O'Rourke Boyle, Marjorie, *Rhetoric and Reform. Erasmus' Civil Dispute with Luther* (Cambridge, Mass.: Harvard University Press, 1983).

Oberman, Heiko A., *Martin Luther: Man Between God and Devil* (New Haven: Yale University Press, 1989).

Ong-Van-Cung, Kim Sang, 'Indifférence et irrationalité chez Descartes', *Dialogue: Canadian Philosophical Review* 42 (2003), 725–48.

Palmer, Kenneth (ed.), *Troilus and Cressida* (London: Routledge, 1982).

Pasnau, Robert, *Thomas Aquinas on Human Nature* (Cambridge: Cambridge University Press, 2002).

Peijnenburg, Johanna, *Acting Against One's Own Best Judgement*. Ph.D Diss. (Groningen: University Library Groningen, 1996).

Pesch, Otto Hermann (ed.), *Humanismus und Reformation—Martin Luther und Erasmus von Rotterdam in den Konflikten ihrer Zeit* (München: Schnell & Steiner, 1985).

—— and Peters, Albrecht, *Einführung in die Lehre von Gnade und Rechtfertigung* (Darmstadt: Wissenschaftliche Buchgesellschaft, 1981).

Peters, Albrecht, *Gesetz und Evangelium* (Gütersloh: Gütersloher Verlagshaus, 1981).

Petersen, Peter, *Geschichte der aristotelischen Philosophie im protestantischen Deutschland* (Leipzig: Meiner, 1921).

Pilvousek, Josef, 'Askese, Brüderlichkeit und Wissenschaft: Die Ideale der Erfurter Augustiner-Eremiten und ihre Bemühungen um eine innovative Umsetzung', in Bultmann, Leppin, and Lindner (2007), 39–56.

Pink, Thomas and Stone, Martin (eds), *The Will and Human Action: From Antiquity to the Present Day* (London: Routledge, 2004).

Pironet, Fabienne, *Jean Buridan et l'acrasie (faiblesse de la volonté). Édition de travail des Questions sur l'Éthique, Livre VII, questions 1–17 avec une brève introduction et des commentaries* (2001) at http://www.mapageweb.umontreal.ca/pironetf/

Pitkin, Barbara, *What Pure Eyes Could See: Calvin's Doctrine Of Faith In Its Exegetical Context* (Oxford: Oxford University Press, 1999).

Pope, Stephen J., *The Ethics of Aquinas* (Washington DC: Georgetown University Press, 2002).

Price, A. W., *Mental Conflict* (London: Routledge, 1994).

Reuter, Karl, *Das Grundverständnis der Theologie Calvins, unter Einbeziehung ihrer geschichtlichen Abhängigkeiten* (Neukirchen: Neukirchner Verlag, 1963).

Ridderikhoff, C. M., 'Orleans and the Dutch Revolt', in C. C. Barfoot and R. Todd (eds), *Great Emporium: Low Countries as a Cultural Crossroads in the Renaissance and the Eighteenth Century* (Amsterdam: Rodopi, 1992), 59–82.

Rist, J. M., *Stoic Philosophy* (Cambridge: Cambridge University Press, 1969).

Roinila, Markku, *Leibniz on Rational Decision-Making* (Helsinki: University of Helsinki, Department of Philosophy, 2007).

Rubiglio, Andrea A., *L'impossibile volere: Tommaso d'Aquino, i tomisti e la volontà* (Milano: Vita e pensiero, 2002).

Rutten, Pepin, 'Secundum processum et mentem Versoris. John Versor and His Relation to the Schools of Thought Reconsidered', *Vivarium* 43 (2005), 292–336.

Saarinen, Risto, 'John Buridan and Donald Davidson on Akrasia', *Synthese* 96 (1993), 133–54.

——, *Weakness of the Will in Medieval Thought: From Augustine to Buridan* (Leiden: Brill, 1994).

——, 'Walter Burley on Akrasia: Second Thoughts', *Vivarium* 37 (1999), 60–71.

——, 'Vorherwissen', in *Historisches Wörterbuch der Philosophie*, Band 11 (2001), 1190–3.

——, 'The Parts of Prudence: Buridan, Odonis, Aquinas', *Dialogue: Canadian Philosophical Review* 42 (2003), 749–68.

——, 'Ethics in Luther's Theology: The Three Orders', in Kraye and Saarinen (2005), 195–215.

——, 'Weakness of Will in the Renaissance and the Reformation', in Hoffmann, Müller, and Perkams (2006), 331–54.

——, 'Klostertheologie auf dem Weg der Ökumene: Wille und Konkupiszenz', in Bultmann, Leppin, and Lindner (2007), 269–90.

——, *The Pastoral Epistles with Philemon and Jude* (Grand Rapids and London: Brazos and SCM Press, 2008a).

——, 'The Pauline Luther and the Law: Lutheran Theology Reengages the Study of Paul', in Lars Aejmelaeus and Antti Mustakallio (eds), *The Nordic Paul* (London: T&T Clark, 2008b), 90–116.

——, 'Renaissance Ethics and the European Reformations', in *Reconsidering Virtue*, ed. Sabrine Ebbersmeyer and David A. Lines (Turnhout: Brepols, forthcoming).

Salles, Ricardo, 'Epictetus on Moral Responsibility for Precipitate Action', in Bobonich and Destrée (2007), 265–82.

Sauer, James B., *Faithful Ethics According to John Calvin: The Teachability of the Heart* (Lewiston: Edwin Mellen Press, 1997).

Savile, Anthony, 'Spinoza, Medea and Irrationality in Action', *Dialogue: Canadian Philosophical Review* 42 (2003), 767–90.

Scheible, Heinz, 'Melanchthon, Philipp' in *Theologische Realenzyklopädie* 22 (1992), 371–410.

——, *Melanchthon: Eine Biographie* (München: Beck, 1997).

Schlabach, Gerald W., 'Continence', in A. D. Fitzgerald (1999), 235–7.

Schmitt, Charles B., *John Case and Aristotelianism in Renaissance England* (Montreal: McGill-Queen's University Press, 1983a).

——, *Aristotle and the Renaissance* (Cambridge, Mass.: Harvard University Press, 1983b).

——, 'The Rise of the Philosophical Textbook', in Schmitt and Skinner (1988), 792–804.

—— and Skinner, Quentin (eds), *The Cambridge History of Renaissance Philosophy* (Cambridge: Cambridge University Press, 1988).

Schneider, Theodor and Wenz, Gunther (eds), *Gerecht und Sünder zugleich? Ökumenische Klärungen* (Göttingen: Vandenhoeck & Ruprecht, 2001).

Schwarz, Reinhard, *Luther* (Göttingen: Vandenhoeck & Ruprecht, 1986).

Seils, Martin, *Der Gedanke vom Zusammenwirken Gottes und des Menschen in Luthers Theologie* (Gütersloh: Gütersloher Verlagshaus, 1962).

Shields, Christopher, 'Unified Agency and Akrasia in Plato's Republic', in Bobonich and Destrée (2007), 61–86.

Shirley, Samuel, 'Translator's Foreword' in Baruch Spinoza, *The Ethics and Selected Letters*, (Indianapolis: Hackett, 1982), 21–9.

Sinnema, Donald M., 'The Discipline of Ethics in Early Reformed Orthodoxy', *Calvin Theological Journal* 28 (1993), 10–44.

Sorabji, Richard, *Emotion and Peace of Mind: From Stoic Agitation to Christian Temptation* (Oxford: Oxford University Press, 2000).

Sparn, Walter, *Wiederkehr der Metaphysik* (Stuttgart: Calwer, 1976).

Spitzley, Thomas, *Handeln wider besseres Wissen: Eine Diskussion klassischer Positionen* (Berlin: de Gruyter, 1992).

Stadter, Ernst, *Psychologie und Metaphysik der menschlichen Freiheit. Die ideengeschichtliche Entwicklung zwischen Bonaventura und Duns Scotus* (München: Schöningh, 1971).

Steinmetz, David, 'Calvin and the Divided Self in Romans 7', in K. Hagen (ed.), *Augustine, the Harvest, and Theology (1300–1650)* (Leiden: Brill, 1990), 300–13.

Strohm, Christoph, *Ethik im frühen Calvinismus* (Berlin: de Gruyter, 1996).

Stroud, Sarah, 'Weakness of Will', in *Stanford Encyclopedia of Philosophy* (2008) http://plato.stanford.edu/

—— and Tappolet, Christine (eds), *Weakness of Will and Practical Irrationality* (Oxford: Clarendon Press, 2003).

Theissen, Gerd, *Psychologische Aspekte paulinischer Theologie* (Göttingen: Vandenhoeck & Ruprecht, 1983).

Thero, Daniel P., *Understanding Moral Weakness* (Amsterdam–New York: Rodopi, 2006).

Tinkler, John F., 'Erasmus' Conversation with Luther', *Archiv für Reformationsgeschichte* 82 (1991), 59–81.

Torrance, Isabelle, 'The Princess's Gruesome Death and *Medea* 1079', *The Classical Quarterly* 57 (2007), 286–9.

Tracey, Martin J., 'Albert on Incontinence, Continence, and Divine Virtue' in Hoffmann, Müller, and Perkams (2006), 197–220.

Trinkaus, Charles, *The Poet as Philosopher. Petrarch and the Formation of Renaissance Consciousness* (New Haven: Yale University Press, 1979).

Vailati, Ezio, 'Leibniz on Locke on Weakness of Will', in *Journal of the History of Philosophy* 28 (1990), 213–28.

Vainio, Olli-Pekka, *Justification and Participation in Christ. The Development of the Lutheran Doctrine of Justification from Luther to the Formula of Concord (1580)* (Leiden: Brill, 2008).

Vasoli, Cesare, 'The Renaissance Concept of Philosophy', in Schmitt and Skinner (1988), 57–74.

Walsh, James J., 'Some Relationships between Gerald Odo's and John Buridan's Commentaries on Aristotle's Ethics', *Franciscan Studies* 35 (1975), 237–75.

Walter, Peter, 'Die bleibende Sündigkeit der Getauften in den Debatten und Beschlüssen des Trienter Konzils', in Schneider and Wenz (2001), 268–302.

Wengert, Timothy J., *Law and Gospel: Philip Melanchthon's Debate with John Agricola over Poenitentia* (Grand Rapids: Baker, 1997).

——, *Human Freedom, Christian Righteousness. Philip Melanchthon's Exegetical Dispute with Erasmus of Rotterdam* (Oxford: Oxford University Press, 1998).

Westerholm, Stephen, *Perspectives Old and New on Paul: The 'Lutheran' Paul and His Critics* (Grand Rapids: Eerdmans, 2004).

Wood, Rega, 'Willing Wickedly: Ockham and Burley Compared', in *Vivarium* 37 (1999), 72–93.

Wriedt, Markus, 'Via Augustini: Ausprägungen des spätmittelalterlichen Augustinismus in der observanten Kongregation der Augustinereremiten', in Bultmann, Leppin, and Lindner (2007), 9–38.

Zeller, Eduard, *Die Philosophie der Griechen in ihrer geschichtlichen Entwicklung*, vol. III–1. (Leipzig: Reisland, 1909).

Zumkeller, Adolar, *Erbsünde, Gnade, Rechtfertigung und Verdienst nach der Lehre der Erfurter Augustinertheologen des Spätmittelalters* (Würzburg: Augustinus Verlag, 1984).

——, *Johannes von Staupitz und seine christliche Heilslehre* (Würzburg: Augustinus Verlag, 1994).

Zupko, Jack, *John Buridan. Portrait of a Fourteenth-Century Arts Master* (Notre Dame: University of Notre Dame Press, 2003).

Zur Mühlen, Karl-Heinz, 'Affekt II', in *Theologische Realenzyklopädie* 1 (1977), 599–612.

Index